This book is dedicated to David Corson (1945-2001), friend, colleague, and tireless campaigner for social justice in education

Table of Contents

Acknowledgements

The central ideas developed in this volume were initially expressed in an article entitled *Empowering Minority Students: A Framework for Intervention* that appeared in the *Harvard Educational Review* in 1986. Subsequently, in 1989, the California Association for Bilingual Education (CABE) published a volume entitled *Empowering Minority Students* that elaborated on the original ideas and tried to link patterns of discrimination and disinformation experienced by culturally diverse communities in North American educational contexts to the realities of exploitation and oppression in the global arena. The first edition of the present volume was published by CABE in 1996. This second edition continues the attempt to elaborate the theoretical ideas and draw implications for classroom practice in light of both new research findings and the many changes that have occurred in political and demographic realities in North America. I would like to express my appreciation to the many committed educators at CABE who have supported the publication and dissemination of these ideas over the past 12 years. I would also like to thank Margo Okazawa-Rey whose editorial feedback helped refine the original *Harvard Educational Review* paper in 1986.

Many colleagues and friends have also contributed to the ideas developed in this volume. Among those who have provided constructive criticism, insight, and information that are reflected in both the first and second editions of this book are: Alma Flor Ada, Kristin Brown, Margarita Calderón, Anna Uhl Chamot, David Corson, Marcel Danesi, Robert DeVillar, David Dolson, David Freeman, Yvonne Freeman, John Gibbons, Pauline Gibbons, Norm Gold, Carolyn Kessler, Stephen Krashen, Antonia López, Sandy McAuley, Lois Meyer, Kazuko Nakajima, Sonia Nieto, Fiona O'Donoghue, J. Michael O'Malley, Robert Phillipson, Delia Pompa, Mary Ann Larsen-Pusey, Dennis Sayers, Tove Skutnabb-Kangas, Merrill Swain, Joan Wink, and Lily Wong Fillmore.

Others who have contributed to the ideas through feedback and encouragement in more recent years include: Colin Baker, Jasone Cenoz, Debra Hopkins, Nancy Hornberger, Ulrike Jessner, Vasilia Kazoullis, Brian Morgan and

Eleni Skourtou. I would particularly like to thank Vasilia for writing the Foreword to this edition and Eleni for organizing and editing the publication of a Greek version of the first edition.

For permission to quote their insightful suggestions about schooling (Chapter 7), I would like to thank Jessica and Julia Rosciglione (ages 9 and 7) and their mother Jane O'Hare.

I would also like to express my appreciation to Carole Aldrich for the design and layout of the volume and for helpful suggestions regarding the final editing process.

Finally, I would like to acknowledge the work of educators throughout North America and elsewhere whose practice has informed and elaborated the theory in the book. In an important sense the book represents a stage in a continuing dialogue about how to create contexts of empowerment in schools. The practice of many educators illustrates far more eloquently than any theory how power can be generated collaboratively in the interactions between educators, students, and communities, and how these interactions can simultaneously challenge structures of injustice in schools. Thus, I see the book as a collaborative effort that draws on the energy, insights, and dedication of many educators.

What did you bring with you to school?

Vasilia Kourtis Kazoullis, University of the Aegean, Rhodes, Greece

One day as I was walking across the classroom, I noticed something familiar in the rubbish bin. It was a small white paper bag. Inside the bag were the small zero-shaped Greek cookies, koulourakia, that my mother had sent to school with me the day before. I, personally, had handed it to my kindergarten teacher who graciously accepted it with a wide smile and warm thank you. I didn't touch the bag, but I could see that it was just as I had given it to her, unopened.

It was then that I must have realized that I couldn't bring anything with me to school. All that I had accumulated from birth to age 5 (language, culture, personality, talent, interests) went straight to the rubbish bin, unopened, not because it was inferior (or superior for that matter), but because it was different, therefore unintelligible, therefore useless.

I entered kindergarten not knowing a word of English. In one year I learned English so well (they thought...) that I became the family interpreter at the age of 5. I carried out all the bank transactions, escorted my parents to the physician, attended the parent-teacher meetings at school, and basically made all the major decisions that had to be made. Language gave me *instant maturity* and immense power. I still can't believe that my parents actually bought a house and started a business because I said so (and I was only in grade school!).

But it wasn't the language that gave me the key to success in the school environment and in the wider society. It was the skill of *metamorphosis*, a skill which *diverse* individuals usually learn to master as a survival tactic in a world that demands conformity. I could enter an environment, immediately calculate the demands of that particular environment and act accordingly. In school I was always creative, but not particularly intelligent, I think. However, I knew what the teacher wanted from me. I knew how I had to act, write, speak. I knew that each teacher had a prototype of excellence. I didn't challenge it—or try to be better than the prototype of excellence for even that was disastrous. I learned to become *just that*. I could do that to some extent. Of course, there are qualities that cannot be acquired, no matter how hard you try, such as blue eyes and natural blond hair. So, with the tools I had, I did the best I could.

But the problem with school, I believe, is the small white paper bag in the rubbish bin. My kindergarten teacher couldn't possibly know that this gift was a symbol of honor. In my home culture, it meant that we recognized the teacher as an authority figure and accepted her position of power. She couldn't possibly know that with that small white paper bag I brought with me a wealth of experience, a rich culture, and a language that was fully developed.

She thought that I brought nothing with me. But I did. So, I began kindergarten ten paces behind the rest of the class and it took me six whole years to catch up with the *moving target*. Looking back at my old report cards, I now understand the "creative student, good at art and music but poor in language skills." I finally did catch up to the rest of my peers. However, I had to throw a lot of things in the rubbish bin along the way because I couldn't carry them all with me. The demands from the teachers and peers (*and* from home) were too great.

If I had been accepted as an individual and if individuality and not conformity had been the key to success in school, society and in the home, things would have been much easier. It is not a question of *multicultural or intercultural* education, which has become very popular lately. I do not believe that we should stress similarities—or differences for that matter. It is a question of acceptance and individuality. Each person is an individual and each person brings something with him or her to school. The teacher's position should be to *accept* and *refine*, first of all, by accepting that she/he is not dealing with *a class of 25* but with 25 individuals. She/he should be the coordinator who organizes methods so that each individual can teach the other. The students should not compete with each other but begin at their own level and enrich their knowledge. If the relationships in the classroom are like this, perhaps relationships in society will one day change.

In society we are constantly accepting and rejecting. We are constantly fighting for a position of power that must be acquired at the expense of someone else, whether this means a position in the job market, economic success of a business or military expansionism of aggressive countries. Power should in fact be *collaborative*, not *coercive*. As a pebble drops in a pond and sets off ripples, the point where the rock breaks the surface of the water—the nucleus—is the individual. The ripples are first the home, then the classroom, the school and ultimately the society. What *ripples* the classroom sends off to some extent define what the end product will be. Therefore, it is up to us as teachers to nurture our *small scale society*, the classroom, in such a way that the relationships of power are generously divided for the benefit of all.

Preface

In the five years since the original version of this book was published, much has happened to illustrate its major themes. In particular, controversy surrounding bilingual and multicultural education in the United States has escalated. Proposition 227, passed in California by a margin of 61% to 39%, severely restricted the extent to which children's first language (L1) could be used as a medium of instruction. Teachers who continue to use children's L1 in the classroom can be held legally liable and sued. In November 2000, the citizens of Arizona followed California's lead in severely restricting bilingual education for linguistic minority children. It seems like we have taken a giant step backward. [1] In the past, bilingual children were frequently punished for speaking their home language in the school; now the focus of coercion has shifted to teachers. Yet many teachers both in bilingual and English-medium classes are actively resisting these coercive relations of power. The present volume analyzes the roots of coercive relations of power as they are manifested in the discourse surrounding the education of bilingual students. It also attempts to chart alternative directions whereby educators can create contexts of empowerment in their interactions with bilingual and culturally diverse students.

The focus of the book is on how power relations operating in the broader society influence the interactions that occur between teachers and students in the classroom. These interactions can be empowering or disempowering for both teachers and students. The basic argument is that culturally diverse students are disempowered educationally in very much the same way that their communities have been disempowered historically in their interactions with societal institutions. The logical implication is that these students will succeed academically to the extent that the patterns of interaction in school reverse those that prevail in the society at large. In other words, a genuine commitment to helping all students succeed academically requires a willingness on the part of educators, individually and collectively, to challenge aspects of the power structure in the wider society.

Thus, the term *empowerment* entails both sociological and psychological dimensions: to create contexts of empowerment in classroom interactions involves not only establishing the respect, trust, and affirmation required for students (and educators) to reflect critically on their own experience and identities; it also challenges explicitly the devaluation of identity that many culturally diverse students and communities still experience in the society as a whole. In concrete terms, when the school affirms the value of students' primary language and encourages them to take pride in their cultural background, it repudiates the escalating societal discourse proclaiming that "bilingualism shuts doors" (Arthur Schlesinger Jr.) and disadvantages both the individual and the wider society.

The title of this volume reflects the fact that relationships between educators and students are at the heart of student learning. The interactions between educators and students always entail a process of negotiating identities. The concept of *negotiating identities* recognizes the agency of culturally diverse students and communities in resisting devaluation and in affirming their basic human rights, but it also focuses on the fact that identities develop in a social context. As articulated by R.D. Laing, the late Scottish psychiatrist: "No one acts or experiences in a vacuum... all 'identities' require an other" (1969, pp. 81-82). The ways in which student-teacher identities are negotiated in classroom and school interactions play a major role in determining students' orientation to self and their orientation to academic effort. The words of Adriana and Rosalba Jasso on the cover of this volume illustrate this process.

As educators, we are constantly sketching an image not only of our own identities and those we envisage for our students, but also of the society we hope our students will form. Students who have been failed by schools predominantly come from communities whose languages, cultures and identities have been distorted and devalued in the wider society. In the past, schools have reinforced this pattern of disempowerment by punishing students for speaking their home language in the school and ignoring or dismissing the knowledge and values of particular communities. Schools viewed culturally diverse students as inherently inferior, a judgment frequently legitimated by culturally-biased IQ tests. Not surprisingly, students often disengaged themselves from school learning under these conditions.

The central argument of the book is that if schools and society are genuinely committed to reversing this pattern of school failure, with its massive human and social costs, the interactions between educators and students in schools must actively challenge historical patterns of disempowerment. This requires that schools respect students' language and culture, encourage community participation, promote critical literacy, and institute forms of assessment that contribute to the school as a learning community rather than pathologize culturally diverse students as scapegoats for the failure of schools and society.

The collaborative creation of power by students and teachers within the classroom is frequently resisted by the power structure of the school and the wider society. This is one of the major reasons why almost 20 years of intense focus on educational restructuring in schools across North America has had minimal impact on the achievement levels of culturally diverse students. Most of the reforms have focused on cosmetic modifications to surface structures, leaving intact the deep structures that reflect patterns of disempowerment in the wider society.

The possibility of genuine reform in the education of bilingual students is limited by xenophobic tendencies that view diversity as "the enemy within"— a threat to nationhood. The discourse related to diversity of all kinds (gender, linguistic, cultural, religious, sexual orientation etc.) is still ruled by the imperatives of *Us versus Them*—what I call in this volume, *coercive relations of power.* Yet, we cannot turn on a television or open a newspaper without seeing the appalling consequences of this way of relating to each other. [2]

Coercive relations of power are not inevitable. In fact, virtually all of us are familiar with an alternative way of relating among people, communities and nations. We have all experienced how power can be generated in interpersonal relationships—how the empowerment of one partner augments rather than diminishes the power of the other. This book is about how to institute these *collaborative relations of power* in the classroom and school.

The book is hopeful because it is based explicitly on the premise that educators, both individually and collectively within particular schools, have a considerable degree of control over how they structure their interactions with culturally diverse students. Although there are usually many constraints and influences on how educators define their roles (as illustrated by Proposition 227), ultimately they have choices in the messages they attempt to communicate regarding students' language and culture, in the forms of parent and community participation they encourage, and in the extent to which they promote collaborative critical inquiry as a dominant form of learning in their classrooms. There are many examples in the book of how communities, educators and students have collaborated to generate power.

The book is also realistic because it acknowledges the enormous pressures that constrict the options available to educators, students, and communities. The portraits of collaborative empowerment in the book are still very much the exceptions. In many schools that serve culturally diverse communities across North America, the "savage inequalities" identified by Jonathan Kozol (1991) are still very much in evidence, despite the best efforts of committed educators.

We have alternatives to the current directions. These alternatives require educators to recognize that relations of power are at the core of schooling and also to recognize that, as educators, we have choices regarding how power is negotiated in our classroom interactions. This volume attempts to sketch how educators and students together can create, through their classroom interactions, a microcosm of the kind of society where everybody feels a strong sense of belonging regardless of race, gender, language, culture, creed or sexual orientation. The creation of these interpersonal and collective spaces represents an act of resistance to those elements within the societal power structure that are intolerant of difference and are motivated to maximize individual profit at the expense of the common good.

Endnotes to Preface

1. The restrictions on bilingual education posed in California and Arizona stand in stark contrast to developments in Europe where bilingual and trilingual education for linguistic minority and majority students is widespread. The year 2001 has been declared by the European Commission as the *European Year of Languages*. This recognition of the link between language diversity and European cultural heritage is designed to raise public awareness of the richness of European language resources and to stimulate language learning and teaching as a high priority for social and economic development.

2. The operation of coercive relations of power is illustrated in Marilyn French's (1992) book *The War Against Women* which documents the universal oppression of women in countries throughout the world. For example, although women do between 65 and 75 percent of the world's work and produce 45 percent of the world's food, they hold only ten percent of the world's income and one percent of the world's property.

Chapter 1

Identity and Empowerment

Relationships dominated all participant discussions about issues of schooling in the U.S. No group inside the schools felt adequately respected, connected or affirmed. Students, over and over again, raised the issue of care. What they liked best about school was when people, particularly teachers, cared about them or did special things for them. Dominating their complaints were being ignored, not being cared for and receiving negative treatment. (Mary Poplin and Joseph Weeres, *Voices from the Inside: A Report on Schooling from Inside the Classroom,* 1992, p. 19)

Although Poplin and Weeres' study focused only on four schools, it represents one of the most in-depth examinations of schooling ever carried out in North America. Their conclusion is based on 24,000 pages of interview transcriptions, essays, drawings, journal entries, and notes. The multicultural urban Californian schools they studied exhibited "a pervasive sense of despair" well summed up by one student who said: "This place hurts my spirit." Teachers in these schools reported that their best experiences were when they connected with students and were able to help them in some way. However, they also reported that they did not always understand students who are culturally different from themselves. They also felt isolated and unappreciated inside schools by students, administrators, and parents as well as within the larger society.

The voices of students, teachers, administrators and parents that line the pages of this report communicate clearly that *human relationships are at the heart of schooling.* The interactions that take place between students and teachers and among students are more central to student success than any method for teaching literacy, or science or math. When powerful relationships are established between teachers and students, these relationships can frequently transcend the economic and social disadvantages that afflict communities and schools alike in inner city and rural areas. Many of us can vividly remember inspiring teachers who, because they believed in us, generated far greater academic effort on our part than did teachers who just taught their subject.

However, the history of education in North America demonstrates equally clearly that relationships established in school can be disempowering for students and communities. Negative messages can be overt or covert, intentional or, more frequently, unintentional. For example, prior to the 1970s, it was extremely common for educators to reprimand bilingual students for speaking their home language (L1) in the school. The clear message to students was that their language, culture, and previous experience have no place within this school or, by extension, within this society. To be accepted within the mainstream society, represented by the school, required that students become invisible and inaudible; culture and language should be left at home. [1]

More subtle forms of unintentional rejection were also common. For example, a large-scale study conducted by the U.S. Commission on Civil Rights (1973) in the American southwest reported that Euro-American students were praised or encouraged 36% more often than Mexican-American students and their classroom contributions were used or built upon 40% more frequently than those of Mexican-American students. It is not hard to see how, under these conditions, many students might come to see themselves as not very bright academically. This is particularly the case when their command of the language of instruction is still at an early stage of development.

The title of this volume points to these interactions, these ways of *negotiating identities*, as fundamental to the academic success of culturally diverse students. When students' developing sense of self is affirmed and extended through their interactions with teachers, they are more likely to apply themselves to academic effort and participate actively in instruction. The consequent learning is the fuel that generates further academic effort. The more we learn, the more we want to learn, and the more effort we are prepared to put into that learning.

By contrast, when students' language, culture and experience are ignored or excluded in classroom interactions, students are immediately starting from a disadvantage. Everything they have learned about life and the world up to this point is being dismissed as irrelevant to school learning; there are few points of connection to curriculum materials or instruction and so students are expected to learn in an experiential vacuum. Students' silence and non-participation under these conditions have frequently been interpreted as lack of academic ability or effort; and teachers' interactions with students have reflected their low expectations for these students, a pattern that becomes self-fulfilling.

In the past, the school's rejection of students' language and culture tended to reflect the broader society's subordination of cultures and languages other than those of the dominant group. In many societies throughout the world, students who experience the most persistent and severe educational difficulties tend to come from communities that, over generations, have been discriminated against and viewed as inherently inferior by the dominant societal group (Ogbu, 1978, 1992). This pattern of relationships between dominant and subordinated groups in the wider society is typical of colonial situations in which the indigenous population is widely disparaged by the colonial power. This is illustrated historically by the attitudes of the British in Africa, India, or Ireland during the heyday of the British empire. The current attitudes of ruling elites in many Latin American countries towards indigenous peoples similarly illustrate this pattern.

The experience of historically subordinated groups in countries around the world reflects their status as *internal colonies* (Blauner, 1969). Schools reflect the values and attitudes of the broader society that supports them and so it is hardly surprising that in the United States students from African-American, Latino/Latina, and Native American communities have experienced extensive devaluation of their cultures and languages within the school context. In some cases, students perceive that their identity is endangered by this process of devaluation and consequently drop out of school in order to preserve their sense of self.

A central argument of the present volume is that this devaluation of identity played out in the interactions between educators and students convinces many students that academic effort is futile. They resist further devaluation of their identities by mentally withdrawing from participation in the life of the school. In inner city areas, they frequently find family and affirmation of identity in the streets as members of gangs. [2]

To turn this scenario around and reverse the pattern of academic failure inevitably requires that educators, students, and communities challenge the historical pattern of subordination that has characterized relations in the broader society. When educators encourage culturally diverse students to develop the language and culture they bring from home and build on their prior experiences, they, together with their students, challenge the perception in the broader society that these attributes are inferior or worthless. When educators and culturally diverse parents become genuine partners in children's education, this partnership repudiates the myth that culturally diverse parents are apathetic and don't care about their children's education. When classroom instruction encourages students to inquire critically into social issues that affect their lives (*e.g.*, racism, environmental deterioration, omissions of groups other than "dead white males" from official histories, etc.), students' intelligence is activated in ways that potentially challenge the societal status quo.

It is important to note at the outset that affirmation of identity is not an uncritical process. It does not imply that educators or students should accept all cultural manifestations in a "liberal" non-evaluative way. Many cultural practices and social structures violate the United Nations Declaration of Human Rights and other United Nations charters (see Skutnabb-Kangas, 2000, and Skutnabb-Kangas & Phillipson, 1995). Students should be encouraged to reflect critically on both their own cultural background and on the culture of the host society in order to identify and resolve contradictions. This process will bring alternative perspectives into the open for both the teacher and students and enable them to understand their world and their identities more coherently than if only one perspective were presented as valid. Affirmation of identity thus refers to the establishment of the respect and trust between educators and students that is crucial for each to reflect critically on their own experience and beliefs. Respect and trust imply that educators listen carefully to their students' perspectives and learn from their students. If teachers are not learning much from their students, it is probable that their students are not learning much from them.

The ways in which negotiation of identity is related to the empowerment or disempowerment of students and communities can be illustrated by contrasting two sets of school-community interactions. The example of a family literacy project in the Pajaro Valley school district in California shows how interactions between educators and parents that affirm student and community identity can result in empowerment of educators, students and parents. The second example draws on the historical experience of First Nations (Native) students in residential schools in the Canadian context; it illustrates in an extreme way how colonial orientations to schooling have shattered the fragile identities of young children and destroyed communities. [3]

Empowerment through Negotiation of Identity: The Pajaro Valley Family Literacy Project

The Pajaro Valley School district serves a mostly rural population in the area surrounding Watsonville, California. More than half the students in the district are Latino/Latina and in the past more than half of these have dropped out before completing high school. During 1986, a group of Spanish-speaking parents varying in size between 60 and 100 met once a month to discuss (among themselves and with Alma Flor Ada) children's literature and to read stories and poems written both by their children, and, increasingly, by themselves. Ada points out that most of these parents had very little schooling and many had never read a book before, much less thought about writing one.

Alma Flor Ada's involvement with the district arose out of an invitation from the school librarian to participate in a "meet the author" program during which she read some of her (Spanish) stories to the children and discussed aspects of what is involved in the process of writing. Children's enthusiasm was enormous and it was decided to follow up the interest that had been stimulated in the children by involving their parents in a similar literacy experience.

The planning of the project (by Alma Flor Ada, Alfonso Anaya, director of the bilingual program, and teachers) was carried out carefully in order to encourage parental participation. For example, meetings were carried out in the library rather than the school itself because of frequent negative associations that culturally diverse parents have with schools; the subject of the meetings was non-threatening, namely children's literature; parents were respectfully invited to participate (through written invitations in Spanish and follow-up personal phone calls); a parallel program for children was offered in a nearby room (films, storytelling, and other activities); and several teachers' aides offered to give rides to parents who lacked transportation. In addition, all the bilingual teachers participated in the meetings, which were conducted entirely in Spanish.

The initial discussion at the first meeting covered the purpose of the program and issues such as the importance of promoting children's proficiency in their home language and pride in their cultural heritage. In addition, parents' crucial role as their children's first and best teachers was stressed. According to Ada (1988a):

> The results of this initial discussion were overwhelming. It was obvious that the parents were deeply moved. One mother stood up and explained: 'What is happening to us is that no one has ever told us that our children are worth something, and no one has ever told us that we are worth something.' (p. 227)

The dialogue on these general themes was followed by a presentation of five children's story books, chosen primarily for their appeal in terms of literary content and presentation. Alma Flor Ada read each of the books aloud to the whole group of parents, dramatizing the action and showing the illustrations. Then parents were invited to select the book they wanted to take home and to join a small group for discussion of that particular book. These discussions were facilitated by the bilingual teachers who were careful to accept and validate everyone's participation while guiding the discussion to more reflective levels of analysis.

In addition to a copy of the book they had chosen, each parent was given a list of questions as a general guide for home discussions with their children. These questions were based on Ada's (1988b) *Creative Reading* methodology (see Chapter 5) and were intended to extend children's and parents' understanding of the story by relating it to their prior experience, critically analyzing aspects of the story, and applying their understandings to real-life situations. In addition, participants were given a list of suggested activities related to the book and a blank book in which children might be encouraged to write their own stories or dictate them for the parents to write. All sessions were videotaped.

From the second session, the parents met first in small groups according to which book they had selected the previous month in order to talk about their experiences in discussing the books with their children. Then in a whole group format they read and listened to some of the stories the children wrote or dictated. Finally, the new books were presented and small groups formed to discuss them.

Ada sums up the major results of the project as follows:

> …parents have begun to read aloud to their children, the children have begun to bring home books from the school library, and parents and children have gone to the public library in search of books. At the first meeting we had a show of hands to find out how many parents had public library cards. None did. At a meeting nine months later almost everyone reported several visits to the library to check out books. (1988a, p. 223)

In addition, the teachers' aides borrowed the videotapes and showed them in the community, thereby giving the children the opportunity of seeing their parents on television, reading aloud the stories created by the children. According to Ada, "the children have felt double pride, both in seeing their parents on the screen, and in hearing their own stories being read aloud." This experience greatly increased children's motivation to write.

Other consequences were an increase in self-confidence and self-expression on the part of the parents, indicated by parents taking over the roles of small-group facilitators, giving presentations on the use of children's literature at the Regional Migrant Education Conference, and requesting the opportunity to purchase books in Spanish for their children, since the one book a month that they took home was insufficient. At the parents' suggestion, a book of stories their children wrote was compiled.

Ada quotes extensively from the parents themselves about their reaction to the program. Two examples will illustrate the empowerment process that took place over the course of these meetings:

> Another mother said: 'Ever since I know I have no need to feel ashamed of speaking Spanish I have become strong. Now I feel I can speak with the teachers about my children's education and I can tell them I want my children to know Spanish. I have gained courage'…

> One of the fathers said: 'I have discovered that my children can write. And I bring another story [written by his child]. But I have also discovered something personal. I have discovered that by reading books one can find out many things. Since my children want me to read them the stories over and over again, I took them to the public library to look for more books. There I discovered books about our own culture. I borrowed them and I am reading, and now I am finding out things I never knew about our roots and what has happened to them and I have discovered that I can read in Spanish about the history of this country [the USA] and of other countries.' (1988a, p. 235–236) [4]

It is clear that these parents are gaining the internal resources, confidence and motivation to exert greater control over the forces that affect their lives. The community's language, culture, and experiences have been acknowledged and validated, a genuine partnership has been established with the school, and the potential of literacy to transform their lives and the lives of their children has been understood. [5] This experience can be described as *empowering*, not because it made the parents or children feel good, but because it challenged and transformed the power relations that are embedded in more typical modes of school-community interactions.

The ways in which these power relations operate can be seen in the discourse surrounding "parental involvement" that has arisen in the North American context during the past 30 years. Despite the fact that this term lines the pages of the many manuals of school effectiveness that have been produced during this period, one can search in vain through most of this literature to find examples of genuine partnerships between schools and parents from culturally diverse backgrounds. [6] Because parents fail to show up to meetings designed to teach them "parenting skills" or other strategies for overcoming their children's "deficits," educators have assumed that they are just not interested in their children's education. This perspective is illustrated by Lloyd Dunn (1987), the author of the widely-used *Peabody Picture Vocabulary Test*, who explicitly blames Latino/Latina parents for their children's academic difficulties when he argues that "teachers are not miracle workers" (p. 65) and "Hispanic pupils and their parents have also failed the schools and society, because they have not been motivated and dedicated enough to make the system work for them" (p. 78). In other words, his argument is that educators are powerless to reverse the debilitating effects of apathetic and incompetent parents (whom Dunn also characterized as genetically inferior [p. 64]).

This form of discourse defines culturally diverse students and parents as inferior in various ways and therefore responsible for their own school failure and poverty. It also takes the focus of critical scrutiny away from schools and society. In this way, the educational and social status quo is legitimated and pressures for change are deflected.

Projects such as the Pajaro Valley example and others (*e.g.,* Balderas, 1995; Delgado-Gaitan, 1994, McCaleb, 1994; Torres-Guzman, 1995; Weinstein-Shr & Quintero, 1995) show that culturally diverse parents strongly desire to contribute to their children's education. The strong parental involvement manifested in these projects exposes the structures of disempowerment that masquerade as "normal" patterns of interaction between schools and culturally diverse communities. Parents who have survived brutal oppression in their home countries, and are experiencing poverty and hardship as they struggle to raise their children, care passionately about their children's education. However, if ability to speak English and knowledge of North American cultural conventions are made prerequisites for "parental involvement," then many of these parents will be defined as apathetic and incompetent and will play out their pre-ordained role of non-involvement.

In contrast to the affirmation of identity and empowerment that are reflected in the interactions between educators and parents in the Pajaro Valley example, the second example describes the disempowerment that indigenous peoples experienced historically in the educational system. Although the primary example is from Canada, equally disturbing accounts could have been drawn from countries such as Australia, New Zealand or the United States.

Disempowerment through Negotiation of Identity: The First Nations Residential School Experience

Residential schools in Canada operated in similar ways to boarding schools in the United States insofar as students were taken from their communities, often against their parents' will, and permitted to return to their communities only sporadically. Some of these schools were still operating into the 1970s.. The story of what happened in these schools for more than one hundred years has begun to emerge in the Canadian context from the first-hand accounts of survivors. Physical, sexual, and psychological abuse were rampant and federal, provincial and Church authorities simply turned a blind eye to what they knew was going on. Eradication of Native identity was seen as a prerequisite to making students into low-level productive citizens.

As expressed more than one hundred years ago by the General Secretary of the Methodist Church of Canada, removal of children from the influence of their homes (for at least five years) was a necessary condition for both salvation and civilization:

> Experience convinces us that the only way in which the Indians of the Country can be permanently elevated and thoroughly civilized, is by removing the children from the surroundings of Indian home life, and keeping them separate long enough to form those habits of order, industry, and systematic effort, which they will never learn at home. ...The return of children to their houses, even temporarily, has a bad effect, while their permanent removal [back home] after one or two years residence results in the loss of all that they have gained. (Letter dated April 2, 1886, from A. Sutherland, General Secretary of the Methodist Church of Canada, Missionary Department to Laurence Vankoughnet, Deputy Superintendent of Indian Affairs. Quoted in Tschantz, 1980, p. 7)

Tschantz goes on to document the extreme violence used in these schools to dissuade children from using their mother tongue, the key to their identity.

Dolphus Shae's testimony to the Berger Inquiry (1977: 90) of his experiences at the Aklavik Residential School describes not only the terrifying experiences which he and many other children endured, but also the resentment which lasted all his life: 'Before I went to school the only English I knew was "hello" and when we got there we were told that if we spoke Indian they would whip us until our hands were blue on both sides. And also we were told that the Indian religion was superstitious and pagan. It made you feel inferior to whites…We all felt lost and wanted to go home…Today I think back on the hostel life and I feel furious.' (Tschantz, 1980, p. 10)

Platero has described similar realities for Navajo students in the United States:

…For nearly a hundred years the policy of the United States government was to acculturate the Navajo, so that the Navajo could be assimilated into the White society. To effect this assimilation Navajo children were taken from the shelter of the family and sent to boarding school. Almost every child who entered the boarding school spoke only Navajo, and most of the people employed at the boarding schools spoke only English. When a Navajo child spoke the language of his family at school, he was punished. …Kee was sent to boarding school as a child where—as was the practice—he was punished for speaking Navajo. Since he was only allowed to return home during Christmas and summer, he lost contact with his family. Kee withdrew both from the White and Navajo worlds as he grew older, because he could not comfortably communicate in either language. …By the time he was 16, Kee was an alcoholic, uneducated and despondent—without identity. Kee's story is more the rule than the exception. (Platero, 1975, pp. 57-58)

The process of identity negotiation in schools is a reciprocal one between educators and students. For example, in the case of First Nations students in residential schools, educators defined their role as dispensers of salvation, civilization and education to students who necessarily had to be defined as lacking all of these qualities. In other words, the self-definition of educators required that students and their communities be defined as heathen, savage and without any valid form of cultural transmission (education). This devaluation of identity was communicated to students in all of the interactions they experienced in schools, ranging from brutal punishment if they were caught speaking their languages to widespread sexual abuse of both boys and girls. The long-term effects of this form of "ethnic cleansing" in education is illustrated in the following newspaper account of a conference focused on the residential school experience in British Columbia:

> A representative of four British Columbia native bands said yesterday that they intend to call churches and governments to account—morally and financially—for the damage done to their communities through the religious residential school system. ...the council of four Shuswap Indian bands decided to mount the conference after the community started to conquer widespread alcoholism and social problems in recent years and realized that the self-destructive behavior had been masking the pain of the residential school experience.

> Most children in the bands were forced to attend the St. Joseph's Mission, a residential school operated by the Roman Catholic Oblate order, until it was closed 10 years ago. Two former officials of the school have been convicted of sexually abusing male students, and its former principal, Bishop Hugh O'Connor of Prince George, is scheduled to go to a preliminary hearing next month on charges of abusing female students. ...

> Bev Sellars, chief of the Soda Creek Indian band of the Cariboo region, said aside from incidents of sexual abuse, residential school children were brutally strapped, sometimes 'until they were black and blue' and permanently scarred. She said they were treated 'like dirt' and made to feel like 'part of a weak, defective race.' 'That to me is not training for success, it is training for self-destruction,' she said. 'And thousands did self-destruct. If they didn't commit suicide, they became addicted to anything that could numb or distract the pain, and the addictions unfortunately only became another thing to be ashamed of.' (Wilson, 1991, *The Globe & Mail*, p. A4) [7]

The destruction of identity that went on in residential schools was rationalized as being in the best interests of the children involved. Although few other examples reach the depth of brutality of the residential school experience, the *process* that these examples illustrate is extremely common. In far too many contexts, the message given to students and communities is that success in school and in the wider society requires that they abandon any identification or affiliation with the culture and experiences they brought to school. Students' prior experiences are seen as an impediment to academic growth rather than as the foundation upon which academic development can be built.

In short, the process of identity negotiation is interwoven into all educator-student interactions. This process is usually non-problematic when there is a cultural, linguistic and social class match between educator and student but often highly problematic when there are mismatches or discontinuities in culture, language or class. In these cases, educators must make special efforts to ensure that students' prior experiences and identities are affirmed rather than devalued.

In the past, the typical pattern has been that the more socially powerful group has devalued the identities of the less powerful group and rationalized this as being in the group's best interests. Under these conditions, the subordinated group often internalizes the ways they are defined or positioned by the dominant group and come to see themselves as inferior. In *Pedagogy of the Oppressed*, Paulo Freire (1970) calls this process *cultural invasion* which he describes as follows:

> In cultural invasion it is essential that those who are invaded come to see their reality with the outlook of the invaders rather than their own; for the more they mimic the invaders, the more stable the position of the latter becomes. For cultural invasion to succeed, it is essential that those invaded become convinced of their intrinsic inferiority. Since everything has its opposite, if those who are invaded consider themselves inferior, they must necessarily recognize the superiority of the invaders. (p. 151)

However, subordinated groups and individuals also actively resist cultural invasion and devaluation of identity. For example, indigenous peoples throughout the Americas (and elsewhere) have been resisting cultural invasion for more than 500 years and this struggle continues unabated (see the volume *Rethinking Columbus* published by Rethinking Schools, [1991]). In the educational context, this resistance can occasionally take the form of excelling academically, as illustrated in the case studies described by Zanger (1994). However, more frequently it results in withdrawal from academic effort and dropping out of school (Darder, 1991; Walsh, 1991). [8]

The ways in which identities are negotiated in the classroom are strongly influenced by the assumptions in regard to culture and language in the wider society. Economically- and socially-powerful groups who have access to, and effectively control the media can manufacture consent for social and educational policies that they see as serving their interests (Chomsky, 1987; van Dijk, 2000). For example, during the 1990s and beyond, groups such as *U.S. English* have escalated a national campaign to promote English-only programs as being in the best interests of bilingual children. Their goal is to change both the way educators interact with bilingual students and the structures that exist within schools (*e.g.,* bilingual education). Arguments such as the following are intended to constrict the identity options for bilingual students in essentially similar ways to the constriction of identity that took place in residential schools for Native students:

- Bilingual students must be prevented from using their first language (L1) in school because "how else will they ever learn English?"

- Monolingual English programs are essential if students are to be given access to what *U.S. English* calls "the language of equal opportunity."

This type of discourse represents a form of "ethnic cleansing" in schools. Teacher-student interactions should cleanse bilingual students of their home language and culture which are constructed as impediments to learning English and assimilating into the full American identity. Sadly, this discourse is also persuasive to many people, as illustrated in the passage of Proposition 227 in California in June 1998 (see Chapter 2). Despite the fact that these media sound bites are contradicted by a vast amount of empirical research (see Chapters 6 and 9), they are capable of dramatically affecting the ways in which educators define their roles with respect to teaching culturally and linguistically diverse students. The ways educators define their roles will, in turn, affect the pattern of educator-student interactions and the process of identity negotiation within these interactions. In short, the pattern of inter-group power relations in the broader society is frequently replicated in the interpersonal power relations played out in the interactions between educators and culturally diverse students within the school.

The constriction of options for identity formation illustrated in an extreme way in the First Nations residential schools is clearly not inevitable. As illustrated in the Pajaro Valley example, there are many educators who define their roles in a very different way in relation to culturally diverse students and communities. They aim explicitly to expand students' options for identity formation by affirming and building on students' prior experience and exploring with them how they can make powerful contributions within their societies. In other words, their pedagogy explicitly takes into account where students are coming from and where they are going. The teacher mediates between students' past and their future. The instructional focus is on empowerment rather than disempowerment.

Terri McCarty provides a contemporary example of the centrality of what she calls the *image of the child* in restructuring schools for empowerment. She describes the changes in pedagogy and assessment initiated by educators and researchers working together in the Navajo-English bilingual program at Rough Rock as fundamentally involving transformations in the images educators held of themselves and of their students:

> In classrooms, curriculum and pedagogy are the mirrors in which children see themselves reflected and through which they construct images of themselves as thinkers, learners, and users of language. The applied research at Rough Rock suggests the potentials children can exploit when the image they see and develop is one of self-affirmation. By engaging students in relevant, content-rich study that builds on their linguistic and experiential capital, whole language pedagogy opens up these potentials. (1993, p. 191) [9]

It is clear that the ways in which identities are negotiated in the school context between educators, students, and communities are intertwined with patterns of power relations in the wider society. In the next section, the nature of these power relations is explored further in order to define what constitutes empowerment in the school context.

Coercive and Collaborative Relations of Power

Coercive relations of power refer to the exercise of power by a dominant group (or individual or country) to the detriment of a subordinated group (or individual or country). The assumption is that there is a fixed quantity of power that operates according to a zero-sum logic; in other words, the more power one group has the less is left for other groups. Coercive relations of power are reflected in and shaped through the use of language or discourse [10] and usually involve a definitional process that legitimates the inferior or deviant status accorded to the subordinated group (or individual or country). In other words, the dominant group defines the subordinated group as inferior (or evil), thereby automatically defining itself as superior (or virtuous). The process of defining groups or individuals as inferior or deviant almost inevitably results in a pattern of interactions that restricts their development and potential. For example, when teachers have low expectations of particular groups of students, they tend to provide fewer opportunities for academic development, thereby confining them intellectually.

The experience of First Nations students in residential schools, discussed above, illustrates the operation of coercive relations of power. In this case, the interactions between individual educators and students (henceforth termed *micro-interactions*) were merely reflecting the pattern of interactions between dominant and subordinated groups in the wider society (henceforth *macro-interactions*) where First Nations communities were widely disparaged. In both micro- and macro-interactions, the process of identity negotiation reflects the relations of power in the society.

Coercive relations of power generally operate to maintain and legitimate the division of resources and status in the society, *i.e.,* the societal power structure. They frequently invoke a particular form of discourse which William Ryan (1972) termed *blaming the victim*. The school failure of subordinated group students is attributed to alleged intrinsic characteristics of the group itself (*e.g.,* bilingualism, parental apathy, genetic inferiority, etc.) or to programs that are seen as serving the interests of the group (*e.g.,* bilingual education).

The relation of coercive power to discourse is clearly expressed by van Dijk (2000):

> We have power over others if they do what we want, or what is in our (and not in their) best interest. Such action control may be based on force, and hence be a form of coercion (such as in male violence against women, or military or police violence against citizens), or on other resources of control (such as money, a job, position) that allow us to 'make' people do what we want.

> Many forms of modern power are more subtle though. They control action indirectly and symbolically, for instance by persuasion. Such power is exerted by mind control. And since the mind is primarily controlled by text and talk, access to discourse as a power resource becomes essential. In other words, if minds are controlled by discourse, control over discourse is an important, though indirect, condition for mind control. Control over influential public discourse

implies more power over other people's minds, hence more symbolic power. (2000, p. 74)

In the present analysis, I am including both overt force and symbolic control as aspects of *coercive relations of power* when they are mobilized by a dominant group to the detriment of a subordinated group.

In contrast to coercive relations of power, collaborative relations of power operate on the assumption that power is not a fixed pre-determined quantity but rather can be *generated* in interpersonal and intergroup relations. In other words, participants in the relationship are *empowered* through their collaboration such that each is more affirmed in her or his identity and has a greater sense of efficacy to create change in his or her life or social situation. Thus, power is created in the relationship and shared among participants. The power relationship is *additive* rather than *subtractive*. Power is *created with* others rather than being *imposed on* or *exercised over* others. [11]

Within this framework, *empowerment* can be defined as *the collaborative creation of power*. Students whose schooling experiences reflect collaborative relations of power develop the ability, confidence and motivation to succeed academically. They participate competently in instruction as a result of having developed a secure sense of identity and the knowledge that their voices will be heard and respected within the classroom.

In other words, empowerment derives from the process of negotiating identities in the classroom. Identities are not static or fixed but rather are constantly being shaped through experiences and interactions. There are multiple facets to our identities. Some of these are difficult or impossible to change (*e.g.*, gender, ethnicity). However, other facets are more malleable or subject to modification as a result of our experiences (*e.g.*, core values, political affiliation, sense of self-worth in relation to intelligence, academic achievements, talents, attractiveness, etc.). For young children growing up, their sense of self-worth is usually cultivated through interactions with caregivers in the home. Ideally, interactions in the school further consolidate students' sense of self-worth but unfortunately, as we have seen, this has frequently not been the case for students whose communities are viewed as inferior or deviant in the wider society. [12]

The dynamic and multi-dimensional nature of identity can be illustrated by considering the concept of self that might be emerging for two bilingual elementary school children. María, from a Latina background in grade 1 of the River Glen dual language program in San Jose, California, might see herself in the following way:

She is *female, a daughter, a sister, American, of Mexican-American heritage, Catholic religion, speaks Spanish, is learning English, becoming bilingual, likes to read, is intelligent/good at school etc.*

Alex, a grade 3 student attending the YALLA (Young Americans Learning Languages Actively) Arabic-English dual language program in Becker Elementary School in Dearborn, Michigan, [13] might see himself as follows:

He is *male, a son, a brother, American, of Lebanese heritage, Christian religion, speaks, reads and writes Arabic in addition to English, intelligent/good at school, wants to be a computer programmer, etc.*

The way these identity options will develop depends fundamentally on the interpersonal experiences children have in school, particularly with their teachers. Furthermore, the identity options that teachers open up for students will dramatically affect the extent and the manner in which they will engage cognitively with academic challenges. A student who has been encouraged and given ample opportunities to write creatively in two languages may come to see herself as an author with something important to say to the world. Students whose writing experiences have not extended much beyond worksheets are unlikely to see themselves in this way.

Educators' interactions with students reflect the ways they have defined their own roles or identities as educators. This *role definition* determines the way they view students' possibilities and the messages they communicate to students in regard to the contributions they can make to their societies. Thus, our interactions with students are constantly sketching a triangular set of images:

• an image of our own identities as educators;

• an image of the identity options we highlight for our students; consider, for example, the contrasting messages conveyed to students in classrooms focused on collaborative critical inquiry compared to classrooms focused on passive internalization of information;

• an image of the society we hope our students will help form.

The ways in which instruction opens up or shuts off identity options can be illustrated in the findings of large-scale studies of classroom interaction in the United States. These studies suggest that teacher-centered transmission of information and skills remains the predominant mode of instruction (*e.g.,* Goodlad, 1984; Ramírez, 1992). Sirotnik (1983), in discussing the implications of Goodlad's study, points to the fact that the typical American classroom contains:

...a lot of teacher talk and a lot of student listening...almost invariably closed and factual questions...and predominantly total class instructional configurations around traditional activities—all in a virtually affectless environment. It is but a short inferential leap to suggest that we are implicitly teaching dependence upon authority, linear thinking, social apathy, passive involvement, and hands-off learning. (p. 29)

In other words, an image of the society that students will graduate into and the kind of contributions they can make to that society is embedded implicitly in the interactions between educators and students. These interactions reflect the way educators have defined their roles with respect to the purposes of education in general and culturally diverse students and communities in particular. Are we preparing students to accept the societal status quo (and, in many cases, their own inferior status therein) or are we preparing them to participate actively and critically in the democratic process in pursuit of the ideals of social justice and equity which are enshrined in the American constitution?

This perspective clearly implies that in situations where coercive relations of power between dominant and subordinated groups predominate, the creation of interpersonal spaces where students' identities are validated will entail a direct challenge by educators (and students) to the societal power structure. For example, to acknowledge that culturally diverse students' religion, culture and language are valid forms of *self*-expression and to encourage their development is to challenge the prevailing attitudes in the wider society and the coercive structures that reflect these attitudes.

Thus, real change in the education of culturally diverse students requires a fundamental shift from coercive to collaborative relations of power. The history of humanity does not augur well for the imminence of such a paradigm shift, but environmental and social deterioration has reached a point where there may be little alternative if our species is to survive. The reality is that in the world of winners and losers, the "winner" ultimately joins the loser. Witness how industrialized societies are threatened by the destruction of the rainforests in the developing countries; or how poverty in the inner cities impacts on the wealthier sectors of society through increased crime, drugs, or costs associated with incarceration or welfare. Historical patterns of coercive relations of power are reaching a point of diminishing returns even for socially powerful groups. Simply put, educating students is a much better investment for our society than incarcerating them.

The challenge is to change the structure of power relations such that they become additive through collaboration rather than subtractive through coercion; in other words, the structure of macro- and micro-interactions needs to shift so that these interactions generate power for all participants rather than increase the disparities of power.

Figure 1.1 outlines the framework that has been sketched thus far. This framework also serves to organize the content of subsequent chapters.

The framework proposes that relations of power in the wider society (macro-interactions), ranging from coercive to collaborative in varying degrees, influence both the ways in which educators define their role and the types of structures that are established in the educational system. Role definitions refer to the mindset of expectations, assumptions and goals that educators bring to the task of educating culturally diverse students. Educational structures refer to the organization of schooling in a broad sense that includes policies, programs, curriculum, and assessment. This organization is established to achieve the goals of education as defined primarily by the dominant group in the society. For example, the historical patterns of educational segregation in the United States, Canada, South Africa and many other countries were designed to limit the opportunities that subordinated groups might have for educational and social advancement. By contrast, bilingual education in the United States was instituted to promote equality of educational opportunity at a time (late 1960s, early 1970s) when there was some degree of consensus in the society that this was a valid and important goal.

Educational structures, however, are not static; as with most other aspects of the way societies are organized and resources distributed, educational structures are contested by individuals and groups. The debates surrounding bilingual education illustrate just how volatile these issues can become.

Educational structures, together with educator role definitions, determine the micro-interactions between educators, students, and communities. These micro-interactions form an interpersonal or an interactional space within which the acquisition of knowledge and formation of identity is negotiated. Power is created and shared within this interpersonal space where minds and identities meet. [14] As such, the micro-interactions constitute the most immediate determinant of student academic success or failure.

These micro-interactions between educators, students and communities are never neutral; in varying degrees, they either reinforce coercive relations of power or promote collaborative relations of power. In the former case, they contribute to the disempowerment of culturally diverse students and communities; in the latter case, the micro-interactions constitute a process of empowerment that enables educators, students and communities to challenge the operation of coercive power structures.

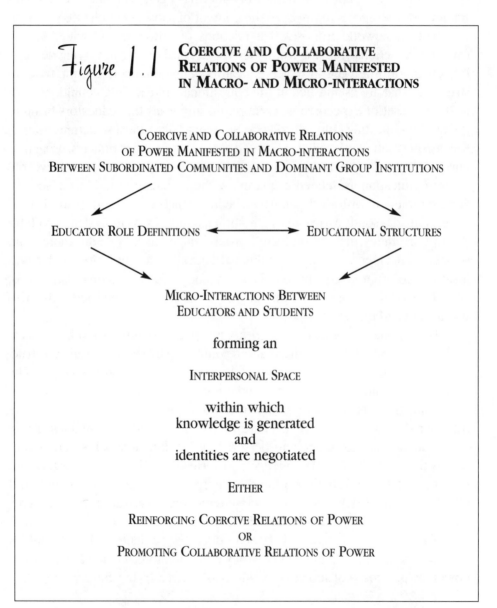

Figure 1.1 COERCIVE AND COLLABORATIVE RELATIONS OF POWER MANIFESTED IN MACRO- AND MICRO-INTERACTIONS

COERCIVE AND COLLABORATIVE RELATIONS
OF POWER MANIFESTED IN MACRO-INTERACTIONS
BETWEEN SUBORDINATED COMMUNITIES AND DOMINANT GROUP INSTITUTIONS

EDUCATOR ROLE DEFINITIONS ⟷ EDUCATIONAL STRUCTURES

MICRO-INTERACTIONS BETWEEN
EDUCATORS AND STUDENTS

forming an

INTERPERSONAL SPACE

within which
knowledge is generated
and
identities are negotiated

EITHER

REINFORCING COERCIVE RELATIONS OF POWER
OR
PROMOTING COLLABORATIVE RELATIONS OF POWER

Conclusion

The pedagogical framework sketched above views the interactions between educators and students as the most immediate determinant of student success or failure in school. These interactions can be viewed through two lens: the lens of the *teaching-learning relationship* in a narrow sense, represented by the strategies and techniques that teachers use to provide the comprehensible input required to promote reading development, content knowledge and cognitive growth; the second lens is the lens of *identity negotiation* which is represented by the messages communicated to students regarding their identities—who they are in the teacher's eyes and who they are capable of becoming.

The chapters that follow highlight the fact that educators, both as individuals and collectively within schools, are never powerless or without choices, although they frequently work in conditions that are oppressive both for them and their students. While they rarely have complete freedom, educators do have choices in the way they structure the interactions in the classroom. They have some degree of freedom in determining the social and educational goals they want to achieve with their students. They are responsible for the role definitions they adopt in relation to culturally diverse students and communities. Even in the context of English-only instruction, educators do have options in their orientation to students' language and culture, in the forms of parent and community participation they encourage, and in the way they implement pedagogy and assessment (see, for example, DeFazio, 1997; Lucas & Katz, 1994).

Sonia Nieto (1999) has expressed well the potential impact of the identity choices that educators adopt. She notes: "the inescapable truth…is that teachers' attitudes and behaviors can make an astonishing difference in student learning" (p. 167) and goes on to elaborate:

> In the end, if teachers believe that students cannot achieve at high levels, that their backgrounds are riddled with deficiencies, and that multicultural education is a frill that cannot help them to learn, the result will be school reform strategies that have little hope for success. On the other hand, if teachers begin by challenging social inequities that inevitably place some students at a disadvantage over others; if they struggle against institutional policies and practices that are unjust; if they begin with the strengths and talents of students and their families; if they undergo a process of personal transformation based on their own identities and experiences; and finally, if they engage with colleagues in a collaborative and imaginative

encounter to transform their own practices and their schools to achieve equal and high-quality education for all students, then the outcome is certain to be a more positive one than is currently the case. (1999, pp. 175–176)

I believe that much of the current discourse on education in the United States and elsewhere is orienting educators towards the first alternative that Nieto outlines. Schools are being pushed to constrict the learning opportunities and identity options available to culturally diverse students as a result of the media dismissal of multicultural and bilingual education as viable educational options. In their place has come the promotion of "one-stop panaceas" such as "phonemic awareness" in the teaching of reading, "structured English immersion" as the solution to academic language learning, and ever increasing layers of accountability and standardized testing designed to ensure compliance and top-down control over teacher-student interactions. This orientation violates any serious interpretation of the term *education*, understood as nurturing and expanding students' potential (Gándara *et al.*, 2000; McNeil, 2000).

My purpose in writing this book is to contribute to making explicit the unease that many educators feel about how their roles are been defined by these constricting trends in recent policy and public debate. In order to resist the prescribed role definitions dictated by these "one-stop panaceas" and the coercive power relations that fuel them, educators must understand the research and theory relating to academic language learning among bilingual and culturally diverse students. The chapters that follow attempt to present, integrate, and interpret for policy and practice the research and theory that exist in this area.

Chapters 2 through 6 focus on aspects of bilingualism, language learning, and bilingual education. The second chapter discusses the history of the education of bilingual students in North America and outlines the way certain forms of discourse are currently being mobilized in the service of coercive relations of power. In order to throw some light on the research realities behind this debate, Chapter 3 focuses on the nature of proficiency in a language and discusses how misconceptions about language proficiency have fueled controversy about bilingual education. Chapter 4 attempts to demystify the volatile controversies concerning reading instruction; specifically, the goal is to put "phonics" and "whole language" in their place and to highlight the influence of broader social factors on reading development. In Chapter 5, the kinds of classroom instructional environments that will accelerate academic language learning are examined. Chapter 6 reviews the research on bilingual education and the theoretical principles that underlie the consistent support for programs that strongly support the development of bilingual students' L1.

In Chapter 7, the focus is on the specific changes necessary to transform the educational experience of culturally diverse students from a historical pattern of widespread academic failure to a pattern of academic success. This change process entails transformations in schools' orientation to students' language and culture, parental participation, pedagogy, and assessment such that the micro-interactions between educators, students, and communities generate collaborative empowerment.

Portraits of how this empowerment process has operated at the preschool, elementary, and secondary levels are presented in Chapter 8. In Chapter 9, I analyze in more detail the recent opposition to bilingual education by academic critics in order to illustrate the disregard for both empirical evidence and logical consistency that underlies their arguments.

The final chapter returns to the issue of how power is negotiated and distributed in both the domestic and international arenas. The goal is to show how the anti-bilingual education discourse mobilized by groups such as *U.S. English* forms part of a broader pattern of coercive relations of power. If educators understand that the purpose of this discourse is (a) to dismantle educational structures that promote student and community empowerment and (b) to limit possibilities for the collaborative creation of power, then they are in a better position to resist this process and more actively promote democratic participation and social justice both in their classrooms and in the wider society.

Endnotes to Chapter 1

1. With the escalation of anti-immigrant rhetoric in the United States during the 1990s, even the home became off-limits to use a language other than English. This is illustrated in the remarks of State District Judge Samuel Kiser to Marta Laureano, a bilingual Mexican-American involved in a child custody dispute in Amarillo, Texas. The judge told Laureano that she was abusing her five-year old daughter by speaking Spanish to her and ordered Laureano to speak only English at home. The father of the child, Timothy Garcia, who was seeking unsupervised visitation rights with his daughter, had complained that she was not proficient in English. As reported in Maclean's magazine (September 11, 1995, p. 13):

> In court, Kiser told Laureano that she was relegating her daughter "to the position of housemaid." After a public outcry, Kiser backed down—a little. He apologized to housekeepers everywhere, "since we entrust our personal possessions and our families' welfare to these hardworking people." But otherwise, Kiser stood by his statements. Excerpts from his comments:

"If she starts first grade with the other children and cannot even speak the language that the teachers and others speak, and she's a full-blooded American citizen, you're abusing that child and you're relegating her to the position of housemaid. Now, get this straight: you start speaking English to that child, because if she doesn't do good [sic] in school, then I can remove her because it's not in her best interest to be ignorant.

"You are real big about talking about what's best for your daughter, but you won't even teach a five-year-old child how to speak English. And then you expect her to go off to school and educate herself and be able to learn how to make a living. Now that is bordering on abuse."

2. R.D. Laing (1969), the Scottish psychiatrist, has written insightfully about patterns of confirmation and disconfirmation in interpersonal relationships. The following quotations from his book *Self and Others* illustrate his perspective:

Even an account of one person cannot afford to forget that each person is always acting upon others and acted upon by others. The others are there also. No one acts or experiences in a vacuum. ...(pp. 81-82)

A woman cannot be a mother without a child. She needs a child to give her the identity of a mother. A man needs a wife for him to be a husband. ...All 'identities' require an other. ...(p. 82)

Every relationship implies a definition of self by other and other by self. ...Other people become a sort of identity kit, whereby one can piece together a picture of oneself. One recognizes oneself in that old smile of recognition from that old friend. ...It is difficult to establish a consistent identity for oneself—that is, to see oneself consistently in the same way—if definitions of oneself by others are inconsistent or mutually exclusive. ...To 'fit in with' them all or to repudiate them all may be impossible. Hence mystification, confusion, and conflict. (pp. 86-87)

This is the situation for many culturally diverse students; the messages about identity they receive from home and school are frequently contradictory. As expressed by Sudia Paloma McCaleb (1994), when a child feels that the culture of the home is not valued by that of the school, she:

...is often forced to make difficult choices about whose teachings she is going to accept and whose she will reject. When the values and teachings of the home and school are quite different, serious intergenerational conflicts can result. ...While some students accept their bicultural identities, others want to deny their home culture completely. ...We are beginning to witness the tragedy that may result when students reject the home culture. As students pull themselves away from their roots and family ties, they need to find or become part of another group for support and care. Growing numbers of young people are succumbing to the attractions of gang involvement. (pp. 32–33)

Schools can go a long way towards preventing this process when educators affirm the home culture and involve parents as partners in the education of their children (see Chapter 7).

3. The term First Nations is the preferred self-descriptor of aboriginal communities in Canada, reflecting their status as the first nations of this continent. First Nations communities in Canada generally view the term *Indian* as reflecting the Eurocentric perspective of Columbus and his followers who thought they had discovered a new route to the Indies.

4. A similar picture emerges from an account of the project in the Santa Cruz Sentinel:

Another parent said she noticed her children are now starting to request that she bring more books home to read, and they are now requesting them in Spanish instead of English. The result, she said, is they are learning about their culture and language, and also realizing that there are as many good ideas in Spanish as there are in English.

Another parent said the reading and writing program has helped her to be more resolute in dealing with teachers and demanding that they teach her child Spanish, her native language.

The biggest benefit, however, may be that the children and their parents are being drawn closer by the constant expression and discussion of ideas and books they are working on together.

'Tell your children every day how much you love them, how much you value them and how much you appreciate them,' Ada said in closing. (Estrada, *Santa Cruz Sentinel*, Friday October 31, 1986)

5. This project is not an isolated one. A variety of other recent projects that have transformed the relationships between schools and communities are described by Balderas (1995), Delgado-Gaitan (1994), McCaleb (1994), and Weinstein-Shr & Quintero (1995).

6. James Comer's (1980) work is a notable exception to this trend.

7. Claims totaling billions of dollars have been filed by First Nations communities against various Churches and the Canadian federal government. Several Churches (*e.g.*, the Anglican Church of Canada) face bankruptcy and may cease operating as a result of this litigation. Efforts to heal the wounds of the past are illustrated by the public apology offered by St. John's (Newfoundland) Roman Catholic Archbishop James MacDonald to First Nations people in September, 2000: "In his apology, Archbishop MacDonald talked of the churches being ashamed of the role they had played in the destruction of native culture. He asked for

forgiveness and sought reconciliation with the native people" (*Globe & Mail*, September 9, 2000, p. A2). More than 25 lawsuits brought by the Innu First Nations community of Labrador claiming abuse by priests are pending against the Roman Catholic Church.

8. Zanger (1994) reports on the insights of a class of academically-successful Latino/Latina high school students into the social dynamics of their schooling experience. Students were asked to discuss the reasons for the high drop-out rate of other Spanish-speaking students at the school and to recommend ways to make the school better for students from Spanish-speaking backgrounds. The student body at the school was about 40% Latino/Latina, 40% African-American, and 20% White. A transitional bilingual program operated in the school and was staffed by Latino/Latina and White teachers but there were no Latino/Latina teachers in the monolingual program.

Three themes emerged from the data: marginalization, cultural respect, and student-teacher trust. Marginalization reflected students' feeling that they existed on the social and academic periphery of the school, were relegated to an inferior status in the school's social hierarchy, and were ignored and felt almost invisible.

Students' perception that their culture was not respected within the school was expressed by Elsa who said "You can't succeed in a place where no one respects you for what you are" (p. 179). Students resented the fact that their culture was not incorporated into the curriculum despite the fact that 40% of the student body was Latino/Latina.

Students' comments also reflected an erosion of trust and cooperation on both sides between teachers and students. Students felt that their teachers' ignorance of their backgrounds contributed to mutual alienation. Elsa, for example, complained that "teachers don't learn from us, they don't learn from anybody. They don't ask" (p. 186). Students expressed the "desire to establish more caring, supportive, even family-like relationships with teachers' (p. 186).

Zanger concludes that school restructuring must focus on transforming the mainstream so that neither students nor teachers feel left out. In Zanger's study, as in the research of Poplin and Weeres (1992), the quality of relationships established across cultural boundaries emerges as a central aspect of students' ability and willingness to become academically engaged. A similar perspective is elaborated by Walsh (1991) in her book *Pedagogy and the Struggle for Voice: Issues of Language, Power, and Schooling for Puerto Ricans*. The central purpose of her study "was to highlight how the past and present intersect in people's voices, infuse pedagogy, and sculpt the conditions and processes involved in coming to know" (p. 133).

The intensity of students' desire for connection and self-expression within the school context is vividly expressed in a piece of writing by a Chinese immigrant high school student in an ethnographic study conducted by Linda Harklau (1999):

> I have no way to project, reveal my persona. Speech is an important part
> of a person's image. All ESL kids when they first come to this country their
> image become: "The foreign students" and that's their persona, all the rest
> are not revealed, are forgotten. For me I cannot stand not to be able to say
> things I want to say. (p. 50)

9. According to McCarty, the instructional changes underway at Rough Rock appear to be bearing fruit with respect to students' academic achievement: "When individual and grade-cohort scores are analyzed for all K–6 students over the past two years, an overriding pattern emerges: Bilingual students who have the benefit of cumulative, uninterrupted initial literacy experiences in Navajo make the greatest gains on local and national measures of achievement" (1993, p. 191).

McCarty's case study of the restructuring process at Rough Rock parallels many other examples of dramatic educational improvement resulting from instruction that emphasizes affirmation of identity. Abi-Nader (1993), for example, documents how Spanish-speaking high school students' academic performance improved dramatically when cultural values associated with *familia* were incorporated into instruction. More than 65 percent of the graduates of this program went on to college, a striking contrast with the massive dropout rates of Latino/Latina students in other school systems.

Hayes, Bahruth, and Kessler (1991) similarly document the impact on student success of incorporating a strong positive affective dimension into a program for migrant Mexican-American students in an agricultural community in South Texas. As expressed in the title of their book (*Literacy con Carino*), the focus was on literacy achieved through a nurturing process:

> Attention to caring about and valuing each student individually was the result of a conscious attempt to incorporate into the school culture the affection and caring the students experienced in their homes. Although many of the parents of these children were illiterate, their home lives often reflected rich oral traditions, deeply felt care and love, and a strong desire on the part of the parents for their children to succeed in school. (p. 2)

The case studies described by Igoa (1995) and Nieto (1996) again show the centrality of issues related to identity in students' orientation to effort and success at school. Finally, a large-scale study of Southeast Asian students carried out by Rumbaut and Ima (1987) reported greater academic success among students who were maintaining traditional values, ethnic pride, and close social and cultural ties with members of their ethnic group.

The clear message from these studies is that the more the school affirms rather than ignores or devalues students' personal and cultural identities, the more likely students are to succeed educationally.

This point has also been made forcefully by Donna Deyhle (1995) in an article entitled: "Navajo Youth and Anglo Racism: Cultural Integrity and Resistance." She analyzes the identity choices that Navajo students were forced to make as a result of a school district's refusal to implement a Navajo-English bilingual program. Administrators and teachers believed that Navajo students' language and culture were the source of their academic difficulties. In the words of one teacher "These kids we get are learning disabled with their reading. Because they speak Navajo, you know" (p. 418). Another teacher argued that "Bilingual education will become the greatest obstacle a Navajo student has to overcome and an impediment to the education of all other students" (p. 418). Deyhle locates these perspectives in the power relations operating in the wider society:

To accept Navajo culture and language would be to confer equal status, which is unacceptable to the Anglo community. Navajo culture and students' lives are effectively silenced by the surrounding Anglo community. Navajo language and traditions are absent from the school curriculum. Teachers' ignorance of Navajo students' lives results in the dismissal of the credibility of Navajo life. (p. 419)

Deyhle documents how maintaining pride in their culture and language (cultural integrity) can contribute to students' academic success in this kind of context, although this path was "fraught with conflict, uncertainty, and pain" (p. 439).

10. I am using the term discourse to refer to the ways in which language is used to create what is generally accepted as *common sense*, thereby orchestrating consent for initiatives that are in the interests of particular groups. Thus, discourses are intimately linked to patterns of power relations in a society. Discourses constitute what can be thought and what counts as truth or knowledge. Internalized discourses constitute cognitive schemata, which might be thought of as computer programs in our heads, that allow for certain propositions to be processed in a highly automatized way and accepted as valid while propositions that are inconsistent with the internalized discourse are automatically rejected. A major focus of schooling in virtually all societies is the transmission of internalized discourses that are consistent with, and reinforcing of, national, cultural or religious identities (see Foucault [1980] for a detailed discussion of discourse and its relation to power).

The relationship between discourse and power is elaborated by Corson (1993) who claims that language is mainly an instrument of power; it is "the vehicle for identifying, manipulating and changing power relations between people" (1993, p. 1). He goes on to argue that "rather than a privilege that is ascribed to the individual, power itself is a network of relations constantly in tension and ever-present in activity; rather than possessed and localized in individual hands, power is exercised through the production, accumulation and functioning of various discourses" (1993, p. 4-5). The ways in which discourse operates to "manufacture consent" (Chomsky, 1987) can be described in terms of Gramsci's notion of *hegemony* which, as summarized by Corson:

> ...describes the organization of consent through invisible cultural dominance, rather than through visible political power. ...This non-coercive 'force' is said to penetrate consciousness itself, so that the dominated become accomplices in their own domination. So it is argued that power hegemonies are reinforced from both sides of the power relationship: in their language usages, the non-dominant adhere to the linguistic norms created by dominant groups, while not realizing that they are being 'voluntarily coerced.' (p. 6)

Within the discipline of psychology, Harré and Gillett (1994) have argued for the centrality of discourse in understanding all aspects of human behavior. They suggest that "the mind of any human being is constituted by the discourses that they are involved in, private and public" (p. 104). Private discourse is thought; public discourse is behavior. It is possible to learn much about private discourse (thought and consciousness) through its public manifestation. According to discursive psychology, each individual's structure of consciousness will appear in the way we converse. Our minds and identities are the confluence of the social relations in which we have participated. In Corson's (1995) terms, "each human individual stands at a unique intersection of discourses and relationships: a 'position' embedded in historical, political, cultural, social, and interpersonal contexts, that largely determines mind" (p. 3).

11. All of us intuitively understand the nature of collaborative relations of power. The notion refers to the kind of affirmation and power that is generated when two people love each other, or in the relations between parents and children, or when teachers connect at a personal level with their students rather than just transmitting content.

I came across a moving example of "collaborative relations of power" in reading a newspaper during a trip to Ireland in May 1995. A news report under the headline "1845 Famine Aid Gesture Is Recalled" read as follows:

> An American Indian tribe which sent aid to Ireland during the Great Famine will be thanked personally by President Robinson [the then Irish President] during a visit to the U.S. The generosity of the Choctaw nation will be marked by the President at the tribal headquarters in Durant, Oklahoma, next Monday. The Choctaw heard of the famine disaster in 1845 and sent aid to Ireland equivalent to [about $1.8] million today, despite their own meagre resources. (*Evening Herald*, Tuesday, May 16, 1995, p. 6)

12. Peirce (1995) has also emphasized the ways in which relations of power affect interaction between language learners and target language speakers. She criticizes current second language acquisition theory for focusing on the individual in isolation from the social context and the power relations embedded in that context. She suggests that the notions of *social identity* and *investment* are key to understanding learners' interactions in the target language. Specifically, she argues that the concept of *motivation* is usually viewed as

> …a property of the language learner—a fixed personality trait. The notion of investment, on the other hand, attempts to capture the relationship of the language learner to the changing social world. It conceives of the language learner as having a complex social identity and multiple desires. The notion presupposes that when language learners speak, they are not only exchanging information with target language speakers but they are constantly organizing and reorganizing a sense of who they are and how they relate to the social world. Thus, an investment in the target language is also an investment in a learner's own social identity, an identity which is constantly changing across time and space. (1995, pp. 17-18)

13. The evaluation of the YALLA 50/50 Arabic-English dual language immersion program reported that 2nd through 5th grade students scored as well as or better than non-immersion students both in Becker Elementary School and in the entire district on standardized tests administered in English. The evaluation report concludes: "Those students who are dominant

Arabic speaking benefit because they get the opportunity to maintain their native language while learning English, and the dominant English speakers benefit because they get the opportunity to become fluent in Arabic. The YALLA program at Becker Elementary School merits continued endorsement and promotion" (EdCon International, February 2000, [Abstract of Report]). At least 95% of students in the YALLA program are of Arabic heritage and the vast majority qualify for free lunch (*i.e.,* come from low income families).

14. I am using the term *interpersonal space* in a way that overlaps with Vygotsky's (1978) influential notion of the *zone of proximal development* (ZPD) which he defined as the distance between children's developmental level as determined by individual problem solving without adult guidance and the level of potential development as determined by children's problem solving under the influence of, or in collaboration with, more capable adults and peers. Expressed simply, the ZPD is the interpersonal space where minds meet and new understandings can arise through collaborative interaction and inquiry. Newman, Griffin, and Cole (1989) label this interpersonal space *the construction zone.* In the present volume, the dual process of reciprocal negotiation of identity and collaborative generation of knowledge take place within this "construction zone" and are seen as being intimately related to each other. Teacher-student collaboration in the construction of knowledge will operate effectively only in contexts where students' identities are being affirmed. Essentially, this conception extends the ZPD beyond the cognitive sphere into the realms of affective development and power relationships (see Chapter 5). It also makes clear that the *construction zone* can also be a *constriction zone* where student identities and learning are constricted rather than extended.

Chapter 2
The Evolution of Xenophobia: Cultural Diversity as the Enemy Within

Many commentators have objected strenuously to the implementation of bilingual education programs because they appear to run counter to the American tradition of assimilating immigrant groups into the mainstream of society. To these commentators, the increased status that accrues to a language (*e.g.,* Spanish) as a result of being recognized for instructional purposes in schools appears likely to hinder the efficient operation of the melting pot. Not only will individuals who speak that language be rewarded with jobs and other incentives, but children will also be encouraged to retain their language. To opponents of bilingual education, the apparent encouragement of ethnic distinctiveness is especially unpalatable at the present time in view of the rapid growth of the Spanish-speaking population. In California, for example, Latino/Latina students are projected to form 50% of the school population by the year 2030. Encouraging these students to retain their home language contributes, according to this view, to what Arthur Schlesinger Jr. (1991) called "The Disuniting of America."

A favorite theme of many commentators is that the melting pot worked well for previous generations of immigrants who "made it" without crutches, and Spanish-speaking students could also make it if they tried.

This attitude shows a profound ignorance of American educational history. The groups that have tended to experience persistent educational difficulty (African-American, Latino/Latina, Native American, and Native Hawaiian students) were never given the opportunity to "melt" into the American mainstream. Unlike immigrant groups, these groups represent what John Ogbu

(1992) terms *involuntary minorities*. Their status has been that of internal colonies insofar as they have been subordinated and regarded as inherently inferior for generations by the Euro-American dominant group.

Ogbu's (1978, 1992) distinction between voluntary and involuntary minorities is important for understanding both the historical and current educational achievement of culturally diverse communities in the United States (and elsewhere).

Voluntary and Involuntary Minorities

Ogbu (1992) defines immigrant or voluntary minorities as people who have moved more or less voluntarily to another society usually because they seek better economic opportunities and/or greater political freedom. He suggests that:

> Voluntary minorities usually experience initial problems in school due to cultural and language differences as well as lack of understanding of how the education system works. But they do not experience lingering, disproportionate school failure. The Chinese and Punjabi Indians are representative U.S. examples. (p. 8)

By contrast, involuntary minorities are people who were originally brought into the United States (or any other society) against their will; for example, through slavery, conquest, colonization, or forced labor. According to Ogbu, "thereafter, these minorities were often relegated to menial positions and denied true assimilation into the mainstream society" (p. 8).

The division between voluntary and involuntary minorities is not always clear-cut. For example, Mexican-Americans who immigrate to the U.S. may initially have many of the characteristics of voluntary minorities; however, they quickly encounter the barriers to full participation that Mexican-Americans have historically experienced and their encounters with the dominant group become very similar to those of previous generations of Mexican-Americans. [1]

Ogbu suggests that voluntary minorities are characterized by primary cultural differences from the dominant group whereas involuntary minorities are characterized by secondary cultural differences. Primary cultural differences are those that existed before two groups come into contact (*e.g.,* differences in language, religion, child-rearing practices, etc.). Secondary cultural differences arise after two populations come into contact, particularly when the contact involves the domination of one group by another. Under these circumstances, the involuntary minority will often develop an ambivalent or oppositional collective identity in relation to the dominant group. Minority group members take on certain cultural behaviors that are opposed to dominant group norms in order to maintain their collective identity and sense of security and self-worth. According to Ogbu:

> Voluntary minorities seem to bring to the United States a sense of who they are from their homeland and seem to retain this different but non-oppositional social identity at least during the first generation. Involuntary minorities, in contrast, develop a new sense of social or collective identity that is in opposition to the social identity of the dominant group after they have become subordinated. They do so in response to their treatment by White Americans in economic, political, social, psychological, cultural, and language domains. Whites' treatment included deliberate exclusion from true assimilation or the reverse, namely, forced superficial assimilation. (p. 9)

Ogbu suggests that a major reason why academic difficulties among involuntary minorities tend to be persistent is that cultural and language boundaries become more rigid than is typically the case for voluntary minorities. As illustrated by Deyhle's (1995) case study of the education of Navajo students, this process is rooted in inter-group power relations:

> The presence of these cultural differences, by themselves, is a politically neutral phenomenon. Navajo youth, securely rooted in their culture, move back and forth between their community and the surrounding Anglo community. …Cultural boundaries, however, are often turned into cultural borders or barriers during inter-group conflict. …The Anglo community uses Navajo culture as a border, a reason to deny equality by claiming the privilege of one kind of knowledge over another. Navajo families are judged by what they don't have—money, middle-class Anglo values, higher education, and professional jobs—rather than by what they do have—extended families, permanent homes, strong Navajo values and religious beliefs. (Deyhle, 1995, p. 438)

Thus, cultural boundaries frequently are entrenched by various forms of discrimination on the part of the dominant group. However, according to Ogbu, they are also maintained by the minority group as a means of insulating themselves culturally from the process of subordination. The cultural and language differences act as markers of the group's collective identity and help the group cope under conditions of subordination.

While the realities of minority group adaptation are likely to be considerably more complex in practice than revealed by Ogbu's typology (see Cummins, 1997, Gibson, 1997), the distinctions he makes do throw light on the general patterns of academic achievement among culturally diverse students. His analysis points to the centrality of issues of identity in understanding school success and failure. Consistent with this perspective, Signitia Fordham's research with academically-successful African-American adolescents highlights the conflict these students feel between loyalty to their peer group and doing well in school, which the peer group regards as selling out to White norms:

> ...within the school structure, Black adolescents consciously and unconsciously sense that they have to give up aspects of their identities and of their indigenous cultural system in order to achieve success as defined in dominant-group terms; their resulting social selves are embodied in the notion of racelessness. Hence, for many of them the cost of school success is too high; it implies that cultural integrity must be sacrificed in order to "make it." For many Black adolescents, that option is unacceptable. For the high achievers identified in this paper, achieving school success is not marked only by conflict and ambivalence...but with the need to camouflage efforts directed at behaviors that the group identifies as "acting White." (1990, p. 259)

In a similar vein, Ladson-Billings (1995) has reviewed research suggesting that academically successful African-American students tended to be social isolates, with neither African-American nor White friends. These students perceived accurately that teachers were likely to devalue their academic competence if they manifested cultural behaviors that were typical of African-American youth. Ladson-Billings points out:

> The problem that African-American students face is the constant devaluation of their culture both in school and in the larger society. Thus, the styles apparent in African-American youth culture—*e.g.,* dress, music, walk, language—are equated with poor academic performance. The student who identifies with "hip-hop" culture may be regarded as dangerous and/or a gang member for whom academic success is not expected. (1995, p. 485).

Ladson-Billings outlines a theory of "culturally relevant pedagogy" that encourages students to maintain their cultural integrity while succeeding academically. The theoretical assumptions underlying "culturally relevant pedagogy" are consistent with the assumptions of the present framework. Both approaches argue that the ways in which identities are negotiated in the micro-interactions between educators and students must challenge the coercive pattern of macro-interactions in the broader society (see Chapter 7).

In the next section, the historical patterns of inter-group contact and academic performance are examined in the context of Ogbu's distinction between voluntary and involuntary minorities.

The Historical Context

Involuntary Minorities. In light of historical realities, the concerns about bilingual education being against American traditions and a potential catalyst for separatist tendencies are highly ironic. In fact, the education of Mexican-Americans in the Southwest was openly dedicated until the late 1960's to *separating* Mexican-American students from the mainstream of American society by means of segregated schooling (conducted exclusively in English). In Texas, for example, the judgment of the court in the United States versus the State of Texas case (1981) documented the "pervasive, intentional discrimination throughout most of this century" against Mexican-American students (a charge that was not contested by the State of Texas in the trial) and noted that:

> the long history of prejudice and deprivation remains a significant obstacle to equal educational opportunity for these children. The deep sense of inferiority, cultural isolation, and acceptance of failure, instilled in a people by generations of subjugation, cannot be eradicated merely by integrating the schools and repealing the 'no Spanish' statutes. (1981, p. 14)

Noel Epstein (1977), although a critic of bilingual education policy, also noted "the widespread discrimination and humiliation that have often been severely inflicted against such students" (p. 55). He goes on to report that:

> As late as 1970, Charles E. Silberman reported, 'In a South Texas school, children are forced to kneel in the playground and beg forgiveness if they are caught talking to each other in Spanish; some teachers require students using the forbidden language to kneel before the entire class.' In the early 1970's, the U.S. Civil Rights Commission reported com-

ments from students who said that getting caught speaking Spanish meant that they were fined, forced to stand on a special black square or made to write 'I must not speak Spanish.' This may help explain why Hispanic Americans speak of the melting pot today in harsh terms which other Americans might not recognize. (p. 55)

This perspective on the melting pot is eloquently expressed in an essay by Isidro Lucas (1981) entitled "Bilingual Education and the Melting Pot: Getting Burned." He argues that

There is in America a profound, underground culture, that of the unmeltable populations. Blacks have proven unmeltable over the years. The only place allowed them near the melting pot was underneath it. Getting burned. Hispanics were also left out of the melting pot. Spanish has been historically preserved more among them than other languages in non-English-speaking populations. It was a shelter, a defense. (p. 21–22)

Segregated/inferior schooling was usually rationalized on the grounds that it was necessary in order to provide effective remedial instruction in English to students who were "language handicapped" (Schlossman, 1983). However, in the Southwest, Latino/Latina children were generally assigned to segregated schools purely on the basis of surname when in fact many knew more English than Spanish since English had been the dominant home language for generations (Sánchez, 1943). George Sánchez, in many articles, pointed to the racism that was rationalized by:

thinly veiled [pedagogical] excuses which do not conform with either the science of education or the facts in the case. Judging from current practice, these pseudo-pedagogical reasons call for short school terms, ramshackle school buildings, poorly paid and untrained teachers, and all varieties of prejudicial discrimination. (1943, p. 16; quoted in Schlossman, 1983, p. 893)

The pattern of physical and/or psychological violence aimed at eradicating students' identity was clearly not a pattern confined to North America (see, for example, Skutnabb-Kangas, 2000). [2] It was, and unfortunately continues to be, more the rule than the exception in many countries around the world in spite of the re-discovery of principles of equity and justice in Western industrialized countries during the 1960s. This pattern is depicted in Figure 2.1.

The historical pattern of inter-group relationships and school performance for voluntary or immigrant minorities shows many similarities with that described for involuntary minorities but also some important differences.

Voluntary Minorities. In the case of voluntary minorities, schooling was generally not segregated but the same overt goals (acculturation to the dominant culture) and methods (punishment for speaking the home language) were used. Contrary to popular belief, many first generation immigrant children experienced considerable difficulty in school. Cohen (1970) sums up the findings of a comprehensive review of the educational achievement of immigrant students in the early part of this century as follows:

> the evidence...suggests that in the first generation, at least, children from many immigrant groups did not have an easy time in school. Pupils from these groups were more likely to be retarded than their native white schoolmates, more likely to make low scores on IQ tests, and they seem to have been a good deal less likely to remain in high school. (1970, p. 24)

Many of these first generation immigrants may have become successful economically since much less education was required for economic and social advancement at the beginning of this century than is the case at the present time.

For the children of these immigrants, there was considerable variability across groups in academic performance; specifically:

> Children whose parents emigrated from England, Scotland, Wales, Germany, and Scandinavia seem to have generally performed about as well in school as native whites. ...The children of Jewish immigrants typically achieved at or above the average for native whites. It was central and southern European non-Jewish immigrants—and to a lesser extent, the Irish—who experienced really serious difficulty in school. (Cohen, 1970, p. 24)

Cohen suggests that these ethnic differences in school performance may arise from cultural/motivational factors and the degree of urbanization of the different groups. [3]

It is clear from these data that a complex array of variables determines the academic achievement of culturally diverse students and that the argument that previous generations of immigrants made it "without the crutch of bilingual education" is seriously oversimplified. However, the data also show that the

Figure 2.1 — BLAMING THE VICTIM IN THE EDUCATION OF BILINGUAL STUDENTS

A. OVERT AIM

Teach English to bilingual children in order to create a harmonious society with equal opportunity for all.

COVERT AIM

Anglicize bilingual children because linguistic and cultural diversity are seen as a threat to social cohesion.

B. METHOD

Punish children for using L1 in schools and encourage them to reject their own culture and language in order to identify with majority English group.

JUSTIFICATION

1. L1 should be eradicated because it will interfere with the learning of English;

2. Identification with L1 culture will reduce child's ability to identify with English-speaking culture.

C. RESULTS

1. Shame in L1 language and culture.

2. Replacement of L1 by L2.

3. School failure among many children.

"SCIENTIFIC" EXPLANATIONS

1. Bilingualism causes confusion in thinking, emotional insecurity and school failure.

2. Bilingual children are "culturally deprived" (almost by definition since they are not Anglos).

3. Some culturally diverse groups are genetically inferior (common theory in 1920's sporadically revived since then (*e.g.* Dunn, 1987).

D. OUTCOMES

1. The educational disablement of bilingual children under these conditions only serves to reinforce the myth of bilingual group inferiority.

2. Even more intense efforts by the school to eradicate the "deficiencies" inherent in bilingual children (i.e. their language and culture).

usual rationale for bilingual education similarly fails to account for the observed pattern. This rationale is that children cannot learn in a language they do not understand and therefore, if there is a home-school "linguistic mismatch," academic retardation will almost invariably result. The historical data show that Scandinavian and German children performed well despite a mismatch between the language of the home and the language of the school whereas Irish children instructed in their native language (English, for the most part) experienced difficulty.

In summary, the historical data reinforce the critical role that inter-group power relations and the negotiation of identity play in determining language learning and academic achievement among culturally diverse students. The major points are as follows:

• Subordinated groups that tend to experience the most severe academic disadvantage have never been given the opportunity to assimilate into the societal mainstream; on the contrary, they were subjected over generations to segregated and inferior schooling, they were punished for speaking their home language in school, and their pride in their cultural identity was systematically eradicated;

• The educational experiences of subordinated group students have reflected the pattern of interactions experienced by their communities in the wider society; both children and adults have been prevented from full participation and advancement in mainstream societal institutions (*e.g.*, schools, the job market, etc.) through segregation and discrimination;

• Although early generations of immigrant children were punished for speaking their L1 and many groups did tend to experience academic difficulties, they were not discriminated against nor segregated educationally to the same extent as involuntary minorities; thus, an ambivalent and/or oppositional identity was not internalized by the group and later generations assimilated to the mainstream society and succeeded academically;

• Among both voluntary and involuntary minorities, school failure on the part of culturally diverse students was generally attributed to some inherent deficiency, either genetic or experiential (*e.g.*, "cultural deprivation," bilingual confusion, etc.); this focus on inherent deficiencies of the bilingual child served to deflect attention away from the educational treatment that children were receiving.

Evolution of the Bilingual Education Debate

The debate about the merits or otherwise of bilingual education has pre-occupied educators, politicians, the media and occasionally the general public in the United States for more than 30 years. Many commentators have warned that bilingual education is not only educationally ill-advised, it also threatens the social and political stability of the nation. Newspaper editorials across the country have detailed a catastrophic scenario of Latino/Latina activists demanding ever more intensive bilingual education as a ploy both to prevent bilingual children from learning English and to fuel separatist tendencies, resulting ultimately in the disintegration of the United States.

To outsiders, this paranoia about bilingual education might seem absurd, especially in view of the prevalence and high status of bilingual programs in many countries around the world (see Baker & Prys Jones, 1998; Cummins & Corson, 1997). However, within the United States, these arguments are taken very seriously. The roots of this bilingual paranoia can be seen in the evolution of the policy debate through four phases during the past 30 years.

Phase I. 1967–1974. Initially, as Troike (1978) has observed, bilingual education was instituted in the late sixties on the basis of what appeared to be a self-evident rationale, namely that "the best medium for teaching a child is his or her mother tongue," but with relatively little hard evidence to back up this rationale. The reaction of many press commentators in the initial years of this experiment was one of "wait-and-see;" they didn't particularly like the idea but were willing to give it a chance to prove its potential for reducing educational inequities. Some were concerned, however, that bilingual education might have the opposite effect, namely of preventing Spanish-speaking students from entering the mainstream of English-speaking America, and also that it might give rise to the divisiveness that appeared to be associated with bilingualism in Canada. However, in general, this first phase of the modern bilingual education debate was marked by a tolerance for the educational potential of bilingual education and, although doubts were certainly raised, its rationale was not disputed in any sustained or systematic way.

An early expression of these views appeared in the *Christian Science Monitor* (Nov. 13, 1967). The editorial noted that several senators were drafting measures for bilingual education because they were concerned, "and very rightly so," about the educational lag among Spanish-speaking children. However, it went on to wonder:

whether such an official recognition of Spanish might not actually worsen the situation rather than improve it. Might it not tend to fasten even more strongly upon children the disadvantage of being Spanish-speaking in an overwhelmingly English-speaking land?

Phase II. 1974–1986. The bilingual education debate became considerably more volatile after the *Lau v. Nichols* case in 1974. The judgment of the Supreme Court in this case acknowledged that the civil rights of non-English-speaking students were violated when the school took no steps to help them acquire the language of instruction.

> …there is no equality of treatment merely by providing students with the same facilities, textbooks, teachers, and curriculum; for students who do not understand English are effectively foreclosed from any meaningful education. Basic English skills are at the very core of what these public schools teach. Imposition of a requirement that, before a child can effectively participate in the educational program, he must already have acquired those basic skills is to make a mockery of public education. We know that those who do not understand English are certain to find their classroom experiences wholly incomprehensible and in no way meaningful. (Crawford, 1992a, p. 253)

The Court did not mandate bilingual education but it did mandate that schools take effective measures to overcome the educational disadvantages resulting from a home-school language mismatch. The Office of Civil Rights, however, interpreted the Supreme Court's decision as effectively mandating transitional bilingual education unless a school district could prove that another approach would be equally or more effective. This interpretation of the Supreme Court decision by the Office of Civil Rights sparked outrage among media commentators and educators in school districts which, for the most part, were totally unprepared to offer any form of bilingual instruction.

The ensuing debate was (and continues to be) volatile. The concern with political divisiveness resulting from bilingual education was articulated clearly in a *New York Times* editorial entitled "Bilingual Danger" on November 22, 1976:

> The disconcerting strength gathered by separatism in Canada contains a relevant lesson for the United States and its approach to bilingual education. …it is no exaggeration to warn that the present encouragement given to making [Spanish-speaking] enclaves perma-

nent, in the mistaken view that they are an expression of positive pluralism, points the road to cultural, economic and political divisiveness. The reason why such a warning appears appropriate is that political splinter groups within the Spanish-speaking community, and among educators, are misinterpreting the goals of bilingual education in New York as a means of creating a Spanish-speaking power base. …Without exaggerating the threat to America's nationhood now that English has prevailed, it nevertheless remains pertinent to warn against a misguided linguistic separatism that, while it may seem to promise its advocates limited political and ideological power, can only have the effect of condemning to permanent economic and social disadvantage those who cut themselves off from the majority culture. (quoted in *The Linguistic Reporter*, January 1977, pp. 1 & 7)

Although his reply was not printed in the *New York Times*, Joshua Fishman refuted the arguments of this editorial as follows:

The *New York Times* seems to fear that something divisive…might grow out of bilingual education in the USA. Having spent many years studying bilingual education throughout the world…I consider this to be highly unlikely, both because ethno-cultural divisiveness, where it obtains, is far too deeply imbedded in a pervasive socioeconomic matrix to be "caused" by any kind of education, as well as because bilingual education per se is unfailingly unifying rather than divisive. The hallmark of all bilingual education (including its compensatory USA variant) is that it includes a unifying supra-ethnic language of wider communication (in our case: English…). Indeed, if any educational pattern can be said to typify Quebec it is the absence (historically as well as currently) of bilingual education (education via two media of instruction), rather than its presence. All of which is not to say that there is no striving for "a Spanish-speaking power base in the USA," or that such strivings may not be justified. …What might counteract such strivings would be genuine opportunity for Hispanic participation in "political power" and a genuine end to the "economic and social disadvantage" of Hispanics in the USA, all of the foregoing having been promised in theory and so obviously denied in practice by the monolingual English establishment. If Hispanic (or rather minority) "divisiveness" increases in the USA, it will be because of the long tradition of English-dominated inequality, such as that long practiced in Quebec, rather than because of bilingual education which functions to link together populations that might otherwise be totally estranged. (The Linguistic Reporter, January 1977, p. 7)

As the debate evolved, the sociopolitical concerns of many commentators were backed up by psychoeducational arguments against bilingual education and in favor of all-English immersion programs. The argument in favor of bilingual education which was reflected in the Supreme Court's decision, namely, that "children can't learn in a language they don't understand," was no longer regarded as self-evident. As Noel Epstein (1977) pointed out, apparent counter-evidence had appeared in the findings from French immersion programs in Canada which showed that English-background children who were taught initially through French in order to develop fluent bilingual skills did not suffer academically as a result of this home-school language switch (see Swain & Lapkin, 1982; Cummins & Swain, 1986). To many commentators in the United States, these results suggested that English immersion programs were a plausible educational alternative to bilingual programs. [4]

The bilingual approach appeared to imply a counter-intuitive "less equals more" rationale in which *less* English instruction is assumed to lead to *more* English achievement. To many opponents of bilingual education it appeared more logical to argue that if children are deficient in English then they need maximum instruction in English, not their native language. School failure is caused by *insufficient exposure* to English (at home) and it makes no sense to further dilute the amount of English to which bilingual students are exposed by instructing them through their L1 at school. Unless such students are immersed in English at school, they will not learn English and consequently will be prevented from participating in the mainstream of American society.

In summary, during this second phase the battle lines were drawn between two opposing but apparently equally plausible arguments: on the one hand, the *linguistic mismatch* hypothesis which argued that children can't learn in a language they don't understand; on the other, the maximum exposure hypothesis that if children are deficient in English, then surely they require *maximum* exposure to English in school. These psychoeducational hypotheses remain prominent in the third phase of this debate; however, in this phase the relatively narrow concern with bilingual education has joined forces with a broader set of concerns in relation to the more general infiltration of cultural diversity into American institutions.

Phase III. 1987–1998. During the 1980s and 1990s, the *U.S. English* organization coordinated much of the opposition to bilingual education, initiating and passing referenda in 19 states to make English the official language (see Cazden & Snow [1990] and Crawford [1992a, 1992b, 1995, 2000] for detailed analysis of the *U.S. English* movement). Inspired by Senator S.I. Hayakawa's (1981) proposed constitutional amendment to make English the official language of the United States, *U.S. English* was formed in 1983 and within five years had grown to a 400,000 member organization with a $6 million annual budget (Crawford, 1992a). By 1995, the membership had mushroomed to more than 600,000.

The urgency of the *U.S. English* mandate was enhanced during the late 1980s by publications of a variety of neo-conservative academics (*e.g.,* Dinesh D'Souza, 1991; E.D. Hirsch, 1987; Arthur Schlesinger, Jr., 1991) who warned about the dangers cultural diversity posed to the American way of life. These authors articulated a form of intellectualized xenophobia intended to alert the general public to the infiltration of the Other into the heart and soul of American institutions. Cultural diversity has become the enemy within, far more potent and insidious in its threat than any external enemy. Most influential was E.D. Hirsch's (1987) *Cultural Literacy: What Every American Needs to Know* which argued that the fabric of nationhood depended on a set of common knowledge, understandings and values shared by the populace. Multilingualism represented a threat to cultural literacy and, by extension, nationhood:

> In America, the reality is that we have not yet properly achieved *mono*literacy, much less multiliteracy. …Linguistic pluralism would make sense for us only on the questionable assumption that our civil peace and national effectiveness could survive multilingualism. But, in fact, multilingualism enormously increases cultural fragmentation, civil antagonism, illiteracy, and economic-technological ineffectualness. (1987, p. 92)

Hirsch's "cultural literacy" represented a call to strengthen the national immune system so that it could successfully resist the debilitating influence of cultural diversity. Only when the national identity has been fortified and secured through "cultural literacy" should contact with the *Other* be contemplated, and even then educators should keep diversity at a distance, always vigilant against its potent destructive power.

It is in this context that we can understand statements such as the following from Arthur Schlesinger Jr. (1991) in his book *The Disuniting of America:*

In recent years the combination of the ethnicity cult with a flood of immigration from Spanish-speaking countries has given bilingualism new impetus. ...Alas, bilingualism has not worked out as planned: rather the contrary. Testimony is mixed, but indications are that bilingual education retards rather than expedites the movement of Hispanic children into the English-speaking world and that it promotes segregation rather than it does integration. Bilingualism shuts doors. It nourishes self-ghettoization, and ghettoization nourishes racial antagonism. ...Using some language other than English dooms people to second-class citizenship in American society. ...Monolingual education opens doors to the larger world. ...institutionalized bilingualism remains another source of the fragmentation of America, another threat to the dream of 'one people.' (1991, pp. 108–109)

The claims that "bilingualism shuts doors" and "monolingual education opens doors to the wider world," are laughable if viewed in isolation, particularly in the context of current global interdependence and the frequently expressed needs of American business for multilingual "human resources." Schlesinger's comments become interpretable only in the context of a societal discourse that is profoundly disquieted by the fact that the sounds of the *Other* have now become audible and the hues of the American social landscape have darkened noticeably.

Despite its disdain for empirical evidence, this discourse is broadcast through the media into every classroom in the nation. There is anger that schools have apparently reneged on their traditional duty to render the *Other* invisible and inaudible. Under the guise of equity programs initiated in the 1960s, diversity infiltrated into the American classroom and became legitimated. In view of demographic projections that diversity will increase dramatically during the next 30 years, there is extreme urgency to curtail the infiltration of diversity and particularly one of its most visible manifestations, bilingual education. [5]

Phase IV. 1998–2000. The bilingual education debate across the United States changed dramatically in June 1998 with the passage in California of Proposition 227. This initiative aimed to eliminate the use of bilingual children's first language (L1) for instructional purposes except in very exceptional circumstances. In its place, a transitional program of structured English immersion, normally to last only one year, was to be implemented. Proposition 227 also mandated that any teacher who willfully and repeatedly refused to implement the law could be personally sued in court.

The debate leading up to the June referendum crystallized all of the arguments that had been advanced for and against bilingual education in the previous quarter century. Both sides claimed "equity" as their central guiding principle. Opponents of bilingual programs argued that limited English proficient students were being denied access to both English and academic advancement as a result of being instructed for part of the day through their L1. Exposure to English was being diluted and, as a result, it was not surprising that bilingual students continued to experience difficulty in academic aspects of English. Only maximum exposure to English (frequently termed "time-on-task") could remediate children's linguistic difficulties in that language on entry to school.

Proponents of bilingual education argued that L1 instruction in the early grades was necessary to ensure that students understood content instruction and experienced a successful start to their schooling. Reading and writing skills acquired initially through the L1 provided a foundation upon which strong English language development could be built. Transfer of academic skills and knowledge across languages was evidenced consistently by the research literature on bilingual development (see Chapter 6). Thus, L1 proficiency could be promoted at no cost to children's academic development in English. Furthermore, the fact that teachers spoke the language of parents increased the likelihood of parental involvement and support for their children's learning. This, together with the reinforcement of children's sense of self as a result of the incorporation of their language and culture in the school program, contributed to long-term academic growth.

In the context of Proposition 227, bilingual advocates argued that bilingual education itself could not logically be regarded as a cause of continued high levels of academic failure among bilingual students since less than 30 percent of limited English proficient students in California were in any form of bilingual education. Less than 18 percent were in classes taught by a certified bilingual teacher, with the other 12 percent in classes most likely taught by a monolingual English teacher and a bilingual aide (Gándara, 1999). Thus, they argued that educational failure among bilingual (particularly Latino/Latina) students was more logically attributed to the absence of genuine bilingual programs than to bilingual education in some absolute sense.

Proposition 227 has not succeeded in eliminating bilingual education from California, although it has reduced the number of programs significantly. Prior to Proposition 227, 29 percent of English learners were in a bilingual program but this figure dropped to 12 percent one year later (Gándara *et al.*, 2000).

A number of school districts have continued to offer bilingual education by using a provision of the law that permits parents to sign a waiver requesting that their child be educated bilingually. However, only 67 percent of districts formally notified parents of this option (Gándara *et al.*, 2000). Some districts have set up charter schools that offer dual language or two-way bilingual programs involving both English-L1 and minority language-L1 (*e.g.* Spanish, Korean) students. Despite the negative social climate around bilingualism and bilingual education, dual language programs increased in California from 95 in 1997–98 to 119 in 1999–2000. According to the California Department of Education (2000), these programs have increased almost 300% since 1990.

Gándara and her University of California colleagues note that the convergence of Proposition 227 and the implementation of new statewide standards and testing have exerted "an extraordinary effect on English Learner instruction" (2000, p. 19). The Stanford 9 (SAT-9) standardized achievement test is administered to all California students who have been in school for at least 12 months regardless of their English language proficiency. The test is administered solely in English and no accommodations are made for English learners. The appropriateness of this measure has been questioned on a number of grounds not least because its norming sample included only 1.8 percent English learners whereas approximately 25 percent of California students are limited English proficient (Gándara *et al.*, 2000). Furthermore the SAT-9 is not aligned with the state's content standards in reading, mathematics and other curricular areas (Gold, 2000).

Teachers observed and interviewed in the Gándara *et al.* study felt compelled to teach to the SAT-9 test, placing much greater emphasis on "English word recognition or phonics, bereft of meaning or context" (2000, p. 19):

> Teachers also worried greatly that if they spent time orienting the children to broader literacy activities like story telling, story sequencing activities, reading for meaning or writing and vocabulary development in the primary language, that their students would not be gaining the skills that would be tested on the standardized test in English. They feared that this could result in the school and the students suffering sanctions imposed by the law. …Heavy emphasis was placed on decoding skills (phonics) and vocabulary development rather than developing broader literacy skills such as reading for meaning, or writing. (2000, pp. 19–21)

This emphasis on teaching to the test can certainly result in improved test scores in the short term. However, it ignores fundamental realities about the nature of reading and the kinds of language proficiencies required to use language for learning in the later grades of elementary school and beyond (see Chapters 3–5).

Not surprisingly, intense debate has also centered on the extent to which state-mandated SAT-9 standardized test scores provide evidence for the efficacy of Proposition 227. Proponents of the measure point to increased test scores in certain school districts (most notably the Oceanside district) as evidence that bilingual students are benefiting from English-only instruction. In August and September 2000, newspaper editorials across the country loudly proclaimed Proposition 227 a success on the basis of these scores, uncritically accepting the "spin" put out by proponents of English-only instruction. A more balanced scientific appraisal by Kenji Hakuta and his colleagues at Stanford University reported little empirical basis for drawing *any* conclusions about the impact of Proposition 227 on student performance. In 1999 and 2000, "scores rose for all students and no clear pattern could be attributable to Proposition 227" (Orr, Butler, Bousquet & Hakuta, 2000, p. 1). They also point out that increases in scores were much greater across the board at the grade 2 level in comparison to grade 3 and beyond. They note that these increases can be attributed to variety of factors such as significant class size reduction in the early grades, increasing familiarity with the test, teaching to the test, and changes in instructional methodology for teaching reading and math.

A preliminary analysis of school level SAT-9 data issued by Californians Together (2000), an advocacy group committed to quality education, compared data for 10 elementary schools with large enrollments of English learners and substantial bilingual instruction, including adequate materials and qualified teachers, with three schools highlighted as effective by proponents of Proposition 227. The report concluded that the bilingual schools reported school-wide performance as strong or stronger than that of the schools providing only structured English immersion in at least 75 percent of the comparisons. In 7 of the 9 cases where complete separate data for English learners was available, the bilingual schools met or exceeded the performance of English learners in the comparison schools in most of the comparisons.

Particularly interesting are data from the Fresno Unified School District showing that English learners in bilingual instruction (Grades 2–6) exceeded the performance of English learners in that district who were enrolled in structured

English immersion in all subject areas: reading, language and mathematics. Between 1998 and 2000, scores for English learners in bilingual instruction grew by 19% in reading and 24% in mathematics whereas scores for English learners in structured English immersion grew by only 11% in reading and 19% in math.

Orr *et al.* (2000) carried out further analysis of the school-level data reported by Californians Together. This analysis confirmed that the 10 bilingual schools selected for the analysis were superior to the English-only schools. The authors also point out that "the much-noted rise in Oceanside scores are indeed not that different from the patterns of increases that can be found in many bilingual schools" and these comparisons show that "there is nothing much at all remarkable about Oceanside" (2000, p. 4).

A further report issued on December 5, 2000, by Californians Together (Gold, 2000), compared 63 elementary schools nominated as having "thoroughly implemented" bilingual education with more than 1,000 schools closely matched on variables such as ethnicity, poverty, mobility, percentage of English learners, and base score on the SAT-9 Academic Performance Index (API). [6] The average Hispanic enrollment in both bilingual and comparison schools was 73 percent. Gold reports that "the bilingual schools exceeded their [API] growth targets for Hispanic students by almost five times, while the comparison schools exceeded their targets by only four times" (2000, p. 2). In an obvious reference to the debate over the Oceanside SAT-9 scores, Gold concludes as follows: "In contrast to widely-discussed anecdotes of student achievement based on the performance of English learners on the SAT-9 in a single school district, the current analysis suggests that well-implemented bilingual programs in many school districts can lead to academic achievement that is at least as strong as the achievement in programs provided mostly in English" (2000, p. 5) [7]

Clearly, this debate will continue. In view of the politicization of the issues and the deep ideological roots that fuel the intensity of emotion on both sides, it is essential for policy-makers and educators who are committed to providing a quality education for culturally diverse students to be aware of what the research is actually saying and what it is not. Results for any individual school or district, considered in isolation, provide very limited information for policy until the impact of various factors have been examined and disaggregated (see Krashen, 2000b). This is equally true for the "success stories" of bilingual education as it is for the "success stories" of English immersion. [8] The following chapters examine what we know about academic language learning and how we can account for the apparently conflicting research findings.

Conclusion

Two general issues can be raised with respect to the psychoeducational arguments for and against bilingual education. First, what underlying assumptions are implied by these arguments and to what extent are these assumptions valid in light of the research evidence? Second, to the extent that the assumptions on either side of the debate are not valid, what sociopolitical functions do they serve? In other words, what policies and programs do they legitimate and to what extent do bilingual students benefit or suffer as a result of these policies and programs?

The arguments about the educational validity of bilingual education embody a variety of assumptions that *can* be tested against the available research evidence. For example, to what extent does research support the "linguistic mismatch" hypothesis that children exposed to a home-school language switch will suffer academic retardation? At the other pole of the debate, is it true that more exposure to English at school increases English academic achievement, or does less English instruction lead to more English achievement, as implied by the bilingual education rationale? Is bilingualism an educational disadvantage (as Arthur Schlesinger Jr. argues) or might it be a positive force in children's development under some conditions? Is there a positive or a negative relationship between children's L1 and L2 academic skills?

At a more basic level, many commentators on both sides of the issue suggest that lack of English proficiency is the major cause of children's academic disadvantage—is there any evidence for this assumption? It is also relevant to ask what exactly is meant by "English proficiency." Specifically, how are academic skills in English related to the acquisition of English conversational skills? Clarification of these issues is important in order to answer the central question regarding the most effective methods of promoting English and overall academic development.

An additional issue concerns the testing of bilingual students in English, either as part of a statewide testing mandate or in the context of special education identification for exceptional status (*e.g.,* learning disabled or gifted and talented). When do such tests become valid for English learners? Are the inferences regarding school or program effectiveness being drawn by media commentators and policy-makers on the basis of such tests appropriate or do they entail potentially negative consequences for program quality?

Finally, the research evidence regarding the impact of broader social factors and patterns of classroom interaction can be examined. In reviewing some of these factors to this point, I have suggested that inter-group power relations have played a major role in determining culturally diverse students' academic progress. If so, why have these variables not been taken into account in the policy debate? What is the relationship between sociopolitical and psychoeducational factors in determining student outcomes?

These issues are discussed in the following chapters. The research on most of these issues is sufficiently clear to show that the major psychoeducational arguments against bilingual education are spurious. In fact, massive amounts of research evidence refute the argument that insufficient exposure to English is the major cause of bilingual students' academic failure and the related assumption that maximum exposure to English will result in academic success.

In view of the overwhelming evidence against the maximum exposure assumption, it is legitimate to ask what sociopolitical function such arguments serve. I argue that the sociopolitical function of such arguments is very similar to the sociopolitical function of previous arguments used to legitimate sink-or-swim (submersion) programs for bilingual students. The argument that bilingualism caused "language handicaps" legitimated eradicating bilingual children's L1 and making them ashamed of their cultural identity. In the same way, current arguments promoting maximum exposure to English serve to subvert bilingual programs such that they are either eliminated or relatively less effective "quick-exit" programs are implemented rather than the considerably more effective programs aimed at promoting biliteracy. In both cases, a patently inferior form of education has been rationalized as being for children's own good and necessary to provide them with access to what *U.S. English* calls "the language of equal opportunity" (see Wong Fillmore, 1992, for a discussion of the attempts to sabotage the implementation of bilingual education). [9]

Endnotes to Chapter 2

1. Any broad categorization, such as Ogbu's voluntary and involuntary minorities, is likely to obscure considerable variation within particular groups. There is enormous variation among different Latino/Latina groups in the U.S. as well as within groups such as Mexicanos (see, for example, Gibson, 1995, 1997; Suárez-Orozco, 1987, 1989; Trueba, 1988; Vásquez, Pease-Alvarez, & Shannon, 1994). In critiquing Ogbu's position, Erickson (1987) and Trueba (1988) point out that it does not explain the success of many involuntary minority students. The ethnographic research of Marcelo Suárez-Orozco among recently arrived students from war-torn Central American countries in the early 1980s also highlights this as an important

issue. He focused not on why students dropped-out or experienced academic problems but on why they remained in school at all. He argues that "becoming a somebody" was an important motivation for students:

> Among many new arrivals in my sample feelings of desperation give way to a harsh sense of responsibility that they must now seize upon any opportunities. Achieving in school and working to ease parental hardships are intimately related to this psychosocial syndrome of propensity to guilt over one's selective survival. (1989, p. 107)

Thus, Ogbu's distinction between voluntary and involuntary minorities should be seen as a broad categorization describing general patterns of power relations between dominant and subordinated groups but allowing for considerable intra-group variation within voluntary and involuntary minorities.

2. A particularly vicious example of punishment for speaking the home language comes from the Welsh context. The "Welsh not" came into existence after the 1870 Education Act in Britain as a means of eradicating the Welsh language. Any child heard speaking Welsh in school had a heavy wooden placard attached by rope placed over his or her shoulders. The placard reached to the child's shins and would bump them when the child walked. If that child heard another child speaking Welsh, he or she could transfer the "Welsh not" to the other child. The child carrying this placard at the end of the day was caned (Evans, 1978). Richard Llewellyn gives an account of this type of punishment in his autobiographical novel *How Green Was My Valley:*

> I heard crying in the infants' school as though a child had fallen and the voice came nearer and fell flat upon the air as a small girl came through the door and walked a couple of steps towards us. ...About her neck a piece of new cord, and from the cord, a board that hung to her shins and cut her as she walked. Chalked on the board, in the fist of Mr. Elijah Jonas-Sessions, I must not speak Welsh in school. ...And the board dragged her down, for she was small, and the cord rasped the flesh on her neck, and there were marks upon her shins where the edge of the board had cut. (Llewellyn, 1968, p. 267)

3. This same variability in academic performance among immigrant students is evident in contemporary data from a number of contexts. For example, Canadian data show many groups of first and second generation immigrant students from non-English-speaking backgrounds performing as well or better academically than English native speakers of the same social class (see Cummins, 1984, for a review). However, involuntary minority groups such as First Nations and francophone students outside Quebec show considerably lower levels of academic performance.

4. Many American commentators who cite the Canadian French immersion programs as counter-evidence to bilingual education and as a means of arguing for "English immersion" for bilingual students fail to realize that French immersion programs are, in fact, fully bilin-

gual programs. These programs are taught by bilingual teachers, the goal is bilingualism and biliteracy, and children's L1 (English) is strongly promoted after the initial grades so that about half the instruction is through L1 in grades 4–6. It is highly illogical to use the success of these bilingual programs to argue for monolingual programs, taught by monolingual teachers, whose goal is to produce monolingualism.

5. The message of the demographic projections has been internalized by the socially-powerful establishment. Poor people currently tend not to vote in the United States. What if bilingual education were to be successful in promoting high levels of critical literacy among the rapidly increasing culturally diverse population and what if these people were to vote? Social control is at stake; hence the escalating campaign on a number of fronts (media, legislative, political) to get rid of bilingual education and revert to traditional forms of assimilation and exclusion that allegedly served the nation well for more than 200 years (see Macedo, 1993, 1994).

Paranoia about the growing Latino/Latina population was vividly illustrated in a memorandum written in the fall of 1988 by John Tanton, chairman of *U.S. English*, who warned about a Latino-Latina political takeover as a result of high immigration and birthrates:

> *Gobernar es popular* translates 'to govern is to populate.' In this society, where the majority rules, does this hold? Will the present majority peacefully hand over its political power to a group that is simply more fertile? …Can *homo contraceptivus* compete with *homo progenitiva* if borders aren't controlled? …Perhaps this is the first instance in which those with their pants up are going to get caught by those with their pants down. (quoted in Crawford, 1995, p. 68)

An example of the rhetoric directed against bilingual education is an advertisement that appeared in some editions of TIME magazine (March 20, 1995) which read as follows:

> Deprive a child of an education. Handicap a young life outside the classroom. Restrict social mobility. If it came at the hand of a parent it would be called child abuse.

> At the hand of our schools and funded primarily by state and local government, it's called *bilingual education.* A massive bureaucratic program that's strayed from its mandate of mainstreaming non-English speaking students. Today more money is spent teaching immigrants in their native languages than teaching them in English.

The claims that more money is spent on L1 instruction than on instruction through English and the equation of bilingual education with child abuse are so patently inaccurate and extreme that they should instantly undermine the credibility of the argument against bilingual education. Unfortunately, as Macedo (1993) has pointed out, "big lies" such as these are often more persuasive than rational debate. This kind of blatant propaganda set the stage for the passage of referenda against bilingual education in California and Arizona in 1998 and 2000 respectively.

6. The Academic Performance Index (API) is derived from a school's scores on the SAT-9 in all subjects for all students, grades 2–6. The content areas are weighted as follows: mathematics, 40%; reading, 30%, language, 15%, and spelling, 15% (see www.cde.ca.gov for further information on the API and API growth reports for individual California schools).

7. Ken Noonan, superintendent of the Oceanside District is reported to have attributed (in a National Public Radio interview on August 22, 2000) the increase of scores in his district partly to the fact that many teachers in Oceanside are bilingual and have qualifications in English language teaching (according to a BILING listserve entry by Dr. Jill Kerper Mora, August 22, 2000). Mora points out that this is not the reality in the vast majority of districts in California where most teachers have no specific qualifications for teaching English learners. She estimates that fewer than 20% of the limited English proficient students in California are currently being taught by a bilingual teacher. She suggests that it is thus highly problematic to generalize the Oceanside results to other California districts, most of which offer only English-only programs taught by monolingual English teachers.

Krashen (2000b) has also noted problems in Oceanside's previous bilingual program:

> We have several reasons to suspect that Oceanside's previous bilingual program, the one that was dropped, was poorly conceived. In an article in the Washington Post (Sept. 2) Oceanside Superintendent Ken Noonan stated that before Proposition 227 Oceanside's bilingual program was all-Spanish, lasting "for up to four years, even longer for some. Only after being designated fluent in English would a child's learning in English begin in earnest." Properly organized bilingual programs, by contrast, introduce children to English from day one, and academic subjects are taught in English as soon as they can be made comprehensible. Failing to provide any English instruction will naturally lead to miserable results on English-language achievement tests. This explains why Oceanside's test scores showed substantial improvement especially for the youngest children, when English was introduced. (2000b, p. 3)

Krashen concludes that "Oceanside dropped an inadequate bilingual program and at the same time focused nearly all its energy on test preparation" (p. 3).

Oceanside was in the news again in late September, 2000, when the California Department of Education (CDE) issued its report on a complaint brought by parents against the Oceanside District. According to a press release issued by Multicultural Education, Training and Advocacy, Inc. (META) on October 2, 2000, the CDE report:

> cites four major areas where the Oceanside District has violated federal and state legal standards applicable to schools with students who are not fluent in English. ...One of the main allegations of the complaint was that the district—in effect—implemented an across the board policy of refusing to grant waivers to immigrant parents whose children needed instruction in their own language as required under Prop. 227. In response to Prop. 227, the district completely dismantled its bilingual education pro-

grams and refused to approve parental waivers. This completely flies in the face of the claims made in the ballot arguments by the proponents of Prop. 227, that Prop. 227 "gives choices to parents, not administrators." ...The report specifically noted that "in many cases, staff were either not qualified and/or not trained to provide either English language development or academic instruction to English learners." ...It also found that as a result of the District's violations of the law "significant numbers" of language minority students at the high school were "doing poorly academically" and that "large numbers" of these students were placed in remedial classes and were receiving "grades of Ds or Fs." (META Press Release, posted by Dr. Jill Kerper Mora on the BILING Listserv, October 2, 2000).

Gándara *et al.* (2000) also note that English learners are much more likely to be taught by a teacher without any credential and "in the districts we studied, we encountered no systematic professional development for teachers of English learners to strengthen their skills at working with these students in either a bilingual or a monolingual English context during the first year [of Proposition 227 implementation]" (p. 26).

Peter Schrag in an editorial published September 6, 2000 in the *Sacramento Bee* (www.sacbee.com/voices/news/voices05_20000906.html) notes that there was actually a decline between second and fourth grade for individual cohorts of students:

And if you take the reading scores for certain cohorts of LEP kids—say the second-graders of 1998 who, presumably, were fourth-graders in 2000— you actually see a decline. Fifteen percent of them scored over the national average in reading in 1998; only 13 percent did in 2000. (In the meantime, second-graders as a whole had gone from 40 percent at or above average to 45 percent.). (2000, p. 2)

6. Delia Pompa, Executive Director of the National Association of Bilingual Education, in an editorial written in *USA Today* (08/28/00, www.USATODAY.com) notes that:

In Arizona and Texas, bilingual students consistently outperform their peers in monolingual programs. Calexico, California, implemented bilingual education and now has dropout rates that are less than half the state average and college acceptance rates of more than 90%. In El Paso, systemwide bilingual education programs have helped raise student scores from the lowest in Texas to among the highest in the nation.

The Calexico program (located close to the Mexican border in California) is featured as exemplary in the report *Transforming Education for Hispanic Youth: Exemplary Practices, Programs and Schools* written by Anne Turnbaugh Lockwood and Walter G. Secada (1999). It is worth quoting at some length from this report to illustrate the transformation in outcomes that can occur when a philosophy of both cognitive challenge and identity affirmation is infused into programs for culturally diverse students:

When Emily Palicio, Calexico's Assistant Superintendent of Instructional Services, looks back at the Calexico schools she saw when she arrived in the district as a teacher in 1969, she remembers a time of low expectations, dismal student performance, and scant understanding of students' native language and culture. Despite Calexico's proximity to Mexico and its constant influx of immigrant students, not only were bilingual teachers virtually nonexistent, immigrant and LEP [limited English proficient] students rarely reached college or achieved even a modicum of academic success.

Teachers, Palicio recalls, didn't expect LEP or non-English-speaking students to succeed in academic work. Primary instructional strategies were remediation: an instructional pace slowed to a crawl, and plenty of drill. Not surprisingly, these approaches failed to yield positive results. ...

Palicio credits the development of a strong research-based bilingual education program—in tandem with a commitment to hiring well-qualified bilingual staff—as the foundation for Calexico's shift to high expectations and academic rigor for all students. In fact, bilingual programs served as the catalyst for substantive reform throughout the Calexico schools.

The presence of bilingual staff throughout the district provides practical and symbolic testimony that students' native language and culture are valued, Palicio explains. It also serves to reflect the district's "value position" that staff respect and understand students' cultural and linguistic background. ..."Today, 85% of our elementary school teachers are bilingual [and] approximately 40% of our high school teachers are bilingual. All our elementary school principals are bilingual [and] one of our two junior high school principals is bilingual as well." (1999, p. 30)

In the bilingual program teachers team-taught with one teacher as the English model and another as the Spanish model. Long-held staff attitudes about the low capabilities of English learners began to change as a result of the implementation of bilingual programs. Palicio notes: "We saw our students as active learners, ...the kids who never participated began to participate. Suddenly they could read, because Spanish is a very easy, phonetic language in which to develop literacy. That created an excitement in all of us" (1999, p. 31).

In their overview of program characteristics common to the exemplary schools for Hispanic students reviewed in their report, Lockwood and Secada note that:

School staff accepted their students at whatever point they came to school—whether they came from poverty, with less than proficient English, or with other intervening variables often cited for lack of success in school. ...these adults prodded and encouraged their students to conceive of productive futures for themselves. They provided numerous mentoring opportunities, both structured and informal, so that these youngsters could benefit from high expectations and personal warmth of appropriately nurturing relationships with adults. They were available to answer—and to provoke—their students' questions. When students need-ed extra help with coursework, staff at these schools had a structure to provide support and a core set of values that insisted upon it. Finally, through an almost inexhaustible supply of inventiveness, they refused to allow these students to fail. If one approach was not effective, they regrouped and tried another. (1999, pp. 17-18)

The centrality of teacher role definitions and the identity options teachers reflect to their students is very evident in this description of successful schools. Also evident is the commitment of educators to challenge the societal power structure that has typically attributed students' academic difficulties to characteristics of the students or their commu-nities (*e.g.,* bilingualism, low parental literacy, etc.) rather than to school policies and instructional practices.

9. In late March 2001 Dr. Maria S. Quezada was interviewed together with Ron Unz on National Public Radio (a WRNI-Providence show called *One Union Station*). Below is her summary of the debate (posted on the BILING Listserve, March 22, 2001 by Luis O. Reyes):

Unz stated:
"After 227 there was a rapid shift to intensive English when bilingual edu-cation was eliminated"

My response:
Not so—more than 70% of students were already in English-only programs and many districts did not have to change their programs very much because they never offered bilingual education.

He stated:
"The majority of Hispanic parents wanted 227."

My response:
Not so—63% of Latinos defeated the measure as did African Americans and many precincts in California overwhelmingly defeated the measure. The only voters who passed the measure were those that did not even have children in schools— only 15% had children in the schools and their children were not impacted by the measure.

He went into his usual tirade about those programs that did not really work. That only researchers who were "bilinguals" said it was effective.

(I countered with the fact that researchers from the American Educational Research Association [AERA]—not your usual "bilinguals" refuted his claims. He then went into the success story of his program in Oceanside. Since I had all testing information from Oceanside in front of me I was able to tell the audience that his figures were meaningless. That he was com-paring 1999 school year 2nd graders to 2000 school year 2nd graders and that was totally misrepresenting the information because they were not the same children. I [also] had information of Limited English Proficient (LEP) students who took the test and were here less than 12 months. I told them that these would be the students in his style of sheltered English immersion classrooms and those second graders scored at the 23rd percentile—a full 10 percentage points below other LEP students in Oceanside at the 2nd grade. And furthermore—the success of the students was not evident in the higher grades—they keep dropping lower.

He then went on to say that "bilinguals" were the ones most interested in keeping the program alive because we profited from having bilingual education and that bilingual education costs more. My response was that in my research on the shortage of qualified teachers I found that only 14 districts of the 137 that I looked at in California offered any kind of stipend. I stated that I was a bilingual teacher that could teach in English and Spanish and that as a bilingual teacher I never received a penny more for the work that I did.

He then stated to the audience that we shouldn't believe him or me, who represented the Association for Bilingual Education but we should believe the New York Times, Newsweek etc (he had his usual list)—to which I responded that since when had newspapers conducted valid educational research—at this point the program ended.

Chapter 3
The Three Faces of Language Proficiency

Appropriate ways of conceptualizing the nature of language proficiency and its relationship to other constructs (*e.g.* "intelligence") have been debated by philosophers and psychologists since ancient times. However, the issue is not just an abstract theoretical question but one that is central to resolving a variety of controversial issues in the education of culturally diverse students. Educational policies are frequently based on assumptions about the nature of "language proficiency" and how long it takes to attain. For example, funding for English as a second language (ESL) and bilingual education classes in North America is based (at least in part) on assumptions about how long it takes bilingual students to acquire sufficient English proficiency to follow instruction in the regular classroom. Proposition 227 explicitly claimed that one year of intensive English support was sufficient to enable English language learners (ELL) to catch up academically. Is this assumption valid or not?

A related contentious issue concerns the validity and appropriateness of administering state-mandated standardized tests to ELL students. Clearly, to administer English reading and writing measures to a grade 5 ELL student who has been learning English for only a few months is unlikely to yield any useful accountability data regarding the quality of instruction in that student's classroom. It is also ethically problematic to require a student to take a high stakes test that she has no possibility of passing. Such a procedure is likely to damage the student's academic confidence and self-esteem. But when does it become reasonable to administer state-mandated assessments to ELL students—after one year, or two years, or three years? What accommodations in administration procedure or interpretation are required to make the test more meaningful?

Underlying these questions is the issue of what exactly constitutes "English proficiency" and how it develops among ELL students. This chapter initially highlights two common misconceptions about the nature of English proficiency and then outlines a framework for considering the nature of English proficiency and academic language learning.

Misconceptions about the Nature of Language Proficiency

Two major misconceptions regarding the nature of language proficiency remain common among educators in North America. These misconceptions have important practical implications for the way educators interact with culturally diverse students. Both involve confusion between the surface or conversational aspects of children's language and deeper aspects of proficiency that are more closely related to conceptual and academic development.

The first misconception entails drawing inferences about children's ability to think logically on the basis of their familiarity with and command of standard English. Children who speak a non-standard variety of English (or their L1) are frequently thought to be handicapped educationally and less capable of logical thinking. This assumption derives from the fact that these children's language is viewed as inherently deficient as a tool for expressing logical relations. Since Labov's (1970) refutation of this position with respect to the language of African-American inner-city children, it has had few advocates among applied linguists, although it is still a common misconception among some educators and academics who have little background in sociolinguistics.

An example of how persistent some of these linguistic prejudices are even among academics comes from Dunn's (1987) monograph on Spanish-speaking children. In expressing his concerns that bilingual education could result in "at least the partial disintegration of the United States of America" (pp. 66–67), Dunn argues that Latino/Latina children and adults "speak inferior Spanish" and that "Latin pupils on the U.S. mainland, as a group, are inadequate bilinguals. They simply don't understand either English or Spanish well enough to function adequately in school" (p. 49). He goes on to argue that this is due to the fact that these children "do not have the scholastic aptitude or linguistic ability to master two languages well, or to handle switching from one to the other, at school, as the language of instruction" (p. 71). He attributes the causes of this lower scholastic ability about equally to environmental factors and "to genes that influence scholastic aptitude" (p. 64). (See the special issue of the *Hispanic Journal of Behavioral Science*, vol. 10, 1988 for critical discussion of Dunn's views.)

The second misconception is in many respects the converse of the first. In this case, children's adequate control over the surface features of English (i.e. their ability to converse fluently in English) is taken as an indication that all aspects of their "English proficiency" have been mastered to the same extent as native speakers of the language. In other words, conversational skills are interpreted as a valid index of overall proficiency in the language.

This implicit assumption has had a major impact on the organization of bilingual education programs in the United States. Historically, bilingual education has been rationalized in the following way:

> *Lack of English proficiency is the major reason for bilingual students' academic failure. Bilingual education is intended to ensure that students do not fall behind in subject matter content while they are learning English, as they would likely do in an all-English program. However, when students have become proficient in English, then they can be exited to an all-English program, since limited English proficiency will no longer impede their academic progress.*

Despite its intuitive appeal, there are serious problems with this rationale. First, it ignores the social and historical factors that influence bilingual students' academic performance. As suggested in previous chapters, these social determinants are more fundamental than linguistic factors alone. Second, this rationale fails to specify what exactly is meant by proficiency in English and this vagueness has contributed directly to bilingual students' academic difficulties.

Some concrete examples will help illustrate how this process operates. These examples are taken from a study conducted in western Canada in which the teacher referral forms and psychological assessments of more than 400 bilingual students were analyzed (Cummins, 1984). Throughout the teachers' referral forms and psychological assessment reports there are references to the fact that children's English communicative skills appeared considerably better developed than their academic language skills. The following example illustrates this point:

DM (105). Arrived from Portugal at age 10 and was placed in a second grade class; three years later in fifth grade, her teacher commented that "her oral answering and comprehension is so much better than her written work that we feel a severe learning problem is involved, not just her non-English background."

This, and many other examples illustrate the influence of the environment in developing English conversational skills. In many instances immigrant students were considered to have sufficient English proficiency to take a verbal IQ test within about one year of arrival in Canada. Similarly, in the United States, bilingual students are often considered to have developed sufficient English proficiency to cope with the demands of an all-English classroom after a relatively short amount of time in a bilingual or ESL program.

There is little doubt that many English language learners can develop a relatively high degree of English conversational skills within about two years of exposure to English-speaking peers, television, and schooling. However, we cannot logically extrapolate from the considerable English proficiency that students may display in face-to-face communication to their overall proficiency in English.

Consider the following example:

PR (289). PR was referred in first grade by the school principal who noted that "PR is experiencing considerable difficulty with grade one work. An intellectual assessment would help her teacher to set realistic learning expectations for her and might provide some clues as to remedial assistance that might be offered."

No mention was made of the fact that the child was learning English as a second language; this only emerged when the child was referred by the second grade teacher in the following year. Thus, the psychologist does not consider this as a possible factor in accounting for the discrepancy between a verbal IQ of 64 and a performance IQ of 108. The assessment report read as follows:

Although overall ability level appears to be within the low average range, note the significant difference between verbal and nonverbal scores. ….It would appear that PR's development has not progressed at a normal rate and consequently she is, and will continue to experience much difficulty in school. Teacher's expectations at this time should be set accordingly.

What is interesting in this example is that the child's English communicative skills are presumably sufficiently well developed that the psychologist (and possibly the teacher) is not alerted to the child's ESL background. This leads the psychologist to infer from her low verbal IQ score that "her development has not progressed at a normal rate" and to advise the teacher to set low academic expectations for the child since she "will continue to experience much difficulty in school." There is ample evidence from many contexts of how the attribution of deficient cognitive skills to culturally diverse students can become self-fulfilling. Ortiz and Yates (1983), for example, report that more than three times as many Latino/Latina students were classified as "learning disabled" in Texas than would be expected based on their proportion in the school population. These classifications usually resulted in a one-way ticket into special education classes where students fell even further behind academically.

In many of the referral forms and psychological assessments analyzed in the Cummins (1984) study, the following line of reasoning was invoked:

> Because bilingual students are fluent in English, their poor academic performance and/or test scores cannot be attributed to lack of proficiency in English. Therefore, these students must either have deficient cognitive abilities or be poorly motivated.

The trend to exit students to all-English instruction as quickly as possible in many bilingual programs inevitably gives rise to a similar line of reasoning. It is commonly observed that students classified as "English proficient" after a relatively short stay in a bilingual program and then exited to an all-English program often fall progressively further behind grade norms in the development of English academic skills. Because these students appear to be fluent in English, their poor academic performance can no longer be explained by the fact that their English language abilities are still in the process of development. Policymakers and educators are also reluctant to blame the school for students' poor performance because the school has accommodated the students by providing a bilingual program (albeit usually one with minimal L1 instruction). Thus, the academic deficiency is typically attributed to factors within the child or his or her community, as in Dunn's (1987) argument outlined above.

Three Dimensions of Language Proficiency

In the case of both of the misconceptions outlined here, a close relationship is assumed between two aspects of language proficiency: the conversational and the academic. Originally termed *basic interpersonal communicative skills* (BICS) and *cognitive academic language proficiency* (CALP) (Cummins,1981a), this conversational/academic distinction builds on a previous distinction between surface fluency and academic proficiency made by Skutnabb-Kangas and Toukomaa (1976). These investigators brought attention to the fact that Finnish immigrant children in Sweden often appeared to educators to be fluent in both Finnish and Swedish but still showed levels of verbal academic performance in both languages considerably below grade/age expectations. Other investigators (*e.g.* Bruner, 1975; Donaldson, 1978; Gibbons, 1991; Olson, 1977; Snow *et al.*, 1991) have made similar distinctions (see Cummins 2000 for a review). For example, in the Australian context, Pauline Gibbons (1991) has given a particularly clear description of the difference between what she terms *playground language* and *classroom language*:

> This playground language includes the language which enables children to make friends, join in games and take part in a variety of day-to-day activities that develop and maintain social contacts. It usually occurs in face-to-face contact, and is thus highly dependent on the physical and visual context, and on gesture and body language. Fluency with this kind of language is an important part of language development; without it a child is isolated from the normal social life of the playground. …

> But playground language is very different from the language that teachers use in the classroom, and from the language that we expect children to learn to use. The language of the playground is not the language associated with learning in mathematics, or social studies, or science. The playground situation does not normally offer children the opportunity to use such language as: *if we increase the angle by 5 degrees, we could cut the circumference into equal parts.* Nor does it normally require the language associated with the higher order thinking skills, such as hypothesizing, evaluating, inferring, generalizing, predicting or classifying. Yet these are the language func-

tions which are related to learning and the development of cognition; they occur in all areas of the curriculum, and without them a child's potential in academic areas cannot be realized. (p. 3)

The conversational/academic distinction has drawn attention to some common misconceptions regarding bilingual children's language and literacy development. However, recent debates regarding the interpretation of standardized test scores in California and elsewhere (see Chapter 2) highlight the need to add an additional dimension of language proficiency to the conversational/academic distinction. Specifically, *discrete language skills* need to be distinguished. The three faces of language proficiency can thus be described as follows:

Conversational fluency is the ability to carry on a conversation in familiar face-to-face situations. This is the kind of proficiency that the vast majority of native speakers of English have developed when they enter school at age 5. It involves use of high frequency words and simple grammatical constructions. Communication of meaning is typically supported by cues such as facial expressions, gestures, intonation, etc. ELL students generally develop fluency in conversational aspects of English within a year or two of exposure to the language either in school or in the environment.

Discrete language skills reflect specific phonological, literacy and grammatical knowledge that students acquire as a result of direct instruction and both formal and informal practice (*e.g.* reading). Some of these discrete language skills are acquired early in schooling and some continue to be acquired throughout schooling. The discrete language skills acquired early include knowledge of the letters of the alphabet, the sounds represented by individual letters and combinations of letters, and the ability to decode written words into appropriate sounds. ELL students can learn these specific language skills at a relatively early stage in their acquisition of English; in fact, these skills can be learned concurrently with their development of basic vocabulary and conversational proficiency.

As students progress through the grades, they will also acquire conventions about spelling, capitalization, and punctuation as well as information about grammatical rules (*e.g.* the fact that pluralization in English generally involves adding –s or –es to words) and exceptions to these rules (*e.g.* the fact that *took* is the past tense of the verb *take* rather than *taked*).

Academic language proficiency includes knowledge of the less frequent vocabulary of English as well as the ability to interpret and produce increasingly complex written (and oral) language. As students progress through the grades, they encounter far more low frequency words (primarily from Greek and Latin sources), complex syntax (*e.g.* passives), and abstract expressions that are virtually never heard in everyday conversation. Students are required to understand linguistically and conceptually demanding texts in the content areas (*e.g.* literature, social studies, science, mathematics) and to use this language in an accurate and coherent way in their own writing.

All three aspects of language proficiency are important. *However, there is an enormous amount of confusion about the relationship among these three aspects of proficiency.* As noted above, many ELL students who have acquired fluent conversational skills are still a long way from grade-level performance in academic language proficiency (*e.g.* reading comprehension). Similarly, discrete language skills can sometimes be learned in virtual isolation from the development of academic language proficiency. ELL (and native-speaking) students who can "read" English fluently may have only a very limited understanding of the words they can decode. As discussed in Chapters 4 and 5, the development of reading comprehension ability in the content areas requires very different forms of instruction than the forms that are successful in teaching discrete language skills.

These three faces of language proficiency can be elaborated in the context of a framework that distinguishes the cognitive and contextual demands made by particular forms of language and communication.

Cognitive and Contextual Demands

The framework outlined in Figure 3.1 is designed to identify the extent to which students are able to cope successfully with the cognitive and linguistic demands made on them by the social and educational environment in which they are obliged to function. These demands are conceptualized within a framework made up of the intersection of two continua, one related to the range of contextual support available for expressing or receiving meaning and the other to the amount of information that must be processed simultaneously or in close succession by the student in order to carry out the activity.

It is important to state at the outset that the degree of contextual support refers not just to characteristics of the language or the instructional presentation in isolation. These dimensions of what I will term *external context* are relevant. However, in most situations they are probably less important in contributing to "contextual support" than the life experiences and prior knowledge of the learner that reflect the *internal context* that they carry around in their heads. Internal context refers to the resources that individuals have acquired as a result of their life experiences and social interactions to actively contextualize (make meaningful) content and language from a range of situations. For example, a physicist has far greater internal resources and prior knowledge to comprehend a technical article on Einstein's theory of relativity that a person whose knowledge of physics is minimal. Such an article may be quite context-embedded for the physicist whereas it is likely to be highly context-reduced to most of us.

The extremes of the context-embedded/context-reduced continuum are distinguished by the fact that in context-embedded communication the participants can actively negotiate meaning (*e.g.* by providing feedback that the message has not been understood) and the language is supported by a wide range of meaningful interpersonal and situational cues. Context-reduced communication, on the other hand, relies primarily on linguistic cues to meaning. Thus, successful interpretation of the message depends heavily both on students' background knowledge and on their knowledge of the specific vocabulary, grammar, and discourse conventions that express the meaning of the message. In general, context-embedded communication is more typical of the everyday world outside the classroom, whereas many of the linguistic demands of the classroom (*e.g.* manipulating text) reflect communicative activities that are close to the context-reduced end of the continuum.

The upper parts of the vertical continuum consist of communicative tasks and activities in which the linguistic tools have become largely automatized and thus require little active cognitive involvement for appropriate performance. At the lower end of the continuum are tasks and activities in which the linguistic tools have not yet become automatized and thus require active cognitive involvement. Persuading another individual that your point of view is correct,

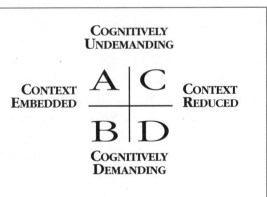

Figure 3.1

RANGE OF CONTEXTUAL SUPPORT AND DEGREE OF COGNITIVE INVOLVEMENT IN LANGUAGE TASKS AND ACTIVITIES

COGNITIVELY UNDEMANDING

CONTEXT EMBEDDED — A | C — CONTEXT REDUCED

B | D

COGNITIVELY DEMANDING

and writing an essay, are examples of quadrant B and D tasks respectively. Casual conversation is a typical quadrant A activity while examples of quadrant C are copying notes from the blackboard or filling in worksheets. Many discrete language skills that have become automatized reflect quadrant C. ...

The framework elaborates on the conversational/academic (or BICS/CALP) distinction by highlighting important underlying dimensions of conversational and academic communication. Thus, conversational abilities (quadrant A) often develop relatively quickly among English language learners because these forms of communication are embedded in students' familiar everyday *lifeworlds* (Gee, 2000). They are also supported by interpersonal and contextual cues (*e.g.* eye contact, intonation, concrete demonstration, etc.) and, as a result, make relatively few cognitive demands on the individual. The vocabulary used in conversational interactions typically involves high frequency words and straightforward grammatical forms.

Mastery of the academic functions of language (quadrant D), on the other hand, is a more formidable task. Students are required to step outside the familiarity of their everyday lifeworld and carry out tasks that are only minimally supported by familiar contextual or interpersonal cues. These tasks also typically require high levels of cognitive involvement for successful completion. Under conditions of high cognitive demand, it is necessary for students to stretch their linguistic resources to the limit to function successfully. As students progress through the grades, they are increasingly required to manipulate language in cognitively-demanding and context-reduced situations that differ significantly from everyday conversational interactions. In writing, for example, they must learn to continue to produce language without the prompting that comes from a conversational partner and they must plan large units of discourse, and organize them coherently, rather than planning only what will be said next.

As the academic demands escalate from grades 1 through 12 and into university, students are expected to master increasingly low frequency specialized vocabulary (*e.g.* the terms *multiplication* and *division* in mathematics) and complex syntax (*e.g.* relative clauses, passive voice, etc.). Within English, this academic vocabulary derives predominantly from Graeco-Latin sources whereas the high frequency vocabulary used in conversational contexts derives largely from Anglo-Saxon sources (Corson, 1995, 1997; Coxhead, 2000; Nation, 1990, 1993). (see Chapters 4 and 5). The differences between conversational and academic language can be illustrated by considering how often children (or adults) will use the passive voice in everyday conversation. This type of grammatical construction is virtually never used in casual conversational interactions. However, in school contexts, students are expected to learn how to understand and eventually produce expository text in which the passive voice is used correctly and appropriately.

The linguistic differences between academic and conversational language can be described in terms of differences of register. The term register is used by linguists to refer to features of speech or writing characteristic of a particular type of linguistic activity (*e.g.* delivering a sermon, telling jokes, teaching a lesson in school, etc.) (Mathews, 1997). Academic language proficiency thus refers to the extent to which an individual has access to and command of the oral and written academic registers of schooling. Academic language can be defined operationally for educational purposes (grades K–12) as the totality of the vocabulary, grammatical constructions, and discourse conventions (*e.g.* paragraph formation) that students are exposed to and expected to learn between Kindergarten and grade 12.

Conversational and academic language registers represent subsets of what James Paul Gee (1996) has termed *primary* and *secondary* discourses. Primary discourses are acquired through face-to-face interactions in the home and represent the language of initial socialization. Secondary discourses are acquired in social institutions beyond the family (*e.g.* school, business, religious and cultural contexts) and involve acquisition of specialized vocabulary and functions of language appropriate to those settings. Secondary discourses can be oral or written and are central to the social life of non-literate cultures as much as they in literate cultures. Examples of secondary discourses common in many non-literate cultures are the conventions of story-telling or the language of marriage or burial rituals which are passed down through oral tradition from one generation to the next. Oral forms of secondary discourses are in no way inferior to written forms, as illustrated in the fact that one of the greatest "literary" achievements of humanity, the Homeric epics of the *Odyssey* and the *Iliad*, existed for many centuries only in oral form prior to being written down. [1]

It is important to emphasize that the context-embedded/context-reduced distinction is not one between oral and written language. Within the framework, the dimensions of contextual embeddedness and cognitive demand are distinguished because some context-embedded activities are clearly just as cognitively-demanding as context-reduced activities. For example, an intense intellectual discussion with one or two other people is likely to require at least as much cognitive processing as writing an essay on the same topic. Similarly, writing an e-mail message to a close friend is, in many respects, more context-embedded than giving a lecture to a large group of people. [2]

The essential aspect of *academic* language proficiency is the ability to make complex meanings explicit in either oral or written modalities by means of *language itself* rather than by means of contextual or paralinguistic cues (*e.g.* gestures, intonation etc.). Experience of these uses of language in oral interactions prior to school clearly helps to prepare children to use and understand the language demands of school. Gee (1999), commenting on the National Academy report *Preventing Reading Difficulties in Young Children* (Snow, Burns & Griffin, 1998), discusses the nature of the early language abilities that relate strongly to success in school:

> So what are these early language abilities that seem to be most important for later success in school? According to the report, they are things like vocabulary (receptive vocabulary, but more especially expressive vocabulary, see p. 107), the ability to recall and comprehend sentences and stories, as well as the ability to engage in verbal interactions. …What appears to cause enhanced verbal abilities are family, community, and school language environments in which children interact intensively with adults and more advanced peers and experience cognitively challenging talk and texts on sustained topics and in different genres of oral and written language. (1999, p. 367)

Gee notes that almost all children regardless of home income level have impressive language abilities and enter school with "large vocabularies, complex grammar, and deep understandings of experiences and stories" (p. 367). Children who experience difficulties in school lack, not these general language abilities, but rather "specific abilities tied to school practices and school-based knowledge" (p. 367). Gee (2000) notes that for advantaged children the trip from their everyday lifeworld to the specialist domain of the school is not very treacherous:

> They are not asked to deny and denigrate their lifeworlds in the process. In fact, from the outset their induction into specialist domains has been built via rich bridges to their lifeworlds. Their lifeworlds have, in fact, incorporated from early on some of the practices and values of specialist domains, though, of course in attenuated forms, for example, the early reading of 'children's literature' provides a bridge to the specialist domain of 'literature' proper. For many minor-

ity and poor children, on the other hand, no such bridges exist or are built. We rarely build on their experiences and on their very real distinctive lifeworld knowledge. In fact, they are very often asked, in the process of being exposed to specialist domains, to deny the value of their lifeworlds and their communities in reference to those of more advantaged children. (2000, p. 66)

We see here in Gee's analysis how, once again, issues of identity and power intersect with issues of learning and instruction. A central theme running though the present volume is that school improvement efforts are likely to be futile if they continue to exclude issues of identity and power from their analyses of the causes of students' academic difficulties and from their recommendations for change. Instructional prescriptions for reading and/or academic language development that base themselves only on technical considerations (*e.g.* how much explicit, systematic, sequenced phonics instruction should early readers receive?) frame the issues far too narrowly to see the big picture. [3]

Within the broader context of societal power relations and identity negotiation, the distinctions incorporated into the framework in Figure 3.1 do have significant implications for instruction of English language learners. The progression of academic tasks should ideally go from quadrant A (context-embedded, cognitively undemanding), to quadrant B (context-embedded, cognitively demanding) and then to quadrant D (context-reduced, cognitively demanding). Cognitive challenge is essential for academic growth but the internal and external contextual support necessary for bilingual students to meet that challenge must also be built into the activities. If instruction stays at the level of quadrant A, there is no cognitive challenge; students are not pushed to go beyond what they already know and can accomplish. If instruction jumps prematurely to quadrant D, students are not given the contextual supports they need to meet the cognitive challenge. Quadrant C activities (context-reduced, cognitively undemanding) can be useful for reinforcement or practice of particular points and for teaching discrete language skills. However, if instruction stays at the level of quadrant C (rather than involving both quadrants B and C), it risks focusing only on out-of-context drills and worksheets. This kind of instruction usually fails to supply certain essential elements to facilitate learning: for example, cognitive challenge, affirmation of identity, and extensive comprehensible input in the target language.

Quadrant B activities provide both cognitive challenge and contextual support and are thus crucial for promoting academic growth. Cooperative learning is an example of a quadrant B activity insofar as the cooperation among students, together with teacher input, supplies the contextual support for students to engage in cognitively challenging projects or activities. Peer tutoring, role-play and drama also fall into this category. Reading and writing activities, when appropriately supported (see Chapters 4 and 5), are also important quadrant B activities.

As noted above, contextual support involves both internal and external dimensions. Internal factors are attributes of the individual that make a task more familiar or easier in some respect (*e.g.* prior experience, motivation, cultural relevance, interests, etc.). External factors refer to aspects of the input that facilitate or impede comprehension; for example, language input that is spoken clearly and contains a considerable amount of syntactic and semantic redundancy is easier to understand than input that lacks these features.

As elaborated in Chapter 5, teachers must focus on both internal and external contextual supports if bilingual students' academic progress is to be accelerated. For example, activating students' prior experience is crucial in making academic input in the target language comprehensible. In addition to facilitating comprehension through mobilizing students' internal resources for contextualizing the content, activating prior knowledge also affirms bilingual students' identities by communicating to them that what they already know is important. In this way, it also challenges the societal power structure that continues to structure schools in ways that excludes bilingual children's language, culture, and lifeworld experiences.

The central point is that language and content will be acquired most successfully when students are challenged cognitively but provided with the contextual and linguistic supports required for successful task completion. The process of providing these supports is usually referred to as scaffolding and is a central component in promoting academic success for English language learners. [4]

The next section considers how long it takes second language learners to master conversational and academic aspects of the target language.

How Long Does It Take English Language Learners to Acquire Different Aspects of Proficiency?

One application of the framework considered in Figure 3.1 is in the interpretation of data regarding the length of time required for bilingual students to develop proficiency in different aspects of English. Several large-scale studies have reported that, on the average, at least five years is required for immigrant students to attain grade norms on academic aspects of English proficiency (*e.g.* Collier, 1987; Cummins, 1981b; Hakuta, Butler & Witt, 2000; Klesmer, 1994; Thomas & Collier, 1997).

Collier's (1987) data are particularly interesting in that most students were from relatively affluent backgrounds attending a district (Fairfax County, Virginia) that was regarded as having an exemplary ESL program (and no bilingual education). She reports that children who arrived in the United States between ages 8 and 12, with several years of L1 schooling, required five to seven years to reach national norms in reading, social studies and science. Those who arrived before age 8 required seven to ten years to attain national norms, while those who arrived after age 12 often ran out of time before they could catch up academically in language-based areas of the curriculum. A considerably shorter period of time was usually required to catch up in math. [5]

Cummins (1981b) also reported that 5-7 years were required for immigrant students from non-English-speaking backgrounds to come close to grade norms in English academic proficiency. Students who had been in Canada for three years were approximately one standard deviation (the equivalent of 15 IQ points) behind grade norms despite the fact that after three years most would have become relatively fluent in English conversational skills. After five years students were within half a standard deviation (7.5 IQ points) of grade norms.

Klesmer's (1994) study involved a representative sample of almost 300 12-year-old ELL students in a metropolitan Toronto school district. Detailed assessments of English proficiency and background data, as well as teacher ratings, were obtained. Klesmer reported that teachers considered most ESL students as average for their age in speaking, listening and reading after 24 to 35 months in Canada. In the area of writing, teachers considered ELL students to have almost reached the mean for Canadian-born students after 5 or 6 years. However, the test data showed significant gaps between the ELL students and a control group of English first language students (N=43) in verbal academic areas (but not non-verbal ability) even after six years length of residence. The control group performed at the level of test norms whereas the ESL students were considerably below test norms on verbal academic measures even after 6 years length of residence. Klesmer (1994) concludes that:

> [T]here is strong evidence to suggest that the academic/linguistic development of ESL students follows a distinct pattern. It requires at least six years for ESL students to approach native English speakers' norms in a variety of areas; and it appears that, even after six years, full comparability may not be achieved. (p. 11) [6]

Outside of North America, Shohamy (1999) reports ongoing research being conducted in Israel that shows a time period of 7–9 years for immigrant students to arrive at similar achievements as native speakers in Hebrew literacy and slightly less in mathematics. Similar data are presented by the Tower Hamlets school district in London, England. Reading scores among ELL students were directly related to the amount of time they had spent in the school system. Students with 4 years in the system obtained a standard score of 88 while those in the system for 7 years were virtually at the average level (99.2). The report concludes: "there are large increases in performance for each additional year in education and those bilingual pupils receiving 7 or more years in education perform close to the Inner London average on the test" (1995, p. 12).

Other research suggests that a much shorter period of time (less than two years) is usually required for immigrant students to attain peer-appropriate levels of proficiency in conversational aspects of their second language (*e.g.* González, 1986, 1989; Snow and Hoefnagel-Höhle 1978). These patterns are depicted in Figure 3.2.

There are two reasons why such major differences are found in the length of time required to attain peer-appropriate levels of conversational and academic skills. First, as outlined above, considerably less knowledge of language itself is usually required to function appropriately in interpersonal communicative situations than is required in academic situations. The social expectations of the learner and sensitivity to contextual and interpersonal cues (*e.g.* eye contact, facial expression, intonation etc.) greatly facilitate communication of meaning. These cues are largely absent in most academic situations that depend on much more extensive vocabulary knowledge and manipulation of language for successful task completion. As noted above, the language of subject matter is fundamentally different from conversational language with respect to vocabulary, syntax, and discourse conventions.

The second reason is that English L1 speakers are not standing still waiting for English language learners to catch up. English L1 speakers come to school fluent in conversational English and yet we spend another 12 years and billions of dollars to expand this initial competence into academic spheres. A major goal of schooling for all children is to develop their ability to manipulate language in increasingly abstract situations. Every year English L1 students gain more sophisticated vocabulary and grammatical knowledge and increase their literacy skills. Thus, English language learners must catch up with a moving target. Specifically, Collier and Thomas (1999) have estimated that in order to catch up to grade norms within 6 years, ELL students must make 15 months gain in every 10-month school year compared to the 10-month gain expected for the typical native-speaking student.

By contrast, in the area of conversational skills, most native speakers have reached a plateau relatively early in schooling in the sense that a typical six year-old can express herself as adequately as an older child on most topics she is likely to want to speak about and she can understand most of what is likely to be addressed to her. While some increase in conversational sophistication can be expected with increasing age, the differences are not particularly salient in

$\mathcal{F}igure\ 3.2$ **LENGTH OF TIME REQUIRED TO ACHIEVE AGE-APPROPRIATE LEVELS OF CONVERSATIONAL AND ACADEMIC LANGUAGE PROFICIENCY**

- - - - NATIVE ENGLISH SPEAKERS
——— ENGLISH LANGUAGE LEARNERS

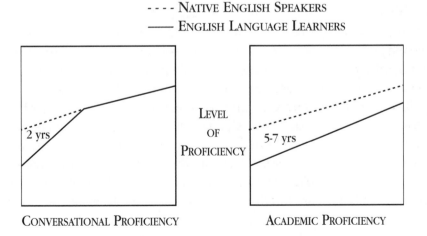

CONVERSATIONAL PROFICIENCY   ACADEMIC PROFICIENCY

comparison to differences in literacy-related skills; compare, for example, the differences in literacy between a twelve and a six year-old student in comparison to differences in their conversational skills.

The preceding discussion of the nature of language proficiency and the length of time required to develop peer-appropriate levels of conversational and academic skills has immediate relevance for two practical issues. First, psychological assessment of bilingual students conducted in English is likely to underestimate their academic potential to a significant extent if any credence is placed in the test norms which are derived predominantly from native English-speaking students.

Second, support for language and academic development will still be beneficial (and frequently necessary) even after students have attained conversational fluency in English and the discrete language skills required for decoding English text. Exiting students prematurely from bilingual or ESL support programs may jeopardize their academic development, particularly if the mainstream classroom does not provide an environment that is supportive of language and content development. The kinds of instructional environment that are supportive of bilingual students' academic development are considered in the next two chapters. [7]

Conclusion

As discussed in Chapter 2, academic difficulties among bilingual students cannot be attributed solely to linguistic factors. However, misconceptions about language on the part of educators have clearly contributed to students' difficulties. [8] In fact, it is argued in Chapter 7 that the persistence of these misconceptions about language is a *symptom* of the underlying educational structure that disables culturally diverse students. For educators, a first step in becoming conscious of the ways in which this underlying structure operates to promote discriminatory assessment, placement, and instruction of culturally diverse students is to examine critically the notion of "language proficiency" and how it affects performance on psychometric tests. Specifically, it is necessary to acknowledge that students' surface fluency in English cannot be taken as indicative of their overall proficiency in English. Similarly, acquisition of discrete language skills in English, while important, is not necessarily predictive of future academic language development. Students usually require most of the elementary school years to develop English academic language proficiency to grade norms. As documented in Chapter 6, research suggests that bilingual students' conceptual foundation in L1 is more fundamental to this process than their English conversational fluency.

It is also crucial for educators and policy-makers to face up to the implications of the fact that students are not failing in school only because of lack of English fluency. Lack of English fluency may be a secondary contributor to children's academic difficulty but the fundamental causal factors of both success and failure lie in what is communicated to children in their interactions with educators. This is clearly expressed by Isidro Lucas (1981) in describing a research study he carried out in the early 1970's with Puerto Rican students in Chicago designed to explore the reasons for student dropout. Although he prepared questionnaires in both Spanish and English, he never had to use the Spanish version. The reason was that:

> All my dropout respondents spoke good understandable English. They hadn't learned math, or social sciences, or natural sciences, unfortunately. But they had learned English...No dropout mentioned lack of English as the reason for quitting. As it evolved through questionnaires and interviews, theirs was a more subtle story—of alienation, of not belonging, of being 'push-outs'...To my surprise, dropouts expressed more confidence in their ability to speak English than did the stay-ins (seniors in high school). For their part, stay-ins showed more confidence in their Spanish than did dropouts...I had to conclude that identity, expressed in one's confidence and acceptance of the native culture, was more a determinant of school stay-in power than the mere acquisition of the coding-decoding skills involved in a different language, English. (p. 19)

In short, understanding why and how bilingual students are failing academically requires that educators dig a little deeper than superficial linguistic mismatches between home and school or insufficient exposure to English. Underachievement is not caused primarily by lack of fluency in English. Underachievement is the result of particular kinds of interactions in school that lead culturally diverse students to mentally withdraw from academic effort.

One of the major reasons why students mentally withdraw from academic effort is that the instructional environment frequently does not facilitate or encourage active participation on their part. The message students get is that academic success is unlikely and thus academic effort is not worthwhile. Their identities disengage from the academic life of the school. What kinds of instructional environments are likely to reverse this pattern? This issue is discussed in the next two chapters.

Endnotes to Chapter 3

1. Secondary discourses depend on well-established cultural institutions for their transmission and sustenance. In contexts where the culture of a marginalized group has been subordinated to that of the dominant group, it is often difficult for the marginalized group to maintain and sustain the secondary discourses central to the culture from one generation to the next. This applies both to the development of academic or literate discourses in the minority language (which depend on schooling in L1) as well as to discourses associated with cultural rituals and traditions. Schooling at least partly through the minority language is usually essential for strong development of academic literacy in that language. Literate parents with a coherent home language policy of reading to the child in L1 on a regular basis and teaching their child to read and write in the L1 *can* sometimes succeed in promoting strong L1 literacy in the absence of L1 schooling, but the challenge is significant. Similarly, participation in the welcoming ceremonies typical of many Polynesian cultures requires apprenticeship in the discourse used in those cultural contexts.

   Sometimes bilingual children get caught in the middle of L1 and L2 secondary discourses competing for their allegiance. Intergenerational transmission of secondary discourses from the home culture may be undermined as a result of contact with the dominant culture while discriminatory educational structures may result in poor development of the secondary discourse types of the dominant culture (*e.g.* literacy in the school language). Primary discourse types (*e.g.* conversational fluency) in both cultures may continue to be sustained.

   The education of Deaf students historically represents an example of bilingual students being denied access to secondary discourses in both their languages. Commenting on the failure of various forms of signed English and "Total Communication" systems to reverse the academic failure of Deaf students, Gibson, Small and Mason (1997) note:

   > People can not sustain a rich conversation with any of these artificial sign systems that distort both ASL and English. Due to the incomplete messages conveyed with these systems, Deaf students were placed at an educational disadvantage. Thus many Deaf students, educated with these systems, left school with low literacy skills in both ASL and English. Many had low self-esteem and lacked indepth knowledge of the world for full participation in life's opportunities...The monolingual philosophy resulted in an ironic socioeducational phenomenon. Deaf students graduated with no exposure to a language which they could have full access to (ASL) had they been permitted. Instead, they were exposed to a language which they could not have full access to (spoken English) and which was being altered (through inconsistent visually coded systems) in an attempt to make it accessible. Thus, students graduated without the secondary discourses necessary for literacy in either ASL or English. (1997, p. 233)

2. In practice, contextual and cognitive dimensions are not totally independent in that many context-reduced activities will tend to be more cognitively-demanding than context-embedded activities. This point is made by Frederickson and Cline (1990) in discussing the applicability of the framework for curriculum-based assessment of bilingual children:

> In observing and analysing classroom tasks, instructions and performances, we have often found it difficult to disentangle the "cognitive" from the "contextual". In some cases, movement along the contextual dimensions has actually been represented on the model as a diagonal shift, as it was found in practice that making tasks or instructions more context embedded also made them somewhat less cognitively demanding. Similarly, changes in cognitive demand may result in tasks actually being presented with greater context embeddedness. (p. 26)

Although there is clearly likely to be a correlation between degree of decontextualization and cognitive demand, I believe it is important to distinguish the two dimensions in order that the extent of this relationship can be investigated. In the one-dimensional distinctions proposed by other investigators (*e.g.* Donaldson's embedded/disembedded distinction), the degree of cognitive demand of particular tasks or activities is not represented and thus the instructional implications are more difficult to discern.

Robson (1995) summarizes some of the ways the framework has been used in the British context as follows:

> We found that the Cummins model was particularly relevant as a tool for formative assessment in that it could offer a framework for ongoing assessment, evaluation of tasks set and the planning of further teaching programmes and tasks for bilingual pupils. ... With reference to a bilingual pupil who may have learning difficulties, the Cummins model offers a framework for assessing progress over time, taking into account context, cognitive demand and language ability in relation to the tasks set. (pp. 41 & 43).

3. On the basis of her extensive ethnographic study among middle-class and lower-class families, Heath (1983) argues that the differences between social classes in learning to read derives from more than just differential access to literacy materials at home. What is more significant is the extent to which literacy activities are integrated with children's daily lives. The black and white *Maintown* (middle-class) children in her study experienced activities such as inventing narratives related to the stories that were read to them and comparing book characters with real people they knew. They learned to view language as an artifact separate from its use in face-to-face communicative contexts.

Heath (1986) points out that students who achieve academic success either bring to school this notion of language as an artifact and the uses of language associated with it or they learn quickly to intuit the rules of this kind of language use for both speaking and writing. Bilingual children who have these functions of language available in their L1 can transfer them easily to English, given appropriate opportunities in English (see Chapter 6). Thus, both in-school and out-of-school occasions (in both L1 and L2) that require explanation of facts and assumptions not shared by others provide practice in the kind of context-reduced and impersonal language that is important for academic success. Heath suggests, for example, that a child who listens to a bank teller explain to her mother the rules for opening a savings account learns something about how to present information to someone who does not already share it, a use of language that will be invoked in much of the child's writing in school.

4. The general distinction that has been made between context-embedded and context reduced language skills is consistent with the psychometric research of Ludo Verhoeven (1992) and Douglas Biber (1986). Verhoeven assessed context-embedded and context-reduced aspects of L1 and L2 proficiency among 72 Turkish-background kindergarten children living in The Netherlands. The context-embedded (or pragmatic in Verhoeven's terms) indices were derived from spontaneous speech whereas the context-reduced (or grammatical in Verhoeven's terms) indices were derived from test data assessing primarily vocabulary and sentence processing skills. Verhoeven found that context-embedded and context-reduced aspects of proficiency were clearly distinguishable (through factor analysis) in both languages. In addition, context-reduced proficiency in both languages was significantly related to non-verbal cognitive ability whereas this was not the case for context-embedded proficiency. Verhoeven concludes:

> The present study suggests that the proficiencies children have developed in L1 and L2 can not be conceived as monolithic traits. The present data show that in either language, context-based pragmatic skills can be distinguished from decontextualized grammatical skills. (1992, p. 134)

Verhoeven also found that both context-embedded and context-reduced proficiencies were significantly related across languages (Turkish-Dutch), a finding that is consistent with the results of Cummins *et al.* (1984) among Japanese-English bilingual students in Toronto, Canada and supportive of the interdependence hypothesis discussed in Chapter 6.

The conversational/academic distinction is also supported by Biber who used psychometric analysis of an extremely large corpus of spoken and written textual material in order to uncover the basic dimensions underlying textual variation. Among the 16 text types included in Biber's analysis were broadcasts, spontaneous speeches, telephone conversation, face-to-face conversation, professional letters, academic prose and press reports. Forty-one linguistic features were counted in 545 text samples, totaling more than one million words.

Three major dimensions emerged from the factor analysis of this corpus. These were labeled by Biber as *Interactive vs. Edited Text, Abstract vs. Situated Content*, and *Reported vs. Immediate Style*. The first dimension is described as follows:

> Thus, Factor 1 identifies a dimension which characterizes texts produced under conditions of high personal involvement and real-time constraints (marked by low explicitness in the expression of meaning, high subordination and interactive features)—as opposed to texts produced under conditions permitting considerable editing and high explicitness of lexical content, but little interaction or personal involvement. ...This dimen-

sion combines both situational and cognitive parameters; in particular it combines interactional features with those reflecting production constraints (or the lack of them) (1986, p. 385).

The second factor has positive weights from linguistic features such as nominalizations, prepositions, and passives and, according to Biber, reflects a "detached formal style vs. a concrete colloquial one" (p. 396). Although this factor is correlated with the first factor, it can be empirically distinguished from it, as illustrated by professional letters, which, according to Biber's analysis, represent highly abstract texts that have a high level of personal involvement.

The third factor has positive weights from linguistic features such as past tense, perfect aspect and 3rd person pronouns which can all refer to a removed narrative context. According to Biber this dimension "distinguishes texts with a primary narrative emphasis, marked by considerable reference to a removed situation, from those with non-narrative emphases (descriptive, expository, or other) marked by little reference to a removed situation but a high occurrence of present tense forms" (p. 396).

Although Biber's three dimensions provide a more detailed analysis of the nature of language proficiency and use than the conversational/academic distinction (as would be expected in view of the very extensive range of spoken and written texts analyzed), it is clear that the distinctions highlighted in his dimensions are consistent with those distinguishing conversational and academic aspects of proficiency. For example, when factor scores were calculated for the different text types on each factor, telephone and face-to-face conversation were at opposite extremes from official documents and academic prose on Textual Dimensions 1 and 2 (Interactive vs. Edited Text, and Abstract vs. Situated Content).

5. Students who arrive after developing literacy in their L1 have a second advantage in that they are less likely to lose their L1 than students who arrive at younger ages (see, for example, Cummins *et al.*, 1984). Bilingual students typically experience rapid loss of L1 in the first few years of learning English in preschool or in the early grades (Cummins, 1991b; Wong Fillmore, 1991a). In short, students who arrive between ages 8 and 12 have the best prospects for developing proficient bilingual and biliterate abilities, a conclusion that agrees with the data of Skutnabb-Kangas and Toukomaa (1976).

6. The Ramírez Report data (Ramírez, 1992) also illustrate the time periods required to catch up in academic aspects of language proficiency: after four years of instruction, grade 3 Spanish-speaking students in both structured immersion (English-only) and early exit bilingual programs were still far from grade norms in English academic achievement. Grade 6 students in late-exit programs who had consistently received about 40% of their instruction through their primary language were beginning to approach grade norms. Further analysis of a subset of these data (from a late-exit program in New York City) showed that the rapidity with which bilingual students approached grade norms in English reading by grade 6 was strongly related to their level of Spanish reading at grade 3. The better developed their Spanish reading was at grade 3, the more rapid progress they made in English reading between grades 3 and 6 (Beykont, 1994).

Gándara (1999), in summarizing data from California, has noted the "large discrepancy" between the developmental patterns for oral L2 skills (measured by tests) as compared to L2 reading and writing during the elementary school years:

> For example, while listening skills are at 80% of native proficiency by level 3 (approximately 3rd grade), reading and writing skills remain below 50% of those expected for native speakers. It is not until after Level 5 (or approximately 5th grade) that the different sets of skills begin to merge. This suggests that while a student may be able to speak and understand English at fairly high levels of proficiency within the first three years of school, academic skills in English reading and writing take longer for students to develop. (1999, p. 5)

Hakuta, Butler and Witt's (2000) analysis of data from two California school districts in the San Francisco bay area showed that "even in two California districts that are considered the most successful in teaching English to LEP [limited English proficient] students, oral proficiency [measured by formal tests] takes 3 to 5 years to develop, and academic English proficiency can take 4 to 7 years" (2000, p. iii). They label the one-year time period of "sheltered English immersion" that Proposition 227 gives ELL students to acquire English "wildly unrealistic" (2000, p. 13).

7. It is interesting to subject the claims of Proposition 227 advocates to a reality check with respect to how long it takes students to learn English (see also Krashen, 2000b, for additional data and discussion). The percentile ranks for the Oceanside district on the SAT-9 test (academic year 1999/2000) are presented below. These data represent the scores for limited English proficient students who had been in the school system for *at least* one year. Many of the students represented in these figures have been in the school system for considerably longer. Oceanside has been touted by Proposition 227 advocates as *the* example that demonstrates the wisdom of the measure. Yet, students show dramatically declining percentile ranks between grades 2 and 11 (32nd percentile at grade 2, 8th percentile at grade 11). If one year is all that is required to learn sufficient English to survive academically then this decline should not be observed and we would expect all students to be close to the 50th percentile after just one year. The Oceanside percentile scores for reading in the SAT-9 (2000) are as follows:

G2:	32	G7:	13
G3:	22	G8:	18
G4:	23	G9:	11
G5:	19	G10:	06
G6:	20	G11:	08

The diminished reading achievement of Oceanside ELL students after the early grades is not unusual and reflects the commonly observed phenomenon of the fourth-grade slump (Chall, Jacobs & Baldwin, 1990; Gee, 1999; Snow, Burns & Griffin, 1998). The data for grade 2 reflect the fact that discrete language skills in an L2 (such as decoding) can be taught to students who are still at relatively early stages of developing proficiency in the language (*e.g.* Kwan & Willows, 1998; Lambert & Tucker, 1972). At higher grade levels, however, standardized tests assess reading comprehension skills to a greater extent than simply the decoding skills tested at early grades. There is substantial research data showing that low-income students taught through drill and practice instruction (*e.g.* in the DISTAR program) drop from between the 30th to 40th percentile in reading at grades 2/3 to about the 15th percentile by grades 5 and 6 (Becker, 1977; Becker & Gersten, 1982; Cummins, 1984—see Chapter 4).

8. Educators are not the only ones who sometimes have misconceptions about language. As I was preparing a paper to present at the American Association of Applied Linguistics (AAAL) in Long Beach, California, in March 1995, my eye was caught by a headline in the Toronto Star entitled "Charles Churlish on U.S. English." Since my presentation focused on the arguments of U.S. English in relation to bilingual education, I was intrigued at the prospect of royal assent for my position. Unfortunately, Prince Charles viewed "U.S. English" as problematic in quite another sense. The Globe & Mail (March 27, 1995) reprinted the following editorial written by Dale McFeatters of the U.S. Scripps Howard News Service:

> Britain's Prince Charles complains that American English is having a "very corrupting" influence on "proper English," which, through the darndest coincidence, happens to be the brand of English he speaks.

> Said the Prince, casually infuriating the Scots, Welsh and Irish as he did so, "We must act now to ensure that English—and that to my way of thinking means English English—maintains its position as the world language well into the next century."

> His problem with Americans is that we tend to "invent all sorts of new nouns and verbs and make words that shouldn't be."

> Our first reaction, as you can well imagine, was, "I say, old chap. Steady on." Think of the American words that have enriched the language: Gridlock. Carjack. Spin doctor. Deadbeat dad. Junk mail. Gangsta rap. Road kill. Cyberpunk. Grunge. Smog. Boombox.

> Our second reaction was: Maybe the Prince has a point. (p. A11)

Bilingual and mother tongue teachers are no less subject to prejudice about language varieties than other members of the public. This was illustrated to me in a workshop I gave during the 1980s to a group of heritage language (mother tongue) teachers in Toronto, Canada. A participant raised the issue of how to deal with children's use of non-standard language in the classroom. Another teacher immediately raised his hand to share his way of helping children learn the standard form of the language (in this case Italian). He suggested that when children use a non-standard form in the classroom, the teacher should immediately stop the child and give her the "correct" term or expression. Another participant then asked what he would do if the child said that the non-standard form was what her parents used. The teacher responded that the child should be told that her parents were using the wrong word and she should go home and tell her parents what the "correct" word was.

It is clear that in this situation the teacher is communicating to the child that her parents not only have problems in English but, in addition, they don't even speak their home language properly. The effect is likely to be to reduce children's pride in their own cultural background and adversely affect their esteem for their parents. An alternative way of dealing with the same issue was suggested by a teacher of Italian at a different workshop. She suggested that when a non-standard word comes up in class the teacher can ask children what other words (in different dialects) they have for this object or idea. Her experience was that children soon realized the need for the standard form of the language in order to facilitate communication between communities whose native dialects are different. The appropriateness of the non-standard variety in its own context is also reinforced.

Chapter 4
Reading and the Bilingual Student: Fact and Friction

The discussion in the preceding chapter of the differences between conversational and academic language proficiency and the length of time required for ELL students to catch up academically carries some clear implications for policy and practice. First, educating ELL students is the responsibility of the *entire school staff* and not just the responsibility of ESL or bilingual teachers. The increasing numbers of ELL students in many districts, together with the time periods typically required for students to catch up, means that "mainstream" classroom teachers must be prepared (in both senses of the term) to teach all the students in their classrooms. Perhaps the most crucial aspect of the classroom teacher's task is to support ELL students in developing strong reading skills because reading is the primary way in which students get access to academic language. This is true across content areas and particularly so as students progress through the grades. The time has long past when linguistic and other "exceptionalities" could be fully addressed by means of "satellite" programs (*e.g.,* ESL, bilingual education, special education, etc.) that revolve around a static mainstream.

A related implication is that school language policies should be developed in every school to address the needs of *all* students in the school, and in particular, those students who require support in English academic language learning (see Corson, 1999, for discussion of school language policies; also see Appendix A for an illustrative language policy statement). This also implies that administrators in schools should be competent to provide leadership in addressing issues of underachievement in culturally and linguistically diverse contexts. In particular, they should know enough about the reading process to guide teachers towards coherent and effective ways of teaching reading to ELL students.

A third set of implications concerns assessment issues. District-, state-, or nation-wide assessment programs that use standardized tests to assess ELL students who are still in the process of catching up academically in English are likely to give a very misleading impression both of students' academic potential and of the effectiveness of instruction. Students who have been learning English for about three years in a school context perform about one standard deviation (the equivalent of 15 IQ points) below grade norms in academic English skills (Cummins, 1981b). If the interpretation of test results fails to take account of these data, effective schools with large numbers of ELL students will appear ineffective to parents and policy-makers. This perception is likely to reduce student and teacher morale. Alternative assessment procedures (*e.g.,* portfolio or performance assessment) that take account of developmental patterns in ELL students' acquisition of academic English, particularly their reading and writing development, are required to provide a valid picture of student progress and instructional effectiveness for accountability purposes (see Cummins, 2000). Similarly, testing of bilingual students who are referred for special education assessment is likely to give distorted results if the tests are administered only in students' L2.

This chapter elaborates on the instructional strategies for teaching reading that are implied by the analysis of power relations and identity negotiation in Chapter 1 and the discussion of academic language in Chapter 3. What *specific* forms of literacy instruction will accelerate ELL students' acquisition of academic language? From one perspective, this question may appear more difficult to answer today than it did ten years ago. There appears to be a never-ending array of instructional prescriptions and requirements that flow down the pipeline from state departments or district offices. The challenges educators face are intensified by the volatile controversies that have characterized debates on education in the 1990s. Maintaining a coherent vision of what we are trying to achieve with our students is difficult when we are bombarded from all sides with conflicting dogmas regarding what constitutes effective reading instruction.

Last year's doctrine has become today's heresy. Fashions in the teaching of reading, math, and science have changed radically in the space of the last decade. For example, in the new orthodoxy of the 1990s, whole language and literature-based approaches to the teaching of reading are out, phonics and phonemic awareness are in. The pendulum has similarly swung back and forth in the teaching of math and science between experiential/constructivist orientations and more teacher-centered didactic approaches. What many of us learned as effective instruction in teacher education courses is now berated by policy-makers and media pundits as the ruination of the next generation.

State-mandated standardized assessments add to the pressure. Many educators fear that such assessments constrict the curriculum and force us to teach to the test, thereby reducing the quality of instruction rather than enhancing it. The empirical data suggest that such fears are well-founded (McNeil, 2000). Standardized tests, such as the SAT-9 in California, also pressure us to reduce the emphasis on L1 literacy in bilingual programs since assessment is conducted only in English (Gándara *et al.*, 2000).

In this cacophony of conflicting ideologies and prescriptions, what can we say with any degree of confidence about effective reading instruction for bilingual/ELL students? Surprisingly, we can say quite a lot. There is actually far more coherence in the research and theory about what works and what constitutes effective literacy instruction for ELL students than we might assume from the volatile controversies about the topic.

First, I outline some central characteristics of second language teaching and learning and then I try to forge a peace treaty in what have been termed the "reading wars." If we understand the relationship of academic language development (particularly vocabulary knowledge) to reading comprehension (and academic achievement generally), then there really should be no controversy in *how* to teach reading. Essentially what I argue is that how we teach phonics and phonemic awareness is not particularly important so long as we ensure that students *do* acquire decoding skills and relevant knowledge about how the sounds of the language relate to the written code. What determines reading achievement in the long-term is how effectively we develop students' reading comprehension. Reading comprehension is overwhelmingly related to the extent to which students engage in extensive reading. Simply put, books are the only place where students get access to the low frequency Graeco-Latin lexicon of English. It follows that a diet of engaging books works much better than a diet of worksheets and drills in developing reading comprehension and academic language.

Second Language Acquisition: A Quick Synthesis

There is general agreement among applied linguists that sufficient *comprehensible input* is a necessary condition for acquisition of a second or third language. The notion of comprehensible input, elaborated by Krashen (1981), refers to the processing of meaning in the target language. Exposure by itself is not enough—it must be exposure that learners can understand. Furthermore, the input should contain structures that are a little beyond what the learner already knows. Despite the presence of "unknown" words and/or structures, learners can utilize context, extra-linguistic information, and their knowledge of the world to understand the meaning. Krashen argued that comprehensible input was not only a necessary condition but also a sufficient condition for target language acquisition. In other words, comprehensible input is *the* central causal variable that determines the extent to which the second language acquisition process is more or less successful.

Apparently persuasive evidence for this strong version of what Krashen termed the *input hypothesis* came from the fact that in naturalistic acquisition-rich contexts children are capable of acquiring native-like fluency in additional languages without formal instruction or any explicit focus on teaching the language itself. Similarly, there is strong evidence that comprehensible input through extensive reading in the second language can be highly effective in promoting L2 proficiency (*e.g.*, Elley, 1991; Krashen, 1993).

These considerations have led Krashen to downplay the role of formal teaching of the target language (*e.g.*, teaching of grammatical rules or vocabulary). He has also argued that use of the target language is not an essential aspect of the acquisition process. Speaking and writing are relevant primarily as a means of generating more comprehensible input within communicative contexts. Writing also has the important additional function of promoting cognitive growth but does not contribute directly to acquisition of the target language.

According to this theoretical perspective, in order to create conditions for more successful second language acquisition, educators must expand opportunities for students to receive comprehensible input in written or oral modalities in these languages. If development of literacy in the target languages is a goal, then extensive reading in these languages is crucial.

I believe that Krashen (1981, 1993) has appropriately highlighted the central importance of comprehensible input in the process of second language acquisition. Also, few would argue with his position that teaching formal features of the language in isolation, out of the context of any meaningful engagement with the language, is not particularly productive. However, the emphasis on issues of identity and societal power relations in the present volume and the focus on *academic* language suggest some additional roles for the teacher than just providing extensive comprehensible input. I believe it is worth asking how we can help students become more efficient processors of that input (in other words, make more of it comprehensible). I also believe that it is worth asking how we can maximize bilingual students' *investment* in the learning process (Kanno, 2000; McKay & Wong, 1996; Peirce, 1995) so that they come to see themselves as powerful users of language with additional insights about language and its potential in comparison to monolingual students. For example, when a student writes and publishes a bilingual book written in both L1 and L2, this achievement holds a mirror up to the student that positively reflects her identity. This, in turn, will motivate more engagement with reading and writing. Active language use thus becomes a critical aspect of learners' personal engagement in the language learning process.

In short, a focus on how societal power relations influence *academic* language development suggests a broader range of determinants of second language acquisition and a more crucial role for the teacher than typically emerges from a focus on comprehensible input in isolation. Specifically, I would assign an important role to (a) the development of critical language awareness through a focus both on formal features of the target language and the societal consequences of particular forms of language use; (b) the development of effective learning strategies to squeeze maximum learning from the input to which we can gain access (*e.g.,* Chamot, Barnhardt, El-Dinary & Robbins, 1999; Chamot & O'Malley, 1994), and (c) actual use of the target language to generate new knowledge, act on social realities, or create literature or art, all of which potentially make a change in our world and open up identity options for the future (see Chapter 5).

Obviously, as Krashen has emphasized, gaining access to *comprehensible input* is essential before we can elaborate the input in the ways outlined above. Three aspects of comprehensible input need to be highlighted: first, the extent to which input will be comprehended depends as much on the cognitive schemata or prior knowledge of the student as it does on the characteristics of the input itself. A migrant student who has a lot of informal background knowledge in her L1 regarding growing and harvesting plants and vegetables is more likely to understand an English science lesson on these topics than a lesson of equal linguistic difficulty on a topic s/he knows very little about. The more background knowledge a student has, the more she understands; and the more she understands, the more she learns. This, in turn, builds up further background knowledge that continues to fuel the learning process. *The implication here is that a crucial component of effective instruction for bilingual/ELL students is the activation of students' prior knowledge, together with building background knowledge, to ensure that the cognitive schemata required for comprehensible input are in place.*

Second, it is clear from the research data (reviewed in Chapter 6) that background knowledge developed in students' L1 helps make input in L2 comprehensible. This suggests that it is important for teachers to tap into and amplify students' L1 background knowledge, particularly in English-only classroom situations where the teacher may not speak the languages of his or her students. *An implication is that teachers should encourage students to continue to develop their knowledge of the world and curriculum content in their L1 while they are acquiring English since this knowledge increases their cognitive power to comprehend and acquire English.*

Third, comprehension is not an "all-or-nothing" phenomenon; our understanding of words, stories, or events deepens the more we relate them to our prior knowledge and personal histories, the more we critically analyze them with respect to their logic and social significance, and the more we express our developing understanding through creative action such as writing on a topic, dramatizing and reinterpreting events, etc. *Thus, the notion of "providing comprehensible input" should be interpreted as encouraging students to engage in a process of collaborative critical inquiry where issues are analyzed and discussed as a way of deepening understanding and motivating further inquiry (e.g., through further reading).*

In summary, comprehensible input is a central determinant of second language acquisition for both conversational and academic purposes. However, comprehensible input is a complex multi-dimensional concept. An instructional focus on providing extensive comprehensible input is in no way incompatible with a focus on demystifying how the target language works and how it is related to students' L1; nor is a focus on comprehensible input in any way incompatible with encouraging active language use (in both L1 and L2) in both oral and written modalities. When students express *themselves* through language, they see their identities reflected in how they use language and the literature they produce through language. A poem written by a student in Spanish (L1) and translated by her with the help of her classmates into English, and then posted in both Spanish and English versions on the class web site, is not just a linguistic creation: it holds a positive mirror up to that student of her present identity and who she can aspire to become in the future. In the process of academic language development, cognitive, linguistic, and academic development are fused together. The fuel that drives this development is the extent to which learners are enabled to invest their identities fully in the learning process.[1] Exactly the same considerations hold for reading development among culturally diverse students.

Reading Development in L1 and L2 Contexts

In a similar way to academic second language acquisition generally, the fuel that drives the development of reading competence is the extent to which students are enabled to invest their identities fully in the process of becoming powerfully literate. The research on how to teach reading is far more consistent than might be apparent from the volatile debates that are still underway on this topic. Part of the confusion derives from the failure of many policy-makers and media warriors to distinguish the process of acquiring decoding skills from the process of developing reading comprehension abilities. The confusion also derives from distortions of opposing views that almost inevitably occur when issues are hotly debated. For example, phonics advocates have erroneously tended to depict whole language as an approach to reading that paid no attention to phonics, while some whole language theorists appeared to argue so strenuously against phonics in isolation that they contributed to the impression that what defined whole language was its opposition to the teaching of phonics. In actual fact, good whole language teaching develops phonemic awareness and phonological skills in a variety of ways (*e.g.,* through some direct instruction and through writing activities where students make hypotheses about sound-symbol relationships [invented spelling]). By the same token, a focus on explicit systematic phonics teaching is not in any way incompatible with a concurrent or later focus on encouraging extensive reading for meaning.

At this point in time, whole language teaching has fallen very much from favor in states such as California and Texas where phonics has been constructed by some policy-makers as *the* solution for all the problems of academic underachievement. It is unfortunate that the central message of whole language teaching regarding the importance of focusing on meaningful engagement with text and encouraging extensive reading of a wide variety of linguistic genres has gotten lost in the ideological conflicts over reading. *All of the research supports the fact that extensive reading and immersion in a literate environment are strongly related to the development of reading comprehension. The research is also clear, however, that some explicit teaching of phonemic awareness and the "alphabetic principle" (relationship of sounds to letters) is useful in developing word decoding skills.*

As noted above, part of the confusion derives from failure to clearly distinguish what the research is saying with respect to decoding, on the one hand, and reading comprehension on the other. These are considered separately below.

Decoding

The alternative positions. The California Department of Education (1996) points out that "Research has shown repeatedly that phonemic awareness is a powerful predictor of success in learning to read" (p. 4). Phonemic awareness is the awareness that spoken words are made up of sounds and includes the ability to segment a word into its constituent sounds. The California report advocates systematic explicit phonics instruction "where letter-sound correspondences for letters and letter clusters are directly taught; blended; practiced in words, word lists, and word families; and practiced initially in text with a high percentage of decodable words linked to the phonics lesson. Teachers should provide "prompt and explicit feedback" (1996, p. 6). This perspective emphasizes the use of decodable texts as the most appropriate initial reading materials:

> Research strongly asserts that from the beginning of first grade and in tandem with basic phonics instruction, the most appropriate materials for independent reading are decodable texts. Toward creating a solid foundation for learning to read, most new words in these texts should be wholly decodable on the basis of the phonics that students have been taught. Sight words should be familiarized ahead of time so that they will not divert this purpose. As soon as children can read such basic decodable texts with reasonable comfort and fluency, they can move on to less controlled texts such as trade books. Some students will be ready to do so sooner than others. (1996, p. 12)

Despite its emphasis on a rigid instructional sequence from phonemic awareness to phonics to decodable texts, this report does acknowledge a crucial role for extensive reading in developing reading comprehension:

> Even so, the single most valuable activity for developing children's comprehension is reading itself. The amount of reading that children do is shown to predict the growth in reading comprehension across

the elementary school years even after controlling for entry-level differences. It predicts the quantity as well as the language, vocabulary, and structure of students' writing. It also predicts the richness of their oral storytelling. Among older students and adults, it predicts receptive vocabulary, verbal fluency, content-area achievement, and all manner of general knowledge even when measures of school ability, general intelligence, age, education, and reading comprehension itself are taken into account. ... Through reading, students encounter new words, new language, and new facts. Beyond that, however, they encounter thoughts and modes of thinking that might never arise in their face-to-face worlds. (1996, p. 11)

This perspective with respect to the importance of extensive reading for the development of reading comprehension is identical to that emphasized by whole language theorists. However, Krashen (1996), McQuillan (1998), Coles (2000) and other whole language theorists strongly dispute the emphasis placed on explicit sequential skills instruction by policy-makers and many reading researchers (see, for example, Foorman, 2000; Stanovich & Stanovich, 1998). They acknowledge that phonemic awareness and phonological knowledge are correlated with reading development but argue that this knowledge can develop without explicit instruction and is a *consequence* of reading experience and print exposure rather than a direct causal factor in explaining the development of either decoding or reading comprehension. In Coles' words, "phonological awareness, although important in early literacy development, needs to be seen as a 'marker' of access to extensive literacy opportunities" (2000, p. 90). These theorists acknowledge a role for some explicit phonics instruction but argue that the teaching of more complex aspects of phonics and phonemic awareness is unnecessary and rapidly reaches a point of diminishing returns.

A research synthesis. My reading of the research is that there is general acknowledgment that phonemic awareness is a significant predictor of word recognition (decoding) skills and that instruction in phonemic awareness can increase performance on tests of phonemic awareness and on some skills related to decoding (Foorman, 2000; Krashen, 1999a; Stanovich & Stanovich, 1998). The link between phonics/phonemic awareness instruction and reading comprehension is much more tentative. There is minimal evidence, in fact, that such training, *by itself,* has any significant or long-lasting effects on the development of reading comprehension (*e.g.,* Allington & Woodside-Jiron, 1999; Coles, 2000; Krashen, 1999a; McQuillan, 1998; Taylor et al., 2000). What the evidence does suggest is that the development of reading comprehension is best promoted by a broadly-based program that combines extensive exposure to meaningful and varied texts with (a) some explicit phonemic awareness and phonics instruction, (b) instruction that encourages students to develop effective learning strategies for both decoding and comprehending text (metacognitive and met-alinguistic awareness) (Cunningham, 1990; Iverson & Tunmer, 1993; Muñiz-Swicegood, 1994; Tunmer & Chapman, 1999).

It is instructive to go back to an earlier influential report that was written at a time when the polemics about reading were less intense. Anderson, Hiebert, Scott and Wilkinson (1985) in *A Nation of Readers*, cited positively by both sides of the issue, expressed the importance of phonics instruction in a less definitive way than is typical of current phonics advocates:

> Phonics is instruction in the relationship between letters and speech sounds. The goal of phonics is not that children be able to state the 'rules' governing letter-sound relationships. Rather the purpose is to get across the alphabetic principle, the principle that there are systematic relationships between letters and sounds. Phonics ought to be conceived as a technique for getting children off to a fast start in mapping the relationships between letters and sounds.

> It follows that phonics instruction should aim to teach only the most important and regular of letter-to-sound relationships because this is the sort of instruction that will most directly lay bare the alphabetic principle. Once the basic relationships have been taught, the best way to get children to refine and extend their knowledge of letter-sound correspondences is through repeated opportunities to read. If this position is correct, then much phonics instruction is overly subtle and probably unproductive. (1985, p. 38)

They go on to suggest that a number of reading programs try to teach too many letter-sound relationships and phonics instruction drags out over too many years. They suggest that phonics instruction should be done early and kept simple. Except in cases of diagnosed individual need, there should be little need for phonics instruction beyond the second grade (p. 43).

In a similar vein, Krashen's (1996) report *Every Person a Reader: An Alternative to the California Task Force Report on Reading* acknowledges that some phonics instruction can contribute to reading development: "some knowledge of the more straight-forward sound-spelling correspondences is certainly useful," (p. 12) particularly initial consonants. However, he suggests that there is a point of diminishing returns with phonics: "many phonics rules are not useful…they are very complex, and have numerous exceptions" (p. 13).

Keith Stanovich, a strong advocate of explicit, systematic phonics instruction, has endorsed what appears to be a similar position. He distinguishes a continuum of phonological sensitivity ranging from shallow to deep sensitivity (Stanovich, 1992). At a deeper level of sensitivity, a child would be able to distinguish explicitly small sound units such as phonemes while at a shallower level of sensitivity the child may be able to distinguish larger sound units such as syllables, or basic letter-sound regularity. Stanovich (1992) suggests that only shallow phonological sensitivity is required for the process of reading acquisition to begin. Krashen (1996) has also quoted Share and Stanovich's (1995) view that "a minimal level of phonological sensitivity and letter-sound knowledge skill may enable a child to acquire rudimentary self-teaching skill" (p. 22). However, Stanovich is also very clear about the importance of "explicit analytic instruction in word decoding in the early years of schooling" (Stanovich & Stanovich, 1998, p. 54). The difference between Stanovich's position and that of whole language theorists with respect to the roles of explicit phonics instruction appears to be primarily a matter of emphasis.

What does this all mean for reading instruction among bilingual/ELL students? Some of what we know can be expressed in the following three statements:

1. The most effective approaches to developing initial reading skills are those that combine extensive and varied exposure to meaningful print with explicit and systematic instruction in phonemic awareness and letter-sound correspondences.

2. Children vary in the extent to which they need and will benefit from intensive phonics instruction. Most children who are immersed in a literate environment in the home are capable of acquiring initial reading skills with minimal explicit phonics instruction. For the same reasons, immersion in a literate environment in school is a crucial component of effective reading instruction. Phonics instruction that is isolated from the search for meaning in authentic text is ineffective in developing and sustaining strong literacy skills.

3. Systematic phonics instruction can enable second language learners to acquire word recognition and decoding skills in their second language to a relatively high level, despite the fact that their knowledge of the second language is still limited. These decoding skills, however, do not automatically generalize to reading comprehension or other aspects of second language proficiency.

Each of these positions is considered in more detail below:

1. Virtually all researchers endorse some variant of a "balanced" view of reading instruction that incorporates varying amounts of explicit phonics instruction together with an emphasis on extensive reading as students progress through the grades. The instructional programs that work best for promoting reading comprehension (as compared to individual word decoding) are those that: (a) emphasize extensive and varied exposure to meaningful print, (b) provide, in the early grades, some explicit and systematic instruction in phonemic awareness and letter-sound correspondences, and (c) provide instruction designed to help students develop metacognitive strategies for recognizing words and improving their own reading abilities. Programs that provide primarily explicit and systematic phonics instruction in the early grades, without extensive exposure to print, work relatively well in developing phonemic awareness and some word recognition skills but are not particularly effective in promoting reading comprehension skills.

The pattern of findings can be illustrated with reference to Cunningham's (1990) study. Cunningham compared three instructional approaches used with kindergarten and grade 1 students. The first involved isolated phonics instruction in which children learned phonemic segmentation and blending and related skills but were not encouraged to apply their knowledge to real reading tasks. This was a typical "skill-and-drill" program that proceeded in a sequential way to teach phonics skills in isolation. The second group also received instruction in phonemic awareness but, in addition, they were directed to try to identify unknown words through sound-symbol relationships and contextual cues. The instruction also encouraged children to think about the story and to reflect on and refine their own strategies for decoding and understanding words (metacognitive awareness) A third group (the control group) only listened to stories and answered questions about them during the time the other two groups were engaged in their specific instructional program. All children received reading instruction in grade 1 from a basal reading program. Coles (2000) summarizes the results of this study as follows:

The group that was taught to reflect and apply knowledge was found to have significantly superior scores on a reading-achievement test, whereas the "skill and drill" group was found to have scores similar to the control group. This study suggests that although phonemic-awareness training by itself does not produce superior reading scores over the receipt of no training, integrating phonemic training with reading and encouraging word-reading strategies that combine both decoding and comprehension can facilitate learning to read. (2000, p. 84)

Tunmer and Chapman (1999) also review research supportive of metacognitive approaches to teaching initial reading and note that: "In general, metacognitive approaches to instruction are in sharp contrast to skill-and-drill approaches in which word-level skills are taught in an isolated, piecemeal fashion with little or no emphasis placed on developing within beginning readers an understanding of how and when to apply such knowledge" (p. 89).

Coles (2000) reviewed the Hatcher, Hulme & Ellis (1994) study that reported superior results from a "reading with phonology" group in comparison to a "phonology training alone" group and a "reading alone" group. The "phonology training alone" students were taught word segmentation, rhyming words, sound synthesis into words and other phonemic awareness skills. The "reading with phonology" group completed about half this program but also devoted time to reading and rereading books, writing stories, and engaging in phonological activities related to the stories. The "reading alone" group performed reading and writing activities similar to the "reading with phonology" group but there was no explicit focus on phonology or letter-sound relationships.

A year after these instructional approaches were completed, the "reading with phonology" group was found to have significantly superior performance in reading comprehension, word identification, and spelling. The "phonology alone" group made significantly more progress in phonological skills but this did not translate into better reading or writing performance. Coles summarizes the study as follows:

The authors conclude, therefore, that 'phonological training alone is not a powerful way of improving children's reading skills.' Moreover, they propose that their findings 'cast doubt on the simple theory that there is a direct causal path from phonological skills to reading skills.' (2000, p. 86).

Coles interprets these studies as supportive of whole language approaches and assumptions because they show the centrality of engagement with text to students' reading progress. He notes that "researchers have moved toward recognizing that phonological abilities are learned best when they are related to reading and writing activities rather than as a singular skill. This shift has moved the phonological awareness paradigm closer to rather than away from whole language theory and practice" (2000, p. 89).

I have deliberately drawn on Coles' (2000) summaries of these research studies to illustrate the fact that whole language theorists do acknowledge the research suggesting that explicit instruction in phonemic awareness and the alphabetic principle, together with a focus on extensive exposure to meaningful text, can contribute to reading development. Unfortunately, some whole language advocates present their position as if they were arguing *against* any role for explicit teaching of phonics in reading instruction. This contributes to the fact that phonics advocates frequently assume that this is, in fact, the defining characteristic of the whole language approach.

To illustrate this point, despite the fact that Coles (2000) interprets the research reviewed above as supportive of whole language, most advocates of explicit phonics instruction interpret this same research as *refuting* whole language approaches and assumptions. Stanovich and Stanovich (1998), for example, acknowledge the criticism that most studies supporting explicit systematic teaching of phonics have focused on decoding skills rather than reading comprehension. However, they cite Cunningham (1990), Hatcher *et al.* (1994), Iverson & Tunmer (1993) among others to show that "children given training in phonological sensitivity and/or alphabetic coding show superior outcomes on measures of comprehension and text reading as well as word recognition" (p. 53). In other words, they claim that phonics training does benefit reading comprehension in addition to decoding and they suggest that the "way now seems clear for whole language advocates to reconstitute their position in a scientifically respectable way" (p. 54). However, what they fail to note in calling for whole language to become "scientific" is that these studies support the whole language emphasis on extensive opportunities to read as a necessary condition for strong reading comprehension just as much as they support the benefits of explicit systematic phonics instruction.

Other advocates of direct and systematic phonics instruction are more tentative in claiming that training in phonological awareness benefits reading comprehension. Snow, Burns and Griffin (1998), for example, in their influential

National Academy report on *Preventing Reading Difficulties in Young Children* acknowledge that "the effects of training, although quite consistent, are only moderate in strength, and have so far not been shown to extend to comprehension" (1998, p. 251). Gee (1999) criticizes the National Academy report's predominant emphasis on phonological awareness training, noting that "surely...it is more plausible to argue that early language abilities cause both phonological awareness and later success in learning to read" (1999, p. 366). The findings reviewed by the report, he argues, do not justify the emphasis on the efficacy of such training:

> Tests of early phonological awareness (or lack of it) do not fruitfully select those students who will later have problems in learning to read (cf., "many of those with weak phonological sensitivity will go on to become adequate readers" [Snow *et al.*, 1998, p. 112]). Interventions based on stressing phonological awareness and phonics do not enhance comprehension, though, of course, comprehension is the basis of learning, and reading is rather pointless without it. Furthermore, although a stress on phonological awareness and overt phonics instruction does initially help at-risk students, it does not bring them up to par with more advantaged students, and they tend to eventually fall back, fueling a fourth-grade or later "slump" (this fact is amply documented in the report, see pp. 216, 228, 232, 248–249, 251, 257). (1999, p. 364)

Clearly, the conflicts regarding early reading instruction have reached a profoundly unproductive stage. There is room at the inn both for an explicit focus on ensuring that all children are developing word analysis skills (some may require more systematic instruction than others) together with a focus on providing ample opportunities for children to engage with meaningful print and relate the wonder of books to their own lives. *Researchers and theorists on both sides of the reading debate agree with this basic position.* However, both sides have set up straw horses in an attempt to prove the other side wrong: phonics advocates have characterized whole language classrooms as focusing on reading only with minimal attempt to demystify how sounds and symbols relate; whole language advocates have characterized phonics-oriented classrooms as focusing on isolated drill-and-skill instruction with no attention to applying these skills to authentic texts. The research appears clear that neither of these extremes is as effective as instruction that focuses both on immersion of students in a literate environment and demystification of how the language works.

Unfortunately, the combination of high stakes standardized testing (*e.g.,* the SAT-9 in California) together with the demonization of whole language has resulted in precisely the **wrong** type of phonics instruction being implemented in many schools. The research cited above is very clear that drill-and-skill phonics instruction that teaches complex subskills in a rigid sequential manner and in isolation from engagement with real text is **not effective** in developing reading comprehension. Yet, this is precisely what appears to be happening in many California schools as a result of that state's three-pronged quick-fix for underachievement: (i) Proposition 227, (ii) the elimination of heretical whole language approaches in favor of phonics instruction, and (iii) the policing of schools and teachers by means of the SAT-9 (Gándara *et al.*, 2000). As noted in Chapter 2, classroom observations and teacher interviews conducted by Gándara and her colleagues suggested that teachers felt compelled to teach to the test, placing much greater emphasis on "English word recognition or phonics, bereft of meaning or context" (p. 19).

Thus, there is considerable merit to the concerns of Taylor *et al.* (2000) that the almost exclusive emphasis in recent research (*e.g.,* Foorman *et al.,* 1998) on the importance of teaching the alphabetic principle, to the exclusion of other central components of the reading process, will have the effect of narrowing the curriculum for students from diverse backgrounds. As one illustration, the requirement in the 1999/2000 Texas reading adoption that there be at least 80% decodable words in reading texts in the early grades suggests that this version of a "balanced approach" is actually quite unbalanced. As pointed out by Allington and Woodside-Jiron (1999) there is no direct research support for emphasizing "decodable" text over "predictable" text in early reading materials. In response, Mathes and Torgeson (2000) acknowledge the lack of direct research on this issue but argue that what we know about transfer and generalization indirectly supports the use of decodable text.

2. Students who are immersed in a literate environment in the home can usually pick up decoding skills with minimal formal instruction in phonics. By the same token, immersion in a literate environment in school is a crucial supplement to phonics instruction for strong literacy (and biliteracy) skills to develop.

Children immersed in a literate home environment usually need some initial help to "break the code" but once they have done so they make rapid progress on their own by relating their knowledge of oral language and their concepts about print to the written text. They know that there is payoff in print so they are highly motivated to become independent readers. With the exception of children who experience some form of reading disability or dyslexia, middle class children rarely experience failure in learning to read, regardless of what type of instructional program they receive in the early grades (*e.g.*, phonics-oriented versus whole-language-oriented).

An example of this phenomenon comes from students in Canadian French immersion programs and English background students in dual language or two-way bilingual immersion programs (see Chapters 7-9). These students are typically introduced to reading instruction through their L2 (*e.g.*, French or Spanish) in which, at the beginning of grade 1, they have relatively minimal fluency. English reading in these programs is not formally introduced until grades 2, 3 or sometimes even 4. It is almost invariably observed that shortly after students have developed some decoding skills in French (or Spanish), they spontaneously start decoding in English (their L1). By the end of grade 1, these students are usually much more fluent readers in English than in their L2 (see Cashion & Eagan, 1990). *They have had no formal phonics instruction in English* but because of their immersion in a literate environment and the support for literacy in school they typically become very fluent readers. This shows clearly that direct instruction in the complex phonics rules for English is not always necessary for students to develop strong decoding and comprehension skills in English.

This is further illustrated by Reyes (2000) in a longitudinal case study of the "spontaneous biliteracy" of four low-income working-class Mexicano/Latino children in a bilingual program, two of whom were taught to read initially only in Spanish and two only in English, according to their language dominance on entry to the program. The children received structured phonics instruction (in English or Spanish) in kindergarten but in first and second grade only minimal phonics was taught. All four children spontaneously transferred their literacy skills from the initial language to their second language without formal instruction. Their "natural, spontaneous, and uncomplicated approach to bilingualism and biliteracy" was supported by their interest in writing in both languages and also by their social play where they challenged each other to read in the language in which they had received no formal reading instruction. This process of spontaneous transfer of literacy across languages parallels what is typically observed in French immersion programs and again illustrates the fact that the goal of phonics instruction should be to get students started on the process of working out the code and to support them as they do so. It is certainly not necessary, and in many cases probably counter-productive, to teach the more complex, exception-ridden phonics rules. Children's time would be much better spent applying their basic phonological awareness to reading engaging texts, with adult support, and beginning to express their identities through personal writing. The centrality of these affective dimensions related to students' identity tend to be omitted from the current "phonics as panacea" dogma. Reyes has strongly emphasized the importance of issues related to identity in the process of spontaneous biliteracy development, noting that the bilingual program:

> legitimated children's bicultural identity, unleashing their potential for bilingualism and biliteracy rather than forcing them to choose between their two cultures. ...There is no doubt that these students felt their languages and their culture affirmed. ...Although each of the girls received instruction in only one language, all their learning from kindergarten to second grade took place in classrooms where the teachers supported and nurtured their cultural and linguistic resources. Each day they heard their teachers and peers use Spanish and English. Their teachers also made great efforts to treat English and Spanish as equally as possible, valuing both languages for personal, social, and academic purposes. (2000, p. 116)

The centrality of identity negotiation to the process of literacy and biliteracy development is clearly compatible with the perspective emphasized in the present volume (see Chapter 1). Reyes concludes that Latino/Latina children's cognitive and linguistic abilities continue to be underestimated in most schools where bilingualism is still constructed as a problem (as illustrated by Proposition 227). She notes that although "many Latinos come to school with the natural potential to become biliterate, that potential frequently is undermined, dismissed, and ignored" (p. 119) resulting in a process whereby children are permitted to develop only half their potential.

Reyes' study shows that school and home can combine to create socioculturally supportive conditions for biliteracy development in working-class contexts in a very similar way to what is typically observed in middle-class contexts. A key element is immersion in a literate environment that enables children to engage their identities with reading and writing.

A final example further illustrates the importance of immersion in a literate environment. Tizard, Schofield and Hewison (1982) reported on a two-year project carried out in six schools in an inner-city area of London, England. Major improvements in children's reading skills were observed simply as a result of sending books home on a daily basis with the children for them to read to their parents, many of whom spoke little English and were illiterate in both English and their L1 (predominantly Bengali and Greek). The grade 1 and 2 children attending the two schools that implemented this "shared literacy" program made significantly greater progress in reading than a comparison group in two different schools who received additional small-group reading instruction from a highly competent reading specialist. Of particular importance is the fact that the differences in favor of the shared literacy program were most apparent among children who were initially having difficulty in learning to read. Both groups made greater progress than a control group in two schools who received no special treatment. Teachers involved in the home collaboration reported that children showed an increased interest in school learning and were better behaved.

The impact of this project in motivating students to read can be seen from the fact that the students in the two "shared reading" schools exhausted the supply of books in the school libraries that were appropriate for early elementary grades simply because they read so much. This project illustrates the fact that far more than just explicit systematic phonics instruction is required to promote strong reading skills in the early grades.

3. Students instructed through a second language can acquire word recognition and decoding skills in their second language to a relatively high level, despite the fact that their knowledge of the second language is still limited. These discrete language skills, however, do not automatically generalize to reading comprehension or other aspects of second language proficiency.

This is an important finding which is highly relevant to interpreting the grade 2 standardized test results from districts such as Oceanside in California (see Chapter 3, note 7). The evidence regarding the acquisition of decoding skills in a second language comes from two sources. The first is research on French immersion programs in Canada (*e.g.,* Lambert & Tucker, 1972). In the original St. Lambert program near Montreal, English-L1 students in grades 1 and 2 who were instructed exclusively through French in Kindergarten and grade 1 and introduced to reading through French, performed either better (grade 1) or at the same level (grade 2) on a French Word Discrimination measure than did native French-speaking control students. In other words, they learned very specific decoding skills in their second language to a level equivalent to that of native speakers.

However, there were major differences in virtually all other aspects of their French proficiency. For example, on a French Picture Vocabulary measure at grade 2 the French immersion (English L1) students obtained a score of 53.85 compared to 63.48 for the French L1 control group, a difference that was highly significant ($F=27.45$, $p<.01$). However, on Word Discrimination, the groups obtained almost identical scores (immersion 25.28, controls 25.60). [3] Students in French immersion programs usually require the entire elementary school period to catch up with French-L1 speakers in French reading comprehension despite the fact that they rapidly catch up in French decoding skills.

The second source of data comes from research conducted on ELL students acquiring English reading skills in all-English programs. Kwan and Willows (1998), for example, examined the effects of the *Jolly Phonics* program among a sample of 240 English-L1 and ELL kindergarten students in Toronto Canada. This program (Lloyd, 1992) is described as a systematic training program aimed at developing phonemic awareness and teaching letter/sound correspondences. The program is playful and multi-modal and designed to appeal to the younger child. It requires minimal teacher training and, since it requires only about 15 minutes per day, can be easily integrated into a regular kindergarten program (Kwan & Willows, 1998). The study found that exposure to the *Jolly Phonics* program resulted in superior performance on a variety of phonological measures both among English-L1 and ELL students. No effects of the program were observed on a broader array of linguistic proficiency measures that assessed linguistic concepts, vocabulary, sentence memory, and word memory. Despite the fact that ELL students performed more poorly than their English-L1 counterparts on all the linguistic proficiency measures and on one of the four phonological processing measures (within treatment groups), they still benefited in phonological processing from participating in the *Jolly Phonics* program. They also out-performed English-L1 students in the control group who received no training in phonological awareness. Kwan and Willows summarize the implications of their findings as follows:

> These results call into question the prevailing assumptions that require second language instructional methods to by-pass perceived acoustic-based processing weaknesses in L2 children and focus solely

on native language literacy development. Indeed, instructional methods that provide explicit and systematic training in English alphabetic coding skills and phonemic awareness are beneficial to L2 learners in that the goal of instruction is tied more to the development, rather than the by-pass, of English phonology and early literacy skills. (1998, Abstract)

These results are clearly consistent with those of Lambert and Tucker (1972) in showing that L2 phonics skills can be taught to second language students in the early stages of schooling. The findings are also consistent with the very positive results obtained in 50:50 (half-time L1 and L2) dual language programs that introduce L1 and L2 reading either simultaneously or in quick succession (see Chapter 6 for a review of the outcomes of these programs). *There is thus no need to delay the introduction of English reading instruction within a bilingual program* (see Cummins, 2000). Furthermore, despite the assumptions of both advocates and opponents of bilingual education, the order in which reading instruction is introduced in a bilingual program is not, in itself, a significant variable. [4]

However, the Kwan/Willows study is also consistent with other results considered above in showing that phonics/phonemic awareness training is no panacea insofar as it does not, by itself, benefit broader aspects of language proficiency that are strongly related to the development of reading comprehension (*e.g.,* vocabulary). The data also in no way contradict the fact that a period of at least 5 years is typically required for ELL students to catch up in academic aspects of L2 proficiency (*e.g.,* reading comprehension). [5]

It is pointless and counter-productive for whole language advocates to argue against the use of programs such as *Jolly Phonics* which succeed well in demystifying important aspects of language among kindergarten children, require only about 15 minutes a day to implement, and are fun for children and teachers alike. A more appropriate target is the dogmatic insistence among some phonics advocates and policy-makers that the vast majority of early reading materials should consist of "decodable text" to the exclusion of more authentic reading material. Some use of decodable text is non-problematic, particularly if the texts have been imaginatively constructed to minimize their contrived nature; however, to insist on near-exclusive use of decodable texts reflects an extreme and antiquated behaviorist learning philosophy that ignores what cognitive science has discovered about the importance of encouraging children to engage in hypothesis-testing and knowledge construction in interaction with supportive adults within the zone of proximal development (Vygotsky, 1978).

The crucial contribution of whole language theory has more to do with the development of reading comprehension than with the development of initial decoding skills. Unfortunately, this contribution risks being ignored despite massive empirical evidence in support of whole language principles regarding the development of reading comprehension.

Conclusion. Students vary widely in the extent to which they require and will benefit from an explicit focus on phonics to develop adequate decoding skills. Some who have been immersed in a literate environment in the home may require minimal formal instruction to start decoding whereas others who have experienced less exposure to print in the home may require much more direct and explicit instruction focused on phonics but also on many other features of language. The purpose of phonics instruction should be to facilitate access to and comprehension of meaningful print. When children start to engage with print in a motivated way they will begin to work out on their own, and with adult help, how letters, sounds, and meaning relate to each other. This is why phonemic awareness instruction succeeds much better when it is integrated with authentic reading activities than when it is implemented in isolation. In addition, it should not be forgotten that it is not only phonemic sensitivity that is related to early reading development but also the wider spectrum of language awareness that Marie Clay has termed *Concepts about Print* and which is assessed by the test of that name. Concepts about Print in both L1 and L2 were strongly related to English reading development among Portuguese background students in a study conducted in Toronto (Cummins, 1991b).

In short, for ELL students who do not come from a highly literate home environment, initial instruction should focus both on developing awareness of how the language works (phonics and beyond) and inducting students into the excitement of books both in school, and to the extent possible, at home. What this might look like in practice is illustrated by Goldenberg's (1998) description of a successful school change project involving bilingual education for Latino/Latina students where both "bottom-up" and "top-down" processes were applied. Among the former for kindergarten and grade 1 students were naming and recognizing letters, recognizing beginning sounds of words, hearing and discriminating rhymes, writing letters and words from dictation, and "estimating" the spellings of words when they wrote (*i.e.,* "invented spelling" in whole language parlance). Top-down strategies included reading or "pseudo-reading" for pleasure, talking about books, and encouraging attempts at communicative writing.

Reading Comprehension

The limitations of viewing phonics as a panacea are immediately apparent from what is probably the largest study of reading achievement and instruction ever conducted. Postlethwaite and Ross (1992) in an evaluation of reading achievement in 32 systems of education around the world showed that the amount of time students reported they spent in voluntary reading activities was amongst the strongest predictors (#2) of a school's overall reading performance. More than 50 variables were ranked in order of importance for reading comprehension at grade 4 and 8 levels. The first ranked indicator was the school's perception of the degree of parent cooperation. This variable is probably a reflection of socioeconomic status. The significance of reading frequency in promoting reading development is evident from the high rankings of variables such as *Reading in class* (#3), *Amount of reading materials in the school* (#8), *Having a classroom library* (#11), and *Frequency of borrowing books from a library* (#12). With respect to teaching methods, a focus on *Comprehension instruction* was ranked #9 and *Emphasis on literature* was ranked #17, both considerably higher than whether or not the school engaged in explicit *Phonics teaching* (#41). The ranking of relevant variables in this study from home, school, and classroom spheres is outlined in Table 4.1.

The low ranking of explicit phonics instruction in determining reading comprehension does not, of course, mean that phonics instruction is not important in the early stages of learning to read. As indicated above, for many students it may be a crucial component. However, at higher levels of reading proficiency, phonics plays a lesser role in comparison to the amount of reading that students engage in and the amount of instruction they receive that is specifically focused on comprehension.

Virtually identical trends emerge from analyses of the 1994 National Assessment of Educational Progress (NAEP) data within the United States. The direct relationship between reading performance and the amount of reading 4th graders report is evident in the fact that those who reported they read almost every day obtained a score of 221, compared to 217 for those who reported they read 1-2 times a week and 198 for those who report reading never or hardly ever (McQuillan, 1998, Table 7.2, p. 69). Ken Goodman (1997) also points to the fact that in the 1994 NAEP data:

> In most cases, kids who read silently [in school] almost everyday score better than those who read silently at least weekly. But the sharp disadvantage is for kids who rarely read silently in school. They

---

Table 4.1

INDICATORS PREDICTING READING COMPREHENSION (GRADE 4)
(Postlethwaite & Ross, *Effective Schools in Reading*, 1992)

HOME

02. Amount of free voluntary reading
12. Frequency of borrowing books from library

SCHOOL RESOURCES

08. Amount of reading materials in school library
14. School resources (school library, reading room for students, student/school newspaper)
19. School library books per student

SCHOOL INITIATIVES

16. Sponsoring of reading initiatives

CLASSROOM CONDITIONS AND TEACHER PRACTICES

03. Reading in class
11. Classroom library
18. Frequency of visiting school library

TEACHER METHODS

09. Comprehension instruction (deliberate emphasis on text understanding)
17. Emphasis on literature (encouragement of silent reading, listened to student reading, focus on library skills, etc.)
41. Phonics teaching

---

scored about thirty points lower on average in both years than daily silent readers. (1997, p. 54)

Treadway (1997), in response to Goodman, acknowledges the importance of extensive reading for the development of reading comprehension but insists that systematic instruction in decoding is a necessary means to achieve that end. He notes that the three strongest predictors of student success in early reading are phonemic awareness, letter knowledge (almost any knowledge about letters), and concepts about print. He disputes the claims by Goodman, Krashen, and other whole language theorists that children learn to read by reading, arguing instead that "children that have phonemic awareness learn to decode. Those that learn to decode, learn to read, enjoy reading, and continue to do it. Those that do not learn to read by the end of first grade find reading frustrating and often quite trying" (1997, p. 58).

Treadway's argument appears convincing if it is interpreted as claiming that phonemic awareness is important in learning how to decode and that decoding ability is a necessary condition for strong development of reading comprehension. However, it is much less convincing if it is interpreted as claiming that phonemic awareness in isolation is a major causal factor in the development of decoding and reading comprehension. This claim is problematic on two counts: (a) research findings cast doubt on the simple theory that there is a direct causal path from phonological skills to reading skills (*e.g.*, Hatcher et al., 1994), and (b) those who come to school with advanced phonemic awareness, letter knowledge, and concepts about print are those who have been immersed in a literate environment at home and have been read to extensively. These students generally require only minimal explicit phonics instruction to break the code. Thus, phonemic awareness can be promoted through immersion in a literate environment as well as through explicit instruction. Treadway's causal sequence could be reformulated as:

- children who are immersed in a preschool literate environment develop phonemic awareness together with other specific language abilities that reflect the expectations of schooling and are predictive of success in schooling;

- those who have phonemic awareness (and other school-related language abilities) learn to decode with appropriate instruction;

- those who do not come to school with phonemic awareness already developed will benefit from immersion in a rich literate environment together with explicit instruction designed to develop concepts about print, including phonemic awareness and the alphabetic principle;

- those who learn to decode will apply and extend their decoding skills to independent reading when they are provided with extensive exposure to varied and meaningful texts.

As I noted earlier, from my perspective it doesn't ultimately matter how children develop phonemic awareness, letter knowledge and general concepts about print. However, it is important for them to develop this knowledge about language. It seems reasonable to advocate that there is an important place for both immersion in a literate environment in the early years of school (*e.g.*, reading Big Books to children, encouragement of writing, etc.) together with explicit demystification of how sounds and symbols relate to each other. This appears to be a position that advocates at opposite poles of the whole-language/phonics debate (*e.g.*, Coles and Treadway) can endorse, albeit grudgingly.

Both of these instructional emphases ([a] a focus on extensive reading and writing for *self*-expression and [b] the development of explicit awareness of how the language works) are also important for reading comprehension instruction. The danger in states that have adopted the "phonics as panacea" mantra is that the importance of immersion in a literate environment gets omitted from both the decoding and comprehension equations. The so-called "balanced" reading approach can easily become a very unbalanced focus on skills, drills, and worksheets with minimal reading of stories and other authentic text and minimal creative writing. In order to emphasize just how overwhelming the data are regarding the importance of extensive reading for the development of reading comprehension, consider some additional evidence.

Consistent with the Postlethwaite/Ross results and the "whole language" arguments of Coles, Goodman, Krashen, and McQuillan, Fielding and Pearson's (1994, p. 62) review of research in this area highlights four components of a reading program that are strongly supported by the research data:

- Large amounts of time for actual text reading;

- Teacher-directed instruction in comprehension strategies;

- Opportunities for peer and collaborative learning; and

- Occasions for students to talk to a teacher and one another about their responses to reading.

The power of extensive reading in a second language to promote knowledge of this language is supported in a wide variety of studies. Elley and Mangubhai (1983), for example, demonstrated that 4th and 5th grade students in Fiji exposed to a "book flood" program during their 30 minute daily English (L2) class in which they simply read books either alone or with the guidance of their teacher, performed significantly better after two years than students taught through more traditional methods. Elley (1991) similarly documented the superiority of book-based English language teaching programs among primary school students in a variety of other contexts (see also Krashen, 1993, 1999b; and McQuillan, 1998, for comprehensive reviews). [6]

How does extensive reading promote the growth of reading comprehension ability and overall second language proficiency? A simple answer is that it is only through reading that children get access to the low-frequency vocabulary and grammatical structures that represent the language of academic success. This becomes clear when we understand the nature of the English lexicon and the ways that vocabulary knowledge are related to reading comprehension.

Vocabulary Knowledge and Reading

As noted briefly in Chapter 3, the English lexicon derives from two main sources. The Anglo-Saxon language (of Germanic origin and related to other languages of northern Europe) had established itself as the major language in England from about the 5th century AD. However, in the 11th century the Normans invaded and their language (derived from Old French, Greek and Latin) became the high status language of the society used among the nobility and in the courts. The Anglo-Saxon language continued to be spoken among the peasants and those in lower status positions in the society. From the 12th through 16th centuries the two languages merged with each other to form the core of what we now call "English." However, the lexicon of each language did not blend evenly across all domains and functions of language. The Anglo-Saxon lexicon continued to be used predominantly in everyday conversation while the Graeco-Latin lexicon became the language of literacy and more formal functions of the society (*e.g.,* legal transactions).

Corson's (1993, 1995, 1997) detailed analysis of this process highlights the fact that today the academic language of texts continues to draw heavily on Graeco-Latin words whereas everyday conversation relies more on an Anglo-

Saxon-based lexicon: "most of the specialist and high status terminology of English is Graeco-Latin in origin, and most of its more everyday terminology is Anglo-Saxon in origin" (1993:13). Graeco-Latin words tend to be three or four syllables long whereas the everyday high frequency words of the Anglo-Saxon lexicon tend to be one or two syllables in length. Corson points out that:

> Academic Graeco-Latin words are mainly literary in their use. Most native speakers of English begin to encounter these words in quantity in their upper primary school reading and in the formal secondary school setting. So the words' introduction in literature or textbooks, rather than in conversation, restricts people's access to them. Certainly, exposure to specialist Graeco-Latin words happens much more often while reading than while talking or watching television. ...Printed texts provided much more exposure to [Graeco-Latin] words than oral ones. For example, even children's books contained 50% more rare words than either adult prime-time television or the conversations of university graduates; popular magazines had three times as many rare words as television and informal conversation (1997, p. 677).

Among the highest frequency Anglo-Saxon nouns are: *time, people, years, work, something, world, children* (Corson, 1997). A listing of 570 word families that are found commonly in academic texts in English but which are not among the most frequent 2,000 words of the language is provided by Coxhead (2000). [7] Some of the words from Coxhead's list are: *analyze, benefit, concept, context, establish, identify, interpret.* Coxhead notes that "more than 82% of the words in the AWL [Academic Word List] are of Greek or Latin origin, indicating that the study of prefixes, suffixes, and stems may be one way to study this vocabulary" (pp. 228–229). The Latin and Greek origins of academic vocabulary in English also means that there are many cognates between this vocabulary and the vocabulary of Spanish and other Romance languages. This reality opens up many possibilities for cross-linguistic language exploration (see Chapter 5). Coxhead, however, cautions that direct study of the vocabulary in isolation is insufficient for effective learning. Direct study "needs to be balanced with opportunities to meet the vocabulary in message-focused reading and listening and to use the vocabulary in speaking and writing" (p. 228).

Paul Nation and his colleagues have carried out the most comprehensive research on the nature and learning of English vocabulary (*e.g.,* Nation, 1990, 1993). Like Corson, he points out that most low-frequency vocabulary comes to English from Latin or Greek. He estimates that about two-thirds of the low-frequency words in English derive from these linguistic origins. He further points out that:

> High frequency vocabulary consists mainly of short words which cannot be broken into meaningful parts. Low-frequency vocabulary, on the other hand, while it consists of many thousands of words, is made from a much smaller number of word parts. The word, impose, for example, is made of two parts, *im-* and *-pose,* which occur in hundreds of other words—*imply, infer, compose, expose, position.* This has clear implications for teaching and learning vocabulary (1990, p. 18).

Nation (1993) suggests that for pedagogical purposes the vocabulary of a language can be classified into four groups:

1. *High frequency words.* In English these consist of around 2,000 word families that provide coverage of more than 80% of most written text. These word families include words such as *put, end, difficult, come.*

2. *General academic vocabulary.* This group of words consists of about 800 word families (527 in Coxhead's more recent research) that provide coverage of about 8-10% of academic text.

3. *Technical or specialized vocabulary.* This usually comprises about 2,000 words for a particular subject area. These words are proportionately much more frequent in a specialized area than they are in the language as a whole and develop as a result of mastery of the field. They account for about 4-5% of academic text.

4. *Low frequency words.* Nation estimates that there remain at least 123,000 low frequency word families. He notes that adult native speakers of English with a post-secondary education have a vocabulary size of about 20,000 word families. Most of this vocabulary is made up of low frequency words that "are learned through diverse and wide-ranging contact with the language" (1993, p. 125). Nation reviews research showing that "informal spoken language does not provide much opportunity for growth in knowledge of

low frequency words" (p. 129). This vocabulary grows slowly and "requires substantial amounts of reading or listening to language that contains more low frequency words than colloquial language does" (p. 129).

Nation emphasizes that learners must be given the opportunity to *use* the language if vocabulary is to develop to its full potential: "If learners have a sufficiently large vocabulary but they are not given the opportunity to put this vocabulary to use and develop skill in using it, their growth in knowledge and further vocabulary growth will not be achieved" (1993, p. 132).

Commenting on the relationship between vocabulary and reading, Nation and Coady (1988) point out that "vocabulary difficulty has consistently been found to be the most significant predictor of overall readability." Once the effect of vocabulary difficulty (usually estimated by word frequency and/or familiarity and word length) is taken into account, other linguistic variables, such as sentence structure, account for little incremental variance in the readability of a text. They summarize their review as follows: "In general the research leaves us in little doubt about the importance of vocabulary knowledge for reading, and the value of reading as a means of increasing vocabulary" (p. 108).

One example of the research illustrating the extent to which vocabulary can be acquired from context is Nagy, Herman and Anderson's (1985) demonstration that the probability of learning a word from context after just one exposure is between 10 and 15 percent. As learners read more in their second language, repeated exposure to unfamiliar words will exert an incremental effect on vocabulary learning. However, there are also limits to inferencing unknown words. Laufer (1992) has shown that learners need 95% "lexical coverage" of the words in a text before they can readily infer from context the meanings of the remaining 5% unknown words. When the proportion of words in a text known by the reader falls below this 95% threshold, the possibility of inferring the unknown words decreases significantly. A Spanish speaker who can supplement the use of context by drawing on cognate connections between Spanish and academic English words (*e.g., encounter-encontrar, predict-predecir*) has an important advantage in the reading process. Similarly, instruction that enables students from all backgrounds to develop strategies for analysis of the morphological structure of words (prefixes, suffixes, and roots) can significantly increase their power to infer the meaning of unknown words (Biemiller, 1999; White, Power & White, 1989; White, Sowell & Yanagihara, 1989).

In short, all of the research evidence suggests that reading extensively in a wide variety of genres is essential for developing high levels of both vocabulary knowledge and reading comprehension. This is particularly the case for ELL students since they are attempting to catch up to students who are continuing to develop their English (L1) academic language proficiency.

The important role that extensive reading itself plays in fueling reading development does not mean that teacher-directed instruction is unimportant. On the contrary, students will become more effective readers if they acquire efficient strategies for text interpretation and analysis and if the teacher directs their attention to how the language of text works (*e.g.,* the role of cohesive devices such as *however, although*, etc.). This is illustrated by the strong showing of *Comprehension instruction* in the Postlethwaite and Ross (1992) study. Fielding and Pearson (1994) similarly rank "teacher-directed instruction in comprehension strategies" second to "large amounts of time for actual text reading" in their review of the implications of reading research for instruction (see Chamot and O'Malley, 1994, and Chamot et al., 1999 for comprehensive reviews of the significance of learning strategies for ELL students' academic learning).

Wong Fillmore (1997) has articulated the role that teachers should play in making texts work as input for language learning:

- Provide the support learners need to make sense of the text;

- Call attention to the way language is used in the text;

- Discuss with learners the meaning and interpretation of sentences and phrases within the text;

- Point out that words in one text may have been encountered or used in other places;

- Help learners discover the grammatical cues that indicate relationships such as cause and effect, antecedence and consequence, comparison and contrast, and so on.

> In short, teachers help written texts become usable input not only by helping children make sense of the text but by drawing their attention, focusing it, in fact, on how language is used in the materials they read. Done consistently enough, the learners themselves will soon come to notice the way language is used in the materials they read. When they do that everything they read will be input for learning. (1997, p. 4)

What Wong Fillmore is discussing here could be described metaphorically as *harvesting the language*. The framework for academic language learning discussed in the next chapter elaborates on the kinds of teacher-student interactions that create classroom conditions for harvesting academic language.

Conclusion

The volatile debates on how to teach reading that continue to occupy researchers, policy-makers, and educators are largely a waste of everybody's time. There is actually a considerable degree of consensus hidden behind the cacophony of ideological debate. For example, (almost)

• everybody agrees that immersion in a literate environment with extensive exposure to both cognitively challenging talk and text either in home or school (and preferably both) is a strong predictor of success in both decoding and reading comprehension;

• everybody agrees that the development of phonemic awareness, letter knowledge, and concepts about print is an important component of the development of initial decoding skills;

• everybody agrees that an explicit instructional focus on developing phonemic awareness, letter knowledge, and concepts about print, *together with a significant instructional focus on actual reading*, contributes to the development of decoding skills and early reading comprehension skills. A combined focus on the code and the meaning works significantly better than instruction that focuses primarily on isolated sequential phonics drills alone or on exposure to authentic text alone.

• everybody agrees that the amount of access to print and the amount of actual reading that students carry out is by far the major determinant of reading comprehension development as students progress through the grades.

The most significant point of contention appears to be the extent to which tight control should be exercised over students' access to authentic text (*i.e.*, text that would not be classified as "decodable"). Those in the phonics advocacy camp emphasize that decodable text should predominate in initial reading materials with only limited access to "non-decodable" text (*e.g.*, children's literature). Mathes and Torgeson (2000), for example, express this perspective as follows:

Likewise, to ask children to read text that they cannot decode using the alphabetic elements and skills that they have been taught is to communicate to them that the alphabetic knowledge and skill they have spent effort learning is not really relevant to reading, and that they must rely heavily on guessing the identity of words from context. (2000, p. 12)

In other words, these authors see it as problematic for children to encounter words in reading materials for which the letter-sound correspondences have not been previously taught in an explicit and systematic way.

By contrast, those who emphasize the importance of phonics skills as a *starting point* for getting into reading have generally little problem with some use of decodable texts but would also encourage students to use the totality of their concepts about print (including knowledge of phonics, contextual clues, and knowledge of the world) to engage with books and other texts that they are motivated to read. When students are motivated to read, and their identities are invested in the process, they will try out their evolving decoding skills on environmental print, stories, and other texts. In doing so, they will receive feedback and scaffolding from teachers, parents, and older siblings and use this feedback to infer more complex letter-sound correspondences that may not have been explicitly taught.

Essentially, the contrast here is between a behaviorist and a sociocultural (Vygotskian) approach to learning. The fact that the research support for behaviorist (or "stimulus-response") approaches came predominantly from watching rats running mazes and teaching pigeons to play ping pong might cause us to question the usefulness of behaviorist principles for complex human activities such as learning how to read. This skepticism is reinforced by the evidence reviewed above showing clearly that children are very capable of developing more complex phonological and decoding skills that have not been explicitly taught when they are in a culturally-responsive learning environment, guided or scaffolded by supportive adults.

The orientation of the present volume is much more consistent with a Vygotskian approach to learning than with the more mechanistic behaviorist approach. Conceptualizing learning as occurring within the interpersonal space of teacher-student interactions (the zone of proximal development) enables us to reflect on how learning to read is affected by identity negotiation rooted in societal power relations in addition to specific instructional strategies or content. Within a Vygotskian framework, there is scope for discussing the centrality of notions such as cognitive engagement and identity investment for children's reading development rather than simply the technical characteristics of instruction (*e.g.,* how many phonics rules should be explicitly taught and in what sequence).

At one level, the differences between the opposing sides in the "reading wars" are profound insofar as they reflect very different notions of what it means to learn. However, as noted above, these differences can also be seen as a matter of emphasis. At a practical level, what this means is *avoid the extremes*. A similar perspective is expressed by Celia Genishi and Dorothy Strickland (1999):

> In practice, teachers who advocate holistic approaches are apt to include strong word-recognition programs with phonics as a key tool for word recognition; and teachers who support intensive, systematic phonics often employ instructional strategies such as reading aloud to children and the encouragement of invented spelling. Although the matter of emphasis is not to be taken lightly, it is unlikely that you will find classrooms that reflect polar ends of an instructional continuum. (1999, p. viii)

I am less confident than Genishi and Strickland that most classrooms are balanced in their approach. The "phonics as panacea" movement has influenced policy-makers in states such as California and Texas to such an extent that what is being implemented in many classrooms is isolated phonics instruction (often combined with exposure to decodable text) to the exclusion of any significant emphasis on extensive reading of authentic text (Gándara *et al.*, 2000). Even worse, in some behavioristically-oriented programs, teachers are expected to read scripts that dictate exactly what they should say to students in order to develop their phonics skills. Deviation from the script is strongly discouraged. There is certainly nothing inappropriate with providing illustrative scripts to *guide* instruction; new or inexperienced teachers may benefit from following the script initially until they gain more confidence. However, the top-down imposition of scripts on all teachers represents an attempt to "teacher-proof" the curriculum. It reflects a profound distrust of teachers and an extremely narrow interpretation of the teaching-learning process. Nowhere in this anemic instructional vision is there room for really connecting with culturally diverse students, affirming their identities, or generating any intrinsic motivation to learn and engage cognitively with the instruction. Teachers and students alike are constructed as programmable robots. This kind of programming reduces instruction to a technical exercise. No role is envisaged for teachers or students to invest their identities in the teaching/learning process. Linda McNeil of Rice University in Houston, commented astutely in *TIME Magazine* that this kind of dictatorial prescriptive programming will "drive out the best teachers and give the weakest a place to hide" (Morse, 2000, p. 61).

In the next chapter, I present a broader and more inclusive vision of the teaching-learning process that integrates literacy learning in culturally diverse contexts both with the interpersonal negotiation of identity between teachers and students and with the sociopolitical power relations in the broader society.

Endnotes to Chapter 4

1. The perspective here is similar to that elaborated in Collier's Prism model (Collier, 1995; Thomas & Collier, 1997). This model has four major components that "drive" language acquisition for school: sociocultural, linguistic, academic, and cognitive processes. Within the prism are the social and cultural processes that impact on the child's experience in home, school, community, and the broader society. These sociocultural processes incorporate the influences and power relations that I have discussed in terms of both macro-interactions and micro-interactions in Chapter 1. Thomas and Collier note that sociopolitical and affective factors will strongly influence the student's response to the new language, "affecting the process positively only when the student is in a socioculturally supportive environment" (1997, p. 42).

   The boundaries of the prism are formed by L1 + L2 language development, L1 + L2 cognitive development, and L1 + L2 academic development. Thomas and Collier note the interdependence of all four components: "If one is developed to the neglect of another, this may be detrimental to a student's overall growth and future success" (1997, p. 44). Thus, programs that focus only on language development in English tend to ignore both cognitive development and sociocultural processes. Furthermore, they typically provide support for overall academic development either minimally or not on grade level.

   The implication of both the Collier/Thomas Prism model and the perspective in the present volume is that it is not particularly useful to try to separate out the unique effects of input (and output) on cognition versus language because the cognitive, linguistic, and academic dimensions of academic language learning are fused. The glue that binds them together in the process of learning is the extent to which broader sociocultural process create the conditions for full identity investment on the part of the learner.

2. Readers with masochistic tendencies may want to explore in detail the arguments/accusations and counter-arguments/accusations surrounding the program of research sponsored by the National Institute of Child Health and Human Development (NICHD), and specifically the Foorman et al. (1998) study and its impact on reading policy in Texas and California (Allington and Woodside-Jiron, 1999; Coles, 2000; Dressman, 1999; Foorman, 2000; Mathes &

Torgesen, 2000; Taylor et al., 2000). I would prefer to emphasize the commonalities between the two sides as illustrated in the following quotes. Mathes and Torgesen note that there is consensus among NICHD-supported researchers that:

> teaching the alphabetic principle is *one* critical component for preventing or remediating reading failure for many children. What NICHD-supported reading researchers do *not* advocate is code-*only* instruction, a focus on skill worksheets, skills taught in a disjointed manner, or skills taught only in isolation. Likewise, NICHD reading researchers do *not* suggest that beginning readers should be deprived of authentic literature and read only decodable text. (2000, pp. 5–6)

Foorman *et al.* (2000) suggest that "it may well be possible to prevent reading failure for large numbers of children if beginning instruction explicitly teaches the alphabetic principle" (p. 52) but they also caution that:

> It is important to keep in mind that the classroom curricula used in this study took place in a print-rich environment with a significant literature base. Instructional programs that provided only phonological awareness or phonics lessons were not used because it was not likely that such training would generalize to actual reading and spelling skills. (p. 52)

From the opposite perspective, Taylor *et al.* (2000) "agree that an extensive body of research exists to support the importance of teachers helping children learn to understand the alphabetic principle" (p. 23) but critique the Foorman *et al.* (1998) research for promoting the idea that "explicitly teaching the alphabetic principle can prevent reading failure" (p. 19). They note that "students of diverse backgrounds already typically receive large doses of instruction in isolated, lower-level skills with little opportunity to engage in higher-level thinking about text" (p. 20). Their concern is that the Foorman *et al.* study "may have the lamentable consequence of leading to more skill and drill and even less thought-provoking experience with meaningful text for children in poor urban schools" (p. 20). They cite the National Reading Panel report (2000, p. 289) to the effect that "Phonics should not become the dominant component in the reading program, neither in the amount of time devoted to it nor in the significance attached." With specific reference to the literacy learning of children from diverse backgrounds they refer to Au (1998):

> She concludes that if students are to achieve at higher levels, educators must emphasize ownership; push for biliteracy rather than using the home language only as a vehicle for English literacy; have students read multicultural literature; and teach skills explicitly, within the context of authentic literacy activities. (Taylor *et al.*, 2000, p. 18)

3. Lambert and Tucker speculate that the significantly better performance of the grade 1 French immersion group compared to the controls on the French Word Discrimination test (in which students were required to associate the sound of a French word with its printed form) may have been due to students developing "a type of linguistic detective capacity to help search out and link up efficiently the written and oral forms of new words" (1972, p. 41). However, this initial superiority was not observed at the grade 2 level.

4. Much more significant than the order in which L1 and L2 reading are introduced in a bilingual program is the extent to which the program focuses on maintaining and developing literacy in the L1. Introduction of reading in L1 is *not* an essential aspect of the rationale for bilingual education for linguistic minority students. However, in many cases it *will* make good sense to introduce reading in students' L1. Spanish, for example, has a more regular sound-symbol relationship than English and is the language Spanish-L1 speakers know better when they enter school, so it will make sense in most circumstances to use that as the language of initial reading instruction. However, the data show clearly that under some circumstances Spanish-L1 students can learn to read first in English or in both languages in quick succession. Reviews of the literature for more than 20 years have shown no clearcut or absolute superiority for introducing reading in L1 as compared to L2 (*e.g.,* Cummins, 1979a; Engle, 1975; Fitzgerald, 1995; Wagner, 1998). To make initial literacy in the L1 central to the rationale for bilingual education places the whole enterprise on very shaky empirical and theoretical grounds because the research data do not show that this, in itself, is the central variable distinguishing successful from less successful programs. For example, programs such as the 50:50 programs in Oyster Bilingual School in Washington DC, and the Amigos program in Cambridge, MA, introduce formal reading instruction in both languages in grade 1.

   Rather than being suspicious of English and delaying its introduction, my belief is that we should encourage the development of biliteracy in classrooms where students are reading extensively in both languages, writing bilingual books (according to well-established whole language procedures), sharing them with parents and peers, and generally augmenting their awareness of language and how it works. Strong and uncompromising promotion of L1 literacy is a crucial component of this approach but we should adopt a *both/and* rather than an *either/or* orientation to L1 and L2. When promoted together, the two languages enrich each other rather than subtracting from each other. Reyes' (2000) research illustrates just how powerful this process of biliteracy development can be for bilingual students.

5. Decoding skills can be taught through drill and practice, as programs such as DISTAR have long demonstrated (Becker, 1977). However, as all advocates for explicit systematic phonics instruction agree, decoding skills may be a necessary condition for the development of reading comprehension but they are not a sufficient condition. In the DISTAR example, students who achieved well on standardized reading measures (particularly decoding tests) up to the 3rd grade dropped significantly in reading comprehension between the 3rd and 6th grades (to the 16th percentile) (see Becker, 1977; Cummins, 1984). Furthermore, as noted previously, the relatively good "reading" performance of grade 2 students in the Oceanside district in California in an all-English program in the wake of Proposition 227, should be considered very cautiously in view of the fact that standardized tests assess primarily decoding skills rather than comprehension abilities at this grade level. The fact that scores of Oceanside students from grades 3-6 were much less impressive illustrates the fact that the acquisition of strong reading comprehension skills is a very different process than acquiring decoding skills. A much more meaningful measure of reading performance will come in later grades when reading comprehension abilities, rather than just decoding, become the focus of assessment. Performance at this level is likely to depend on the extent to which the program incorporates the "whole language" emphasis on extensive reading and writing activities.

6. Working with Japanese university students of English as a foreign language (EFL), Mason and Krashen demonstrated in three experiments that extensive reading in English

> proved to be superior to traditional approaches on measures of reading comprehension, as well as on measures of writing and reading speed, and according to teacher observations, was much more popular with students. ...Extensive reading resulted in significantly superior gains in six out of seven comparisons for cloze and reading comprehension tests and extensive readers did better on measures of writing and reading speed. Extensive reading allowed "reluctant" students of EFL to catch up to traditional students...(1997, p. 101).

> In a similar vein, Lightbown (1992) reported on a study that examined the power of reading in L2 compared to more traditional L2 teaching among francophone elementary school students in New Brunswick, Canada. In the experimental program, students learned English as a second language through listening to tape-recorded stories and other material while following the written text with no formal teaching. These students learned at least as much between grades 3 and 6 as did students in a more traditional aural-oral program. Both programs lasted for 30 minutes per day and in the experimental program student autonomy was strictly respected insofar as there was "no teaching, no testing, no probing students' comprehension" (p. 356).

7. For purposes of creating the Academic Word List, Coxhead notes that "a word family was defined as a stem plus all closely related affixed forms" (2000, p. 218). For example, the word family associated with the word *concept* includes the forms: *conception, concepts, conceptual, conceptualization, conceptualize, conceptualized, conceptualizes, conceptualizing, conceptually*.

Chapter 5

Understanding Academic Language Learning: Making It Happen in the Classroom

In this chapter, I try to pull the research and theory on academic language learning together in such a way that major controversies are resolved and the implications for instruction become apparent. As noted in the previous chapter, the demographics of diversity together with the length of time required for ELL students to catch up academically means that virtually all teachers in urban areas will be required to teach culturally and linguistically diverse students in their "mainstream" classrooms. In order to implement effective instruction in this context, educators must re-define their roles both individually and collectively. This implies that schools must take seriously the fact that they are "learning institutions." In other words, in addition to being places where students learn, schools must also acknowledge that they are required to adapt to changing demographic and social circumstances if they are to carry out their mission effectively. In particular, schools must learn how to teach a diverse student body that is dramatically different from the "generic" white, middle-class, monolingual, monocultural students for whom curriculum was developed in the past.

Thus, policy-makers and administrators must ensure that all educators in the school have the opportunity to develop the knowledge base to teach culturally and linguistically diverse students appropriately. A high school teacher may take pride in her ability to teach science but unless she knows how to teach science to students who are at varying stages of acquiring academic English, her science teaching skills may amount to very little. Her role definition must change from being an effective science teacher for the "generic" white, middle-class, monolingual, monocultural student to being an effective teacher of science *and*

English academic skills to the new culturally and linguistically diverse mainstream student. Universities across North America are only beginning to take account of these new realities in the way they prepare pre-service teachers and other educators (*e.g.*, administrators, psychologists, etc.) (see Merino, 1999).

What this perspective implies is that schools must develop policies to reorient their instruction with respect to culturally and linguistically diverse students. These policies relate to the roles not only of ESL and bilingual teachers but of *all* teachers in the school. If all teachers are to buy into these policies, then they should have a role in formulating and monitoring them within the school. In other words, effective instruction for ELL students requires that all educators within a school become informed about relevant research and theory and take responsibility for implementing appropriate practices that address students' language learning and academic needs.

The instructional framework in the present chapter is intended to serve as a convenient starting point for discussing the development of language and equity policies in schools. It represents just the beginning, not the end-point, of such a process. Any policy should be dynamic rather than static; in other words, it should draw on the collective experience of educators in the school and be subject to ongoing refinement and modification based on that collective experience (Corson, 1999). An example of the kinds of considerations that might contribute to a culturally-sensitive language policy process, based on suggestions from the Scottish Consultative Council on the Curriculum (Landon *et al.*, 1994), is provided in Appendix A.

The present framework incorporates the emphasis on identity negotiation and cognitive challenge, and their intersection with patterns of societal power relations, discussed in previous chapters. It also highlights three focus areas for instruction aimed at developing academic language proficiency: instruction must incorporate a focus on meaning or message (comprehensible input), it must aim to demystify how academic language works and develop a critical language awareness among students, and finally, it must provide ample opportunities and encouragement for students to express themselves—their developing identities—through varied forms of creative oral and written language use.

A Framework for Academic Language Learning
The Interpersonal Space of
Cognitive Engagement and Identity Investment

The central sphere in Figure 5.1 represents the interpersonal space creat-ed in the interactions between teachers and students. Within this interpersonal space or what Vygotsky (1962, 1978) termed the *zone of proximal develop-ment* (Chapter 1, note 14), knowledge is generated (learning occurs) and iden-tities are negotiated. In contexts of cultural, linguistic, or economic diversity where social inequality inevitably exists, these interactions are never neutral: they either challenge the operation of coercive relations of power in the wider society or they reinforce these power relations. At the other end of the sphere, we can visualize the discourse of societal power relations which is broadcast into the classroom and directly affects how identities are negotiated between teachers and students. For example, the discourse that asserts bilingual children

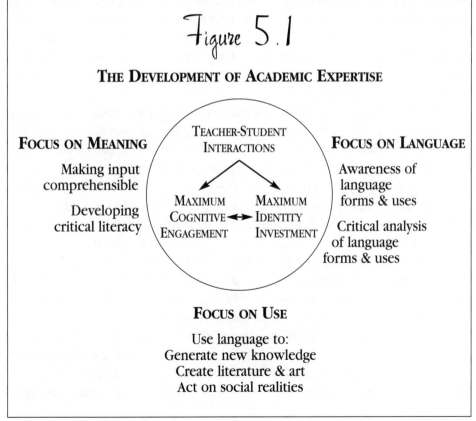

Figure 5.1

THE DEVELOPMENT OF ACADEMIC EXPERTISE

FOCUS ON MEANING

Making input
comprehensible

Developing
critical literacy

TEACHER-STUDENT
INTERACTIONS

MAXIMUM
COGNITIVE ←→ IDENTITY
ENGAGEMENT   INVESTMENT

MAXIMUM

FOCUS ON LANGUAGE

Awareness of
language
forms & uses

Critical analysis
of language
forms & uses

FOCUS ON USE

Use language to:
Generate new knowledge
Create literature & art
Act on social realities

need to assimilate and give up their L1 if they are to succeed in the society is not a neutral scientific statement of fact; on the contrary, it contradicts the scientific data on this issue and derives directly from patterns of coercive power relations in the wider society. This construction of children's bilingualism as a problem to be resolved frequently results in patterns of teacher-student interaction that communicate to students that they should leave their language and culture at the schoolhouse door.

The framework argues that within the interpersonal space of teacher-student interactions, students' cognitive engagement must be maximized if they are to progress academically. Similarly, teacher-student interactions must *affirm* students' cultural, linguistic, and personal identities in order to create classroom conditions for maximum identity investment in the learning process.

There is a reciprocal relationship between cognitive engagement and identity investment. The more students learn, the more their academic self-concept grows, and the more academically engaged they become. However, students will be reluctant to invest their identities in the learning process if they feel their teachers do not like them, respect them, and appreciate their experiences and talents. In the past, students from marginalized social groups have seldom felt this sense of affirmation and respect for language and culture from their teachers. Consequently their intellectual and personal talents rarely found expression in the classroom.

In short, a starting point in the framework is the assertion that the learning process must be observed through the twin lens of cognitive engagement and identity investment. What this means in practice can be illustrated with respect to the process of activating students' prior knowledge.

Activating prior knowledge/building background knowledge. There is general agreement among cognitive psychologists that we learn by integrating new input into our existing cognitive structures or schemata. Our prior experience provides the foundation for interpreting new information. No learner is a blank slate. In reading, for example, we construct meaning by bringing our prior knowledge of language and of the world to the text. As Fielding and Pearson (1994) point out, research conducted in the late 1970s and early 1980s consistently revealed a strong reciprocal relationship between prior knowledge and reading comprehension ability: "The more one already knows, the more one comprehends; and the more one comprehends, the more one learns new knowledge to enable comprehension of an even greater array of topics and texts" (1994, p. 62). More recently, Spires and Donley (1998) have shown that ninth-grade students instructed in a prior knowledge activation strategy showed significantly better performance in reading comprehension than comparison groups (those instructed in a main idea strategy and a control group). The prior knowledge strategy group also demonstrated more positive attitudes towards reading than the other groups. Chamot (1998) has expressed very clearly the "dramatic effect that prior knowledge has on learning new information and skills" and how this is particularly important for second language learners:

> Nowhere is the role of prior knowledge more important than in second language educational contexts. Students who can access their prior knowledge through the language and culture most familiar to them can call on a rich array of schemata, whereas students who believe they can only use that knowledge they have explicitly learned in the second language are limited in their access. (1998, p. 197)

Thus, in second language learning, our prior knowledge plays a major role in helping to make the second language input comprehensible. Imagine, for example, that you have intermediate Spanish skills and you take advantage of an opportunity to take a course on child development in a Mexican university in order to improve your knowledge of the language. You already know a lot about child development from courses you have taken in English and from raising your own children. As you struggle to understand the lectures in Spanish, your prior knowledge of child development allows you to understand far more than if you had no knowledge of the content. Because you know much of the content already, you can make intelligent guesses or inferences about the meaning. By contrast, if you had enrolled in a course on South American literature, about which you knew very little, your intermediate Spanish would not have carried you nearly as far. And furthermore, because you understood far less of the input, you would have learned far less Spanish (see Krashen, 1991).

Thus, a major rationale for activating students' prior knowledge, or if there is minimal prior knowledge on a particular topic or issue, building it with the students, is to make the learning process more efficient. Prior knowledge represents one central aspect of what students bring to the learning situation that makes input more context-embedded and comprehensible. It is important to *activate* students' prior knowledge because students may not explicitly realize what they know about a particular topic or issue; consequently, their prior knowledge may not facilitate learning unless it is brought to consciousness. As

Jessner (1999) argues, activating students' metalinguistic knowledge of their L1 and encouraging them to relate their L1 knowledge to their L2 is an important aspect of this process.

Lois Meyer (2000) has expressed in a particularly clear way the importance of prior knowledge (familiarity with the topic) in reducing the cognitive load of the instruction and how L1 instruction can contribute to this process:

> The number of new concepts embedded in a lesson or text is its cognitive load. Whether or not a learning activity is "cognitively loaded" is not so much a factor of the specific content of the lesson but rather depends on the student's initial familiarity with that content. If the English learner has little entry knowledge about the subject matter, the cognitive load of the lesson will be heavy, for many concepts will be new and unfamiliar. The student will have little basis from which to generate hypotheses regarding the meanings the teacher is conveying through English.
>
> If the student's entry knowledge of the topic is considerable, this will lighten the cognitive load. Learners can draw on their knowledge to interpret linguistic and non-linguistic clues in the lesson in order to make educated guesses about the meanings of the teacher's talk and text. Instruction through the student's primary language contributes in important ways to lowering the cognitive barrier, for content knowledge acquired through the first language aids the English learner to interpret the meanings of lessons received through English. (2000, p. 229)

In a classroom with second language learners from diverse backgrounds, prior knowledge about a particular topic may vary widely. Thus, simple transmission of the information or skill will fail to connect with the prior knowledge and previous experience of many students. As a result, the input will be much less comprehensible for those students. Some students may have relevant information in their L1 but not realize that there is any connection with what they are learning in their L2. In other cases, there may be a considerable cultural gap between what is assumed by the text and what students know from their prior experience. This is particularly the case for older students whose previous schooling has been interrupted and who may have minimal L1 literacy skills.

Thus, a first step in making any input more context-embedded is to activate students' prior knowledge through brainstorming as a whole class, or in small groups or pairs. This is an appropriate situation for students to use their L1 in small groups or in pairs when their proficiency in English is limited. [1]

Finding out what students know about a particular topic allows the teacher to supply relevant concepts or vocabulary that some or all students may be lacking but which will be important for understanding the upcoming text or lesson. Building this context permits students to understand more complex language and to pursue more cognitively demanding activities. It frees up brain power.

One useful technique for ensuring that students have the necessary background knowledge to understand the lesson is the *preview, view, review* procedure (Freeman & Freeman, 1998, 2000). The preview is provided to students in the L1 (by the teacher, a bilingual aide, a bilingual peer, a cross-age tutor, or a parent volunteer) in order to give the students an overview of what the upcoming lesson is about. The preview could be an oral summary, reading a book, showing a film or visuals (*e.g.* poster, photographs), asking key questions etc. According to Freeman and Freeman:

> During the view the teacher conducts the lesson using strategies to make the input comprehensible. With the help of the preview, the students can follow the English better and acquire both English and academic content. Finally, it is good to have a short time of review during which students can use their native language. For example, students who speak the same first language could meet in groups to review the main ideas of the lesson and then report back in English. (2000, p. 11)

In short, activation of students' prior knowledge and building background knowledge increases students' cognitive engagement and enables them to function at an intellectually and linguistically higher level. Students understand more and consequently they learn more language and academic content.

However, just as important for the learning process as these cognitive considerations is the fact that activation of prior knowledge enables teachers to validate culturally diverse students' background experiences and affirm their cultural knowledge. Inviting students to contribute what they already know to the class discussion communicates to students that the cultural and linguistic knowledge they are bringing into the classroom is important. Both the teacher and other students are interested in the unique cultural experiences of individual students. A community of sharing is created in the classroom; identity is being negotiated in ways that motivate students to express their growing sense of self and participate actively in the learning process. The sharing of cultural knowledge among teacher and students is multicultural education in action in a far more profound way than the more typical "heroes and holidays" approach.

In this regard, it is important to emphasize that curriculum materials and texts should be chosen carefully to ensure their relevance to students' cultural background and prior experience. If students' prior experience is excluded by virtue of the cultural loading of the text or material, it will be far more difficult for students to relate to it, or for teachers to build background knowledge. Lisa Delpit has eloquently expressed this point:

> If we plan to survive as a species on this planet we must certainly create multicultural curricula that educate our children to the differing perspectives of our diverse population. In part, the problems we see exhibited in school by African American children and by children of other oppressed minorities can be traced to this lack of a curriculum in which they can find represented the intellectual achievements of people who look like themselves. Were that not the case, these children would not talk about doing well in school as "acting White." Our children of color need to see the brilliance of their legacy, too. (1992, p. 245)

In summary, activating bilingual students' prior knowledge:

- Increases cognitive engagement and makes language and concepts more meaningful to students by enabling them to interpret new information in relation to what they already know;

- Enables teachers to get to know their students better as individuals with unique personal histories; in turn, this permits teachers to tune their instruction to the needs and interests of individual students;

- Creates a context in the classroom where students' cultural knowledge is expressed, shared and affirmed, thereby motivating students to invest themselves more fully in the learning process.

The reciprocal relationship between affirming students' identity and maximizing their cognitive engagement is also evident in many other aspects of instruction. For example, when students write, revise, and publish stories in the classroom, they are simultaneously stretched cognitively and also affirmed as individuals with something important and interesting to contribute. Identity investment and cognitive engagement are two sides of the same coin.

The teacher's role in maximizing cognitive engagement and identity investment. If students are primarily involved in rote memorization in the classroom, only a fraction of their cognitive capacity is engaged in learning. From an academic perspective, they are chugging along in second gear. Engagement of higher level cognitive processes such as analysis, synthesis, and evaluation—critical thinking—is clearly likely to produce much more learning for the simple reason that much more of students' brains is involved in the process of learning. By the same token, this kind of stimulation will develop students' brains, and their cognitive capacity, much more than instruction that involves only low-level cognitive processes. This clearly points to a major limitation of traditional orientations to pedagogy that focus primarily on low-level memorization and application skills (see Chapter 7).

In terms of Figure 3.1, discussed in Chapter 3, the primary "target zone" or zone of proximal development for pitching instruction for second language learners should be quadrant B—context-embedded and cognitively demanding. The rationale is that instruction must evoke intellectual effort on the part of students, *i.e.,* be cognitively demanding and engaging, if it is to develop academic and intellectual abilities. If the instruction is cognitively undemanding (quadrants A and C), students will learn very little and quickly become bored in the process; if the instruction goes beyond what students can process cognitively (because of lack of contextual support), then they will also learn very little and become frustrated and mentally withdraw from academic effort. As indicated in Figure 3.1, the crucial dimension in helping students succeed in cognitively demanding tasks and activities is the contextual support that is (a) activated in the learner (*e.g.,* motivation, prior knowledge etc.) and (b) embedded in the instruction.

Expressed differently, an English L1 student may succeed in a particular task (*e.g.,* writing a science experiment report) with relatively little contextual support because English is her L1 and she has acquired the rules of this genre of writing from previous instruction; however, the same task may be much more cognitively challenging for a second language learner because of limitations in her current English language abilities and lack of previous instruction in how to write up science reports. The second student will require considerable contextual support or scaffolding if she is to succeed in the task.

Faced with this situation, some teachers who are unfamiliar with instructional strategies for second language learners have tended to "dumb down" the task (*i.e.,* revert to quadrants A or C). This permits students to work within their level of English and academic competence but never pushes them to go beyond that level, which they must do if they are to catch up academically to English L1 students.

Effective teaching for ELL students is often conceived as a collection of techniques or strategies for making input comprehensible to students and developing their literacy skills. Knowledge of, and effective classroom implementation of techniques such as use of graphic organizers, cooperative learning, total physical response, developing learning strategies, peer tutoring, dialogue journals, authentic assessment, and so on are important but they do not necessarily translate into effective instruction. Much more crucial is the recognition that human relationships are fundamental to students' academic engagement. This is true for all students, but particularly so in the case of second language learners who may be trying to find their way in the borderlands between cultures. They frequently don't have either the means or the desire to go back to their original culture but don't yet have the language skills or cultural understanding to participate fully in their new culture. For students to invest their sense of self, their identity, in acquiring their new language and participating actively in their new culture, they must experience positive and affirming interactions with members of that culture.

Nobody is more important in this process than the teacher. Teachers have the opportunity to nurture students' growing understanding of who they are and who they want to be. It is the teacher who guides students towards powerful ways of expressing themselves in their new language and communicates to them possibilities of who they can become and the roles they might play within their new society.

In other words, techniques and strategies will be effective only when teachers and students forge a relationship of respect and affirmation; when students feel that they are welcomed into the learning community of the classroom and supported in the immense challenges they face in catching up academically; and when students feel that their teachers believe in them and expect them to succeed in school and in life.

Respect and affirmation are the basis of any relationship and, in classroom interactions, respect and affirmation are central to motivating second language learners to engage actively and enthusiastically in academic effort. This perspective entails two implications for how teachers define their role: first, it implies that teachers must see their role as creating instructional contexts in which second language learners can become active partners in the learning process; second, it implies that teachers must view themselves as learners—in order to teach effectively they must learn from their students about students' culture, background, and experience.

When we look at the learning process through the twin lens of cognitive engagement and identity investment, what comes into focus are teacher-student interactions that:

- provide ample opportunities for students to process meaningful language and concepts;

- provide ample opportunities for students to deepen their awareness of how their languages work and how language use intersects with power relations to affect their lives (*e.g.*, through advertisements, political rhetoric, etc.);

- provide ample opportunities for students to use their languages in powerful ways to connect with other people and make a difference in their world.

These three focus areas are discussed below.

Focus on Meaning

The framework highlights the fact that effective instruction in a second language must focus initially on meaning or messages. As noted in the previous chapter, virtually all applied linguists agree that access to sufficient comprehensible input in the target language is a necessary condition for language acquisition. However, for purposes of *academic* language development, our interpretation of the construct of comprehensible input must go beyond just literal comprehension. Depth of understanding of concepts and vocabulary, as well as critical literacy, are intrinsic to the notion of comprehensible input when we are talking about the development of academic language proficiency. This implies a process whereby students relate textual and instructional meanings to their own experience and prior knowledge (*i.e.*, activate their cognitive schemata), critically analyze the information in the text (*e.g.*, evaluate the validity of various arguments or propositions), and use the results of their discussions and analyses in some concrete, intrinsically-motivating activity or project (*e.g.*, making a video or writing a poem or essay on a particular topic). In short, for effective learning of academic content, the notion of comprehensible input must move beyond literal, surface-level comprehension to a deeper level of cognitive and linguistic processing.

The following outline of the kinds of teacher-students interactions that promote critical literacy (Table 5.1) is derived from the Au's (1979) *experience-text-relationship* approach and Ada's (1988a, 1988b) *creative reading* approach. It attempts to show how interpersonal spaces can be created between teachers and students that encourage students to share and amplify their experience within a collaborative process of critical inquiry. Each of the five phases progressively opens up possibilities for strengthening students' personal and academic identity. The texts that are the focus of the interaction can

---

Table 5.1

FOCUS ON MEANING:
FROM COMPREHENSIBLE INPUT TO CRITICAL LITERACY

Experiential Phase. Activate prior knowledge and build background knowledge; For example, in a science unit on photosynthesis, teachers and students brainstorm on "What makes plants grow?"

Literal Phase. Focus is on information contained in the text; Typical questions might be: When, where, how, did it happen? Who did it? Why?

Personal Phase. Students relate textual information to their own experiences and feelings; Teachers might ask: Have you ever seen (felt, experienced) something like this? Have you ever wanted something similar?

Critical Phase. Critical analysis of issues or problems arising from the text; involves drawing inferences and exploring generalizations. Teachers might ask: Is what this person said valid? Always? Under what conditions? Are there any alternatives to this situation?

Creative Phase. Translating the results of previous phases into concrete action; How can the problem or issues be resolved? What role can *we* play in helping to resolve the problem. This phase might involve drama, role play, letters to editor, school principal, web site or newsletter publication of research/analysis/art, poetry, stories.

---

derive from any curricular area or from newspapers, popular songs, or current events. The process is equally applicable to students at any grade level and the phases can be intertwined rather than follow a strict sequence. A basic assumption is that collective action to transform aspects of our social realities results in a deeper understanding of those realities.

Much conventional reading instruction in both L1 and L2 has focused only on the *literal phase* or on comprehensible input in a very narrow sense. The *experiential, personal, critical, and creative phases* are essential if we are to speak of knowledge generation or transformative pedagogy rather than just transmission of information.

The ways in which maximizing cognitive engagement are intertwined with maximizing identity investment have been illustrated earlier with reference to the importance of activating students' prior knowledge and, where necessary, building background knowledge. These instructional activities reflect the *experiential* and *personal* phases of the scheme outlined above. Some further elaboration of these phases is outlined below.

Schifini (1994) suggests five strategies for tapping, focusing, and building on students' background knowledge:

- **Use visuals to stimulate discussion.** Students work in small groups to make observations or speculate about visual stimuli that are in the text or supplied by the teacher. For example, in a science class, the teacher may show a picture of waves breaking on a beach and ask students to write down or discuss how ocean water moves. The most frequent responses from students are highlighted and used as an introduction to the text itself.

- **Use manipulatives and multimedia presentations.** Schifini points out that "concrete objects such as historical artifacts, posters, replicas of newspaper coverage of major historical events, and laboratory experiences with everyday objects such as thermometers, rocks, leaves, batteries, and bulbs all build background through interaction" (p. 165).

- **Sharing prior experiences with students from diverse backgrounds.** Schifini gives the example of students listening to the songs "We Shall Overcome" and "De Colores" and sharing their personal experiences or prior knowledge of discrimination and prejudice. Teachers can focus the discussion through questions such as "Why do you think people discriminate against other people?" "Have you ever felt discriminated against?" "How have we tried to decrease discrimination in this country?" etc. On the basis of this discussion, the teacher might then ask students to predict what they might read about in a text on the Civil Rights movement in the United States.

- **Writing activities that focus students' prior knowledge.** Schifini suggests that quick-writes (*e.g.*, one-minute brainstorming on paper), journal writing, and responding to written prompts (*e.g.*, "People make war because _____") help students to become aware of their prior knowledge and extend their schemata.

- **Linking prior knowledge to new concepts.** A technique proposed originally by Ogle (1986), K-W-L charts, is useful in relating prior knowledge to new information and concepts. A page is divided into three sections which students can fill out individually or in groups. "K" stands for "What I know;" Schifini points out that this activates prior knowledge and can help students clarify misconceptions when discussed within groups. "W" stands for "What I want to find out" and helps students establish their own purposes for reading and can guide their interpretation of and extraction of information from text. "L" stands for "What I have learned and still need to learn" and encourages students to monitor their own learning and become actively involved in the assessment process. Anna Uhl Chamot (1996) has suggested that "H" can be added to the chart to signify "How I learned what I learned" in order to build students' awareness of learning strategies.

Although these strategies for activating prior knowledge constitute good instruction for all students, they are particularly important for second language learners because the activation and building of context permits them to function at a cognitively and linguistically higher level. These strategies also stimulate students to use the target language since extended discussion is usually required rather than single word answers to teacher questions.

The intersection of cognitive engagement and identity investment is also apparent in the critical and creative phases. Students who are given the opportunity and encouragement to use higher-order thinking and to solve problems not only develop these cognitive abilities but also come to see themselves as individuals who are capable of intellectual insights and creative work. Their sense of who they are and who they can become expands as a result.

This deepening of comprehension represents a progressive expansion of conceptual horizons. Thus, the more we process input or information, the more potential there is for deepening our understanding of the phenomena in question. In other words, for purposes of academic language development, the notion of comprehensible input merges into the notion of critical literacy. Critical literacy is required to make literature and complex social issues comprehensible. Furthermore, the more critically literate students become, the more they generate the power to define their own identities and realities rather than being subject to the kinds of external definitions that historically have served to disempower subordinated groups.

Focus on Language

The Focus on Language component in Figure 5.1 attempts to put controversial issues such as the appropriate time and ways to teach L2 grammar, the role of phonics in reading instruction, the place of corrective feedback to students, etc. under the "umbrella" of *Language Awareness.* The development of language awareness includes not just a focus on formal aspects of the language but also the development of *critical language awareness* which encompasses exploration of the relationships between language and power. Students, for example, might carry out research on the status of different varieties of language (*e.g.,* colloquial language versus formal "standard" language) and explore critically why one form is considered by many educators and the general public to be "better" than the other. They might also research issues such as code-switching and the functions it plays within their own lives and their bilingual communities. Or they might analyze letters to the editor on controversial issues such as immigration and examine how the language used in these letters positions and potentially stereotypes bilingual learners such as themselves and their parents.

In short, a focus on formal features of the target language should be integrated with critical inquiry into issues of language and power. Also, to be effective, a focus on language must be linked to extensive input in the target language (*e.g.,* through reading) and extensive opportunities for written and oral use of the language.

A number of scholars and educators have focused on the importance of developing language awareness not only as a means of demystifying language and how it works but also as a way of reinforcing students' sense of identity. Lisa Delpit (1998), for example, talks about encouraging African American speakers of Ebonics to become "language detectives" investigating similarities and differences between their own vernacular and other forms of English such as that found in school texts. For example, groups of students can work together to create bilingual dictionaries of their own language forms and Standard English. A significant goal is to reinforce students' understanding that their language is legitimate and powerful in its context of use but that other forms of English are necessary in different contexts of use. She also illustrates how an affirmation of identity can be associated with a focus on language by referring to the practice of a teacher who has her middle school students (grades 7–8) listen to rap songs in order to develop a rule base for their creation:

Table 5.2

FOCUS AREAS FOR CRITICAL INQUIRY INTO LANGUAGE

- The structure of language systems (*e.g.,* relationships between sounds and spelling, regional and class-based accents, grammar, vocabulary, etc.);

- Ways of accomplishing different functions and purposes of language;

- Conventions of different musical and literary forms (*e.g.,* rap, rock, folk music, poetry, fiction, etc.);

- Appropriateness of expression in different contexts (cultural conventions of politeness, street language versus school language, the language of everyday speech versus the language of books, language variety as a badge of identity in groups as diverse as gangs, political parties, fraternities, etc.);

- Ways of organizing oral or written discourse to create powerful or persuasive messages (*e.g.,.* oratorical speeches, influential written documents, political rhetoric, advertisements, etc.);

- Cross-lingual comparison of languages (*e.g.,* proverbs in L1 and L2, differences in orthography among languages spoken by children in the class, cognates between English and L1, etc.)

- Diversity of language use in both monolingual and multilingual contexts (code-switching in bilingual communities, language maintenance and loss in families, political controversies surrounding

The students would teach her their newly constructed "rules for writing rap," and she would in turn use this knowledge as a base to begin a discussion of the rules Shakespeare used to construct his plays, or the rules poets used to develop their sonnets. (Delpit, 1995, p. 67)

Table 5.2 outlines some aspects of language that might be the focus of collaborative inquiry among students. Encouraging this collaborative inquiry in the classroom clearly goes beyond just the teaching of forms and functions of the language. The goal is to develop among students an awareness of language and how it works in different social situations. [2]

A systematic focus on developing critical language awareness requires that teachers organize instruction to enable students to *harvest the language* so that it becomes available for their use. Computer technology can be useful in helping students (either individually or in groups) to collect, internalize, and consolidate their knowledge of language and then use it powerfully to extend their intellectual horizons and personal identities. For example, along the lines suggested by Norah McWilliam's (1998) *word-weaving* project, students could set up templates in computer files to enter words that they have come across in their reading or everyday experiences that they want to explore. A variety of categories could be entered along the left hand side of the page and students could use various resources and strategies to complete the database as illustrated in Table 5.3 (*e.g.,* brainstorming, use of conventional or electronic dictionaries or thesauri, world wide web pages devoted to language issues, discussion with parents or teachers, etc.). Obviously, computers are not necessary to carry out this type of activity (as illustrated in McWilliam's work) but the technology, if available, would certainly increase the scope and impact of this kind of project and permit easy updating of the file as new aspects or dimensions of the words are discovered. The kind of information that might be gathered is illustrated in Table 5.3 for the word ***Big***. Word exploration files could be printed out for each group member at the end of the week and shared with parents and other family members. Students could be encouraged to use, in their own writing, words they have explored (*e.g.,* rather than using "big", use one of the more vivid synonyms).

The categories chosen in the example above represent only some of the avenues for language exploration. Other categories that might be chosen include, in the Meaning category, *Homonyms, Cognates/Related Words in L1.* Under Form, language exploration could pursue words with the *Same Prefix, Same Suffix, Related Root Words* while Use might include *Idioms, Proverbs,*

Jokes, Puns, Advertisements, etc. The goal here is not just to collect these examples of language use but to analyze them critically. For example, students might analyze the ways in which language is used to exclude alternative perspectives, persuade, and frequently deceive in commercial or political advertisements. They might brainstorm "survival strategies" to avoid being manipulated by these forms of language.

Table 5.3

BIG WORDS FOR BIG MINDS: COLLECTING LANGUAGE SPECIMENS

Word: Big

Meaning	
L1 Equivalents:	grande (in Spanish)
Synonyms:	huge, gigantic, enormous, vast, mammoth, immense, gargantuan, large, massive, great, grand (*e.g.* "on a grand scale"), extensive, bulky;
Antonyms:	small, little, tiny, miniscule, petite, insignificant;
Examples of:	Empire State Building, the sun, etc.
Form	
Grammatical Category:	adjective
Comparatives:	big, bigger, biggest
Use	
Metaphoric Usage:	She has a big heart (= she's generous) Big Brother is watching you! He's gotten too big for his boots; He's got a big mouth; His eyes were bigger than his stomach The big issue of the presidential campaign is.... That's big of you! (sarcastic)

Language exploration, where students assume the role of *linguistic detectives*, is likely to be particularly fruitful in analyzing more complex words. Frequently words that derive from Graeco-Latin origins entail a stem or a root form that is joined with a variety of prefixes and suffixes. These prefixes and suffixes behave in predictable ways across languages. For example, European languages that derive from Latin and Greek have many cognates in common

Table 5.4

BIG WORDS FOR BIG MINDS: COLLECTING LANGUAGE SPECIMENS

WORD: PREDICT

Meaning

L1 Equivalents:	L1 Equivalents: predecir (in Spanish)
Synonyms:	forecast, foresee, foretell, envisage, expect, guess, prophesy
Prefix/Root Meanings:	pre = before; "dict" from Latin dicere = say. Predict = say before

Form

Grammatical Category:	verb
Grammatical Patterns:	predict (verb), prediction (noun), predictable (adjective), predictably (adverb)
Words with Same Prefix:	prefer, prehistoric, prejudge, premature, premeditate, preoccupy, prepare, etc.
Words with Same Root:	contradict, contradiction, dictate, dictation, dictator, diction, dictionary, etc.

Use

Seismologists try to predict where and
when earthquakes are going to happen

and charts such as that in Table 5.4 for the word ***predict*** could be compared across languages. Grade 1 students will encounter the word *predict* in their Science curriculum (as well as the other process words in Science (*e.g.,* investigate, communicate, observe, etc., all of which have cognates in Spanish). Teachers could explain the Latin (or Spanish) meaning for the prefix *pre* (before) and the root word (*dict*) which derives from the Latin *say*. Thus, *predict* means to *say before*. In a bilingual classroom or an enlightened "English-only" classroom, the teacher could encourage Spanish-speaking students to construct a chart in Spanish similar to Table 5.4. Students could use a variety of resources such as parents, community volunteers, dictionaries, on-line dictionaries, etc. to complete this task. [3]

In addition to exploring cognate connections across languages, students can compare similarities in the way abstract nouns are formed from verbs in different languages (*e.g., predict/prediction= predecir/predicción*). They will soon see that for the Graeco-Latin lexicon, consistent rules govern the behavior of these suffixes both within and across languages. For example, words ending in *-tion* in English end in *ción* in Spanish and words ending in *-ity* in English end in *-dad* in Spanish (*e.g.,* identity/identidad). Students or groups could also be asked to brainstorm and/or research other examples of the same pattern (*e.g., accelerate/acceleration; contradict/contradiction; investigate/investigation, etc.*). An alternative graphic organizer for exploring words with similar roots is presented in Figure 5.2.

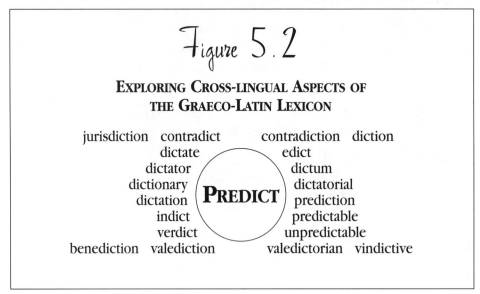

Figure 5.2

EXPLORING CROSS-LINGUAL ASPECTS OF THE GRAECO-LATIN LEXICON

jurisdiction contradict   contradiction diction
        dictate   edict
        dictator   dictum
        dictionary   dictatorial
        dictation   **PREDICT** prediction
        indict   predictable
        verdict   unpredictable
benediction valediction   valedictorian vindictive

The contrast in the exploration categories for *Big* and *Predict* illustrate a point made earlier. Many of the high frequency monosyllabic words derived from the Anglo-Saxon lexicon are *polysemous*—they have multiple meanings and are frequently used metaphorically or figuratively in everyday language. Compare, for example, the literal meaning of *high* (=*far above the ground*) with the many metaphoric uses of the term (*e.g., high=feeling happy* or *in a drug-induced state*) or its use in expressions such as *high quality, high speed train,* etc.). Many of the multisyllabic low-frequency words derived from the Graeco-Latin lexicon, on the other hand, have more stable and fixed meanings and are less subject to metaphoric usage. These words often are embedded in *word families* where the same core word can be transformed into many different grammatical categories (*e.g., predict, prediction, predictable, predictably*).

Clearly, each type of word presents its own unique challenges to second language learners. It is crucial that teachers provide ELL students with ample opportunities to develop what McWilliam (1998) calls *semantic agility* by means of exploring metaphoric usage in the English they are reading and hearing and also by using metaphorical language in their own writing of prose and poetry. Semantic agility also includes an awareness of how root words combine with prefixes and suffixes to generate an extensive array of words and word families.

This type of explicit focus on how academic language works can reinforce the modeling of language that teachers provide in their content instruction. Gibbons (1991) emphasizes that explicit modeling of academic language is particularly important in schools with large numbers of bilingual students:

> In such a school it is very easy to fall into the habit of constantly simplifying our language because we expect not to be understood. But if we only ever use basic language such as *put in* or *take out* or *go faster*, some children will not have any opportunity to learn other ways of expressing these ideas, such as *insert* or *remove* or *accelerate*. And these are the words which are needed to refer to the general concepts related to the ideas, such as *removal, insertion* and *acceleration*. (p. 18)

The point of harvesting the language in the manner suggested in this section is to make it available for students to use in their own production of language.[4]

In this regard, bilingual students from Romance language backgrounds have a significant advantage over their monolingual counterparts. The most difficult, low-frequency words in English are overwhelmingly derived from

Latin and Greek sources and most of these words have cognates in Spanish and other Romance languages. Encouraging bilingual students to explore cognate connections across their languages not only communicates to students the value of their home language and culture (identity affirmation) but also deepens their knowledge of English in ways that are academically highly significant.

Focus on Use

The Focus on Use component is based on the notion that L2 acquisition will remain abstract and classroom-bound unless students have the opportunity to express themselves–their identities and their intelligence–through that language. In order to motivate language use there should ideally be an authentic audience that encourages two-way communication in both oral and written modes. The three examples of language use presented in Figure 5.1 (*generate new knowledge, create literature and art, act on social realities*) are intended to illustrate important components of critical literacy. Language must be used to amplify students' intellectual, aesthetic, and social identities if it is to contribute to student empowerment, understood as the collaborative creation of power. Unless active and authentic language use for these purposes is promoted in the classroom, students' grasp of academic (and conversational) aspects of their second language is likely to remain shallow and passive.

Language use can stimulate linguistic growth, cognitive development, and affirmation of identity. Each of these three processes is important for academic language learning. With respect to linguistic growth, Swain (1995) notes three ways in which active use of the target language stimulates acquisition:

- Students must try to figure out sophisticated aspects of the target language in order to express what they want to communicate;

- It brings home to students and to their teachers what aspects of language they need assistance with;

- It provides teachers with the opportunity to provide corrective feedback to build language awareness and help students figure out how the language works (for a recent review of the effects of output on L2 acquisition see Izumi and Bigelow, 2000).

One example of how this process operates in the teaching of content areas is provided by Gibbons (1991). She emphasizes the importance of *reporting back* as a strategy for promoting academic language development. For example, after a concrete hands-on group experience, such as a science experiment, students are asked to report back to the class orally about what they did and observed and then to write about it. As students progress from concrete hands-on experience to more abstract language use, they must include sufficient information within the language itself for the meaning to be understood by those who did not share in the original experience. She notes that:

> while hands-on experiences are a very valuable starting point for language development, they do not, on their own, offer children adequate opportunities to develop the more 'context-free' language associated with reading and writing. ....a reporting back situation is a bridge into the more formal demands of literacy. It allows children to try out in speech—in a realistic and authentic situation—the sort of language they meet in books and which they need to develop in their writing. Where children's own language background has not led to this extension of oral language, it becomes even more important for the classroom to provide such opportunities. (1991, p. 31)

From the perspective of cognition, active language use is endorsed as central to cognitive development by the majority of theorists across North America today who operate from a Vygotskian or sociocultural perspective. Vygotsky (1978) emphasized that intellectual functions develop within a matrix of social interaction and are mediated by the child's inner speech. Language use and social interaction through language are thus crucial for intellectual development both in home and school (for elaborations of this perspective see Pérez, 1998a, 1998b, and the work on *instructional conversations* [*e.g.,* Patthey-Chavez, Clare & Goldenberg, 1995; Tharp & Gallimore, 1988]).

As one illustration of how closely linked active language use is to intellectual functioning, consider the role of teacher-mediated discussion in developing critical literacy through experiential, literal, personal, critical, and creative phases (Table 5.1). Writing about or discussion of complex issues with their teacher and peers encourages students to reflect critically and refine their ideas. As learners connect new information with what they already know, their cognitive power increases. They are enabled to understand more of the content and language that they hear or read. Cognitive and linguistic growth are seriously impeded when students are confined to passive roles within the classroom.

In addition to its cognitive and linguistic benefits, active language use in the classroom encourages students to express *themselves*; in other words, to explore their feelings, ideas, and experiences in a supportive context and thereby become more aware of their goals, values, and aspirations. Two examples of language use that have the potential to strongly promote affirmation of identity are drama/role-play and creative writing.

Drama/Role-Play. Shirley Brice Heath (1993) has argued that drama is a powerful means of enabling language learning through collaboration and cognitive apprenticeship. She documents how inner city youth organizations have used dramas that young people write, cast, and direct to enable them to retain their first language or dialect while acquiring standard English and preparing for job entry. In the Canadian context, Regnier (1988) has also documented how inner city First Nations (Native) youth have written and performed dramas that reflect their lives and how this process has exerted a powerful impact on their sense of self and on their academic development.

Creative writing and publishing. The process approach to writing, advocated for more than 20 years by Donald Graves (1983) and his colleagues, brought about a major change in the way writing was taught in North American schools. Graves' approach emphasizes writing as a communicative activity in which there is a real purpose (*e.g.,* publication of a book within the classroom), a genuine audience (*e.g.,* peers, teachers, parents), and support systems to assist children to work through the editing of successive drafts. This type of writing, in a variety of genres, can be highly effective in creating a sense of academic power, particularly among bilingual children who are developing literacy in two languages (see, for example, Brisk, 1985; Brisk & Harrington, 2000; Edelsky, 1986). There is probably no clearer illustration of what the term *empowerment* means than when a student's published story is placed in the class library and this student sees her friend borrowing the book from the class library to bring home and read with her parents. Daiute (1985) has expressed the potential of creative writing to promote a sense of academic efficacy among students:

> Children who learn early that writing is not simply an exercise gain a sense of power that gives them confidence to write—and write a lot. ....Beginning writers who are confident that they have something to say or that they can find out what they need to know can even overcome some limits of training or development. Writers who don't feel that what they say matters have an additional burden that no skills training can help them overcome. (1985, pp. 5-6)

Once again it is clear how a student's sense of self is affected by the opportunities provided in the classroom for active language use and creative effort.

Writing on a daily basis is especially important for second language learners because it requires them to engage with the most sophisticated aspects of academic language. It brings home to them and to their teachers what aspects of language they need assistance with and encourages them to become familiar with supports such as dictionaries, computer spell checkers, word banks they may have kept on particular topics etc. Despite its cognitively challenging nature, if the appropriate supports are in place, writing can be highly satisfying and motivating for second language learners.

Dialogue journals (where teachers respond in writing to students' journals) are an excellent way of encouraging second language learners' writing development in a genuinely communicative manner (Peyton & Stanton, 1993). This type of personal interaction between teacher and student provides an authentic context for students to express themselves and for teachers to provide both affirmation and guidance. Within the interpersonal space provided by dialogue journals teachers and students learn from each other and collaborate in extending conceptual horizons (see Brisk and Harrington, 2000, for a variety of very useful hands-on and identity-affirming literacy activities).

In the current era of "knee-jerk accountability," many teachers and administrators are concerned that if they devote too much time to authentic classroom reading and writing activities, their students will suffer on the standardized tests used to police instruction. This concern is legitimate but teachers should be reassured by the fact that extended reading is by far the strongest predictor of reading comprehension test scores (see Chapter 4, Table 4.1). There is also at least anecdotal evidence that extended writing across curricular areas can boost standardized test scores. [5] Observations by the staff of the highly successful Oyster Bilingual School in Washington DC highlight the importance of writing for academic achievement in general but also more specifically for performance on the SAT-9 test:

> Further analysis of test scores on a class-by-class basis indicated that the teachers who were most successful in raising test scores provided a very strong writing program for their students. Schoolwide priorities this year include reading 25 books a year and writing two books, one in English, one in Spanish. We will hold, for the first time, a Young Authors' Night where students will have the opportunity to read their books to parents and to other students. ...a schoolwide

Writing Process is being implemented across all classes and grades. Teachers are required to implement the Writing Process to enable students to write two books. (Oyster Bilingual School, 1999, p. 4)

Here again, we see the positive effects of integrating students' sense of self with active language use and engagement with literacy. A student who sees herself as a Young Author, capable of writing creatively in two or three languages, will read more extensively and write more enthusiastically than one who is confined to a passive role within the classroom.

Another example of a language use activity that clearly promotes identity exploration together with literacy skills development is the writing of critical autobiographies in which culturally- and linguistically-diverse students write about experiences and events in their lives (*e.g.*, Brisk, 1998; Brisk & Harrington, 2000). Brisk points out that in writing the autobiographies, students should examine and discuss their lives from a variety of perspectives: linguistic, cultural, political, economic, sociological, and psychological, and try to understand why things are the way they are. In the course of class discussion exploring various themes, teachers can ask questions to students to probe deeper into issues. Parents can also be interviewed for relevant information and resources (*e.g.*, photographs) (see McCaleb, 1994).

A variation of the critical autobiography is to have pairs of students collaborate to write each others' biography. In some cases, a more fluent speaker of the target language will collaborate with a less fluent student to construct and write the biography of the less fluent student. Publication of the biographies in paper or electronic format (*e.g.*, class web page) can also be pursued for sharing with a wider audience (*e.g.*, parents, other students, etc.).

Students can be encouraged to write in their stronger language and then work with other students or the teacher or a volunteer to produce a bilingual or trilingual text. Edwards documents how this process simultaneously develops writing expertise and affirms bilingual students' identities:

While it is clearly very difficult for language learners to write in English in the early stages, there is no reason why they cannot draft, revise and edit in their first language. This approach allows them to develop their skills while joining in the same activity as their peers. It can also enhance their status in the class. Instead of emphasizing what they cannot do, the focus shifts to their achievements. This is precisely what happened with Julia, a ten year old girl who had recently arrived from Russia. Classmates—and teacher—were fascinated by the appearance of the Cyrillic script on the page and very impressed by her beautiful handwriting. A Russian-speaking member of staff provided a translation so that she was able to share her story with the class. (1998, p. 67)

Once again, the impact of this type of initiative derives from its dual and complementary focus on knowledge generation and identity negotiation. [6]

Even in the case of students who have significant gaps in their formal schooling, writing can play a major role in promoting academic growth. This is vividly documented by Ofelia García (1999) in an article entitled *Educating Latino high school students with little formal schooling* which examined the academic progress of students in Dual Literacy programs in New York City:

And it became obvious that these students, despite their limitations with academic skills, had an ability for poetic metaphor and written expression that exceeded that of many of their schooled adolescent peers. Their images were complex, their metaphors forceful. Standard language did not constrain them, and students felt free to construct their own language to write poetry. (p. 70)

Unfortunately, the structure of most high schools frequently turns off bilingual students' voice and capacity for literary self-expression rather than amplifying it. García concludes:

When students are encouraged to write freely and are made to understand that writing is a system of expression of thoughts and feelings, language flows fluidly and communicates appropriately, even if it contains errors. But…when students are allowed only correct form, their writing becomes limited and fails to communicate. (1999, p. 77)

Guadalupe Valdés (1999) has also documented that middle school students who start with minimal or no English can, within 2 years and with appropriate instruction, "reach the point where they can carry out communicative acts—like explaining, describing, and narrating—in writing" (p. 173). Many bilingual students, however, are never given the opportunity to develop the power of self-expression through writing. Linda Harklau (1999) notes that in an attempt to increase their chances of academic success, bilingual/ELL students are frequently placed in low-track classrooms rather than the more demanding high-track classrooms. However, these low-track classrooms tend to socialize students into language behaviors and practices that limit their access to future educational and occupational opportunities. Whereas high-track students were frequently assigned extensive reading from authentic sources and were asked to synthesize, analyze, and interpret this reading material, low-track students were seldom given these opportunities and rarely engaged in extended reading or writing. According to Harklau, the typical high school program with its compartmentalization of instruction organizes "ESL as one more subject area to be affixed to students' schedules until they can function in mainstream classrooms" (p. 56). The weakness of such a structure is that it provides "little support for students' special linguistic needs outside the confines of ESL classrooms, little recognition of fostering of linguistic and ethnic diversity in the school at large, and a strong tendency to confound bilingualism with academic deficiency (p. 56).

In short, extensive writing in a variety of genres, on a daily basis, should be a central part of ELL students' instructional experience at all grade levels and across curricular areas. Writing articulates self in a way that is cognitively challenging and linguistically enriching. To ensure that bilingual/ELL students have ample opportunities for extended writing (and reading), schools must engage in a language policy process that involves *all* educators as active participants. Ideally, parents and students should also be invited to participate actively in shaping the school's identity along these lines.

Conclusion

A framework for academic language learning has been outlined that views the interactions between educators and students as the most immediate determinant of student success or failure in school. These interactions can be viewed through two lens: the lens of *the teaching-learning relationship* in a narrow sense, represented by the strategies and techniques that teachers use to provide comprehensible input and reading instruction as well as promote content knowledge and cognitive growth. Effective instruction viewed through this lens will maximize students' cognitive engagement.

The second lens is the lens of *identity negotiation* which is represented by the messages communicated to students regarding their identities—who they are in the teacher's eyes and who they are capable of becoming. Perhaps the most important thing that teachers can do to promote students' mastery of academic English is to organize the classroom as a learning community where the voices of all students can be heard. When students feel strong respect and affirmation from their teachers and peers, it generates a powerful sense of belonging to the classroom learning community and motivation to participate fully in the society beyond.

Maximum cognitive engagement and maximum identity investment are realized in instruction that provides opportunities for students to focus on meaning, language, and extensive use of both oral and written language. In this regard, the importance of extensive reading and writing in the development of both academic self-confidence and academic language proficiency cannot be over-emphasized. Reading texts that students can relate to their personal histories or their understanding of the world generates the motivation to keep on reading. Writing narratives and analyses that express their growing sense of self, their identity, allows students to map out where they have come from and where they are going. However, students will also benefit from an explicit focus on developing an awareness of language and its pervasive role in all aspects of our society. This focus on language itself and its intersection with various kinds of power relations in society encourages students to *harvest the language*. In this way, they absorb much more academic language from what they read and are enabled to use this language powerfully and effectively in their own speaking and writing.

The following two chapters elaborate on these themes in the context of bilingual education and educational restructuring. These chapters highlight crucial aspects of the instructional environment that have not been considered in depth in this chapter; for example, the role of L1 instruction in promoting L2 literacy development, and the importance of establishing strong partnerships to encourage culturally-diverse parents to participate actively in their children's education.

Endnotes to Chapter 5

1. Handscombe and Becker (1994) provide a telling example of the powerful messages conveyed to bilingual students when they are encouraged to use their L1 and share their prior knowledge with the teacher and other students. Taraneh was a student of Iranian background in a culturally diverse grade 3/4 class in the Metropolitan Toronto area taught by Nancy Becker. She had been in Canada for 10 months but had been educated prior to this through Urdu in Pakistan:

     While Tareneh's previous schooling had been in Urdu, her parents had taught her to read and write in Farsi/Persian and Nancy encouraged her to bring a book to school in what Tareneh always referred to as "my language" so that she could hear Tareneh read it. Tareneh was delighted to do this and chose to bring a book about a stuffed Panda. The book had appealing drawings to help the monolingual English users with the meaning, while Tareneh rattled her way fluently through the text. The girls in the class were particularly impressed with her skill at deciphering the impossible-looking squiggles on the pages. Their demonstrated interest did much to bolster Tareneh's self-esteem. The very next week, when Nancy asked if she would like to bring another book in Farsi, she arrived with one in English, making it clear that she knew what she needed to learn at this moment and would take all the help she could get, especially now that everyone knew how literate she really was. (1994, pp. 25-26)

It is particularly important to communicate strong reinforcing and welcoming messages to refugee children who may have survived considerable trauma prior to arriving in North America (see Criddle & Mam, 1987, and Kaprielian-Churchill & Churchill, 1994, for moving accounts of refugees' struggle for survival in their homeland and the challenges they face trying to reestablish their lives and identities in a new society).

2. Three useful resources for fascinating information about language are John Edwards' (1994) book *Multilingualism*, David Crystal's (1987) *Cambridge Encyclopedia of Language*, and Norah McWilliam's (1998) *What's in a Word*. Among the facts included in Crystal's volume are the following:

- There are about 5,000 languages co-existing in fewer than 200 countries around the world. This explains why most countries in the world are multilingual.

- One of the most multilingual people ever to have lived was Cardinal Giuseppe Mezzofanti who lived between 1774 and 1849 and was the librarian at the Vatican. The eminent Cardinal could speak 50 languages, understand 70 and translate 114!

- Chinese has the most mother tongue speakers (1,000 million), English comes next with 350 million, and then Spanish with 250 million. Although fewer in mother tongue speakers, English is estimated to exceed Chinese in terms of total number of speakers (1400 million) (Edwards, 1994).

Discussion of "fun facts" such as these can stimulate a variety of language awareness activities in the classroom. For example, students could research how many languages are spoken and understood by students in the class (these could then be graphed by languages); which student in the class speaks the most languages (give student a certificate or some form of recognition); what are the major countries in which Chinese, English, and Spanish are spoken (identify on a world map and connect with voyages of discovery/colonization etc.). In other words, the facts are not inert but rather act as catalysts for further student investigation.

3. Two potentially useful web-based resources that can facilitate ELL students, access to the curriculum and support the transfer of L1 writing expertise to L2 writing are: http://www.babylon.com and http://world.altavista.com. The Altavista site uses "Babel Fish" as a translator to translate text across a variety of languages. Babylon, on the other hand, does not do extended translations but rather provides either on-line or downloaded access to dictionaries in 12 languages (including Spanish, Chinese, and Japanese). Students can highlight a word in an English text and get either a pop-up translation in their L1 or an English dictionary definition.

The Babel Fish site provides machine translation across 7 languages (English, French, German, Italian, Portuguese, Russian, Spanish). Using Babel Fish (or some other computer translation service or program), a recently-arrived Spanish L1 student could write a story or autobiography in Spanish and the teacher could cut and paste her writing into Babel Fish and receive an English translation. The translation will be rough (as machine translations tend to be) but it will usually be sufficient to provide Ïthe teacher with the sense of what the student is trying to express. Also, teachers and students can have some fun editing the computerese variety of English (or other languages) into coherent prose. This classroom-edited version provides the ELL student with a self-generated text in English to accompany her Spanish L1 text. It also permits her to share her experiences and insights with her teacher and classmates.

To illustrate how Babel Fish works, consider a passage written in Spanish from the book *El Canto de las Palomas* written by Juan Felipe Herrera and included in the Scott Foresman *Lectura* Spanish Reading Program (grade 3):

> Mi mamá me decía esto
> Cuando teníamos que mudarnos a otro campo de labor.
> Mi mamá Lucha, mi papá Felipe y yo.
> Divisaba a los campesinos trabajando en los files
> Mientras mi papá manejaba nuestra vieja troca del Army
> Por los caminos olvidados de California.(Lectura Scott Foresman, Grade 3,
> Volume 2, Teacher's Guide, p. 138).

Babel Fish has some difficulty rendering this passage into English, as the following attempt at translation shows:

> My mother said this to me
> When we had to change us to another field of work.
> My mother Fight, my papa Felipe and I.
> She descried to the farmers working in you case out them.
> While my papa handled our old troca of the Army
> By the ways forgotten California.

Although garbled, this "translation" provides enough entry into the passage to enable students with varying degrees of Spanish-English bilingualism to brainstorm about the correct meaning and to "teach" the computer "proper English". For example, Spanish-speakers will know immediately why the computer translated the mother's name as "Fight" and will likely be amused at the computer's "misunderstanding". Interesting discussions might also ensue regarding the computer's inability to translate *troca* into *truck*. If the word in the text had been camión rather than the "borrowed" form *troca*, the computer would have had no difficulty getting the meaning.

The last phrase *By the ways forgotten California* would likely also stimulate some creative brainstorming about what the computer is trying to say. Students might be encouraged to don their linguistic detective cloaks and explore the different meanings of the word *way* or *ways* and the many idiomatic and figurative uses of the term.

This kind of language exploration (of L1 and L2) can increase students' awareness of language and their understanding of the evolution of their own language. It also shows students the value of their bilingualism since students who have more developed bilingual and biliteracy abilities have a clear advantage in this kind of classroom activity.

The "official" translation of the text (from the *Lectura* Teacher's Manual [p. 138]) is provided below. Once again, where polished translations such as this exist for texts submitted to Babel Fish, students can be encouraged to discuss in groups or brainstorm as a whole class what makes the professional translation a coherent and elegant piece of writing (as compared to Babel Fish's stumbling effort or possibly their own initial attempts). They might also question the accuracy of "official" translations (such as the way *trabajando en los files* is rendered in the English version) and come to understand that literal translations are not always possible or most effective in rendering the author's meaning.

> My mother would tell me this
> when we had to move on to another labor camp.
> My mother Lucha, my father Felipe, and me.
> I would gaze across the fields at the *campesinos*—
> the farmworkers—as my father drove our old army truck
> through the backroads of California.

The same translation engine operates from the *SYSTRAN* web site but an alternative can be found at the *Transparent Language* site (www.transparentlanguage.com/ets). As the following example shows, it has similar difficulties to Bablefish/SYSTRAN in translating the Spanish text above:

> My mom told me this.
> When we had to move us to another field of work.
> My mom Fights, my dad Felipe and I.
> He made out the peasants working in the files.
> While my dad handled our old one he exchanges of the Army
> By the roads forgot of California

A wide-range of technology resources relevant to bilingual education (including other translation resources) can be found in Ana Bishop's excellent article *Technology trends and their potential for bilingual education* (National Clearinghouse for Bilingual Education, No. 7, September 2000. www.ncbe.gwu.edu).

4. Two web sites that might be useful to explore as a means of expanding students' language awareness are:

The Human Languages Page (http://www.ilovelanguages.com/), a comprehensive catalogue of language-related Internet resources with more than 1900 links to related sites (including the Altavista Babel Fish site. These sites offer online language lessons, translating dictionaries, literature, translation services, software, language schools, or information on particular languages.

Languages Made Clear (http://www.languagesmadeclear.cjb.net) offers information about English, Spanish, French, German, Dutch, Portuguese, Italian, and Esperanto languages. Users can find information about and practice Grammar, Vocabulary and Pronunciation in these languages. The site includes lists of vocabulary on specific topics (*e.g.,* Animals, Education, etc.) that permit words in different languages to be compared. This might be a useful source for language exploration activities focused on cognate relationships across languages.

A number of web sites that can support ELL students' vocabulary expansion have been identified by Christine Meloni in an article in *TESOL Matters* (October/November, 2000, 10:4, p. 14): These are summarized below:

Wordwizard (http://www.wordwizard.com/) permits users to peruse pages on word origins, slang, insults, and quotations as well as study vocabulary used in both prose and poetry.

A.Word.A.Day (http://www.wordsmith.org/awad/index.html) offers a new word everyday together with its pronunciation, meaning, and examples of use.

Cool Word of the Day (http://www.edu.yorku.ca/wotd) offers a variety of word games to develop English vocabulary.

The Monthly Idiom (http://www.comenius.com/idioms) presents a new idiom every month together with an archive of more than 60 idioms.

Common Errors in English (http://www.wsu.edu/~brians/errors/index. html) clarifies common errors that learners of English frequently make.

Words in the News (http://www/bbc/co.uk/worldservice/learningenglish/ words) focuses on the language used in recent British Broadcasting Corporation news reports.

English Vocabulary (http://xahlee.org/PageTwo_dir/Vocabulary_dir/vocabulary.html) organizes words in various categories such as "SAT Words," "Slang" etc.

Vocabulary Quizzes (http://www.aitech.ac.jp/~iteslj/quizzes/vocabulary. html) is one of a number of useful pages available at the TESL Internet Journal.

ESL Slang Page (http://www.eslcafe.com/slang) is offered as part of Dave's ESL Café which also offers a wealth of other useful resources. For example, there is also an idiom page and a phrasal verb page at (http://www.eslcafe. com/idioms) and (http://www. eslcafe.com/pv) respectively.

5. One way to involve students actively in demystifying the construction and social functions of standardized tests is to provide opportunities for them, working in groups, to construct their own tests on topics with which they are familiar or on which they have carried out research. For example, the teacher might explain how multiple-choice items are constructed (*e.g.,* the role of distractors) and groups might construct a set of items on topics such as baseball, popular music, television programs, popular slang etc., and administer their items to the other groups. Alternatively, each group might research aspects of a particular topic (*e.g.,* the American Civil War, the European arrival in North America, endangered species, etc.) and construct items based on their research. Groups could also construct items that focus on the unit of study that has just been completed.

Within this conception, standardized tests are viewed as one particular genre of language. Students should be familiar with the conventions of this genre if their academic worth is to be recognized. In generating multiple-choice items, students are developing language awareness in the context of a highly challenging (but engaging) cognitive activity. I believe that this strategy would develop "test-taking skills" (and a lot more) far more effectively than current drill and practice approaches.

6. Another set of examples of language use in the context of transformative pedagogy comes from the computer-mediated sister class projects documented by Brown (1999), Cummins and Sayers (1995) and Brown, Figueroa, Sayers, and Cummins (1998). Brown, for example, describes a project dubbed "New Places" by the participating classes in which students who had moved described their experiences. Students who hadn't moved interviewed peers at their school about how they were received in their new schools and communities. Students from a dozen countries were involved in this project, including those who had moved from rural China to Beijing, African Americans who had moved from the south to the north within the United States, and immigrant students who had moved from many countries to the United States. Students investigated what motivates migration and how people from different cultural, racial, and linguistic backgrounds were received by their new communities. Brown concludes:

> One of the outcomes of this project was that together the students analyzed the linguistic, cultural, and institutional barriers at their schools and drew up guidelines for teachers and students about how to make their schools better places for newcomers. The idea that collaborative problem solving might make the world a better place motivates much online learning. (1999, p. 312)

Chapter 6
Bilingual Education: What Does the Research Say?

As we have seen, both opponents and advocates of bilingual education in the United States justify their positions in terms of what is in the best interests of children. Advocates argue that bilingual education can help make instruction comprehensible for English language learners and facilitate parental participation in their children's education. Opponents, by contrast, have suggested that bilingual education reduces children's exposure to English, thereby limiting their academic opportunities. These claims are frequently clothed in vivid rhetoric: for example, the claim by *U.S. English* that bilingual education constitutes child abuse or Schlesinger's (1991) suggestion that "bilingualism shuts doors" whereas "monolingual education opens doors to the larger world."

In this chapter, these opposing claims are examined in relation to the research evidence. An extensive body of research on bilingualism and bilingual education exists within the United States. When this research is combined with the research carried out worldwide for more than 70 years on these issues, the evidence is truly monumental. As far back as 1963, entire volumes were being filled with reviews of the research on bilingualism (*e.g.,* Vildomec, 1963).

Thus, I have always been puzzled by the frequent lament from policy-makers that "research on bilingual education is sparse" or that "the research evidence is conflicting and therefore no conclusions regarding the efficacy of bilingual education can be drawn." What has been missing from the policy debate is any attempt to think theoretically about the research evidence. By *theoretical thinking* I mean articulating predictions based on the opposing claims and evaluating these predictions in relation to the research evidence. For example, what predictions can be derived from the opposing *linguistic mismatch* and *maximum exposure* hypotheses and how do these predictions stack up against the research evidence?

In order to evaluate what the research evidence on bilingual education is saying, it is necessary first to examine the relationship between theory, research, and policy decisions. I suggest that when the role of theory is understood, there is overwhelming consistency in the research on bilingualism and bilingual education. Following this, a definition of bilingual education is offered and the different types of bilingual programs that have been implemented in various parts of the world are described. The third section makes explicit the theoretical positions underlying the claims of opponents and advocates of bilingual education in the United States and then predictions derived from these theoretical positions are examined, first in relation to recent large-scale studies carried out in the United States, and then in relation to the international research on bilingual education.

Theory, Research, and Policy

A major reason why many policy-makers and educators in the United States regard the research basis for bilingual education as inadequate is that they have failed to realize that data or "facts" from bilingual programs (or any other programs) become interpretable for policy purposes only within the context of a coherent theory. It is the *theory* rather than the individual research findings that permits the generation of predictions about program outcomes under different conditions. Research findings themselves cannot be *directly* applied across contexts. For example, the fact that kindergarten and grade 1 Punjabi-background students in a Punjabi-English bilingual program in Bradford, England, learned English just as successfully as a control group in a traditional English-only program (Rees, 1981), tells us very little about what might happen in the case of Latino/Latina students in the United States.

Yet when this pattern is repeated across a wide range of situations, it suggests that some stable underlying principle is at work. This principle can then be formally stated as a theoretical proposition or hypothesis from which predictions can be derived and tested. For example, the *linguistic mismatch* hypothesis would predict that in every situation where there is a switch between home language and school language, students will encounter academic difficulties. The *maximum exposure* hypothesis would predict that any form of bilingual education that reduces the amount of instructional time through the medium of English will result in academic difficulties in English. These predictions can be tested against the research evidence.

Similarly, if we observe that across a wide variety of social, political, and linguistic contexts, instruction through a minority language for part or all of the school day does not result in any long-term academic loss in the majority language, it suggests that some theoretical principle is operating that can account for the consistency of findings despite wide variation in contexts. This is, in fact, what the research data clearly show and the underlying principle has been termed the *linguistic interdependence* principle (Cummins, 1981a, 1984). I suggest in this chapter that it provides a reliable, albeit partial, basis for policy decisions regarding the education of bilingual students. In short, although research findings cannot be applied directly across contexts, the accumulation of research findings does have relevance for policy. This relevance is achieved by means of the integration of the findings within a coherent theory from which predictions regarding program outcomes under different conditions can be generated. In contrast to research findings, theories are almost by definition applicable across contexts. The validity of any theoretical principle is assessed precisely by how well it can account for the research findings in a variety of contexts. If a theory cannot account for a particular set of research findings, then it is an inadequate or incomplete theory. Thus, if there is counter-evidence to predictions derived from the linguistic mismatch, maximum exposure, or interdependence hypotheses, then they must be rejected as inadequate theoretical principles to explain the research data.

Types of Bilingual Education Programs

The term *bilingual education* usually refers to the use of two (or more) languages of instruction at some point in the student's school career. In other words, it is generally defined in terms of the *means* through which particular educational goals are achieved. When used in this sense, proficiency in two languages is not necessarily a goal of bilingual education. For example, the most common form of bilingual education in the United States, transitional bilingual education, aims only to promote students' proficiency in English. When it is assumed that students have attained sufficient proficiency in the school language to follow instruction in that language, home language instruction is discontinued.

However, the term *bilingual education* is sometimes defined in relation to *goals*, to refer to educational programs that are designed to promote bilingual proficiency among students. When used in this broader sense, bilingual education may entail instruction primarily or exclusively through only one language, as for example, when instruction is delivered through a minority language in order to provide students with the maximum opportunity to learn that language. Second language immersion programs of this type are implemented widely in certain countries.

For example, French immersion programs have operated across Canada for almost 40 years and currently involve approximately 300,000 students. There are three broad types of French immersion program: *early*, starting usually in Kindergarten with 100% French until English is introduced in grades 2, 3 or 4; usually about half the time is spent through each language by grade 5 or 6; *middle*, starting in grades 4 or 5 with between 50% and 100% French initially; and *late*, starting in grade 7 or 8 with 50% to 100% French initially. The early immersion program is the most common variant and countless evaluations have shown that students make good progress in acquiring French fluency and literacy at no cost to their English (L1) academic skills despite considerably less instructional time through English (Lambert & Tucker, 1972; Swain & Lapkin, 1982).

Dual language programs (sometimes called *two-way bilingual programs*) implemented in the United States are modeled after the early French immersion programs but involve students from English home backgrounds together with students from another language background (*e.g.,* Spanish, Korean, Chinese, etc.). There are two major patterns of language allocation in dual language programs:

- 90/10 programs deliver approximately 90% of the instruction initially through the minority language with a gradual transition to equal use of the two languages in the later grades of elementary school. English reading is usually introduced in grade 3.

- 50/50 programs have equal use of each language from grade 1-6 (sometimes kindergarten is conducted predominantly through the minority language). Reading is usually introduced in both languages in grade 1. Sometimes the alternation of languages takes place on a morning/afternoon basis and sometimes on an alternate day basis. This model also allows for a team teaching approach where the English part of the program is taught by a monolingual English teacher and the minority language part by a bilingual teacher. However, often the same bilingual teacher teaches both parts of the program.

Typologies of bilingual education programs have generated a myriad of different types depending on the combination of program goals, status of the student group (*e.g.,* dominant/subordinated, majority/minority etc.), proportion of instructional time through each language, and sociolinguistic and sociopolitical situation in the immediate community and wider society (see Skutnabb-Kangas, 1984, for a review). [1] For our purposes, it is sufficient to distinguish five broad types based on the population groups the program is intended to serve. Four of these program types are intended primarily for minority or subordinated group students while the fifth is intended for majority or dominant group students.

Type I programs involve the use of indigenous or Native languages as mediums of instruction; examples are the various Native language bilingual programs in the U.S. (*e.g.,* McCarty, 1997) and Maori bilingual or immersion programs in New Zealand (Bishop & Glynn, 1999). The indigenous group has usually been conquered or colonized at some time in the past and the bilingual programs are often aimed at revival or revitalization of languages that have become endangered.

Type II programs involve the use of a *national minority language* which sometimes has official language status in the society. Examples are the use of Gaelic in Ireland and Scotland, and Welsh in Wales as well as Basque and Catalan in Spain. The rights to L1 instruction for official language minorities (both French and English) in Canada constitute another example. Many other examples exist across the world, from China and Singapore in Asia to a variety of programs in Africa and other continents (Cummins & Corson, 1997; see Skutnabb-Kangas, 2000 and Skutnabb-Kangas & Phillipson, 1994, for discussion of linguistic human rights related to bilingual education around the globe). The minority language or languages involved usually have long-term status in the society and often some degree of official recognition. Maintenance or revitalization of these languages is usually the primary goal of such programs. Some programs could be classified as either Type I or Type II; for example, the Basques are usually regarded as the indigenous population of the northern parts of the Iberian peninsula and thus programs aimed at revitalization of Basque could also be classified as Type I.

Type III programs involve *international minority languages* that are the languages of relatively recent immigrants to a host country. Many of the bilingual programs in countries such as the United States, The Netherlands, Australia, or Sweden fall into this category. Most of these are transitional programs designed to facilitate students' academic progress. In some situations, Type II and Type III programs merge into one another, as in the case of some Spanish-English bilingual programs in the United States that may serve both long-term Spanish-speaking groups as well as more recent immigrant groups.

Type IV programs serve children who are deaf or hard-of-hearing Bilingual/bicultural programs for Deaf children are a relatively recent phenomenon. This is not surprising in view of the fact that the manual languages of the Deaf were recognized by linguists (and somewhat later by policy makers) as genuine languages only in the 1970s. Bilingual/bicultural programs involving American Sign Language (ASL) started in North America only in the early 1990s (Gibson *et al.*, 1997). Scandinavian countries were more advanced in implementing bilingual/bicultural programs for Deaf students (Mahshie, 1995). However, bilingual/bicultural programs for Deaf children are still in their infancy in most places around the world.

Type V programs are intended for dominant or majority group students and aim to develop bilingual and biliteracy skills among such students. French immersion programs in Canada and dual language programs in the United States are examples of Type V. Dual language programs also fall into the category of Type II or Type III since they also serve linguistic minority students. The European Schools model (Beardsmore, 1993; Skutnabb-Kangas, 1995) which involves instruction through four languages at various points in the students' school career also qualifies as Type V, as do Swedish immersion programs for Finnish students in Finland (Buss & Laurén, 1995).

Contrary to the impression one might get from the current U.S. debate on the issue, bilingual programs are not a recent innovation. In fact, bilingual education was common in Greek and Roman times (Lewis, 1976) as well as in the United States prior to the first world war (Kloss, 1977; Schlossman, 1983). Currently some form of bilingual education is implemented in the vast majority of countries around the world (Fishman, 1976). [2] In the next section, theoretical positions underlying the opposing claims related to bilingual education in the United States are outlined.

Theory Underlying Opposition to Bilingual Education

Three major psychoeducational claims have been articulated to argue against bilingual education: (a) the claim that "time on task"(or "maximum exposure") is the major variable underlying language learning and hence immersion in English is the most effective means to ensure the learning of English; (b) the claim that under these conditions of immersion, language minority students will quickly (within 1–2 years) pick up sufficient English to survive academically without further special support; (c) the claim that English immersion should start as early as possible in the student's school career since younger children are better language learners than older children. Examples of each of these claims are presented below.

Rosalie Pedalino Porter (1990) clearly articulates the "time-on-task" principle in stating:

> My personal experience and professional investigations together impel me to conclude that the two overriding conditions that promote the best learning of a second language are (1) starting at an early age, say at five, and (2) having as much exposure and carefully planned instruction in the language as possible. Effective time on task—the amount of time spent learning—is, as educators know, the single greatest predictor of educational achievement; this is at least as true, if not more so, for low-socioeconomic-level, limited-English students. Children learn what they are taught, and if they are taught mainly in Spanish for several years, their Spanish-language skills will be far better than their English-language ones. (1990, pp. 63-64)

Gary Imhoff (1990) in outlining the U.S. English position on bilingual education suggests that while native language instruction might be acceptable "for the first few months" (p. 51), the educational rationale for bilingual education beyond this initial adjustment period is seriously deficient. Especially problematic is the rejection by bilingual education advocates of the "time on task" principle:

> Bilingual-education advocates also tend to dismiss the idea that practice makes perfect, expressed in educational terms as "time on task," and hold instead that non-English-speaking students will learn English better if less time is spent teaching it. (1990, p. 51)

Nathan Glazer (Glazer & Cummins, 1985) has articulated his position in regard to teaching methodology and length of time required to develop English proficiency in responding to questions posed by the editors of the journal *Equity and Choice*:

> all our experience shows that the most extended and steady exposure to the spoken language is the best way of learning any language. …How long? It depends. But one year of intensive immersion seems to be enough to permit most children to transfer to English-language classes. (1985, p. 48)

These claims are in direct contrast to those made by academic advocates of bilingual education, as outlined below.

Theory Proposed by Bilingual Education Advocates

It is important first to highlight the fact that most bilingual education theorists have distanced themselves from the usual rationale for bilingual programs, namely the *linguistic mismatch* hypothesis, outlined earlier. While the claim that children cannot learn through a language they do not understand has been persuasive to many policy-makers and educators (and, in fact, underlies the quick-exit transitional focus of most U.S. bilingual education), it is seriously flawed. It fails to account either for the success of English background children in Canadian French immersion or in U.S. dual language programs or the fact that, under certain conditions, English language learners can succeed academically in English-only programs (see Cummins, 1984).

Related to the rejection of the linguistic mismatch hypothesis by bilingual education advocates is the fact that bilingual education theory does not assign a central role to the language of initial reading instruction. As noted in Chapter 4, initial reading instruction in Spanish is a reasonable strategy in many situations in Spanish-English bilingual programs due to the relatively consistent sound-symbol relationship in Spanish compared to English and the fact that it is the language most Spanish-speaking students know best on entry to school. However, bilingual and ELL students *can* acquire decoding skills through a second language in all-English contexts and several 50/50 dual language programs that introduce reading in Spanish and English simultaneously or in quick succession have been highly successful (*e.g.,* Oyster Bilingual School in Washington DC).

Academic advocates of bilingual education have consistently rejected compensatory (or transitional) bilingual programs; instead, they have argued for enrichment (or two-way) bilingual programs that promote biliteracy for all children, regardless of language background (*e.g.,* Collier, 1995; Fishman, 1976; Lambert, 1975; Swain, 1979). They suggest that reinforcing children's conceptual base in their L1 throughout elementary school (and beyond) will provide a foundation for long-term growth in English academic skills. Based on the time periods required to catch up academically with English L1 peers, researchers have also cautioned that we should not expect bilingual children to approach grade norms in English academic skills before the later grades of elementary school.

The two theoretical principles proposed in support of bilingual education have been termed the *additive bilingualism enrichment principle* and the *interdependence or common underlying proficiency principle*. Each will be considered in turn.

The Positive Effects of Additive Bilingualism

There are close to 150 empirical studies carried out during the past 30 or so years that have reported a positive association between additive bilingualism and students' linguistic, cognitive, or academic growth. The most consistent findings among these research studies are that bilinguals show more developed awareness of the structure and functions of language itself (metalinguistic abilities) and that they have advantages in learning additional languages. The term *additive bilingualism* refers to the form of bilingualism that results when students add a second language to their intellectual tool-kit while continuing to develop conceptually and academically in their first language.

This pattern of findings suggests that the proficiency attained by bilingual students in their two languages may exert important influences on their academic and intellectual development. Continued development of both languages into literate domains (additive bilingualism) appears to be a precondition for enhanced cognitive, linguistic, and academic growth. Some illustrative studies focusing on the effects of bilingualism on metalinguistic abilities and on the learning of additional languages are considered below.

Bilingualism and Metalinguistic Abilities. The findings of a series of Australian studies (Ricciardelli, 1992, 1993) illustrate the types of advantage that bilingual information processing might confer on the developing child. Ricciardelli conducted two studies to investigate the influence of bilingualism on children's cognitive abilities and creativity. The first involved 57 Italian-English bilingual and 55 English monolingual children who were aged 5 or 6 at the time of the study. This study found that children who were proficient in both Italian and English performed significantly better than children who were proficient in English only (the high English monolingual group) and those bilinguals who were proficient in English but less proficient in Italian, on several measures reflecting creative thinking (the Torrance Fluency and Imagination measures), metalinguistic awareness (Word Order Correction), and verbal and non-verbal abilities.

The second study was conducted in Rome with 35 Italian-English bilingual and 35 Italian monolingual 5 and 6 year-old children. Again, those children who were proficiently bilingual in Italian and English performed significantly better than the other groups on the Torrance Fluency and Imagination measures as well as on Word Order Correction and Word Reading.

Another series of seven studies, carried out between 1978 and 1987 in a totally different socio-cultural context (Orissa, India), shows a consistent pattern of results. Mohanty (1994) studied large numbers of monolingual and bilingual Kond tribal children who had varying degrees of contact with the dominant language of Orissa, namely Oriya. The monolingual children came from areas where the original Kui language of the Konds had given way to Oriya monolingualism as a result of contact with speakers of the dominant language. In other areas, a relatively stable form of Kui-Oriya bilingualism exists where Kui is used predominantly in children's homes but contact with Oriya through peers and others in the neighborhood results in most children having a considerable degree of bilingualism by the time they start school, which is conducted through the medium of Oriya. Despite the differences in language use, the Konds are relatively homogenous with respect to Kond identity, socioeconomic status, and cultural characteristics. The context thus provides a unique opportunity to study the impact of bilingualism in relative isolation from the social, political and economic factors which frequently confound comparisons between monolingual and bilingual groups.

Mohanty's studies show a clear positive relationship between bilingualism and cognitive performance including measures of metalinguistic ability. He suggests that bilinguals' awareness of language and their cognitive strategies are enhanced as a result of the challenging communicative environment in which their bilingual abilities have developed.

Bialystok (1987a, 1987b, 1988) has also carried out a series of studies that suggest a positive influence of bilingualism on children's metalinguistic awareness. The advantages are more evident for bilinguals who are more fully fluent in their two languages. She suggests that "the level of bilingualism is decisive in determining the effect it will have on development" (1988:567).

The cognitive benefits of bilingualism are also supported by research carried out in the Basque country. Lasagabaster (1998) investigated a trilingual school situation (Basque, Spanish, English). Participants were 126 grade 5 and 126 grade 8 students. The grade 5 students were in their second year of studying English and the grade 8 students were in their third year. Students' academic knowledge of Basque, Spanish, and English was assessed together with a nonverbal ability test (Raven's Progressive Matrices) as a control measure and a test of metalinguistic abilities as dependent variable. Groups were formed based on median splits carried out on the three language measures (Basque, Spanish, English) and comparisons made between those "highly competent" (*i.e.,* above the median) in three languages, those highly competent in two languages, those highly competent in one language, and those below the median in all three languages.

Lasagabaster reported that performance on the metalinguistic ability test was directly related to the levels of bilingualism/trilingualism in the order outlined above. Those above the median in three languages performed significantly better than all other groups with those below the median in all three languages demonstrating less well-developed metalinguistic abilities than the other three groups. Although in the predicted direction, differences were not significant between those above the median in two languages as compared to those above the median in just one, possibly, as Lasagabaster suggests, because those who had become highly proficient in three languages would have been the ones who might have made the differences between the other two groups significant. The differences between the groups could not be attributed to nonverbal ability or socioeconomic or sociocultural status.

A variety of explanations have been suggested to account for the observed superiority of bilingual children on certain types of cognitive and linguistic measures: for example, the fact that bilinguals have two words for the same idea or object and two ways of expressing the same thought may lead them to "objectify" or become more aware of their linguistic operations, as suggested by Vygotsky (1962) (see Cummins, 1976; Diaz & Klinger, 1991; and Lambert & Tucker, 1972, for reviews). [3]

In general, it is not surprising that bilingual children should be more adept at certain aspects of linguistic processing. In gaining control over two language systems, the bilingual child has had to decipher much more language input than the monolingual child who has been exposed to only one language system. Thus, the bilingual child has had considerably more practice in analyzing meanings than the monolingual child.

The evidence is not conclusive as to whether this linguistic advantage transfers to more general cognitive skills; McLaughlin's review of the literature, for example, concludes that:

> It seems clear that the child who has mastered two languages has a linguistic advantage over the monolingual child. Bilingual children become aware that there are two ways of saying the same thing. But does this sensitivity to the lexical and formal aspects of language generalize to cognitive functioning? There is no conclusive answer to this question—mainly because it has proven so difficult to apply the

necessary controls in research (1984, p. 44).

An important characteristic of the bilingual children in the more recent studies (conducted since the early 1960's) is that, for the most part, they were developing what has been termed an *additive* form of bilingualism (Lambert, 1975); in other words, they were adding a second language to their repertory of skills at no cost to the development of their first language. Consequently, these children were in the process of attaining a relatively high level of both fluency and literacy in their two languages. [4] The children in these studies tended to come either from dominant language groups whose L1 was strongly reinforced in the society (*e.g.,* English-speakers in dual language or second language immersion programs) or from minority groups whose L1 was reinforced by bilingual programs in the school. Bilingual children who lack this educational support for literacy development in L1 frequently develop a subtractive form of bilingualism in which L1 skills are replaced or "subtracted" by L2 (Wong Fillmore, 1991a). [5]

Enhancement of Third Language Learning. Two studies carried out in Canada suggest that development of bilingual students' L1 academic proficiency can positively influence the learning of additional languages. Both studies were conducted in a large Metropolitan Toronto school board that offers French as a second language for 20 minutes a day from grades 1 through 4 followed by the option of a French-English bilingual program (50% English, 50% French) from grades 5 through 8. Students also have the option of participating in a heritage language program involving the teaching of languages other than English or French from Kindergarten through Grade 8.

The first study (Bild & Swain, 1989) reported that Grade 8 students from heritage language backgrounds who were enrolled in the French-English bilingual program performed better than an English-background group in the same program on a variety of grammatical measures of French but not on measures of lexical knowledge. A significant positive correlation between the number of years in heritage language classes and indices of French proficiency was also noted in this study.

The second study (Swain & Lapkin, 1991; Swain, Rowen and Hart, 1991) involved more than 300 grade 8 students in the same bilingual program. Swain *et al.* compared four groups of students on various measures of French proficiency: (1) those who had no knowledge of a heritage language (HL); (2) those with some knowledge but no literacy skills in the HL; (3) those with HL literacy skills but who mentioned no active use of HL literacy; and finally, (4) those who understood and used the HL in the written mode. The first group had parents with higher educational and occupational status than the other three groups who did not differ in this regard.

Highly significant differences in favor of those students with HL literacy skills (groups 3 and 4) were found on both written and oral measures of French. These differences are particularly noteworthy in view of the fact that these students came from considerably lower socio-economic backgrounds than students who spoke English as their first language. There was also a trend for students from Romance language backgrounds to perform better in oral aspects of French but the effect of this variable was much less than the effect of literacy in the heritage language. The authors conclude that there is transfer of knowledge and learning processes across languages and development of L1 literacy entails concrete benefits for students' acquisition of subsequent languages.

These two studies taken together suggest that trilingualism is a feasible educational goal and that the development of literacy in the minority language spoken in the home facilitates the learning of a third language in school.

Two studies carried out in Spain that focused on the learning of English within Basque/Spanish or Catalan/Spanish bilingual programs also found evidence that literacy in two languages facilitates the acquisition of a third language (Cenoz & Valencia, 1994; Sanz, 2000). Cenoz and Valencia reported that, in the Basque Country, students in Basque-medium schools who were becoming bilingual and biliterate in Basque and Spanish performed significantly better than monolingual Spanish students in Spanish-medium schools on measures of English. Sanz reported a similar pattern in Catalonia. She concludes:

> These results replicate those of Cenoz and Valencia (1994). As in the case of the Basque immersion program, students in the Catalan immersion program showed an advantage as L3 learners compared with students in a monolingual school. Catalan bilingualism, like Basque bilingualism, explains superior English achievement independently from other variables. Another commonality between Cenoz and Valencia's results and those presented in here is the significant role that both motivation and exposure play as factors predicting L3 proficiency. ...results from the present study [show that] immersion programs in the minority language, whether in the Basque Country or in Catalonia, produce more efficient L3 learners. (2000: 33-34)

Sanz relates the advantage of literate bilinguals in learning a third language to their greater metalinguistic awareness:

> The weak interface position in L2 acquisition theory (Ellis, 1994) proposes that, while explicit knowledge cannot be transformed into implicit knowledge of the L2, it can help in the acquisition process by acting as an advance organizer, focusing learners' attention on the relevant features of the language. That is, heightened metalinguistic awareness, which results from exposure to literacy in two languages, gives bilinguals the capacity to focus on form and pay attention to the relevant features of the input. (2000: 36)

The pattern of research findings suggests that the level of proficiency attained by bilingual students in their two languages may be an important influence on their academic and intellectual development (Cummins, 1976; 1981a). Specifically, there may be threshold levels of proficiency in both languages that students must attain in order to participate effectively in instruction and avoid falling behind academically and a second, higher, threshold necessary to reap the linguistic and intellectual benefits of bilingualism and biliteracy.

Diaz (1985; Diaz & Klinger, 1991) has questioned the threshold hypothesis on the grounds that the effects of bilingualism on cognitive abilities in his data were stronger for children of relatively low L2 proficiency (non-balanced bilinguals). This suggests that the positive effects are related to the initial struggles and experiences of the beginning second-language learner. This interpretation does not appear to be incompatible with the threshold hypothesis since the major point of this hypothesis is that for positive effects to manifest themselves, children must be in an additive situation where both languages are developing. If beginning L2 learners do not continue to develop both their languages, any initial positive effects are likely to be counteracted by the negative consequences of subtractive bilingualism. Thus, positive effects will not be sustained unless high levels of bilingual proficiency are attained (see Figure 6.1).

In summary, the research strongly suggests that, rather than "shutting doors" as Schlesinger (1991) claimed, literacy in two languages enhances the intellectual and academic resources of bilingual students. At an instructional level, we should be asking how we can build on this potential advantage in the classroom by focusing students' attention on language and helping them become more adept at manipulating language in abstract academic situations.

Figure 6.1   EFFECTS OF BILINGUALISM

One wheel (one language) can get you places…

So can a big wheel and a little wheel…

However, when your wheels are nicely balanced and fully inflated you'll go farther…

Provided, of course, the people who made the wheels knew what they were doing.

The Role of First and Second Language Interdependence in Explaining the Outcomes of Bilingual Programs

A major concern of parents and policy-makers in contexts where bilingual programs have been implemented is that spending instructional time through a minority language will result in lower achievement in the majority language. The majority or dominant language is usually the language associated with power and status in the society and thus it is not surprising that parents and policy-makers are concerned that children's development in this language should not suffer as a result of bilingual education. The argument proposed by opponents of bilingual education that deficiencies in English should be remediated by intensive instruction in English appears intuitively logical at first sight. The alternative argument that some initial instruction in L1 will be more effective than total instruction in English in promoting English skills appears to invoke a "less equals more" type of logic that is unlikely to convince skeptics.

However, when empirical evidence rather than "common sense" is made the criterion for evaluating the merits of these two positions, it becomes very clear that the maximum exposure or time-on-task claim is seriously flawed. The research data from contexts around the world show clearly that students in bilingual education programs develop academic skills in the majority language that are at least equivalent to students who are taught exclusively through that language. We can understand how this process works by means of the linguistic interdependence principle.

The interdependence principle has been stated as follows (Cummins, 1981a):

> To the extent that instruction in Lx is effective in promoting proficiency in Lx, transfer of this proficiency to Ly will occur provided there is adequate exposure to Ly (either in school or environment) and adequate motivation to learn Ly. (1981a, p. 29)

The issues revolve around two alternative conceptions of bilingual proficiency, termed the Separate Underlying Proficiency (SUP) and Common Underlying Proficiency (CUP) models.

The SUP and CUP models of bilingual proficiency. The argument that if bilingual children are deficient in English, then they need instruction in English, not in their L1, implies: (a) that proficiency in Ll is separate from proficiency in English, and (b) that there is a direct relationship between exposure to a language (in home or school) and achievement in that language. The SUP model is illustrated in Figure 6.2.

The second implication of the SUP model follows from the first: if L1 and L2 proficiency are separate, then content and skills learned through L1 cannot transfer to L2 and vice versa. In terms of the balloon metaphor illustrated in Figure 6.2, blowing into the L1 balloon will succeed in inflating L1 but not L2. When bilingual education is approached with these "common-sense" assumptions about bilingual proficiency, it is not at all surprising that it appears illogical to argue that L2 proficiency can be more effectively developed through L1 instruction.

However, despite its intuitive appeal, the empirical evidence clearly refutes the SUP model by showing significant transfer of conceptual knowledge and skills across languages. In order to account for the evidence (reviewed below), we must posit a *common underlying proficiency* (CUP) model in which the literacy-related aspects of a bilingual's proficiency in L1 and L2 are seen as common or interdependent across languages. In other words, the common underlying proficiency refers to the cognitive/academic knowledge and abilities that underlie academic performance in both languages.

Two ways of illustrating the CUP model (the linguistic interdependence principle) are shown in Figures 6.3 and 6.4. Figure 6.3 expresses the point that experience with either language can promote development of the proficiency

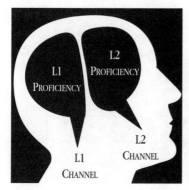

Figure 6.2

THE SEPARATE
UNDERLYING PROFICIENCY
(SUP) MODEL OF
BILINGUAL PROFICIENCY

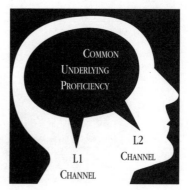

Figure 6.3

THE COMMON
UNDERLYING PROFICIENCY
(CUP) MODEL OF
BILINGUAL PROFICIENCY

underlying both languages, given adequate motivation and exposure to both either in school or in the wider environment. In Figure 6.4 bilingual proficiency is represented by means of a "dual iceberg" in which common cross-lingual proficiencies underlie the obviously different surface manifestations of each language. In general, the surface features of L1 and L2 are those conversational features that have become relatively automatized or less cognitively demanding whereas the underlying proficiency is that involved in cognitively demanding tasks. [6]

In concrete terms, what this principle means is that in, for example, a Spanish-English bilingual program, Spanish instruction that develops Spanish reading and writing skills (for either Spanish L1 or L2 speakers) is not just developing *Spanish* skills, it is also developing a deeper conceptual and linguistic proficiency that is strongly related to the development of literacy in the majority language (English). In other words, although the surface aspects (*e.g.,* pronunciation, fluency, etc.) of different languages are clearly separate, there is an underlying cognitive/academic proficiency that is common across languages. This common underlying proficiency makes possible the transfer of cognitive/academic or literacy-related skills from one language to another.

Another illustration involves telling the time: a 9-year old immigrant student who arrives from Mexico knowing how to tell the time in Spanish does not have to learn all over again the principles underlying this process (*e.g.,* the meaning of seconds, minutes, hours, and the fact that there are 60 seconds in a minute, 60 minutes in an hour, and 24 hours in a day). She does have to learn the English

Figure 6.4
THE "DUAL ICEBERG" REPRESENTATION OF BILINGUAL PROFICIENCY

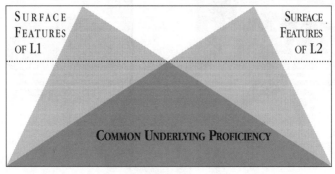

equivalents for the words and concepts she knows in Spanish but she doesn't have to learn the concepts themselves which form part of her knowledge base— her common underlying proficiency. This student's 6-year old sister who does not already know the principles involved in telling time has a more difficult task: she has to learn both the *concepts* and the English vocabulary involved in telling time through a language that, at this point, she doesn't understand.

In general, transfer is more likely to occur from the minority to the majority language because of the typically greater exposure to literacy in the majority language outside of school and the strong social pressure to learn it. However, when the sociolinguistic conditions are right, two-way transfer across languages *does* occur. This has been demonstrated in both minority contexts (Verhoeven, 1991a, 1991b) and majority contexts (Cashion & Eagan, 1990).

In short, the development of academic skills in English depends not just on exposure to English (as "time-on-task" advocates argue) but equally on the knowledge and concepts that children have inside their heads that help them make sense of English. Thus, instruction that builds up Latino/Latina children's reading and writing in Spanish is creating a conceptual foundation upon which academic skills in English can be built. A student who knows how to write sentences and paragraphs in Spanish doesn't have to learn what sentences and paragraphs are all over again in English.

Clearly, the notions of *time-on-task/maximum exposure* and *interdependence/common underlying proficiency* make diametrically opposite predictions in relation to the effects of bilingual education. If the time-on-task notion were valid we would expect that all students in bilingual programs would suffer academically in English when less instructional time was spent through English. By contrast, the interdependence notion would predict that transfer of underlying conceptual knowledge across languages would offset any impact of less instructional time through English.

Maximum Exposure v. Linguistic Interdependence: The Research Evidence

Consider the following research data that support the linguistic interdependence principle:

• In virtually every bilingual program that has ever been evaluated, whether intended for linguistic majority or minority students, spending instructional time teaching through the minority language entails no academic costs for students' academic development in the majority language (Baker, 1996; Cummins & Corson, 1997).

- An impressive number of research studies have documented a moderately strong correlation between bilingual students' L1 and L2 literacy skills in situations where students have the opportunity to develop literacy in both languages. It is worth noting that these findings also apply to the relationships among very dissimilar languages in addition to languages that are more closely related, although the strength of relationship is often reduced (*e.g.,* Arabic-French, Dutch-Turkish, Japanese-English, Chinese-English, Basque-Spanish) (Cummins, 1991d; Cummins *et al.*, 1984; Genesee, 1979; Huguet, Vila & Llurda, 2000; Sierra & Olaziregi, 1991; Verhoeven & Aarts, 1998; Wagner, 1998).

A comprehensive review of U.S. research on cognitive reading processes among bilingual students concluded that this research consistently supported the common underlying proficiency model:

> considerable evidence emerged to support the CUP model. United States ESL readers used knowledge of their native language as they read in English. This supports a prominent current view that native-language development can enhance ESL reading. (Fitzgerald, 1995, p. 181) [7]

The most clear-cut large-scale evidence with respect to the validity or otherwise of time-on-task versus interdependence notions comes from the Ramírez report, so-named after its principal investigator, J. David Ramírez, and from the Thomas and Collier (1997) report which involved more than 40,000 students. The findings of these reports are reviewed in the next section and then some of the international evaluations of bilingual education are examined.

The Ramírez Report

The Ramírez report was released on February 11th, 1991, by the U.S. Department of Education. The study involved 2352 Latino elementary schoolchildren in nine school districts, 51 schools and 554 classrooms. It compared the academic progress of children in three program types: (a) English immersion, involving almost exclusive use of English throughout elementary school, (b) early-exit bilingual in which Spanish was used for about one-third of the time in kindergarten and first grade with a rapid phase-out thereafter, and (c) late-exit bilingual that used primarily Spanish instruction in kindergarten, with English used for about one-third of the time in grades 1 and 2, half the time in grade 3, and about sixty per cent of the time thereafter. One of the three late-

exit programs in the study (site G) was an exception to this pattern in that students were abruptly transitioned into primarily English instruction at the end of grade 2 and English was used almost exclusively in grades five and six. In other words, this "late-exit" program is similar in its implementation to early-exit. Students were followed through to the point where each program model assumes they would be ready for mainstreaming into the regular program; in the case of the early-exit and immersion students this was grade 3 while late-exit students were followed to the end of grade 6.

It was possible to compare directly the progress of children in the English immersion and early-exit bilingual programs but only indirect comparisons were possible between these programs and the late-exit program because these latter programs were offered in different districts and schools from the former. The comparison of immersion and early-exit programs showed that by the end of grade 3 students were performing at comparable levels in English language and reading skills as well as in mathematics. Slightly more of the early-exit bilingual students were reclassified as fully English proficient by the end of grade 3 than was the case for immersion program students (72% vs. 67%). Students in each of these program types progressed academically at about the same rate as students in the general population but the gap between their performance and that of the general population remained large. In other words, they tended not to fall further behind academically between first and third grade but neither did they bridge the gap in any significant way.

While these results do not demonstrate the superiority of early-exit bilingual over English immersion, they clearly do refute the argument that there is a direct relation between the amount of time spent through English instruction and academic development in English. If the "time-on-task" notion were valid, the early-exit bilingual students should have performed at a considerably lower level than the English immersion students, which they did not.

The "time-on-task" notion suffers even further indignity from the late-exit bilingual program results. In contrast to students in the immersion and early-exit programs, the late-exit students in the two sites that continued to strongly emphasize primary language instruction throughout elementary school (at close to 40% of instructional time) were catching up academically to students in the general population. This is despite the fact that these students received considerably less instruction in English than students in early-exit and immersion programs and proportionately more of their families came from the lowest income levels than was the case for students in the other two programs. It was also found that parental involvement (*e.g.,* help with homework) was greater in the late exit sites, presumably because teachers were fluent in Spanish and students were bringing work home in Spanish.

Differences were observed among the three late-exit sites with respect to mathematics, English language (*i.e.,* skills such as punctuation, capitalization etc.) and English reading; specifically, according to the report:

> As in mathematics and English language, it seems that those students in site E, who received the strongest opportunity to develop their primary language skills, realized a growth in their English reading skills that was greater than that of the norming population used in this study. If sustained, in time these students would be expected to catch up and approximate the average achievement level of this norming population (Ramírez, 1992, pp. 37-38).

By contrast, students in site G who were abruptly transitioned into almost all-English instruction in the early grades (in a similar fashion to early-exit students) seemed to lose ground in relation to the general population between grades 3 and 6 in mathematics, English language and reading.

The report concludes that:

> Students who were provided with a substantial and consistent primary language development program learned mathematics, English language, and English reading skills as fast or faster than the norming population used in this study. As their growth in these academic skills is atypical of disadvantaged youth, it provides support for the efficacy of primary language development in facilitating the acquisition of English language skills (1992, pp. 38-39).

An additional conclusion highlighted by Ramírez (1992) was that learning English language skills by limited English proficient students requires six or more years of special instructional support, a finding clearly consistent with the results of studies reviewed in Chapter 3 (*e.g.,* Collier, 1987; Cummins, 1981b; Hakuta *et al.,* 1999; Klesmer, 1994).

These findings are entirely consistent with the results of other bilingual programs and show clearly that, as predicted by the interdependence principle, there is no direct relationship between the instructional time spent through the medium of a majority language and academic achievement in that language. On the contrary, there appears to be an inverse relation between exposure to English instruction and English achievement for Latino/Latina students in this study. [8]

Beykont's analysis of Ramírez Site E data. Beykont (1994) has carried out further analyses of the Ramírez data from Site E which involved Puerto Rican students in New York City. The sample of two cohorts for whom data were available from grades 3 through 6 consisted of 139 students (74 girls and 65 boys), the majority of whom were born in the United States. The progression of Spanish and English reading scores from grades 3 through 6 was related to a variety of predictor variables (preschool attendance, parental attitudes towards bilingual education, classroom organization [grouping patterns]). Beykont used sophisticated methodology for measuring change over time that relied on repeated measures of growth (Rogosa & Willett, 1985).

Among the findings of her study are the following:

• Students made significant progress between grades 3 and 6 in both English and Spanish reading. Spanish reading scores remained higher than English reading throughout this period but students approached grade norms rapidly in both languages.

• Academic progress in English reading was faster for those students whose initial (grade 3) Spanish reading scores were high and slower for those with low initial Spanish reading scores. A strong relationship was also observed between English and Spanish reading at the grade 3 level.

• Students whose parents held favorable attitudes towards bilingual education made faster progress in both English and Spanish reading between grades 3 and 6 than those whose parents held unfavorable or ambivalent attitudes.

• Students tended to show higher English and Spanish academic performance in classrooms that relied on smaller groups rather than on larger or whole class grouping.

Beykont concludes that:

In fact, children's consistently rapid progress in both English and Spanish reading through the sixth grade is remarkable, considering that the academic performance of native speakers typically levels off starting in the fourth grade, when children are expected to move beyond "learning to read" and start "reading to learn" difficult content matter. ...Of those Puerto Rican children who stayed in the program, about 50% of cohort 1 read at or above the sixth grade level in both English and Spanish; an additional 21.4% read at or above grade level in Spanish only and the rest read one or two years below grade level in English and Spanish. In cohort 2, which was followed for three years [to the end of grade 5], about 37% read at or above fifth-grade level in English and Spanish; an additional 31% read at or above fifth-grade level in Spanish only by the end of the study. ...These results clearly indicate that early assessment of English skills conceals the long-term benefits of extensive Spanish instruction for biliteracy development (p. 140). [9]

The Thomas/Collier (1997) Study

The study entitled *School Effectiveness for Language Minority Students* carried out by Wayne Thomas and Virginia Collier (1997) is undoubtedly one of the largest investigations of educational effectiveness ever conducted. It involved analysis of more than 700,000 student records compiled from five large school systems during the years 1982-1996. Student progress was examined both cross-sectionally and longitudinally. The core analyses were carried out on 42,317 students who had attended the participating schools for at least four years. More than 150 home languages were represented in the sample with Spanish the largest language group comprising 63 per cent overall.

Thomas and Collier investigated two central questions: (1) How long does it take ELL students to reach the 50th Normal Curve Equivalent (NCE), taking account of age on arrival in the U.S. and type of program attended? (2) What is the influence of school program and instructional variables on the long-term academic achievement of ELL students? With respect to the first question, Thomas and Collier report that:

[I]t takes typical bilingually schooled students who are achieving on grade level in L1, from 4-7 years to make it to the 50th NCE [normal curve equivalent] in L2. It takes typical "advantaged" immigrants with 2-5 years of on-grade-level home country schooling in L1 from 5-7 years to reach the 50th NCE in L2, when schooled all in L2 in the U.S. It takes the typical young immigrant schooled all in L2 in the U.S. 7-10 years or more to reach the 50th NCE, and the majority of these students do not ever make it to the 50th NCE, unless they receive support for L1 academic and cognitive development at home. (1997, p. 36)

They report that the amount of formal schooling in L1 that students have received is the strongest predictor of how rapidly they will catch up academically in L2. This factor is a stronger predictor than socioeconomic status or the extent to which parents may or may not speak English. [10]

With respect to the second question, Thomas and Collier report major differences in long-term academic outcomes (in English) across programs. They point out that their results are aggregated from a series of 4–8 year longitudinal studies from well-implemented, mature programs in five school districts. Students whose achievement is represented in the following chart are those who began schooling in the U.S. in kindergarten with no proficiency in English and whose background is low socioeconomic status as measured by eligibility for free or reduced lunch. However, a similar pattern was found for other cohorts from different socioeconomic levels. The pattern of mean NCE findings for students at the grade 11 level is presented below. The proportion of the samples (at the elementary school level) in each of these program types is represented in parentheses.

Two-way developmental bilingual education programs (two-way bilingual immersion):	NCE 61 (3%)
One-way developmental bilingual education (late-exit) with content-based ESL support:	NCE 52 (7%)
Transitional bilingual education with content ESL:	NCE 40 (9%)
Transitional bilingual education together with ESL, both taught traditionally:	NCE 35 (17%)
ESL taught through academic content:	NCE 34 (13%)
ESL pullout, taught traditionally:	NCE 24 (51%)

Thomas and Collier interpret the differences in programs in terms of the fact that the developmental bilingual programs address students' linguistic, cognitive, academic, and sociocultural realities whereas less successful programs tend to focus narrowly only on students' linguistic or academic needs. [11]

International Evaluations of Bilingual Education

As mentioned above, the international literature on bilingual education is voluminous (for example, see reviews by Baker, 1996; Baker & Prys Jones, 1998;

Cummins & Corson, 1997; Cummins, 2000; Krashen, 1999a; Reid & Reich, 1992; Spolsky & Cooper, 1978). We provide just two examples here to illustrate the database that does exist. The first study was conducted in The Netherlands and the second in the Basque country.

Verhoeven's Turkish-Dutch bilingual program evaluation. Verhoeven (1991a, 1991b, 1994) reported the results of two experimental programs in transitional L1 literacy instruction with Turkish-background students in The Netherlands. He summarizes the results as follows:

> With respect to linguistic measures, it was found that a strong emphasis on instruction in L1 does lead to better literacy results in L1 with no retardation of literacy results in L2. On the contrary, there was a tendency for L2 literacy results in the transitional classes to be better than in the regular submersion classes. Moreover, it was found that the transitional approach tended to develop a more positive orientation toward literacy in both L1 and L2. …Finally, there was positive evidence for…[the] interdependence hypothesis. From the study on biliteracy development it was found that literacy skills being developed in one language strongly predict corresponding skills in another language acquired later in time (1991a, p. 72).

Verhoeven (1994) reports stronger cross-lingual relationships for literacy and pragmatic language skills than for lexical knowledge. Phonology (as measured by phoneme discrimination tests) was also significantly related across languages which Verhoeven interprets as reflecting the influence of metalinguistic factors on phonological performance in both languages. [12]

Evaluations of Basque-Spanish bilingual programs. A series of evaluations of Basque-Spanish bilingual programs in the Basque Country of Spain (Gabina *et al.*, 1986; Sierra and Olaziregi, 1989; 1991) similarly showed a minimal relationship between instructional time spent through the medium of a majority language (in this case, Spanish) and academic achievement in that language. The three studies were similar in design in that each compared the Basque and Spanish achievement of elementary school students in three program types: (a) Spanish language instruction with Basque taught as a second language (Model A); (b) Spanish and Basque both used for instruction about 50% of the time (Model B); and (c) Basque as the language of instruction with Spanish taught as a subject (Model D). Students in Model D came from both Basque- and Spanish-speaking homes whereas the majority of students in the other two programs came from Spanish-speaking homes. In all three studies, stratified random samples were chosen that were representative of the population of the Basque Country.

A similar pattern of results emerged in the three studies and at both grade levels studied (Grades 2 and 5). Extremely large differences were evident between Models D and A in command of both oral and written Basque, with Model B in an intermediate position. With respect to Spanish, however, the program differences at both grade levels were small. For example, in the second study involving Grade 5 students (Sierra and Olaziregi, 1989) there was only a six-point difference in overall Spanish scores between Models A and D (79.81, standard deviation 7.99, versus 73.77, standard deviation 9.31) compared to a 56 point difference in Basque scores (23.17 versus 79.04).

The goals of the Basque bilingual (Model B) and minority language immersion (Model D) programs are different than those of most bilingual programs in the United States insofar as promotion of additive bilingualism is the major objective in the Basque Country whereas academic achievement in the majority language is the primary goal of U.S. bilingual programs. Nevertheless, the findings are remarkably consistent in showing that instruction through the medium of a minority language for a substantial part of the school day entails no long-term academic disadvantage with respect to achievement in the majority language. [13]

In summary, the research evidence shows consistent support for the principle of linguistic interdependence in studies investigating L1-L2 relationships and in evaluations of bilingual education from around the world. The consistency and strength of research support indicates that highly reliable policy predictions can be made on the basis of this principle. Specifically, the data imply that instructional time can be focused on developing bilingual students' literacy skills in their first language without adverse effects on the development of their literacy skills in the majority language. Furthermore, the relationship between first and second language literacy skills suggests that effective development of first language literacy skills can provide a conceptual foundation for long-term growth in majority language literacy skills. This does not imply, however, that transfer of literacy and academic language knowledge will happen automatically; there is usually also a need for formal instruction in both languages to realize the benefits of cross-linguistic transfer. Also, as argued in Chapter 5, there should be an explicit instructional focus on language itself in order to demystify the structure, functions, and status relations of the bilingual student's two languages. [14]

Conclusion

This review of psychoeducational data regarding bilingual academic development shows that a theoretical and research basis for at least some policy decisions regarding bilingual students' education does exist. In other words, policy-makers can predict with considerable accuracy the probable effects of educational programs for bilingual students implemented in very different sociopolitical contexts.

First, they can be confident that if the program is effective in continuing to develop students' academic skills in both languages, no cognitive confusion or handicap will result; in fact, students may benefit in concrete ways from access to two linguistic systems.

Second, they can be confident that spending instructional time through the minority language will not result in lower levels of academic performance in the majority language, provided of course, the instructional program is effective in developing academic skills in the minority language and there is also adequate instruction in the majority language. It is possible to spend instructional time developing literacy in the minority language because at deeper levels of conceptual and academic functioning, there is considerable overlap or interdependence across languages. Conceptual knowledge developed in one language helps to make input in the other language comprehensible.

The *additive bilingualism enrichment* principle and the *linguistic interdependence* principle open up significant possibilities for the planning of bilingual programs by showing that, when programs are well-implemented, students will not suffer academically either as a result of bilingualism itself nor as a result of spending less instructional time through English. If optimum academic development of bilingual students is the goal, then students must be encouraged to acquire a conceptual foundation in their L1 in addition to English.

This does not mean, however, that exposure to literacy in English should be delayed. The interdependence principle posits that transfer of academic skills and knowledge will occur across languages under appropriate conditions of student motivation and exposure to both languages. It does *not* argue that initial instruction in the early grades should be totally through the minority language nor that literacy should necessarily be introduced first in the minority language (see Chapter 4). Such an approach may be effective under certain conditions, as the outcomes of many 90/10 dual language programs and second language immersion programs suggest. However, in other situations where bilingual students may have varying levels of proficiency in their L1 and English on entry to the program, it may be more effective to promote literacy in both L1 and English simultaneously or in close succession. The goal here would be to work for two-way transfer across languages from an early stage by encouraging students to read literature in both languages and write in both languages (*e.g.,* produce and publish bilingual books). This type of approach has been implemented very successfully since 1971 in the Oyster Bilingual School dual language program in Washington, DC. (see Cummins, 2000; Freeman, 1998, for reviews of this program).

In short, the data reviewed in this chapter clearly imply (a) that bilingualism and biliteracy should be promoted as central educational goals for all students and (b) that bilingual instruction should place a strong emphasis on developing literacy in the minority language. However, there is no one prescribed model for achieving these goals and flexibility of approach is necessary to take account of the varying entry characteristics of students, the availability of resources (*e.g.,* bilingual teachers, minority language curriculum materials) and the political and economic climate within which the program is being instituted. [15]

While the psychoeducational principles discussed in this and the previous chapter clarify many of the disputed issues related to bilingual education, they do not, by themselves, constitute a fully adequate basis for planning educational interventions for bilingual students who come from groups that have been characterized by persistent school failure. The psychoeducational principles do not address the fundamental causes of bilingual students' educational difficulties, which, as noted in Chapters 1 and 2, are sociopolitical and sociohistorical in nature. Also, they do not fully explain the fact that, under some circumstances, bilingual programs have been dramatically successful in *reversing* students' academic difficulties. Thus, a framework for intervention is required that takes account of the interactions between sociopolitical and psychoeducational factors and that allows us to specify the essential components of an effective education for culturally-diverse students. Promotion of an additive form of bilingualism and biliteracy is one significant component but there are others that are equally significant. The components of effective programs for ELL students are discussed in the next two chapters.

Endnotes to Chapter 6

1. Among the typologies of bilingual education that have been proposed, the most elaborate is Mackey's (1970) which distinguishes 90 different potential varieties depending on the intersection of home language(s), curricular organization of languages, and language(s) of the neighborhood and country.

Perhaps the most useful typology for understanding the intersections between educational and sociopolitical factors in bilingual/multilingual education for both minority and majority students is that developed by Skutnabb-Kangas (1984). According to this typology, the *language of instruction* can be primarily the majority language, the minority language or both; the *program* can be designed for the majority group, the minority group or both together (a "two-way" or dual language program); *societal goals* of bilingual education can include direct assimilation of minority students, segregation of minority students (possibly with a view to deportation or repatriation), equality for minority students, or enrichment and/or instrumental benefits (*e.g.,* jobs) for both minority and majority students; finally, the *linguistic aims* include monolingual (or strongly dominant) in the majority language (*e.g.,* transitional bilingual programs in the United States), monolingual (or strongly dominant) in the minority language (*e.g.,* some primarily L1 programs for children of guest-workers in Europe), and bilingualism.

Another useful typology of policy responses to linguistic diversity and minority group rights is elaborated by Churchill (1986). These policy responses range from viewing the minority group as experiencing a "deficit" as a result of their lack of proficiency in the majority language (Stage 1) to viewing the issues in terms of promoting language equality where the majority and minority languages are seen as having equal rights in the society and special supports are provided to reinforce the status of the minority language.

2. A variety of bilingual program evaluations conducted in Canada during the past 20 years involving languages other than English and French are reviewed in Cummins & Danesi (1990). The results of all of these studies are consistent with the notion of linguistic interdependence. Two Australian studies of note document a Lebanese-English bilingual program (Gibbons, White, & Gibbons, 1994) and an Aboriginal language program (Gale *et al.*, 1981). A small part of the vast experience with bilingual education in India is documented by Mohanty (1994) while a considerable number of international bilingual education programs are described in Baker and Prys Jones (1998) and in Cummins & Corson (1997). In recent years, bilingual programs in the Basque Country, Catalonia, and other parts of Spain have been documented; all of these evaluations are consistent with predictions derived from the interdependence hypothesis (Cenoz, 1999; Huguet, Vila & Llurda, 2000; Sierra & Olaziregi, 1991; Vila, 1995).

3. Diaz and Klinger (1991) have outlined an explanatory model to account for the empirical data. Their first proposition states that exposure to two languages at an early age in a systematic additive fashion results in an objective awareness of grammatical rules and language functions. The second proposition holds that this greater awareness of the cognitive functions of language leads to increased and more efficient use of language as a tool for thought. Finally, they suggest that bilinguals' increased reliance on private speech and verbal mediation will promote the development of cognitive executive functions. Along the same lines, Bialystok (1991) and Bialystok and Hakuta (1994) have interpreted the research data as indicating that bilingual children have enhanced awareness of the analysis and control components of linguistic processing. They argue that processing systems developed to serve two linguistic systems are necessarily different from the same processing systems that operate in the service of only one.

Malakoff and Hakuta (1991) have further explored the relation between bilingualism and metalinguistic awareness in two studies that investigated minority students' translation from one language to another. They report that translation skill is widely found in bilingual children in late elementary school. This ability appears to be related both to language proficiency in the two languages and to a separate metalinguistic ability that is unrelated to proficiency in the two languages. They also suggest that translation offers an excellent pedagogical tool to enhance students' metalinguistic awareness and their pride in bilingualism.

4. Landry and Allard (1991) have suggested that the additive/subtractive distinction should be viewed not as a linguistic dichotomy but as extremes on a continuum that encompasses the cognitive, affective, and behavioral aspects of language experience. Landry and his colleagues have conducted a series of large-scale studies of minority francophone students in various parts of Canada. He summarizes the conclusions of these studies as follows:

> Recent research studies …have demonstrated that the attainment of additive bilingualism among minority francophones is strongly related to the proportion of schooling through French [students' L1]. Students who experienced more French-medium schooling developed higher levels of both conversational and academic proficiency in French, they desired to integrate more with the francophone community, they identified more as francophone, and they utilized the French language to a greater extent. Furthermore, students' English proficiency was not in any way diminished through participation in a strong French-medium bilingual program, a result that illustrates the additive nature of their bilingualism. …Among anglophone students who are members of a community with extremely high ethnolinguistic vitality, spending a large proportion of instructional time through French [their L2] had a positive impact on both their French proficiency and attitudes towards the francophone community without any negative impact on their mother tongue. (1993, p. 893) [translation by Jim Cummins]

The findings of Landry's studies are consistent with other large-scale Canadian evaluations of bilingual programs for minority francophone students outside Quebec (*e.g.,* Hébert *et al.,* 1976) and provide strong support for the interdependence of bilingual academic skills across languages. In other words, they demonstrate that minority students who are educated for up to 80% of the time through their L1 (as in the case of most Canadian bilingual programs for minority francophone students) develop literacy skills in English (the majority language) that are equivalent to similar students who have been instructed entirely through English.

In light of these data, Landry and Allard (1991) propose a *counterbalance model of bilingual experience* which states that "additive bilingualism for a minority group's members is only possible when the frequency of opportunities for linguistic contact in L1 can compensate for the dominance of L2" (p. 205). In most cases, this will require that the school and family context be almost completely unilingual in L1. While L1 schooling is an essential contributor to additive bilingualism, by itself it is inadequate to compensate fully for low levels of linguistic vitality at the sociological level or for low levels of linguistic contact in the family or social milieu. Despite French-medium schooling, most francophone students in their studies were dominant in English.

5. For bilingual students without the benefit of L1 literacy promotion in school, language shift can be extremely rapid. This pattern is illustrated in a small-scale longitudinal study of Portuguese-speaking children in Toronto, Canada (Cummins, 1991a). The developing bilingual skills of 20 children were monitored from Junior Kindergarten [JK] (a two hour program for 4 year-olds) through Senior Kindergarten and grade 1. Language use in the home was tape-recorded, interviews with the children were conducted in both languages, and English reading measures were administered at the end of grade 1. It was found that even at the JK level, language shift was already well underway. Although parents used Portuguese predominantly with their children, a significant minority of children were already using more English with their parents, especially with mothers. In addition, English had already become the dominant language among siblings. Only seven of the 4-year old children (out of 20) showed a marked preference for Portuguese, three showed roughly equal use of each language, while the remainder (10) used English as their predominant language. By the time the children completed grade 1, only 2 (out of 14) were rated as more conversationally proficient in Portuguese than in English and only three were rated as equally proficient in each language.

There were indications that the development of conceptual knowledge in both languages was closely related and that loss of Portuguese was associated with lower academic achievement in English. For example, the various preschool indices of language development in Portuguese and English were positively related across languages and about equally related to English reading performance at the grade 1 level. This pattern suggests a general developmental process encompassing conceptual growth and oral skills in both languages. There was also a very significant difference (about one standard deviation) in English reading skills in favor of children who were maintaining Portuguese language skills (N=6, ratings of 3–5 on Portuguese oral proficiency) as compared to those who were losing the language (N=8, ratings of 1–2 on Portuguese oral proficiency).

Wong Fillmore (1991a) has also documented the loss of language skills in early childhood in an interview study involving more than 1,000 families. More than 60% of the families judged monolingual English daycare or preschool provision to have exerted a negative impact on family communication as a result of loss of L1 skills on the part of children. By contrast, preschool programs that utilized children's L1 exclusively were associated with significantly less language loss. Wong Fillmore argues on the basis of both the quantitative and qualitative data of this study that communication between children and parents in the home frequently breaks down as children progress through the grades as a result of the fact that they no longer share a common language.

6. The metaphor of language proficiency as an iceberg was first proposed by Roger Shuy (1978) to distinguish between surface and deeper levels of language proficiency. Basic grammar, vocabulary, and phonology are "visible" above the surface but the less obvious semantic and functional proficiencies below the surface are much more significant for academic progress.

The idea of representing bilingual proficiency (and the interdependence hypothesis) as a dual-iceberg came to me in discussion with Roger Shuy and John Oller at a workshop organized by Margarita Calderón on a very hot February 1979 day in Riverside, California.

7. Many studies conducted since the mid-eighties support the interdependence principle. Kemp (1984), for example, reported that level of Hebrew (L1) cognitive/academic abilities strongly predicted English (L2) academic skills among 196 seventh grade Israeli students.

In a three-year longitudinal study conducted in Newark, New Jersey, Ramírez (1985) followed 75 Latino/Latina elementary school students enrolled in bilingual programs. He reported that Spanish and English academic language scores were so strongly related that they represented the same underlying dimension over the three years of data collection.

Hakuta and Diaz (1985) with a similar sample of Latino/Latina students found an increasing correlation between English and Spanish academic skills over time. Between kindergarten and third grade the correlation between English and Spanish went from 0 to .68 (representing close to 50% of shared variance). The low cross-lingual relationship at the kindergarten level is likely due to the varied length of residence of the students and their parents in the United States which would result in varying levels of English proficiency at the start of school.

A case study of five schools attempting to implement the theoretical framework for the education of language minority students developed by the California State Department of Education (1985) showed consistently higher correlations between English and Spanish reading skills (range $r= .60-.74$) than between English reading and oral language skills (range $r= .36-.59$) (California State Department of Education, 1985). It was also found that the relation between L1 and L2 reading became stronger as English oral communicative skills grew stronger ($r=.71$, $N=190$ for students in the highest category of English oral skills). See Crawford (1995) for a detailed account of the Case Studies project and its highly positive outcomes for bilingual students' achievement in schools such as the Eastman Avenue school in Los Angeles.

Geva and Ryan (1993) have reported evidence with Hebrew-English bilinguals in Toronto that L1 cognitive/academic skills are significantly related to L2 cognitive/academic skills. They show that not only underlying non-verbal intellectual factors are involved in this process but also memory storage capacity and analytic processes required in performing academic tasks. In other words, they have made explicit some of the cognitive processes that are involved in mediating the transfer from L1 to L2.

European research also supports the interdependence hypothesis. McLaughlin (1986), for example, reviewed research carried out by German linguist Jochen Rehbein (1984) which found that:

> the ability of Turkish children to deal with complex texts in German was affected by their ability to understand these texts in their first language. Rehbein's investigations suggest that there is a strong developmental interrelationship between the bilingual child's two languages and that conceptual information and discourse strategies acquired in the first language transfer to the second (McLaughlin, 1986, p. 34-35).

Ricciardelli's study of Italian-English bilinguals in Australia and Italy (Ricciardelli, 1989) reported significant relationships between Italian and English proficiency among both the Australian and Italian samples. In the Italian data, for example, she reported:

> there is a large degree of overlap between the standard cognitive measures which were given in the two languages. ...These [findings] suggest that bilinguals' linguistic abilities are interdependent and are not separate, and therefore any instruction which bilingual children receive in either language is capable of promoting academic skills in both languages (1989, p. 137).

Medina and Escamilla (1992) compared the outcomes of a transitional bilingual program for 125 Vietnamese-speaking students with a maintenance program for 298 Latino/Latina students between kindergarten and grade 2. The data indicated that students in maintenance programs retained oral command of their L1 significantly better than those in transitional programs while performance in English was equivalent for the two programs. These data again suggest that the amount of time through the majority language is largely unrelated to achievement in that language.

Cummins, Harley, Swain and Allen (1990) reported highly significant correlations for written grammatical, discourse and sociolinguistic skills in Portuguese (L1) and English (L2) among Portuguese grade 7 students in Toronto. Cross-language correlations for oral skills were generally not significant. Significant cross-linguistic relationships for reading and writing skills were also observed among Japanese-background students in the Cummins *et al.* study as well as in an earlier study (Cummins, Swain, Nakajima, Handscombe, Green & Tran, 1984). This latter study also found a strong cross-lingual relationship for a variable labelled "interactional style" which reflected fluency and ease in interpersonal situations. It was suggested that personality constituted the underlying attribute that accounted for the similar interactional styles in each language just as cognition accounted for the cross-lingual interdependence of context-reduced language abilities.

More recently, in the Spanish context, Huguet, Vila and Llurda (2000) examined the academic performance of almost 400 grade 7 students in predominantly bilingual (Catalan/Spanish) and monolingual (Spanish-only) areas of Aragon. Within the bilingual area where all students had Catalan as their L1, the performance of students who received Spanish-only instruction was compared with the performance of students who received optional Catalan language instruction (3 hours per week taught by teachers with a degree in Catalan and who are from Eastern Aragon). The measures of Catalan and Spanish included group administered tests of listening comprehension, morpho-syntax, spelling, reading comprehension and writing as well as individually administered tests of speaking, pronunciation, and reading. The first five tests were combined into an index of written measures (SC1). A second index (SC2) combined all eight tests. IQ was controlled in all comparisons. Huguet *et al.* report their findings as follows:

> Students in Eastern Aragon [the bilingual area] who attend Catalan classes, although knowing less Catalan than their counterparts in Catalonia, are not negatively affected in their knowledge of Spanish. What is more, this improves notably with the Catalan classes, up to the point where no

significant differences can be observed between them and their monolingual counterparts in Aragon. In addition, in the SC1 index, they even perform slightly better than monolinguals. On the other hand, students of Eastern Aragon who do not attend Catalan classes perform significantly worse in Spanish than those who do attend optional classes (p=0.0001 for SC1 and p=0.0045 for SC2); the differences with their monolingual counterparts are even higher. (2000, pp. 325–326)

The positive consequences on Spanish academic development were greater for students at low and medium IQ levels than at high IQ levels. At low and medium IQ levels, differences in Spanish scores were statistically significant in favor of those who attended the Catalan classes as compared to those who received instruction only in Spanish. A similar trend was observed with respect to socioeconomic status (SES). Students of low and medium SES who attended Catalan classes performed significantly better in Spanish than those who attended only Spanish classes.

Huguet *et al.* also reported significant correlations between Catalan and Spanish proficiency for both the SC1 index (r=0.631) and the SC2 index (r=0.594). These correlations are lower than those reported for the same measures in Catalonia (r=0.796 for SC1 and r=0.838 for SC2) a fact that the authors attribute to the reduced transfer from L1 to L2 in the sociolinguistic situation of Eastern Aragon as compared to the situation in Catalonia where there is much greater exposure to Catalan both in school and in the society as a whole.

The authors conclude as follows:

These results point to the conclusion that, considering knowledge of Spanish, the students in Eastern Aragon that attend Catalan classes, regardless of their IQ and their family social status, do significantly better than those who do not attend those classes. Thus, besides being totally harmless for their normal language development, Catalan classes contribute to the students' learning of the other language. (2000, pp. 328)

8. Wayne Thomas (1992) has conducted supplementary analyses of the Ramírez data which lead him to view the report's conclusions as very conservatively worded. He argues that:

In fact, late-exit success across sites seems directly proportional to the degree of use of primary language instruction. Based on this author's supplementary analyses, it appears that both structured-immersion and early-exit students can be expected gradually to fall behind the norm group by amounts that fall slightly short of statistical significance over a three-year period. (p. 235)

Thomas goes on to point out that standardized test items "tend to sample more cognitively complex skills with more sophisticated usage of English with each passing grade, especially at secondary levels" (p. 238). He suggests that this may explain how second language learners "may appear to make quick progress in the early elementary years, even relative to the national norm group, but may quickly fall behind their native-speaking counterparts in the post-elementary school period as their initial acquisition of mostly low-level English skills becomes inadequate to cope with the increasing cognitive demands of the tests, as well as the requirements of more advanced courses that lead to higher education" (p. 238). Thus, initial gains made by students in English-only programs may be illusory:

> Because the structured-immersion students have sacrificed cognitive development and content in their early emphasis on learning English, their long-term ability to deal with increasingly complex material may be hampered, especially as they enter their years of post-elementary school instruction. ...The Ramírez study found that late-exit students, with both L1 and L2 support, were catching up to the norm group even as their academic work became cognitively more complex in the upper elementary grades. (p. 239)

In contrast to Thomas's assessment that the Ramírez report findings are expressed in an overly cautious manner, a review of the study by an expert panel of the National Research Council (NRC) considered many of the group comparisons to be inadequately controlled when strict experimental criteria were invoked. The review questioned whether comparability had been achieved between programs in different school districts and even in different schools within the same district. Thus, direct comparisons of growth curves across programs were rejected by the NRC panel. This, however, does not in any way invalidate the general patterns of growth that were observed within programs and the fact that the late-exit students were approaching grade expectations in English academic skills by the end of elementary school despite considerably less English-medium instruction than alternative programs. Crawford (1995) notes one additional finding highlighted by the NRC panel:

> The NRC did, however, accept as "compelling" one finding of the Ramírez report: when comparisons were made between kindergarten and 1st grade classrooms in the same school, early-exit bilingual students scored significantly higher in English reading than the immersion students. More generally, the panel found no evidence that native-language instruction impedes the acquisition of English. To the contrary, it noted the "convergence" of evidence in the Ramírez report and other research that "suggests, under certain conditions, the importance of primary-language instruction in second-language achievement in language arts and mathematics." (1995, p. 152)

9. It is worth noting that attrition and socioeconomic status were controlled in these analyses. Students who left the study by the end of third grade had somewhat higher (marginally significant) levels of English achievement and those who left by the end of the fifth grade had somewhat higher levels of Spanish achievement. Thus, the impressive progress revealed by the analyses is not caused by weaker students leaving the program. If anything, the opposite is the case.

10. Thomas and Collier (1997) interpret this pattern of findings in terms of Collier's (1995) Prism Model. This model has four major components that "drive" language acquisition for school: sociocultural, linguistic, academic, and cognitive processes. Within the prism are the

social and cultural processes that impact on the child's experience in home, school, community, and the broader society. These sociocultural processes incorporate the influences that I have discussed in terms of both macro-interactions and micro-interactions in Chapter 1. In a similar way to the discussion of negotiating identities in Chapter 1, Thomas and Collier note that sociopolitical and affective factors will strongly influence the student's response to the new language, "affecting the process positively only when the student is in a socioculturally supportive environment" (1997, p. 42).

The boundaries of the prism are formed by L1 + L2 language development, L1 + L2 cognitive development, and L1 + L2 academic development. Thomas and Collier note the interdependence of all four components: "If one is developed to the neglect of another, this may be detrimental to a student's overall growth and future success" (1997. p. 44). Thus, programs that focus only on language development in English tend to ignore both cognitive development and sociocultural processes and provide support for overall academic development either minimally or not on grade level.

11. The Thomas and Collier study has been critiqued by Christine Rossell (1998) on several grounds. She characterizes them as arguing that treatment and control groups are unnecessary and claims that this represents an "unscientific" position. She further criticizes them for the lack of detailed statistical and sampling information in their report; and finally, she argues that their results do not conform to the outcomes of small-scale two-way bilingual immersion programs and are thus not credible.

In response to Rossell's (1998) first point, Wayne Thomas (personal communication, January 2000) notes that:

> Actually, we said that true control groups are unavailable (each program group is a treatment group) and that the portion of the test norm group with the same pre-test scores as the program (treatment) groups can serve as a suitable 'no treatment' comparison group in the necessary absence of true 'no treatment' control groups. Rossell mangled this into 'treatment and control groups are unnecessary'. She further muddied the water by confusing the concepts of comparison groups and 'no treatment' control groups by using them interchangeably, by asserting incorrectly that one cannot construct a comparison group from the subset of the norm group with the same pretest scores. ...[This is] possibly true in a short-term study but not in a long-term study, and ours is a long-term study.

Thomas (personal communication, January, 2000) also points out that, in their literature review, Rossell and Baker's (1996) use of "the outmoded and primitive vote counting technique, instead of cumulative probabilities or effect sizes is prima facie evidence of unscientific analysis."

The credibility of the Thomas/Collier results is clearly related to their consistency with other data. If Rossell's (1998) claim were valid that the outcomes of individual two-way bilingual immersion programs are much more modest than the trends reported by Thomas and Collier, then this inconsistency would require explanation. However, in contrast to what

Rossell (1998) claims, the trends emerging from dual language (*e.g.,* Oyster Bilingual School, 1999) and developmental programs (*e.g.,* Beykont, 1994; Ramírez, 1992) are entirely consistent with the trends reported by Thomas and Collier (see Cummins, 2000, for a detailed review).

The Thomas/Collier study was summarized prior to publication in a November 1995 article in TIME magazine:

> Though some states end bilingual education after three years, the study found that children who had received six years of bilingual education in well-designed programs performed better than 70% of all 11th graders, including native speakers, on standardized English tests. One of the report's authors, professor Virginia Collier, says children placed in an English-language environment before they are fluent "are just left out of the discussion in their mainstream classes. It shows up in the long term, when the academic going gets tough."
>
> The George Mason study also found that the highest achievers are products of the avant-garde experiment in so-called two-way schools, where half the curriculum is taught in English, half in a foreign language. An example is the Oyster Bilingual Elementary School in the District of Columbia, whose students are 58% Hispanic, 26% white, 12% black, and 4% Asian. After six years of Spanish-English curriculum, the school's sixth-graders score at ninth-grade level in reading and 10th-grade level in math. (Hornblower, 1995, p. 45)

12. Verhoeven (1994) suggests that his data only partially support the interdependence hypothesis. Strong support is evident for interdependence on tasks that require metalinguistic skills or that assess literacy development. However, he suggests that the much more limited degree of transfer on lexical and morphosyntactic tasks is inconsistent with the theory, as is the transfer that was evident in pragmatic aspects of language proficiency. The pragmatic index was derived from the number of different content words and the mean length of utterance in children's spontaneous speech.

The small relationship across languages for oral syntactic functioning is not surprising to me. Consistent findings were reported by Harley, Allen, Cummins, and Swain (1990) in studies involving French immersion and Portuguese-speaking students in Toronto. Syntactic functioning in conversational contexts represents very specific linguistic knowledge that appears largely independent of the common underlying proficiency which is more conceptual and cognitive in nature. By contrast, the limited cross-relationship Verhoeven observed for lexical knowledge is more surprising and at variance with the results of a number of other studies reviewed above (see Note 7).

The strong cross-lingual relationship Verhoeven observed for pragmatic language proficiency is not in any way at variance with the interdependence hypothesis. In fact, as noted above (Note 7), a similar finding was reported by Cummins *et al.* (1984) who hypothesized that personality traits could account for the similar pragmatic behavior in both languages.

Verhoeven also suggests that the interdependence hypothesis largely neglects the role of social factors in explaining differential literacy success. This is simply inaccurate. I have always posited the interdependence of L1 and L2 as an intervening factor strongly influenced by broader societal factors (Cummins, 1981a, 1986, 1989, 2000) and the present volume continues the elaboration of these relationships between social (macro-interactional) and cognitive/linguistic factors.

13. The review of literature on bilingual education is not meant to imply that all bilingual programs, as implemented, have been successful. In fact, the results of many so-called bilingual programs are mixed. The majority of bilingual programs instituted in the United States are quick-exit programs that make minimal or no attempt to promote literacy in students' L1. This weak variety of bilingual education is a consequence of the political pressure to remove students from bilingual programs as quickly as possible. Other programs may involve little more than a classroom assistant who works with the bilingual students (in either L1 or L2) while the classroom teacher instructs those who are fluent in English (Gándara, 1999). Under these conditions, it is hardly surprising that students fall behind since they seldom interact with the teacher nor get access to mainstream curriculum content.

In general, many programs have been set up to fail and, as Lily Wong Fillmore (1992) has argued, there have been concerted attempts to subvert bilingual education in a large number of school districts. She suggests that "a close examination of bilingual education where it has performed poorly will often show the extent to which it has been sabotaged from within by the people who were supposed to make it work" (p. 370). As reflected in the Thomas/Collier (1997) data, only a minority of programs have attempted to promote strong literacy skills in students' L1 which the research reviewed in this chapter suggest is central to students' prospects for success in English academic skills.

Despite the mixed quality of many bilingual programs, overall trends, even before the release of the Ramírez report, show the program to be more successful than English-only programs. Willig's (1985) meta-analysis of the research suggested that:

> When statistical controls for methodological inadequacies were employed,
> participation in bilingual education programs consistently produced small
> to moderate differences favoring bilingual education for tests of reading,
> language skills, mathematics, and total achievement when the tests were in
> English, and for reading, language, mathematics, writing, social studies, listening comprehension, and attitudes toward school or self when tests
> were in other languages (Willig, 1985, p. 269).

More recently, Jay Greene's (1997, 1998) meta-analysis of bilingual education research reported that participation in a bilingual program over a period of two years made a difference of about 1/5 of a standard deviation in achievement. Thus, if a student in an English-only program performed at the 26th percentile at the end of those two years, the bilingual student would be at the 34th percentile.

Krashen and Biber (1988) similarly reviewed the results of several bilingual programs in California in which bilingual students approached grade norms during the elementary school years and surpassed the academic performance of similar students in English-only programs.

In general, both large-scale and small-scale studies consistently show that strong promotion of bilingual students' L1 throughout elementary school contributes significantly to their academic success. However, bilingual education, by itself, is no panacea. Bilingual programs that are remedial in orientation or that fail to promote literacy skills in L1 will experience much less positive outcomes. Even programs that incorporate strong L1 promotion must also include active encouragement of parental participation and cognitively challenging instruction if optimum results are to be obtained.

14. Some cautions with respect to the instructional implications of the interdependence principle are in order. First, while considerable evidence has accumulated for transfer of literacy skills from one language to another, instruction oriented to promoting this form of transfer may not always be appropriate in bilingual education contexts. This, at least, is the persuasive argument made by Harris (1990) in his analysis of Aboriginal schooling in Australia. He suggests that the gap in world views between Aboriginal and western cultures is so great that bilingual education programs should clearly separate western and Aboriginal cultural domains, with English used exclusively for the former and Aboriginal languages for the latter. Using the Aboriginal language as a means of teaching the concepts of western schooling risks undermining the Aboriginal culture and contributing to language and cultural shift. This analysis has implications for indigenous groups around the world who are concerned that bilingualism is but a step towards monolingualism in the majority societal language.

15. Related to the misconception that the teaching of English literacy skills should be delayed for several years is an inappropriate linking of the threshold and interdependence hypotheses (see Cummins, 2000, Chapter 7). For example, it is not uncommon to see these hypotheses interpreted as implying that "English reading should be delayed until students have attained a threshold level of proficiency in their L1." I can understand how it may be tempting to connect the two hypotheses in this way but I have never advocated this type of linkage. The threshold and interdependence hypotheses developed independently and were proposed to account for two very different sets of data: the threshold hypothesis attempted to account for the effects of bilingualism on children's cognitive development, while the interdependence hypothesis focused on the relationship between L1 and L2 academic proficiencies, accounting for data in the areas of bilingual education, immigrant language learning, age and L2 learning, and correlational and experimental studies of L1/L2 relationships. The fact that L1 academic proficiency is a significant predictor of L2 proficiency suggests that, optimally, schools should strongly promote L1 literacy but it does not specify when L1 or L2 literacy should be introduced nor in what instructional proportions. There are many viable options for bilingual programs in this regard (Cummins, 2000).

Chapter 7
The Deep Structure of Educational Reform

S ince the mid-1960s, educators in the United States have implemented a series of educational reforms aimed at reversing the pattern of school failure among culturally diverse students. These have included Head Start programs at the preschool level, myriad forms of bilingual education and all-English programs, Chapter I programs for low-income students, imposition of curricular standards and standardized assessment procedures, etc.

These reforms have probably had some impact but the achievement gap between students from dominant and subordinated groups remains extremely large as documented by periodic reports from agencies such as the National Center for Educational Statistics (NCES) and the National Assessment of Educational Progress (NAEP).

Why has the rhetoric of "equality of educational opportunity" failed to translate into equity of educational outcomes? There are obvious reasons related to the persistence of poverty in American inner cities and rural areas and the huge disparities in educational spending between affluent and impoverished districts. For example, in many states high-expenditure districts spend almost three times as much per pupil as low-expenditure districts (Taylor & Piché, 1991). These disparities in the distribution of resources reflect the power structure of the society. Despite the rhetoric of equity, coercive relations of power are still evident in the distribution of resources and differential access to quality education among social groups. As Andrew Hacker (1995) concluded in his book *Two Nations: Black and White, Separate, Hostile, Unequal*, "legal slavery may be in the past, but segregation and subordination have been allowed to persist" (p. 229).

Since schools reflect the societies that support them, it is hardly surprising that issues related to equity are hotly contested in schools. Inter-group power relations in the broader society are reflected in the organization of schooling (curriculum, language of instruction, assessment practices, tracking, degree of parental participation, etc.) and in the mindset that educators bring to the teaching of culturally diverse students. These educational structures and the role definitions that educators adopt directly affect the interactions that culturally diverse students experience in schools.

I argue in this chapter that one of the major reasons why previous reform efforts have had only limited success is that the relationships between teachers and students and between schools and communities have remained largely unchanged. Interventions have often resulted in only superficial change, leaving the deep structure of relationships between educators and culturally diverse students untouched. Individual educators have attempted to challenge inequities in schools, but in many school contexts, this kind of advocacy for culturally diverse students has not been encouraged. The result has been that the power relations operating in both schools and the wider society have usually been accepted unconsciously rather than challenged. These power relations were powerfully documented in Jonathon Kozol's (1991) book *Savage Inequalities* and have remained largely unchanged through the 1990s. Gerald W. Bracey, for example, in a November 1999 article in *USA Today* pointed to the hypocrisy of educational reformers who have shown minimal interest in addressing issues of child poverty which he argues has a "devastating impact" on school performance:

> Poor children get off to a bad start before they are born. Their mothers are likely to get prenatal care late, if at all, which can impair later intellectual functioning. They are more than three times as likely as nonpoor children to have stunted growth. They are about twice as likely to have physical and mental disabilities, and are seven times more likely to be abused or neglected. And they are more than three times more likely to die.
>
> What these kids need are high standards, right? (1999: 19A)

Payne and Biddle (1999) have recently demonstrated the independent effects of school funding levels and child poverty on mathematics achievement in the United States. Together these variables accounted for 25% of the variance in achievement. Level of curriculum challenge (ranging from remedial to advanced algebra curriculum) was also significantly related to achievement. Payne and Biddle point out that despite continuous economic growth during the past decade, the child poverty level in the most affluent country in the world is still more than 20 percent, substantially higher than any other industrialized nation. They suggest a far more likely explanation for the relatively poor showing of U.S. schools in international comparisons than the "declining standards" usually invoked by politicians:

> Since poorly funded schools and communities with high levels of poverty are very rare in other industrialized nations, education in America is uniquely handicapped because of the singular tolerance for large numbers of poorly funded schools and massive amounts of child poverty in our country. And as long as this tolerance continues, *none* of the present programs being touted for "reforming" American education—educational vouchers, "setting high standards," "accountability" schemes, charter schools—are likely to improve America's aggregate math achievement substantially. (1999, p. 12)

A central assumption of the present analysis is that implementation of genuine educational reform aimed at reversing centuries of discrimination requires *personal redefinitions* of the ways in which *individual educators* interact with the students and communities they serve. In other words, legislative and policy reforms aimed at changing educational structures may be necessary conditions for effective change, but they are not sufficient. Implementation of change is dependent on the extent to which educators, both collectively and individually, redefine their roles with respect to culturally diverse students and communities. This is the deep structure of educational reform. I suggest that reversal of the pattern of school failure requires that educator-student interactions be oriented towards *empowerment*, defined as the collaborative creation of power. Creating contexts of empowerment in the classroom entails a direct challenge to the coercive relations of power operating in the wider society that are at the root of culturally diverse students' school failure.

The empowerment framework described in this chapter (Figure 7.1) elaborates on the framework sketched in Chapter 1. The framework proposes that the causes of underachievement are rooted in the continuation of historical patterns of coercive relations of power between dominant and subordinated groups. These relations of power are reflected in the culture of the school. The culture of the school refers to the structural organization of the school and to the collective role definitions that educators adopt in relation to culturally diverse students and communities. Educational structures and educator role definitions together determine the interactions that students experience in the school system. Culturally diverse students will succeed educationally to the extent that the patterns of interaction in school challenge and reverse those that prevail in the society at large.

In Figure 7.1, the term *Exclusionary/Assimilationist* refers to the general orientation to education characteristic of most countries prior to the 1960s and still characteristic of many today. The goal of education was either to exclude certain groups from the mainstream of society or assimilate them completely. The term *Transformative/Intercultural* refers to the orientation required to challenge the operation of coercive relations of power in the school and wider society. This form of pedagogy entails interactions between educators and students that foster the collaborative creation of power; in other words, *empowerment*. Although *exclusionary* and *assimilationist* may appear to be opposites insofar as "exclusionary" focuses on segregation of subordinated groups from the mainstream of schools and society while "assimilationist" focuses on total integration into the society, in reality they are frequently two sides of the same coin: both orientations aspire to make subordinated groups invisible and inaudible. Minority groups constructed as "racially different" have historically been subjected to exclusionary rather than assimilationist policies for the simple reason that "disappearance" could not readily be achieved through assimilation. In addition, if assimilationist policies were applied to "racial" minorities, it would imply inter-marriage across "races" within the same "melting pot." This mixing of "races" would implode the myths of racial superiority that have characterized most dominant groups in societies around the world.

It is easy to recognize the Exclusionary/Assimilationist patterns outlined in Figure 7.1 as characteristic of historical realities in many countries. The extent to which they still characterize educator-student interactions is a matter for debate and school-by-school analysis.

By contrast, *Transformative/Intercultural* orientations are based on principles of racial and cultural equality and a commitment to educate students for full participation within a democratic society. This implies providing opportunities for students to develop a form of critical literacy where they become capable not only of decoding the words, but also reading between the lines in order to understand how power is exercised through various forms of discourse (advertisements, political rhetoric, textbooks, etc.). The focus is on understanding not only what is said in the surface structure of the text but also whose perspectives are represented and whose have been excluded.

The ways in which identities are negotiated between educators and students can be analyzed in relation to four overlapping dimensions of schooling: (a) incorporation of bilingual students' language and culture; (b) community participation; (c) orientation to pedagogy; and (d) assessment of bilingual students. The extent to which culturally diverse students and communities either accept or resist the societal power structure will also directly affect the ways in which identities are negotiated in the school context.

Central to the framework is the claim that the process of identity negotiation and the challenge to coercive relations of power are at least as important for students' academic development as any particular program or instructional technique. Instructional techniques become effective only to the extent that they contribute to the collaborative creation of power.

Macro-Interactions and the Culture of the School

When patterns of school success and failure among culturally diverse students are examined within an international perspective, it becomes evident that power and status relations between dominant and subordinated groups exert a major influence. As noted in Chapter 2, several theorists (e.g., Blauner, 1969; Ogbu, 1978, 1992) have pointed to the fact that subordinated groups that fail academically have generally been discriminated against over many generations. They react to this discrimination along a continuum ranging from internalization of a sense of ambivalence or insecurity about their identities to rejection of, and active resistance to, dominant group values. At both extremes, alienation from schooling and mental withdrawal from academic effort has been a frequent consequence.

The educational effects of this pattern of macro-interactions are strikingly evident in many situations where formerly subjugated or colonized groups are still in a subordinated relationship to the dominant group. Examples abound from around the world. For example, most indigenous groups fall into this pattern (e.g., Australian Aboriginals, Maoris in New Zealand, Inuit and First Nations in Canada, Sami in Scandinavian countries, as well as indigenous populations in the United States and Latin America). Other examples are Burakumin in Japan who perform poorly in Japanese schools as a result of their low social status but perform well after immigration to the United States because educators are unaware of their low social status in their home country. Thus, educators tend to have the same high academic expectations of them as they do for other Japanese students (Ogbu, 1992).

$\mathcal{F}igure$ 7.1 **INTERVENTION FOR COLLABORATIVE EMPOWERMENT**

COERCIVE RELATIONS OF POWER MANIFESTED IN THE MACRO-INTERACTIONS BETWEEN DOMINANT GROUP INSTITUTIONS AND SUBORDINATED COMMUNITIES → AMBIVALENT/INSECURE OR RESISTANT SUBORDINATED GROUP IDENTITY

EDUCATOR ROLE DEFINITIONS ⟷ EDUCATIONAL STRUCTURES

MICRO-INTERACTIONS BETWEEN EDUCATORS AND STUDENTS

reflecting a

Transformative/ Intercultural Orientation	Exclusionary/ Assimilationist Orientation
CULTURAL/LINGUISTIC INCORPORATION	
Additive	Subtractive
COMMUNITY PARTICIPATION	
Collaborative	Exclusionary
PEDAGOGY	
Transformative	"Banking"
ASSESSMENT	
Advocacy	Legitimation
↓	↓
Academically and Personally Empowered Students	Academically Disabled or Resistant Students

Similar patterns existed in the 1970s and 1980s in Sweden where Finnish-background students experienced severe academic difficulties. This phenomenon reflected the lower status of the Finnish community in Swedish society resulting from the fact that Finland was ruled by Sweden for several hundred years. The institution of Finnish-Swedish bilingual schools in the 1980s and 1990s dedicated to promoting bilingualism and biliteracy has dramatically improved achievement levels of the Finnish students in those schools (see Peura, 2000, and Skutnabb-Kangas, 2000, Chapter 8, pp. 600–611). Skutnabb-Kangas notes that there are today 11 private (but state-financed) Finnish schools in Sweden focused on language maintenance that are producing "excellent results in terms of high levels of multilingualism and multiculturalism and academic success" (2000, pp. 607–608). A more detailed description of these schools is provided in Chapter 8.

Central to understanding the framework proposed in Figure 7.1 is the fact that coercive relations of power can operate only through the micro-interactions between educators and students. *Thus, educators, students, and communities can challenge this coercive process.* Although educational and social structures will impose constraints on resistance, these structures can never stifle the pursuit of empowering interactions on the part of educators and students. In short, educators always have options in the way they negotiate identities with students and communities.

Educational Structures. Inter-group macro-interactions give rise to particular forms of educational structures that reflect the relations of power in the broader society. For example, the historical segregation of culturally diverse students from "mainstream" educational opportunities in many countries constituted one form of structural discrimination. As documented by Kozol (1991) for African-American students and by Berman *et al.* (1992) for recent immigrants in California, similar patterns of segregation still characterize the education of many subordinated groups. Olsen and Minicucci (1992) discuss the implications of the Berman *et al.* (1992) findings with respect to the degree of integration/segregation of culturally diverse students in 27 California secondary schools:

> On an integration/segregation continuum, the majority of the schools in our study are moving increasingly towards the use of sheltered English classes with a resultant formal curricular separation of limited English proficient students. Despite calling the LEP program 'transitional,' and despite recurring and persistent rhetoric about preparing the students to enter the mainstream, the evidence appears to run

contrary to an integration orientation. LEP students are tracked into separate classes, spend the great percentage of the school day in these LEP classes, and appear to rarely be reclassified into the mainstream. Thus, it appears that through the use of English as a language of instruction students are being channeled away from their native language and culture, and they are simultaneously also being kept separate from their English speaking peers and denied access to the track which houses mainstream English speaking students. We would conclude from our small sample that secondary school LEP programs are thus segregatory. (1992, p. 18)

Other examples of educational structures that might systematically discriminate against culturally diverse students are:

• imposition of English-only programs that not only fail to provide comprehensible instruction but also communicate to bilingual children that their home language and culture have no place in the school (*e.g.,* Proposition 227 in California and Proposition 203 in Arizona);

• state mandated high-stakes assessment programs that take no account of the time periods required for ELL students to catch up academically in English; these assessment practices furthermore have the effect of narrowing the curriculum such that cognitively unchallenging drill and practice instruction is implemented rather than cognitively challenging instruction designed to promote critical literacy in two languages (Gándara *et al.*, 2000; McNeil, 1999);

• the medical model of special education that uncritically locates the source of academic difficulties within students rather than within the pattern of interactions that students experience in school (Cummins, 1984, Harry, 1992; Ortiz & Yates, 1983; Rueda, 1989);

• ability grouping and tracking practices that deny students in low-ability groups access to quality instruction (Oakes, 1985);

• the use of culturally- and linguistically-biased IQ tests to give culturally diverse students a one-way ticket to special education or low-track programs (Cummins, 1984; Harry, 1992; Ortiz & Yates, 1983);

- teacher education institutions that still treat issues related to culturally diverse students as marginal and send new teachers into the classroom with minimal information regarding patterns of language and emotional development among such students and few pedagogical strategies for helping students learn;

- curriculum that reflects only the experiences and values of middle-class English-speaking students and effectively suppresses the experiences and values of culturally diverse students;

- the absence from most schools of professionals and/or para-professionals capable of communicating in the languages of culturally diverse students and their parents; these staff members could assist in functions such as: primary language instruction; primary language assessment for purposes of placement and intervention, and parent/school liaison;

- criteria for promotion to positions of responsibility (*e.g.*, principals) that take minimal account of the individual's experience with or potential for leadership in the education of culturally diverse students.

These educational structures constitute a frame that sets limits on the kinds of micro-interactions that are likely to occur between educators and students. As one illustration of the impact of these structures, Jeanie Oakes (1985) has shown that tracking results in major differences in the quality of instruction that students receive; those in lower tracks receive instruction that is less challenging and motivating than those in higher tracks. She concludes that when schools are structured according to tracks, the academic progress of those in average and low groups is retarded. Tracking also lowers educational aspirations, fosters low self-esteem and promotes dropping-out.

Educator Role Definitions. Societal macro-interactions will also influence the ways in which educators define their roles in relation to culturally diverse students and communities; in other words, they influence the mindset of assumptions, expectations and goals that educators bring to the task of educating students. The notion of *educator role definitions* is proposed as a central explanatory construct in the present framework. The framework suggests that culturally diverse students are empowered or disabled as a direct result of their interactions with educators in the schools. These interactions are mediated by the implicit or explicit role definitions that educators assume in relation to four institutional dimensions of schools. These four dimensions outlined in Figure

7.1, *language/culture incorporation*, *community participation*, *pedagogy*, and *assessment* represent sets of educational structures that will affect, but can also be influenced by, educators' role definitions.

A concrete example will illustrate the ways in which educators' role definitions can combine with educational structures to the detriment of bilingual students' academic progress. The following psychological assessment was one of more than 400 assessments of culturally diverse students carried out in a western Canadian city (Cummins, 1984). It illustrates the assumptions that school psychologists and teachers frequently make about issues such as the appropriateness of standardized tests for culturally diverse students and the consequences of bilingualism for students' development.

Maria (not child's real name) was referred for psychological assessment by her grade 1 teacher, who noted that she had difficulty in all aspects of learning. She was given both speech and hearing and psychological assessments. The former assessment found that all structures and functions pertaining to speech were within normal limits and hearing was also normal. The findings were summarized as follows: "Maria comes from an Italian home where Italian is spoken mainly. However, language skills appeared to be within normal limits for English."

The psychologist's conclusions, however, were very different. On the Wechsler Preschool and Primary Scale of Intelligence (WPPSI), Maria obtained a Verbal IQ of 89 and a Performance IQ of 99. In other words, non-verbal abilities were virtually at the average level while verbal abilities were 11 points below the mean, a surprisingly good score given the clear cultural biases of the test and the fact that the child had been learning English in a school context for little more than a year. The report to Maria's teacher read as follows:

> Maria tended to be very slow to respond to questions, particularly if she were unsure of the answers. Her spoken English was a little hard to understand, which is probably due to poor English models at home (speech is within normal limits). Italian is spoken almost exclusively at home and this will be further complicated by the coming arrival of an aunt and grandmother from Italy.

> There is little doubt that Maria is a child of low average ability whose school progress is impeded by lack of practice in English. Encourage Maria's oral participation as much as possible, and try to involve her in extra-curricular activities where she will be with her English-speaking peers.

Despite the fact that the speech assessment revealed no deficiencies in Maria's spoken English, the psychologist has no hesitation ("There is little doubt..") in attributing Maria's academic problems to the use of Italian at home. The implicit message to the teacher (and parents) is clear: Maria's communication in L1 with parents and relatives detracts from her school performance, and the aim of the school program should be to expose Maria to as much English as possible in order to compensate for these deficient linguistic and cultural background experiences. In other words, the psychologist's assessment and recommendations reflect the assumptions of the separate underlying proficiency model of bilingualism (see Chapter 6).

How does this assessment (which was not atypical of the sample) represent institutionalized discrimination in action? In several ways:

- The structure of special education identification, assessment, and placement not only permits, but in many cases mandates the use of IQ tests which are characterized almost invariably by serious cultural and linguistic biases when used with culturally diverse students;

- The structure of psychologist training and certification frequently pays only lip-service to the implications of diversity for assessment and placement;

- The psychologist's role definition shows little sensitivity to the fact that the child's cultural background and linguistic talents differ significantly from those of the sample upon whom the test was normed. The psychologist is not conscious that the child's culturally-specific experiences (in L1) might have any implications for the administration or interpretation of the test. There is also no hesitation in drawing inferences about the negative effects of L1 use in the home nor in making recommendations about language use in school despite the fact that the psychologist has likely had no training whatsoever on issues related to bilingualism or language learning.

What are the probable consequences of this type of assessment? As a result of the assessment, there is an increased likelihood that Maria will be reprimanded for any use of Italian with other Italian students in school, thereby promoting feelings of shame in her own cultural background. It is also probable that the child's parents will be advised to use English rather than Italian at home. If parents adhere to this advice, then they are likely both to expose the child to poor models of English, and also reduce the quality and quantity of communication between adults and children in the home since they are likely to be much less comfortable in English than Italian. The importance of adult-child home interaction for future academic achievement has been demonstrated repeatedly (*e.g.*, Wells, 1986), and thus the advice to switch to English in the home has the potential to exert serious negative effects on children's development. Furthermore, it is likely to drive an emotional wedge between children and parents (including the recently arrived aunt and grandmother who will know no English) since parents may feel that communication of affection and warmth in Italian will reduce the child's future academic prospects. [1]

In summary, the example of Maria illustrates how students can become educationally disabled as a direct result of their interactions with well-intentioned educators. These interactions are mediated by the role definitions of educators which, in turn, are molded by a variety of influences: for example, the broader policy and legal structure within which educators operate, the institutional structure within which they have been trained, and the state and school district structures that determine priorities for action on a day-to-day basis (*e.g.*, Proposition 227, high-stakes assessment, etc.).

Micro-Interactions as Reflections of Coercive or Collaborative Relations of Power

The framework argues that the micro-interactions between educators and students form an interpersonal or an interactional space within which the acquisition of knowledge and formation of identity is negotiated. In the past, schools have required that subordinated groups deny their cultural identity as a necessary condition for success in the "mainstream" society. The historical pattern of dominant-subordinated group interactions has been one where educators have constricted the interactional space in an attempt to sanitize deviant cultural identities. For educators to become partners in the transmission of knowledge, culturally diverse students were required to acquiesce in the subordination of their identities and to celebrate as "truth" the cultural literacy (Hirsch, 1987) of the dominant group (*e.g.*, the "truth" that Columbus discovered America). The constriction of the interactional space by educators reflected a process whereby they defined their role as "civilizing," "saving," "assimilating," or "educating" students whose culture and values they viewed as inherently inferior. Through these micro-interactions they reproduced the pattern of societal macro-interactions and limited students' possibilities to define and interpret their own realities and identities.

Becker (1990) documented how this process operated in an urban New England high school to shape the ethnic identity and academic engagement of Portuguese-background students. She interprets the 50% dropout rate among Portuguese-background students in the school as a function of the negative teacher attitudes towards Portuguese students and their culture. This resulted in identity conflict among students and internalization of a sense of academic inferiority. Students simply lived down to their teachers' expectations regardless of which identity orientation (Anglo or Portuguese) they attempted to adopt.

It is important to note that students (and communities) do not passively accept dominant group attributions of their inferiority. Frequently, they resist this process of subordination actively through disruptive or oppositional behavior. While for some students, resistance may contribute to academic development (Skutnabb-Kangas, 1988; Zanger, 1994), in many situations resistance has severe costs with respect to academic success and upward mobility, often culminating in students dropping out of school prematurely (Ogbu, 1992; Willis, 1977). Other students may modify their cultural identity by "acting White" (Fordham, 1990) and buying educational success at the expense of rejection by their peers and ambivalence about their identity. Still others are never given the opportunity in school to gain either academic confidence or pride in identity and, over time, internalize the negative attributions of the dominant group and live down to their teachers' expectations.

There is ample research evidence regarding the kinds of school structures, educator role definitions and instructional interactions that are effective in reversing the traditional patterns of educational disempowerment experienced by culturally diverse students. For example, García's (1991) synthesis of research highlights the importance of support for primary language and literacy development as well as the importance of the way educators define their roles. He points out that educators in effective schools demonstrated a coherent pattern of high academic expectations for their students and perceived themselves as advocates for students. They also saw themselves as instructional innovators and had a strong commitment to school-home communication. They felt they had the autonomy to innovate and support from their principals to do so.

Stedman (1987) similarly highlights the importance of a positive orientation to cultural pluralism in schools that were effective in promoting academic achievement among low-income students. He argues that effective schools acknowledge the ethnic and racial identity of their students through having role models in high status positions and offering opportunities for students to develop their linguistic and cultural talents through programs such as bilingual education. Among the other factors stressed by Stedman are *parental participation* and *academically rich programs*. Parents are encouraged to become involved in their children's education and students are actively engaged in their own learning through cognitively challenging projects and tasks that capitalize on their prior experiences.

Lucas, Henze, and Donato's (1990) study of six successful high schools serving primarily Latino/Latina students in Arizona and California documented eight factors that appeared to distinguish these schools. These factors are as follows:

• Value is placed on students' languages and cultures;

• High academic expectations are communicated to bilingual students;

• School leaders make the education of bilingual students a priority;

• Staff development is explicitly designed to help teachers and other school staff to serve bilingual students more effectively;

• A variety of advanced and basic courses and programs for bilingual students is offered;

• School counselors are committed to and capable of providing appropriate guidance to bilingual students as a result of speaking students' language and coming from similar cultural backgrounds;

• Parents of bilingual students are encouraged to become involved in their children's education;

• School staff members share a strong commitment to create contexts both inside the school and in the community wherein a sense of empowerment can be generated among bilingual students.

The factors highlighted by Lucas and her colleagues are very similar to those elaborated by the Scottish Consultative Council on the Curriculum (Landon *et al.*, 1994) in their discussion of language policies that address the learning needs of bilingual students (see Appendix A).

The picture that emerges from these studies of school effectiveness for culturally diverse students has three specific and one general component that contribute to student academic success. The three specific components are:

- Affirmation of students' cultural identity and encouragement of L1 literacy and language development;

- Encouragement of active parental participation; and

- Cognitively-challenging instruction that provides opportunities for students to draw on their background experiences while working collaboratively to explore issues and topics that are relevant to their lives.

These specific interventions are implemented in a school context where issues related to the education of culturally diverse students have moved from the periphery to the center of concern for the entire school. Educators, both individually and collectively, have defined their roles in such a way that their interactions with culturally diverse students actively affirm students' identities. The educational structures established in the school reflect these role definitions.

The affective dimension of these interactions between educators and students is clear in student comments reported by Lucas and her colleagues:

> At all of the schools, students mentioned teachers who had given them special help and attention, often crediting them with providing personal counseling as well as academic support. Typical student comments included the following: 'The teachers here don't just teach; they care about you' and 'Teachers stay after school to explain what we didn't understand.' (p. 336)

For each of the four dimensions of school organization outlined in Figure 7.1, the role definitions of educators can be described in terms of a continuum with one end of the continuum promoting the empowerment of students while the other contributes to the disabling of students. In the sections that follow, the dimensions are described and examples of the discourses that have been mobilized to support both exclusionary/assimilationist and transformative/intercultural orientations are outlined.

Cultural/Linguistic Incorporation
As noted in Chapter 6, considerable research data suggest that for subordinated group students, the extent to which students' language and culture is incorporated into the school program constitutes a significant predictor of academic success (see for example, Beykont, 1994; Campos & Keatinge, 1988; Ramírez, 1992). Students' school success appears to reflect both the more solid

cognitive/academic foundation developed through intensive L1 instruction and also the reinforcement of their cultural identity.

Educators' role definitions with respect to students' language and culture can be characterized along an *additive-subtractive* dimension. Educators who see their role as helping students to add a second language and cultural affiliation while maintaining their primary language and culture are more likely to create interactional conditions of empowerment than those who see their role as replacing or subtracting students' primary language and culture in the process of assimilating them to the dominant culture. Bilingual programs that aim explicitly to promote L1 literacy clearly communicate a strong additive orientation to students and have greater scope for creating conditions of empowerment than monolingual programs.

However, an additive orientation is not dependent upon actual teaching of students' primary language. In many cases this may not be possible for a variety of reasons (*e.g.,* low concentration of particular groups of bilingual students). Even within a monolingual school context, powerful messages can be communicated to students regarding the validity and advantages of primary language development. For example, a teacher who decides to learn just one word per day of the various languages represented in her classroom communicates a strong message of respect for students' language and culture. Each day, one student can be invited to bring in a word that is particularly meaningful to him or her and all students in the class can learn this word and talk (in English) about its meaning and cultural connotations. In this way, students share their background experiences with other students and with the teacher and develop a greater awareness of how languages map out the world in different ways.

Along the same lines, Lucas and Katz (1994) have demonstrated that exemplary Special Alternative Instructional Programs (SAIPs), that use primarily English for instructional purposes, also make considerable use of students' primary language. The investigators studied language use patterns in nine SAIPs (operating in six states) that had been nominated as exemplary in terms of student outcomes. They found that although the programs were designed to provide instruction primarily in English, teachers made considerable use of students' L1 for instructional purposes:

> In practice, however, the classrooms were multilingual environments in which students' native languages served a multitude of purposes and functions. They gave students access to academic content, to classroom activities, and to their own knowledge and experience;

gave teachers a way to show their respect and value for students' languages and cultures; acted as a medium for social interaction and establishment of rapport; fostered family involvement; and fostered students' development of, knowledge of, and pride in their native languages and cultures. (1994, p. 545)

Among the concrete ways in which teachers drew on the linguistic resources of their students were the following:

• Teachers set up activities that specifically called for students to use their L1 with each other; for example, a group writing assignment that used the L1 or, working in groups, translating stories from the L1 into English to tell to other students.

• Less fluent students were paired with more fluent students from the same L1 background so that the more fluent students could assist those who were less fluent.

• Bilingual dictionaries and L1 library books were provided to assist students comprehend instruction and to encourage development of L1 literacy skills. In addition, journal writing in L1 was encouraged in some schools.

Furthermore, when teachers or teaching assistants were fluent in students' L1, they used it for instructional purposes to clarify content and concepts originally presented in English or to teach content directly in the L1. Courses in L1 language arts were also offered in some sites and awards were given for excellence in languages that are not commonly studied (*e.g.,* a senior award in Khmer language skill in one school).

Lucas and Katz conclude that "alternatives to bilingual education need not be English-only programs. There is no reason to assume that programs for students who speak many languages must use only English in ESL classes and content classes" (p. 557). They reinforce Elsa Auerbach's (1993) claim that the inclusion of students' L1 can reduce the degree of language and culture shock and strengthen students' self-esteem and identity. The *deep structure* of these programs is similar to that of genuine bilingual programs in that an additive orientation to students' language and culture is communicated to both students and parents. Thus, Lucas and Katz argue for going beyond the divisive debate on the merits or otherwise of bilingual education versus English-only programs; they suggest focusing instead on providing as much reinforcement for students' identity formation and academic development as the constraints of particular situations permit (*e.g.,* availability of bilingual teachers, teaching assistants, L1 curriculum resources etc.). At the same time that Lucas and Katz' important article appeared, a similar perspective was being articulated across the Atlantic by the Scottish Consultative Council on the Curriculum (Landon *et al.*, 1994) with respect to the significance of developing school language policies that respected the linguistic diversity of the students and community and used this diversity as a resource to enrich all students (see Appendix A).

Lucas and Katz' conclusion is reinforced by the findings of an earlier year-long ethnographic study of an ESL classroom in which a variety of linguistic backgrounds were represented (Saville-Troike, 1984). It was found that opportunities to use the primary language were significantly related to the learning of English:

> Most of the children who achieved best in content areas, as measured by tests in English, were those who had the opportunity to discuss the concepts they were learning in their native language with other children or adults. (Saville-Troike, 1984, p. 216) [2]

In summary, as documented in Chapter 6, the most powerful ways of incorporating students' language and culture into the curriculum are through dual language (two-way) or developmental (late-exit) bilingual programs that aim explicitly to promote bilingualism and biliteracy. However, in situations where genuine bilingual programs are not possible, an additive orientation to students' language and culture can still be communicated to students and parents in a variety of ways. This reinforcement of students' identities is crucial for motivating students to engage with academic content. By contrast, when the implicit or explicit message given to students is that they should leave their language and culture at the schoolhouse door, many students will accurately perceive the schooling process to be coercive and may resist it actively by not learning. Pauline Gibbons (1991) has eloquently expressed a similar point:

> A second language and culture is not learned by destroying the first. By ignoring the mother tongue, we run the risk of slowing down children's learning and encouraging, often unintentionally, the beginning of a one-way journey away from their families. (p. 69) [3]

Community Participation

Students from subordinated communities will be empowered in the school context to the extent that their parents are empowered through their interactions with the school. When educators and parents develop partnerships to promote their children's education, parents appear to develop a sense of efficacy that communicates itself to children with positive academic consequences (*e.g.*, Ada, 1988a; McCaleb, 1994; Tizard, Hewison & Schofield, 1982). The positive impact of parental involvement and support, documented in the Ramírez (1992) and Beykont (1994) studies, illustrates the importance of pursuing these partnerships.

The teacher role definitions associated with community participation can be characterized along a *collaborative-exclusionary* dimension. Teachers operating at the collaborative end of the continuum actively encourage parents to participate in promoting their children's academic progress both in the home and through involvement in classroom activities. A collaborative orientation may require a willingness on the part of the teacher to work closely with classroom assistants or community volunteers in order to communicate effectively and in a non-condescending way with parents. Teachers with an exclusionary orientation, on the other hand, tend to regard teaching as *their* job and are likely to view collaboration with culturally diverse parents as either irrelevant or actually detrimental to children's progress.

Clearly, initiatives for collaboration or for a shared decision-making process can come from the community as well as from the school. Under these conditions, maintenance of an exclusionary orientation by the school can lead communities to challenge the institutional power structure. This was the case with the school strike organized by Finnish parents and their children at Bredby school in Rinkeby, Sweden. In response to a plan by the headmistress to reduce the amount of Finnish instruction, the Finnish community withdrew their children from the school. Eventually (after eight weeks) most of their demands were met. According to Skutnabb-Kangas (1988), the strike had the effect of generating a new sense of efficacy among the community and making them more aware of the role of an exclusionary orientation in the educational system in reproducing the powerless status of subordinated groups. A hypothesis that the present framework generates is that this renewed sense of efficacy will lead to higher levels of academic achievement among culturally diverse students in this type of situation.

Even simple initiatives that permit parents to participate actively in aspects of their children's education can have profound effects. For example, a two-year project carried out in six schools in an inner-city area of London, England, showed major improvements in children's reading skills simply as a result of sending books home on a daily basis with the children for them to read to their parents, many of whom spoke little English and were illiterate in both English and their L1 (predominantly Bengali and Greek) (Tizard, Schofield, & Hewison,

1982). The children attending the two schools that implemented the "shared literacy" program made significantly greater progress in reading than a comparison group in two different schools who received additional small-group reading instruction from a highly competent reading specialist. Of particular importance is the fact that the differences in favor of the shared literacy program were most apparent among children who were initially having difficulty in learning to read. Both groups made greater progress than a control group in two schools who received no special treatment. Teachers involved in the home collaboration reported that children showed an increased interest in school learning and were better behaved. The impact of this project in motivating students to read can be seen from the fact that the students in the two "shared reading" schools exhausted the supply of books in the school libraries that were appropriate for early elementary grades simply because they read so much.

Several reasons can be suggested for the success of this project. First, it changed fundamentally the relationship between the schools and community. Partnerships were established that enabled parents to play an important role in helping their children succeed academically. Second, the project motivated students to read more and, as documented in Chapter 4, the more students read, the stronger their reading skills become (Fielding & Pearson, 1994; Krashen, 1993; Postlethwaite & Ross, 1992). Third, it is likely that many students would have translated or paraphrased the story for their parent in their L1 since the parent would have had limited knowledge of English. This constitutes a cognitively demanding activity that may have increased students' overall ability to analyze the semantic and syntactic aspects of text.

Whatever the underlying reasons for the dramatic impact of this program, it surely points to the role of parents as largely untapped resources in accelerating students' academic skills development. Clearly, books can be sent home in students' L1 as an alternative to, or in addition to, books in English. The crucial aspect of this type of family literacy project is that students become motivated to read for pleasure outside of school because only in books will they find the academic language they need to succeed in school. [4]

In summary, when educators define their roles in terms of collaboration with culturally diverse parents and communities, they are challenging the all-too-prevalent coercive discourse that attributes students' academic difficulties to apathetic and uninvolved parents (*e.g.*, Dunn, 1987). By refuting the myth of parental apathy, they expose the exclusionary structures that have prevented culturally diverse parents from productive involvement in their children's education.

Pedagogy

Three major orientations can be distinguished with respect to pedagogy. These differ in the extent to which the teacher retains exclusive control over classroom interaction as opposed to sharing some of this control with students. The dominant instructional model in most western industrial societies has been termed a "banking" model (Freire, 1970; Freire & Macedo, 1987) on the grounds that teachers are expected to deposit information and skills in students' memory banks. This traditional model can be contrasted with constructivist and transformative models of pedagogy. Constructivist pedagogy historically is associated with the "progressive" pedagogy of John Dewey (1963) who emphasized the centrality of student experience and the importance of encouraging active student learning rather than passive reception of information. Although a variety of labels have been used, I am using the term "constructivist" as an umbrella term to refer to the pedagogical assumptions that are associated not only with Dewey's work, but also the work of sociocultural theorists whose pedagogical focus derives primarily from the work of Vygotsky (1962, 1978) (*e.g.,* Tharp & Gallimore, 1988; Wells, 2000). Current whole-language approaches to language and literacy also embody many constructivist principles.

In philosophical debates about education throughout this century, traditional and constructivist orientations have vied for ascendancy at regular intervals. The focus on the transformative potential of education is a more recent phenomenon and is strongly influenced by Paulo Freire's work. Each of the three orientations incorporates a set of instructional and social assumptions. Instructional assumptions are concerned with the conceptions of language, knowledge, and learning that underlie various forms of teaching while social assumptions focus on the ways in which relations of culture and power are addressed in the curriculum.

Most proponents of traditional and constructivist pedagogies tend to focus more on instructional than on social dimensions. They tend to see their instructional recommendations as socially-neutral and non-ideological. By contrast, advocates of transformative pedagogy argue that all forms of instruction entail social assumptions, whether acknowledged explicitly or not. The forms of thinking and literacy that are encouraged in school anticipate the forms of civic participation that students are being prepared to undertake upon graduation. Transformative pedagogy explicitly aims to prepare students to participate fully in the democratic process and to uphold principles of human rights and social justice that are enshrined in the constitutions of most western industrialized countries (see Frederickson, 1995).

The instructional and social assumptions of traditional (banking), constructivist, and transformative pedagogy are outlined in Figure 7.2. Although these orientations are expressed as distinct categories in Figure 7.2, it is more appropriate to see them as points on a continuum that merge into one another. For example, a transformative orientation will usually include considerable explicit instruction and much classroom interaction will be constructivist in nature rather than focused directly on social realities. However, a transformative orientation will also actively seek opportunities to relate instruction to students' experience and identity and to the social realities within which their experiences and identities are embedded. Similarly, as Eleni Skourtou points out (personal communication, April 2001), constructivist approaches will tend to merge into transformative pedagogy if carried to their logical conclusion. The emphasis within constructivism on constructing knowledge on the basis of students' experience within a community of learners should logically extend into the power relations that shape what counts as knowledge and whose knowledge counts. Frequently, however, constructivist approaches (*e.g.,* whole-language) decline to cross this threshold, preferring to remain within the confines of the classroom rather than venturing into the social landscape beyond.

Traditional pedagogy. The basic premise of the traditional model is that the teacher's task is to impart knowledge or skills to students. This implies that the teacher initiates and controls the interaction, constantly orienting it towards the achievement of instructional objectives. The instructional content in this type of program derives primarily from the internal structure of the language or subject matter; consequently, it frequently involves a predominant focus on surface features of language or literacy and emphasizes correct recall of content taught. Content is frequently transmitted by means of highly structured drills and workbook exercises, although in many cases the drills are disguised in order to make them more attractive and motivating to students.

Within this instructional orientation, language is decomposed into its component parts (*e.g.,* phonics, vocabulary, grammatical rules) which are then transmitted in isolation from each other; learning is assumed to progress in a hierarchical manner starting with simple elements and progressing to more complex forms. Thus, explicit phonics instruction is a prerequisite for reading development; grammar, vocabulary, and spelling must be taught before students can start writing; and knowledge is viewed as static or inert, to be internalized and reproduced by students when required.

The social assumptions of traditional pedagogy are straightforward. Curriculum should present the "cultural literacy" of the society—in Hirsch's terms "what every American needs to know." However, by virtue of what it omits, this type of curriculum also operates to restrict access to alternative perspectives on historical and contemporary events (Macedo, 1993, 1994; Peterson, 1994). The

Figure 7.2 **INSTRUCTION AND SOCIAL ASSUMPTIONS UNDERLYING TRADITIONAL, CONSTRUCTIVIST AND TRANSFORMATIVE PEDAGOGY**

Traditional	Constructivist	Transformative
Instructional Assumptions		
LANGUAGE		
Decomposed	Whole	Whole
KNOWLEDGE		
Static/Inert	Catalytic	Catalytic
LEARNING		
Hierarchical internalization from simple to complex	Joint interactive construction through collaborative inquiry	Joint interactive construction through critical inquiry
Social Assumptions		
CURRICULUM		
Transmission of "cultural literacy;" explicitly sanitized with respect to power relations	Celebrates differences but implicitly sanitized with respect to power relations	Focused on critical examination of student experience and social realities; explicit attention to power relations
STUDENT OUTCOMES		
Compliant/Uncritical	Liberal but Uncritical	Empowered/Critical

curriculum is sanitized with respect to issues of historical and current power relations, and students are expected to emerge from schooling as "good citizens" who will comply with the expectations of the societal power structure.

With respect to the education of culturally diverse students, the major problems with this form of "banking" education are:

• It promotes cultural ambivalence among subordinated group students by providing no opportunity for students to express and share their experience with peers and teachers; in other words, students are silenced or rendered "voiceless" in the classroom (Giroux, 1991; Walsh, 1991). Their prior knowledge is untapped and there are few if any opportunities to reflect critically on social issues of direct relevance to their lives.

• It contravenes central principles of language and literacy acquisition in that it is impossible to learn language or develop literacy in the absence of ample opportunities for meaningful communicative interaction in both oral and written modes.

Cummins and Sayers (1995) summarize the limitations of traditional pedagogy as follows:

> In summary, traditional pedagogy aims to indoctrinate, both in its instructional and social goals. Facts are to be memorized, religious or cultural truths internalized, inquiry circumscribed, and contradictions obscured. The goal may appear laudable—to build a strong culture—but a culture whose identity is based on ignorance of all around it is living in a fool's paradise. (p. 150)

Constructivist pedagogy. Whereas traditional approaches decompose language—break it up into its component parts for easier transmission—constructivist approaches, as embodied in whole-language pedagogy, insist that language can be learned only when it is kept "whole" and used for meaningful communication either in oral or written modes. Knowledge within traditional curriculum is viewed as fixed and inert whereas in constructivist pedagogy it is seen as catalytic in the sense that new information acts as a catalyst for further inquiry. Learning in traditional pedagogy is largely memorization whereas in constructivist pedagogy learning is constructed collaboratively through interaction with peers and teachers.

Within a constructivist approach, teachers encourage students to use both written and oral language actively as a means of learning content and promoting cognitive growth. Students' experience is expressed and shared within the classroom context creating an interpersonal space within which their identity can be validated. By contrast, "banking" approaches usually employ textbooks that reflect only the values and priorities of the dominant group, thereby effectively suppressing the experience of culturally diverse students. Constructivist approaches highlight the role of collaborative inquiry and the construction of meaning as central to students' academic growth. The classroom is seen as a community of learning where knowledge is generated by teachers and students together (Wells, 2000). [5]

There is considerable research evidence supporting the general principles underlying a whole-language, inquiry-based constructivist pedagogy (see Cummins and Sayers, 1995 for a review). Such an approach is not in any sense incompatible with a strong focus on providing explicit feedback to students on formal aspects of language. It can also accommodate the explicit teaching of learning strategies to help students become efficient and independent learners. As noted in Chapter 5, an instructional focus on language itself is an important part of effective pedagogy. Some forms of whole-language and constructivist pedagogy have tended to neglect this explicit focus on demystifying language in favor of an exclusive focus on meaning and use. [6]

While the instructional assumptions underlying constructivist pedagogies are generally appropriate and supported by research, the social assumptions underlying constructivist pedagogy are seldom articulated. With some exceptions, contemporary whole-language theorists have tended to focus on instructional rather than social realities. Their focus is on the child, either as an individual or within the classroom learning community. An unfortunate consequence of this, as Maria de la Luz Reyes (1992) has pointed out, is that without explicit attention to the social realities of diversity, many whole-language classrooms will be just as monocultural and blind to students' cultural realities as are more traditional classrooms. Similarly, issues of power and status are rarely the focus of instruction within whole-language classrooms. Any focus on multiculturalism is frequently limited to "celebrating diversity"—promotion of tolerance and acceptance that is aimed at increasing students' self-esteem but does little to challenge inequities of power and status distribution in the society.

In short, constructivist pedagogy usually focuses narrowly on the teaching-learning relationship and fails to articulate a coherent vision of the broader social implications of instruction. Tolerance and acceptance of cultural difference are often implied but critical reflection on students' own experience, and critique of social realities are not.

Transformative pedagogy. The instructional assumptions of transformative pedagogy are similar to those of constructivist pedagogy. However, they diverge with respect to social assumptions. Transformative pedagogy uses collaborative critical inquiry to enable students to relate curriculum content to their individual and collective experience and to analyze broader social issues relevant to their lives. It also encourages students to discuss ways in which social realities might be transformed through various forms of democratic participation and social action.

Thus, transformative pedagogy will aim to go beyond the sanitized curriculum that is still the norm in many schools. It will attempt to promote students' ability to analyze and understand the social realities of their own lives and of their communities. It will strive to develop a critical literacy which Ira Shor (1992) has defined as follows:

> Habits of thought, reading, writing, and speaking which go beneath surface meaning, first impressions, dominant myths, official pronouncements, traditional cliches, received wisdom, and mere opinions, to understand the deep meaning, root causes, social context, ideology, and personal consequences of any action, event, object, process, organization, experience, text, subject matter, policy, mass media, or discourse. (p. 129)

In short, critical literacy reflects the analytic abilities involved in cutting through the surface veneer of persuasive arguments to the realities underneath and analyzing the methods and purposes of particular forms of persuasion. Clearly, the ability to think critically in these ways is crucial for meaningful participation in a democratic society. If consent can be manufactured effortlessly through media persuasion, then democracy merges into totalitarianism.

A transformative orientation to pedagogy inevitably means that educators must be willing to explore the ways in which dominant groups both historically and currently have maintained their power. In order to challenge the operation of coercive relations of power in their own lives, students and communities must understand how it works. This is why the (transformative) instructional framework elaborated in Chapter 5 incorporates an emphasis on the intersections of power and language in all its phases (Focus on Meaning, Focus on Language, Focus on Use). [7]

Assessment. In the past, assessment has played a central role in legitimating the instructional disabling of culturally diverse students. Biased standardized tests have located the "problem" within the student, thereby screening from critical scrutiny the subtractive nature of the school program, the exclusionary orientation of teachers towards subordinated communities, and "banking" models of teaching that suppress students' experience and inhibit them from active participation in learning.

This process is virtually inevitable when the conceptual base for the assessment process is purely psychoeducational. If the psychologist's task (or role definition) is to discover the causes of a student's academic difficulties and the only tools at her disposal are psychological tests (in either L1 or L2), then it is hardly surprising that the child's difficulties will be attributed to psychological dysfunctions. The myth of bilingual handicaps that still influences educational policy was generated in exactly this way during the 1920's and 1930's.

A number of studies suggest that despite the appearance of change with respect to nondiscriminatory assessment, the underlying structure has remained essentially intact. Mehan, Hertweck and Meihls (1986), for example, reported that psychologists continued to test children until they "found" the disability that could be invoked to "explain" the student's apparent academic difficulties. The Cummins (1984) study, discussed earlier, also revealed that although no diagnostic conclusions were logically possible in the majority of assessments, psychologists were most reluctant to admit this fact to teachers and parents. In short, the data suggest that the structure within which psychological assessment takes place orients the psychologist to locate the cause of the academic problem within culturally diverse students themselves.

The alternative role definition that is required to reverse the traditional "legitimating" function of assessment can be termed an "advocacy" role. Educators must be prepared to become advocates for the student in critically scrutinizing the societal and educational context within which the student has developed. This implies that the conceptual basis for assessment should be broadened so that it goes beyond psychoeducational considerations to take account of the student's entire learning environment. To challenge the disabling of culturally diverse students, assessment must focus on the extent to which children's language and culture are incorporated within the school program, the extent to which educators establish genuine partnerships with culturally diverse parents, and the extent to which students are encouraged to use language (both L1 and L2) actively within the classroom to amplify their experiences in interaction with other students and adults. In other words, the primary focus should be on remediating the educational interactions that culturally diverse students experience.

It is worth noting that assessment and pedagogy are closely linked in that classroom teachers have considerable opportunity to observe children undertaking a variety of cognitive and academic tasks when the instruction is individualized and interactional. This information can and should play an important role in assessment/placement decisions. Within a "banking" instructional model student learning activities are teacher-imposed rather than expressive of students' own experience; consequently, this form of instruction limits the extent to which students' knowledge and abilities can find expression in the classroom. Similarly, most standardized tests exclude bilingual students' culturally-specific knowledge and abilities. Under these conditions of silencing, there is much less opportunity for teachers to observe students' academic strengths and weaknesses.

In short, many forms of standardized assessment focus on what culturally diverse students have not had the opportunity to learn. These tests also ignore the culturally-specific knowledge that students have learned. For example, a grade 5 immigrant student who has been in an English-speaking school environment for only one year has not had the opportunity to learn as much of the English language or English academic content as students whose native language is English and who have been learning through English for 6 years. The immigrant student may have extensive literacy in Spanish, Chinese or Farsi, and related cultural and academic knowledge, but this knowledge and literacy ability is not tapped by the grade 5 test. Consequently, such a test not only discriminates against the student but also provides highly inaccurate and misleading information if the test results are interpreted as reflecting the quality of instruction in a particular school (which they are in states such as California and Texas).

There are alternatives to forms of standardized assessment that fail to assess what students know and have learned. Various forms of performance and portfolio assessment can assess students' progress over time in a culturally- and instructionally-sensitive way (O'Malley & Pierce, 1996). In Chapter 8, the impact of portfolio assessment in dramatically transforming the educational outcomes of ELL students at the International High School in Laguardia Community College in New York City is reviewed (DeFazio, 1997). Cummins (2000, Chapter 6) and Gottlieb (1999) also discuss issues regarding the inclusion of ELL students in state-mandated assessment programs.

In summary, an advocacy approach to assessment of culturally diverse students will involve a willingness to locate the "problem" in the societal power relations between dominant and subordinated groups, in the reflection of these power relations between school and communities, and in the suppression of students' experience and identities within classrooms oriented only towards transmission of information and skills. These conditions are a more probable cause of the threefold overrepresentation of Latino/Latina students in Texas in the learning disabled category than any intrinsic processing deficit unique to these students (Ortiz & Yates, 1983).

In most industrialized countries the training of psychologists and special educators does not prepare them for this advocacy role. To advocate for bilingual students in this way frequently entails challenging the societal and educational power structure. Thus, in the past, rather than challenging a social and educational system that acts to disable bilingual students and communities, educators have accepted a role definition and an educational structure that makes discriminatory instruction and assessment virtually inevitable.

Conclusion

Alternative visions of society have emerged in the debate during the past two decades in regard to the education of culturally diverse students in North America. At issue is the extent to which the educational system will take seriously notions such as *equity* and *social justice* and promote academic achievement for all students regardless of race, class or income; or will the educational system continue its traditional function of reproducing the power structure such that the existing division of status, resources and income is reinforced?

In spite of considerable rhetoric endorsing equity and justice, little has changed in terms of educational outcomes. Culturally diverse students are still massively over-represented in low-achieving categories.

In order to understand why so little has changed in the big picture, a theoretical framework was proposed for analyzing culturally diverse students' academic difficulties and for predicting the effects of educational interventions. I have argued that the patterns of micro-interactions that culturally diverse students experience in the educational system are a function of the power relations operating between dominant and subordinated groups in the wider society. The power structure in the wider society strongly influences the culture of the school which is expressed in the educational structures implemented in the school and in the ways educators define their roles with respect to culturally diverse students and communities. Thus, it is not surprising that most educational reforms have remained at a surface level where they do not seriously challenge the societal power structure.

Genuine reform, at a deep structure level, requires that the culture of the school change in ways that potentially challenge coercive relations of power. Individual educators are by no means powerless; they have many opportunities within the school to challenge the operation of the societal power structure. Specifically, they can become advocates for the promotion of students' linguistic talents, actively encourage culturally diverse parents to participate in developing students' academic and cultural resources, and implement pedagogical approaches that encourage students to use oral and written language to reflect critically on and amplify their experience. When educators define their roles in terms of promoting social justice and equality of opportunity, then their interactions with culturally diverse students are more likely to embody a transformative potential that challenges coercive relations of power as they are manifested in the school context. [8]

The outcome of this process for both educators and students can be described in terms of *empowerment*. Conditions of collaborative empowerment are created when educators attempt to organize their interactions with culturally diverse students in such a way that power is generated and shared through these interactions. This involves becoming aware of, and actively working to change, educational structures that limit culturally diverse students' opportunities for educational and social advancement. Teaching for empowerment, by definition, constitutes a challenge to the societal power structure. Interventions that fail to challenge the power structure simply erect a cosmetic facade that obscures the continuing reality of disempowerment.

Genuine educational reform requires that innovations permeate and transform the entire culture of the school. If innovations are restricted to a single classroom and affect only a small number of teachers and school staff, the culture of the school will remain largely unchanged. Neither educational structures nor collective role definitions will be affected. By contrast, when most educators in the school "buy into" and take ownership of the approach or innovation, it becomes part of the school's mission. The culture of the school becomes infused with this mission; structures and collective role definitions change to accomplish a set of explicitly articulated goals related to culturally diverse students and communities (Hopkins, 1987; Olsen *et al.*, 1994; Organization for Economic Cooperation and Development, 1991).

In the next chapter, portraits of schools and educators that have created conditions of collaborative empowerment are sketched. Not only have most of these schools moved towards the transformative/intercultural end of the continua of Figure 7.1, they have done so in such a way that their innovations become part of the collective identity of the entire school. As a result, the interactional spaces in these schools, where minds and identities meet, generate power for both educators and students. [9]

Endnotes to Chapter 7

1. Rodriguez (1982) provides an autobiographical account of the emotional schism brought about by teachers' advice to parents to switch from Spanish to English in the home:

> One Saturday morning three nuns arrived at the house to talk to our parents …I overheard one voice gently wondering, 'Do your children speak only Spanish at home, Mrs. Rodriguez?' …With great tact the visitors continued, 'Is it possible for you and your husband to encourage your children to practice their English when they are at home?' Of course, my parents complied. What would they not do for their children's well-being? And how could they have questioned the Church's authority which those women represented? In an instant, they agreed to give up the language (the sounds) that had revealed and accentuated our family's closeness. The moment after the visitors left, the change was observed. 'Ahora, speak to us en inglés', my father and mother united to tell us. (p. 20-21)

Rodriguez goes on to describe the effect of this language switch for the family's interaction at home:

> The family's quiet was partly due to the fact that, as we children learned more and more English, we shared fewer and fewer words with our parents. Sentences needed to be spoken slowly when a child addressed his mother or father. (Often the parent wouldn't understand.) The child would need to repeat himself. (Still the parent misunderstood.) The young voice, frustrated, would end up saying, 'Never mind'—the subject was closed. Dinners would be noisy with the clinking of knives and forks against dishes. (p. 23)

Rodriguez (1982) argues that this schism between children's lives in home and school, their private and public selves, is necessary and that bilingual programs are potentially detrimental to bilingual children because they create the illusion that it is possible for children to become fully integrated into American society while maintaining aspects of their cultural identity. An examination of the research data on bilingual education from virtually any country in the world shows that this argument is totally without foundation (see Chapter 6).

2. Other countries have similarly sought ways of incorporating students' L1 into what are essentially English language programs (see Appendix A). For example, the New Zealand Department of Education (1988) has suggested a variety of strategies such as:

- Provide signs in the main office and elsewhere that welcome people in the different languages of the community;

- Encourage students to use their L1 around the school and to write contributions in their L1 for school newspapers and magazines;

- Provide opportunities for students from the same ethnic group to communicate with one another in their L1 where possible (*e.g.*, in cooperative learning groups on at least some occasions);

- Provide books written in community languages in both classrooms and the school library; Provide opportunities for students to study their L1 in elective subjects and/or in extracurricular clubs;

- Encourage parents to help in the classroom, library, playground, and in clubs;

- Invite second language learners to use their L1 during assemblies, prize givings, and other official functions;

- Invite people from culturally diverse communities to act as resource people and to speak to students in both formal and informal settings.

In the Australian context, Pauline Gibbons (1991, pp. 67–69) has suggested a variety of additional ways in which students' primary language and cultural identity can be reinforced in the classroom. Some of her ideas are paraphrased below:

- Build mother tongue stories into the program, using tapes at listening posts or making available books in the mother tongue. Older children or parents may help produce tapes.

- Display the children's mother tongues in the classroom. Label objects around the classroom and display the children's writing.

- Build up a stock of bilingual books based on the children's own writing. Children who are literate in their mother tongue, or parents, may help with translation. If the English and the mother tongue are on facing pages, all children will have access to the text.

- Invite children to teach you and the class a little of their language, such as a song, a greeting, colors or how to count. Each morning for a week say 'good morning' to the class in one of the class languages, and encourage all children to reply.

3. David and Yvonne Freeman (1994) provide several concrete examples of an intercultural orientation in practice in their book *Between Worlds: Access to Second Language Acquisition*. These include student explorations of their own communities and family histories as well as in-depth study of the history of particular cultural groups. For example, in one sixth-grade class, students examined the significant contributions made by Mexican-Americans in a vari-

ety of spheres of endeavor. The impact on both Anglo and Mexican-American students is described as follows:

> When Anglo students in Rusty's class read about the rights promised Mexicans living in the United States by the Treaty of Guadalupe Hidalgo, the treaty written when the war between Mexico and the United States ended in 1848, they also feel the indignation of their Hispanic classmates over the broken promises. Students study the changing geography of the Southwest between 1810 and 1848, and they begin to understand the strong roots that Spanish-speaking peoples claim in this country. Studying about political activists like César Chavez and Gloria Molina, as well as writers and artists, gives Hispanic students a pride in their culture and people. (1994, p. 282)

4. A useful resource for parental involvement initiatives is Sudia Paloma McCaleb's (1994) book *Building Communities of Learners: A Collaboration Among Teachers, Students, Family and Community*. The projects and initiatives documented in the book were inspired by Alma Flor Ada's pioneering work in the Pajaro Valley School District (described in Chapter 1).

Another outstanding project also inspired by Alma Flor Ada's work is the *The Family Connection: Hmong Parent Education Project* carried out with the support of Title VII funds in Merced County, California (Eccles, Kirton & Xiong, 1994). The project has translated a variety of children's literature into Hmong, produced Hmong "Big Books" and published an extensive collection of stories and accounts of life in Laos written and illustrated by Hmong parents in the Merced County area. Most of these books are cerlox bound and have a "story cloth" set of illustrations on the left facing page and Hmong and English versions of the story on the right facing page.

Frances Eccles describes how parents discovered their voice in the unfamiliar medium of written language:

> In working with our Hmong parents, most of whom had never been to school and didn't know how to read and write their own language, much less English, we found that they thought they could not write, and that they had nothing to say that anyone would want to read. ...Once the parents realized they did indeed have stories to tell, and that they could tell their stories to a tape recorder and someone else could transcribe them we were off and running.

> The easiest stories to elicit were stories from their own lives and personal experience. So we developed some questions to help them organize their writing. (1994, p. 1)

Writing of personal histories was facilitated by questions about home and family life as a child and teenager in Laos as well as questions related to cultural conventions and the experience of war and migration to the United States. These oral histories were transcribed and published in both Hmong and English with parents themselves illustrating "story cloths" that depicted events in the stories.

Questions were also asked about topics that would be suitable for children's stories (*e.g.,* things that scared the parents as children) and books on these topics were produced and are used extensively in the district's bilingual programs. North American folktales (*e.g.,* The City Mouse and the Country Mouse) were also translated into Hmong and discussed among the parents in relation to their own experiences. A variety of imaginative lesson plans for use by teachers in school and activities for both parents and children at home have been developed by the project. These activities focus directly on the texts written by the parents.

Crucial to the success of the project has been the involvement of a bilingual/bicultural Parent Education Facilitator (Blong Xiong) and the fact that parents see quick and powerful results (their books in print, in the school library, and being used in classrooms). The project directors also point out that parents like learning about North American cultures and about the literature used in school, and they enjoy stories of all kinds because theirs is a culture of learning through oral tradition.

Of related interest is the fact that resources related to Hmong history, culture, language, and current events are now available on the World Wide Web. The Hmong Home Page address is: http://www.hmongnet.org.

5. The importance of creating classroom and school-wide communities of learning that focus on acceleration of student progress rather than remediation is reinforced by the success of the Accelerated Schools Project, initiated by Stanford University professor Henry Levin (1998). This project, implemented in about 1,000 schools across North America, rejects remediation for low-income students and instead argues that what works for so-called gifted and talented students will work for all students. Curriculum and instruction build on students' experiences, interests, motivations, culture, and observed abilities. Language use is emphasized across the curriculum and the development of higher-order literacy skills is fostered from an early age. A focus on experiential learning (*i.e.,* learning-by-doing rather than learning-by-listening), problem-solving, peer tutoring and cooperative learning are also central to instruction in Accelerated Schools. There is a strong focus on parents as partners in a shared educational enterprise, with parents expected to contribute significantly to their children's engagement in learning.

Accelerated schools (at both elementary and middle school level) have shown substantial increases in student achievement in places as diverse as San Francisco, Los Angeles, Seattle, New Orleans, Missouri and Illinois. Levin cautions, however, that usually about six years is required for a school to make the full transformation from a conventional to an accelerated school because major changes in school organization are required. Central among these changes is a shift from "top-down" to "bottom-up" decision making with teachers taking collective responsibility for decisions which they will implement and evaluate. More information on the Accelerated Schools project can be found at www-leland.stanford.edu/group/ASP.

6. Several critics of whole-language approaches (*e.g.,* Delpit, 1988; Kalantzis & Cope, 1993) have argued convincingly that some children require more explicit forms of instruction and corrective feedback than is the case in many whole-language classrooms. Specifically, there is a need for explicit instruction in how to use language powerfully to achieve social goals. This would entail developing competence in the conventions of different genres (*e.g.,* report writing, formal letters etc.) and an awareness of how language is used in a wide variety of

social contexts. In Lisa Delpit's words, teachers must learn not only how to "help students to establish their own voices, but to coach those voices to produce notes that will be heard clearly in the larger society" (1988, p. 296).

Reyes (1992) has also criticized the "one size fits all" assumptions of some whole-language classrooms, arguing that there is a need to affirm more explicitly culturally diverse students' cultural knowledge and to promote multicultural awareness.

These critiques of whole-language pedagogy are important but they appear to apply more to the way whole-language has been interpreted and implemented inappropriately in certain contexts rather than to any central theoretical assumptions underlying whole-language pedagogy. Many educators whose views are generally consistent with whole-language approaches would also endorse strongly an explicit focus on critical literacy and on developing students' language awareness. This would include providing relevant explicit instruction and corrective feedback on formal aspects of language in order to ensure that students' voices will be heard and understood in the wider society. This orientation would also strive to affirm students' primary language and culture and challenge educational structures that devalue these and other aspects of students' identity (see, for example, Freeman & Freeman, 1992, 1998).

In short, it does not seem difficult to avoid the excesses occasionally identified in the implementation of whole-language and process writing approaches by insisting on the importance of explicit instruction to guide students' critical inquiry and their use of both written and oral language (see Chapter 5). Similarly, an explicit focus on developing a wide-ranging knowledge of language among students is not in any way incompatible with whole-language or constructivist approaches. For example, with respect to phonics, direct teaching of phonemic awareness and phonics is not in itself problematic nor is it in any way incompatible with the basic principles of whole-language (see Chapter 4). But within a whole-language or constructivist approach, any direct instruction of components of language (*e.g.,* phonics, grammar, etc.) should be aligned to the social construction of knowledge (*e.g.,* encouragement of extensive reading and writing) rather than taught in isolation from experience and meaning.

7. A number of excellent teacher-friendly resources for promoting critical literacy have been published by the editors of *Rethinking Schools*. For a catalogue contact Rethinking Schools, 1001 E. Keefe Avenue, Milwaukee, WI 53212 (fax: 414-964-7220; tel. [toll-free] 1-800-669-4192; website: www.rethinkingschools.org). Many of their publications focus on how critical literacy can be promoted in the classroom as a central component of a multicultural anti-racist curriculum.

The urgency of promoting critical literacy can be gauged from Donaldo Macedo's (1993, 1994) provocative and sobering account of how educational systems frequently promote "literacy for stupidification" and sanitize the curriculum through "the pedagogy of big lies."

8. In view of the fact that educational failure is concentrated among culturally diverse communities, it is surprising that issues of diversity remain at the periphery of much of the restructuring process in California and elsewhere. This is true even for schools that are attempting to engage in a participatory and democratic restructuring process rather than a

"top-down" process. This pattern is illustrated by the findings of a major research project conducted by the advocacy group *California Tomorrow* involving 73 Californian schools that were in the process of restructuring. The sample included a variety of restructuring models based on the work of James Comer (1980), Henry Levin (1998), Theodore Sizer (1984) as well as other initiatives funded through California's 1991 school restructuring legislation (SB 1274). The study revealed a silence about issues of culture and identity and "heavy barriers to bringing diversity and equity issues into the school's plans to better serve their students" (Olsen *et al.*, 1994, p. 31). In spite of genuine commitment, the agenda for the reform process was largely determined by the concerns of dominant group educators and the voices of culturally diverse educators and parents were rarely heard around the table. Parents and instructional aides who were capable of adding to the knowledge base about issues of language, culture and race in the lives of the students were excluded from significant participation in the restructuring process in a large number of schools. The report suggests some of the reasons why dialogue about diversity and equity was missing:

> Four-fifths of California's teachers are white. Most do not come to work with firsthand knowledge of the communities and cultures of their students. Most speak only English…Teacher education programs are far behind the times in providing teachers with the knowledge about second language acquisition, about the impact of racism in students' lives, and about the diverse cultural backgrounds of the students in the public schools. We found more direct, lively dialogue and consideration of issues of race, culture and language in schools where prior to restructuring, there had been a tradition of strong bilingual programs or multicultural education and community embeddedness. …Generally, however, it appeared to us that in many schools, people were unaware that there is a perspective, a knowledge base that is missing around their table. They do not know that they do not know (1994, p. 30).

Unfortunately, the situation in California has, in all likelihood, degenerated further since the passage of Proposition 227 and the imposition of state-mandated high-stakes testing.

9. One set of voices conspicuously absent from educational reform debates are the voices of students. We would do well to heed the views of students such as 9-year old Jessica Rosciglione and her 7-year old sister, Julia. Both girls are bilingual in Italian and English and spent the initial years of their life in Italy before moving to Toronto. Their mother, Jane O'Hare, interviewed them as part of a class project at the Ontario Institute for Studies in Education. Here are some of their likes, dislikes, and suggestions regarding schooling:

> I wish we could work with younger kids and older kids, so we'd help younger kids and older kids would help us;

> I wish we could decide some of the topics instead of the teacher telling us what to do. We're always doing animals;

> I wish school was half a day and they'd give us lots of homework;

I wish school was like an Open House so that parents and grandparents could come in and help us and teach us some of the things they've learned;

I wish I knew or could know about the other kids' families or backgrounds and stuff like that to know what they're like;

I wish we could teach each other our languages;

I wish we could learn what's going on in the world, like: *Why do people have wars? Why do we have a food bank? Why are rich people—people at the top—mean to people at the bottom? Why do people sell drugs? Why do people take drugs? Why do people smoke? Why are some people poor?*

I don't like it when the teacher tells us to be quiet all the time—maybe we have good ideas that we'd like to share with the class;

I don't like it when the teacher tells us to be silent when I'm talking to my friend because maybe he or she doesn't understand something and I'm trying to explain it.

Chapter 8
Collaborative Empowerment at the Preschool, Elementary, and Secondary Levels

T his chapter presents portraits of programs that have succeeded, to a significant extent, in creating contexts for collaborative empowerment in the interactions between educators and culturally diverse students. These portraits demonstrate that transformation of culturally diverse students' educational opportunities is not only possible, but is happening, in schools throughout North America. They also illustrate that what is fundamental is not what a particular program is called, but the extent to which genuine change occurs in the role definitions of educators and in the structures that frame the interactions between educators and students. The portraits in the text derive from the United States but relevant international examples are sketched in the endnotes. [1]

The Preschool Level
The Foundation Center Preschools
Among advocates for culturally diverse children and families, there is widespread agreement that the network of 23 preschool centers operated by the Foundation Center for Phenomenological Research, a non-profit organization based in Sacramento, California, was one of the most outstanding North American examples of early childhood education (*e.g.* Chang & Sakai, 1993). The Foundation Center's network of centers was de-funded by the California State Department in June 1995. [2] The Foundation Center's programs served children from low-income and migrant agricultural working families. The programs were based on the Montessori Method, delivered in children's home languages, and

staff came predominantly from the communities being served. The Foundation Center trained almost 100 of its staff as credentialed Montessori teachers and became the largest officially designated Montessori school system in the United States. This represents a remarkable achievement in view of the fact that many staff members had minimal education before joining the centers as teaching assistants. The Montessori training program was offered through Spanish, teachers' dominant language. Antonia López, Co-Director of the Foundation Center, explained the rationale for training teachers from the community:

> When we first started, we found that most of the existing teachers were not from the same culture as the children. The teachers were frustrated because they weren't getting the results they wanted. There was an invisible distance created by barriers of language and culture. Children were acting out and teachers were having difficulty forming relationships with parents. …We realized that in order to have an emotionally safe environment, we needed to find a way to bring people from the community into the center as staff. But we did not want them to simply become teacher's aides—children are already too accustomed to seeing members of the community in secondary, subservient roles. (Chang & Sakai, 1993, p. 31) [3]

Because of the fact that the centers were staffed by community members, issues of cultural conflict never arose. In Antonia López' words:

> Everything about how the centers run is embedded in the culture of the people—what is an acceptable noise level, what are appropriate adult-child interactions, how they talk about problems, what they say at parent meetings. Because the staff come from the communities, we don't have to worry about "cultural conflicts" or to plan in-services on cultural awareness. They relate to the families and respond to them naturally. Staff is often not even conscious of what they do that is culturally appropriate. (Chang & Sakai, 1993, p. 28)

In addition to use of the Montessori Method and exclusive use of children's primary language for instructional purposes, the program focused on children's nutrition and on supporting family health care. Only organic foods were served in the centers on the grounds that families working in agricultural settings are already exposed to excesses of noxious chemicals without also eating pesticide-treated food. A comprehensive program of family health education was in place at all the centers and all members of the child's family underwent free health screening on a regular basis. This resulted in the detection of serious life-threatening illness such as hypertension, diabetes and major hearing impairments in about 25% of the fathers of children in the preschool programs (López, 1988).

Although no formal evaluation was ever conducted of the Foundation Center's preschool programs, anecdotal accounts suggest a program that was exceptional in promoting children's social and conceptual development. Lily Wong Fillmore, one of the most credible voices in American education, expressed eloquently what many people (including this author) have felt on visiting one of the Foundation Center's programs:

> There are few honest-to-god epiphanies in the education business or in life, for that matter. I experienced one a couple of months ago in Winters, California. I visited a child development center located in a Winters public housing project. The Center, which is sponsored by a group called the Foundation Center for Phenomenological Research, serves the children of seasonal and migrant farm workers. The children range in age from two to six. The program is just about the best I have ever seen: it is exactly what I would have chosen for my own children. Indeed, it is the kind of child development program Yuppie couples seek out before they even consider having a child...It has a family health services program that can easily be a model for early education programs throughout the country. Parents and children attend clinics and health education programs that are designed to keep the entire family in good shape and to establish good health as a family affair. The facilities are beautifully designed and maintained...The physical environment is bright and attractive. Paintings and drawings are hung at child-eye-level. They are meant to be seen, touched, and enjoyed by the children...

> Was this program a miracle? How was it achieved? The teachers at this center are mostly women from the same background as the parents of the children in the center. The lead teacher had just one year of formal schooling before joining the staff of the Winters Child Development Center. After eight years on the job, she is a highly skilled professional educator. That's the genius of this program... [Many of the children coming out of the Foundation Center's

programs] have been judged to be 'gifted' after they leave the Center. From what I saw, they certainly are.

Here then is the kind of program that Latino children, indeed all children, need. It is a program that begins with the assumption that children and their parents want and deserve the best education that can be provided. But good education such as I have described must be very costly, you must be thinking.

I too was a bit worried that this program was too good to be true. It had to be terribly expensive. It could never be replicated on a wide scale, I thought. This turned out to be the biggest surprise of all. While the not-so-hot-programs that one finds across the country cost around $23 per child per day for a three and a half hour program, the programs run by the Foundation Center operate on just $19 per child per day for an 11-hour a day program, including two hot meals and two snacks. (1990a, pp. 32–35)

The Foundation Center was able to offer this outstanding program by paring administrative costs to the bone. While California early childhood education centers were limited to spending 15 percent of their budgets on administration, the Foundation Center spent only 7–9 percent (Chang & Sakai, 1993, p. 34). [4]

The Elementary School Level

Three programs are reviewed briefly here. Two are dual language programs while the third exemplifies the kind of transformative pedagogy discussed in Chapter 7. The information presented below is accurate as of the time of the publications cited. However, schools evolve and personnel change so it is quite likely that the portraits presented here do not fully represent these schools as they are now. The point, however, is that they illustrate what educators, students, and communities *can* achieve when the collective role definitions of educators effect structural changes that challenge the constricting and devaluing messages that subordinated groups have historically experienced in the wider society (and still do as illustrated by Propositions 227 and 203).

Oyster Bilingual School, Washington DC

This school, established in 1971, is one of the earliest Spanish-English dual language programs in the United States. Its major goal is to enable students to become fully bilingual and bicultural. In 1998/99 the student body was as follows: 59% Hispanic (primarily Salvadorean), 24% White, 14% African-American and 3% Asian; 31% are Language Majority and 69% Language Minority; 28% limited English proficient and 46% Free/Reduced Lunch (low-income background) (Oyster Bilingual School, 1999).

The school philosophy focuses on linguistic equality and consequently instruction is approximately 50% Spanish, 50% English. Each class is taught by two teachers, one responsible for English-medium instruction and one for Spanish-medium instruction. This organization is achieved through larger class sizes and by assigning ancillary or resource teacher allocations to classroom instruction. [5] In line with the philosophy of linguistic equality, students read in both languages each day.

The academic results obtained by the Oyster Bilingual School have been consistently outstanding over a period of 30 years. For example, in 1991, Grade 3 Reading, Mathematics, Language and Science scores were more than one grade equivalent above norms (percentiles 74–81). Grade 6 grade equivalents were more than 3.5 years above norms (percentiles 85–96) (Freeman, 1998). The school was ranked in the top 8% of Washington DC schools in reading and mathematics on the SAT-9 test (1997/1998 data). Spanish achievement scores have also been consistently above grade level.

Rebecca Freeman (1998) provides detailed discourse analyses that illustrate how the micro-interactions between educators and students in Oyster bilingual school "refuse" the discourse of subordination that characterizes the wider society and most conventional school contexts. She points out that the discourse practices in the school "reflect an ideological assumption that linguistic and cultural diversity is a resource to be developed by all students, and not a problem that minority students must overcome in order to participate and achieve at school" (p. 233). Specifically, educators have *choices* in the way they organize discourse practices and these choices entail significant consequences for both language minority and majority students. The school *requires* all students to become bilingual and biliterate in Spanish and English, and "to expect, tolerate, and respect diverse ways of interacting" (1998:27).

> Oyster's bilingual program has two complementary agendas that together challenge the unequal distribution of rights in mainstream US schools and society. First, the dual-language program is organized so that language minority and language majority students have the opportunity to develop the ability to speak two languages and to achieve academically through two languages. Second, the social

identities project is organized so that language minority students gain experience seeing themselves as having the right to participate equally in the academic discourse, and the language majority students gain experience respecting that right. (1998, p. 231)

In other words, the school "aims to promote social change on the local level by socializing children differently from the way children are socialized in mainstream US educational discourse" (1998, p. 27). According to Freeman, the school has evolved a *social identities project* that communicates strongly to students the value of linguistic and cultural diversity. In the words of one of the teachers: "It's much more than language:"

> Rather than pressuring language minority students to assimilate to the positively evaluated majority social identity (white middle-class native English-speaking) in order to participate and achieve at school, the Oyster educational discourse is organized to positively evaluate linguistic and cultural diversity. …this socializing discourse makes possible the emergence of a wide range of positively evaluated social identities, and offers more choices to both language minority and language majority students than are traditionally available in mainstream US schools and society. The Oyster educators argue that students' socialization through this educational discourse is the reason that [limited English proficient], language minority, and language majority students are all participating and achieving more or less equally. (1998, p. 27)

The Oyster Bilingual School Local School Plan for the school year 1999–2000 provides more information about the outstanding achievement levels of the students and insight into the conditions that nurture this achievement. It notes that Oyster has moved from being ranked 25th out of 119 Washington DC elementary schools in the results of standardized tests in 1982 (top 21%) to being ranked 9th out of 111 elementary schools in the results of the SAT-9 reading and mathematics assessment in 1998 (top 8%). On the Spanish achievement test (APRENDA), 51% of Oyster students scored at the proficient or advanced levels in reading and 77% scored at the proficient or advanced levels in mathematics (Oyster Bilingual School, 1999).

The Local School Plan also notes that

The hallmark of Oyster's dual-language immersion program is that it nurtures students' valuing of themselves and their valuing of others. That cherishing of human growth comes in significant measure from the way that the dual language immersion program is delivered at Oyster. From Pre-Kindergarten, students learn in an atmosphere where language and culture are integrated. ...the equal valuation of two languages communicates to the children that cultures and the people who are products of those cultures are also to be equally valued. (1999, p. 3)

There is an obvious congruence between these accounts of why and how the Oyster Bilingual School succeeds so well and the *empowerment/negotiating identities* framework presented in previous chapters.

The Dual Language Program of Manhattan's District 3
This program was initiated in Public School 84 in 1984 and by 1993 had expanded horizontally to eight other schools in the District and vertically beyond elementary school to middle school (Foster & Swinney, 1995; Morison, 1990). The program has been implemented in some of the richest and some of the poorest schools in the district.

In order to desegregate the bilingual program and to provide linguistic role models in both languages, schools strive to attain a 50/50 ratio of Spanish and English dominant students. The program operates on an alternative day basis with English and Spanish being used on succeeding days for all content instruction. The program philosophy is student-centered with considerable emphasis placed on cooperative learning and hands-on activities designed to foster both learning and cross-cultural understanding. The separation of Spanish and English is central to the language policy of the Dual Language Program.

At the middle school level, the traditional middle school structure does not allow for an alternate day design. Thus, the curriculum is organized in thematic units with specific goals for each language. About 35 percent of the instructional time is spent through Spanish and 65 percent through English. Morison describes the development of reading and writing in the program as follows:

Older children have been writing plays and poetry in two languages with the help of a poet-consultant from the Teachers and Writers Collaborative...The question of whether or not children will become confused learning to read in two languages simultaneously is no longer even discussed. After five years of experience, it is taken for granted that learning to read is one process. Each class library has collections in both Spanish and English, and the teacher reads to the children every day. The children eagerly follow along, especially when big books are used. The teacher also records experiences so that children can see their words being put to print. The children also write little books of their own, on letters of the alphabet, colors, collective stories, and so on. In the beginning, second-language reading lags behind, but that is expected and no pressure is applied to hasten the balance. (1990, p. 167)

Considerable emphasis is placed on reading literature in the two languages (with the focus on Caribbean and Latin American literature in the Spanish component) and Latino/Latina artists and writers work directly with students and teachers to enrich the program. With their help, many classes in the dual language program have written and performed their own theatrical works in Spanish.

The picture that emerges from the program descriptions provided by Morison (1990) and Foster and Swinney (1995) is of a dual language program dedicated to building on the bilingual nature of the community and enabling all students to use both languages of the community in authentic and powerful ways. The potential of such a program to unite communities across cultural and linguistic boundaries is expressed by Morison: "As a result of word of mouth and other publicity, we are inundated with requests for information and tours, especially from white middle-class parents who are attracted by the enrichment offered by such a program" (1990, p. 168).

The Bilingual Bicultural Mini-School in East Harlem

The achievements of this program were featured in the periodical *Electronic Learning* in September 1995 (Siegel, 1995). The school is a "mini-school" of 560 students located within another school. The mini-school was founded in 1973 in response to Latino/Latina parents' requests for a bilingual program that enhanced students' knowledge of their own language and cultural heritage together with teaching them English and other core subjects. Students in the school come from many South and Central American countries and from the Caribbean. All of the teachers in the school are bilingual. The school transitions students into greater amounts of English instruction over the course of elementary school but maintains a strong focus on developing students' language and culture. In the words of Lourdes Arroyo, the school's director: "We strive to make them feel proud and knowledgeable about their own history, though not at the expense of learning about American history" (p. 27). The focus of language learning is two-way: English dominant students in the school learn Spanish just as Spanish dominant students learn English.

What attracted *Electronic Learning* to the school was its innovations in using technology to promote collaborative critical inquiry among its students. The school was one of 11 winners of the Apple Computer Partners in Education Grant for 1994-5. The hardware and software they received permitted them to implement their proposal which called for an extensive revision of the entire curriculum, using El Barrio (East Harlem) as its focus.

Students' work for the 1994-95 year was displayed for three days at the end of May at the school fair. Prominent among the project exhibits was a huge model of East Harlem itself. Technology facilitated the process of cultural exploration and self-definition that students engaged in over the course of the year:

> Third graders in their social studies class looked at what defined the neighborhood as a community. In fourth-grade science, students tested water quality in the school; in fifth-grade math they created graphs measuring immigration flow into the neighborhood and compared the results to other eras. In each grade, technology fit like another puzzle piece into the overall plan. Students produced *HyperStudio* living histories of El Barrio, learned *Lego Logo* to move the elevated train across the model of the neighborhood, and videoed El Barrio's landmarks. (Siegel, 1995, p. 28)

Among the other projects carried out by students in the school were:

- A project on "The Trees of East Harlem" (Los Arboles del Barrio) that used HyperStudio to create text, drawings, photographs, and sound relating to six different trees found in East Harlem. Students also produced a 1995 calendar on this topic which they sell to raise money for the school.

- A telecommunications project carried out by the third/fourth-grade class with 15 other schools in the area monitoring the water quality of Harlem Meer, a body of water in the northern stretch of Central Park. Students collect water samples on a regular basis which they test and send on-line to the Central Park Conservatory.

- A survey carried out by grade 6 students on the countries of origin of students in their school which they integrated with U.S. census data.

- A survey of different ethnic groups' home remedies integrated into a *HyperStudio* database.

What is remarkable about the achievements of the Bilingual Bicultural Mini School is not the technology that they used but the pedagogical vision that unleashed students' and teachers' creative intellectual energies. Students and teachers engaged in collaborative critical inquiry to gain insights into their identities as individuals, as a neighborhood community, and as a school community.

Opponents of bilingual education might argue that the successes of this school have very little to do with its bilingual bicultural program. Yet, how much real communication would be going on in the school, or between teachers and parents, if all the teachers were monocultural and monolingual and students were prohibited from using Spanish in the classroom? To what extent could students have planned and implemented their complex projects if communication among them had been limited to their weaker language? To what extent could students have carried out parent and community surveys if they had not developed the Spanish literacy to record their responses and data? Finally, would it even have been possible for educators to conceive of integrating the curriculum with community and encouraging students to take pride in their "neighborhood as laboratory" if the school culture had been focused on assimilation and exclusion of students' language and culture from the school? Why would students take pride in their neighborhood or community if the culture of the school communicated clearly to them that the language of that community has no place within the walls of the school?

The pedagogical innovations undertaken at the Bilingual Bicultural Mini-School serve as a model of what can be achieved when bilingual students are encouraged and enabled to use their entire linguistic repertoire for purposes of collaborative critical inquiry. An implication is that any program—transitional bilingual, two-way bilingual, ESL, mainstream—will achieve its potential for accelerating students' academic development only when collaborative critical inquiry becomes the central pedagogical focus of the entire school (Cummins & Sayers, 1995). [6]

The Secondary School Level

The academic difficulties of immigrant and ELL students are often particularly acute at the secondary level for several reasons: (a) students risk running out of time before they have caught up sufficiently in academic English and subject knowledge to attain graduation requirements; (b) traditional departmentalized high schools are organized in rigid ways that often track ELL students into lower-level programs and construct their bilingualism as an academic deficiency (García, 1999; Harklau, 1999); and (c) a large majority of secondary school teachers have had minimal training to enable them to teach ELL students effectively; Waggoner (1999), for example, points out that "43% of secondary teachers had LEP students in their classes in 1994 and...only half of them had received any training to teach them"(p. 39).

The three programs profiled here have one major element in common: they all acknowledge that bilingual adolescents have "so much to say" (to borrow the title of Faltis and Wolfe's [1999] book), and they provide organizational structures and interpersonal spaces within which students' voices can find expression. The first example comes from an analysis of educational changes implemented in a school in a Navajo reservation community (McLaughlin, 1992). The second focuses on the transformative journey undertaken by one Latino teacher and his students in Oxnard, California (Jasso & Jasso, 1994; Terrazas, 1995). Finally, we look at the International High School in Laguardia Community College in New York City as an example of how the educational experience and academic outcomes of ELL students can be transformed when the school shifts from exclusionary to transformative patterns of cultural/linguistic incorporation, community involvement, pedagogy, and assessment.

A Navajo-English Applied Literacy Program

Dan McLaughlin first came to "Mesa Valley" (a pseudonym) as a teacher of secondary level gifted-and-talented students. A large majority of students designated as gifted and talented were children of school staff members (and presumably non-Navajo) and were making good academic progress. By contrast, students in the mainstream program were falling further and further behind as they progressed from one grade level to the next. In order to remedy this situation, the school abolished the gifted-and-talented program and instituted a program for all students based on specifying products that students would produce for particular audiences. Thus, curriculum was conceived as product plus audience (C = P + A). The approach was seen as congruent with Navajo cultural learning style, characterized by McLaughlin as "practice privately and in small groups first, then perform." In McLaughlin's terms:

> The climate of community control and community participation at the school was such that we also felt intuitively the need to create products for viable audiences. The need was to "hook in" not only the students but also their parents and other community members. Because most people in the community spoke only Navajo, inserting the students' first language into instruction was an obvious first requirement. (1992, pp. 245–246)

The curriculum focused on four areas: Navajo Research, English Research, Computers, and Performance which students rotate through in nine-week cycles over the course of the year. All of the activities incorporate cognitive challenges. As described by McLaughlin:

> In 12th grade, for example, students divide equally into the project's four classes. In Navajo Research, they develop an editorial-style article in Navajo, first articulating research questions, next interviewing at least two experts (with contrasting points of view) on their research topic, then evaluating and synthesizing opinions, and finally writing editorial articles for publication in the bilingual community newspaper. Seniors in English Research follow the same set of procedures, only in English, to develop editorial-style articles for the same newspaper. In computers, with the Navajo-smart word processors, students learn to use different word processing and page layout programs, which they may encounter at work or in higher education. In Performance, they analyze a topic of critical importance to the individual, the school, the community, the Navajo Tribe, and prepare comprehensive videotape products to be aired over the community's low-power television station. (pp. 246–247)

In summary, the Navajo-English Applied Literacy program provided students with an opportunity to use their lived experiences as a basis for acquiring language, literacy and critical thinking skills. Consistent with the critical literacy framework discussed in Chapter 5 (see Ada, 1988a, 1988b), students were enabled to relate community social issues to their own experience, analyze alternative perspectives on these social issues, and generate new syntheses in written or video form that extended the horizons of community dialogue. The fact that students' first language was validated within the high school, on an equal basis with English, appears to have been a central component of the program's success.

The portraits of empowerment pedagogy to this point have been characterized by a strong whole school commitment to validating students' language and culture, encouragement of parent and community participation, and approaches to pedagogy and assessment that promote critical and independent learning among students. The innovations infused the culture of the school at a deep structure level.

The following example focuses on innovations that were instituted by one teacher in one classroom and viewed with a certain ambivalence by other staff members. The example illustrates very clearly how the creation of contexts for collaborative empowerment almost inevitably constitutes a challenge to power structures that operate in the school and wider society.

Students for Cultural and Linguistic Democracy

One gets a glimpse of what a high school education could and should be like from two chapters in the book *Reclaiming Our Voices: Bilingual Education, Critical Pedagogy & Praxis* (Frederickson, 1995). Both accounts document the events and dialogue leading up to the formation of Students for Cultural and Linguistic Democracy (SCaLD) in a high school in Oxnard, California. Adriana and Rosalba Jasso describe the personal transformations they experienced as students in Bill Terrazas Jr.'s high school classroom:

> We had heard before about a different classroom at our high school, and we were about to step inside it for the first time in our junior year. Mr. Terrazas was a different teacher, you felt special in his class, like a "somebody." You could honestly say it was your class. We were surrounded by butcher paper hanging from the walls with bright colors, beautiful drawings, and big letters. There were no desks or rows, instead there were big round tables. You could choose your own seat and you were responsible for your own work and production.
>
> The most exciting thing we can remember is going into the classroom and having one of those deep and powerful dialogues. In these powerful dialogues we also shared and examined our own lives. ...As students we were taking control of our lives, getting to know ourselves, and we were able to share our feelings with others. If we had known that sharing and looking closely at our cultures, our lives, and society was so transforming, we would have done it sooner!...

Our classroom was full of human knowledge; all of us knew something different and we were confident enough to share it with each other. We had a teacher who believed in us; he didn't hide our power, he advertised it. He gave us the opportunity we truly needed to reclaim our voices. He too was sharing his oppressive life experiences, his human knowledge, his cultural truth—this is what we appreciated the most. He shared information about oppression, discrimination, and exploitation of oppressed peoples in the United States. We had never heard this history before. (1995, p. 255)

Bill Terrazas Jr. describes the same reality from the perspective of a teacher who became more a colleague of his students in a search for insight and identity than an "instructor" who has information, skills, and values to transmit:

As you look around our classroom, the walls, ceiling, and four-by-eight foot pieces of plywood literally are covered with butcher paper. These huge sheets are filled with students' writings, projects, research, and dialogue questions on their life experiences, social issues of importance to them, text book information, cultural art, cultural history of the common people, and the life experiences of famous leaders from social justice movements like Marcus Garvey, Malcolm X, Dolores Huerta, and César Chavez. We use tons of butcher paper. We always display our critical work, because all our investigations connect with real life situations and knowledge that can dramatically affect and change the living conditions of someone in class. (1995, pp. 286-287)

Terrazas goes on to describe critical incidents in the cultural and social explorations of students in the school. He concludes his account as follows:

Many of my students return to visit me after being in my classes. In every case they never mention the grammar, vocabulary, writing, or reading lessons we studied. Instead, they always remember the critical dialogues we voiced in class. All of them have said that their classroom experiences changed their life and their way of looking at the world. At times, this baffles me. This wasn't what the university teacher training programs had taught me to do, nor to expect. I had learned how to design a lesson plan, to organize a good lecture, to select appropriate worksheets and assignments. I had learned how to keep my students quiet, managed, and passive. To listen silently. With my students I have learned another view of education, another approach to educating. I no longer practice a curriculum made for failure and poverty. (pp. 307-308) [7]

The International High School at
Laguardia Community College, New York City

This high school was founded in 1985 and offers learners of English a four-year comprehensive program where they can satisfy state mandated subject matter requirements while they are learning English (DeFazio, 1997; DevTech Systems, 1996). The students come from over 60 countries and speak more than 50 different languages. According to DeFazio, entering students score in the lowest quartile on tests of English proficiency, yet more than 90 percent of them graduate within four years and move on to post-secondary education. As a result of the success of the original program, the philosophy and vision have been extended to two other international high schools in different boroughs of New York City.

The philosophy underlying instruction and school organization at the International High School includes the following beliefs:

• Language is key to learning and increasing proficiency in academic language emerges most naturally in experiential, language rich, interdisciplinary study;

• Fluency in two languages represents a resource for the student, the school, and the society;

• Students learn best from each other in heterogeneous, collaborative group-ings and learning is facilitated when collaboration exists between the school and the larger community;

• Assessment must support individual growth and offer a variety of opportunities for students and faculty to demonstrate what they know and what they can do.

Among the innovations of the school is an emphasis on career education throughout the curriculum to encourage students to explore their future life options and motivate them to continue to expand their language sophistica-tion. In addition, cohesion of the school's educational vision is reinforced by the fact that new teachers are selected and hired by the teachers already working in the school. The teachers themselves have developed procedures for collabo-ration with each other to provide support and evaluative feedback.

Rather than being organized according to traditional subject matter, the curriculum is structured in an interdisciplinary way. The teaching staff has organized itself into six interdisciplinary teams with each team responsible for developing at least two interdisciplinary programs. Each of these programs runs for 13 weeks with the team of teachers in the program responsible for overseeing a group of approximately 75 students. An example of the kind of interdisciplinary focus is one labeled *Origins, Growth, and Structure* that involves chemistry, mathematics, linguistics, and art.

Rethinking the assessment of students has been a fundamental component of the restructuring process. Portfolios and exhibitions incorporating self, peer, and instructor evaluations play a major role. DeFazio notes that

> Students at the International High School undergo portfolio assessment where they demonstrate their academic, linguistic and social proficiencies. Traditional testing is eschewed because it is often unfair and counterproductive to linguistically diverse populations who often know much more than they may be able to articulate in English. Portfolio assessment encourages retention, higher-level cognitive skills, development of internal standards, creativity and variety in solving problems. ...Students undergo these assessments informally during the course of a semester and more formally at the end. Students also present a master portfolio as they prepare to graduate. (1997, p. 102)

Although English is the usual language of instruction, the school is very much a multilingual learning environment. Students' first languages are integrated into all phases of learning and assessment. In developing their portfolios in the various interdisciplinary programs, students write in both their first language and English, according to their choice. Teachers will often ask other students or members of the wider community for assistance in translating material that has been written in a language they themselves do not know. For example, in the *American Reality* program students formally explore their native language, human development, and career education, spending at least half their school day doing academic reading and writing in their native language. The first language resources to enable students to do this "include abundant native language materials that teachers, students, and parents purchased for the school" (DeFazio, 1997, p. 104)

Parents have also become significantly involved in the school. Teachers have asked students to write letters home in their native languages to describe the interdisciplinary program the student is involved with, to explain what they are learning, and to explain the portfolio/grading process. Parents are encouraged to respond to the letters in either the native language or English. When parents' letters come back in the native language, the student is requested to translate the letters for the teacher into English. According to DeFazio:

> The letter writing campaign helped instantiate several aspects of the school's language philosophy: the importance of the native language; the need for the parent/guardian and school to work together regardless of language; the development and importance of bi- and multi-lingualism; language respect. (1997, p. 103)

In other projects, students produce both native language and English language magazines and articles; their writing is read by teachers and students proficient in the native language and if no one on the school staff is proficient in the students' language "teachers go into the community to find volunteers willing to spend time reading and commenting on the students' work" (p. 104). DeFazio notes that students often comment on how much of their native language they had forgotten.

Other projects that students carry out in the *Origins/Growth/Structures* program include writing an autobiography or a biography of another student (again in English, their L1, or both) and investigations into comparative linguistics. For example, students work with the International Phonetic Alphabet to practice the sounds in each others' languages, to write cartoon strips in phonetics, and to attempt tongue twisters and riddles in the various languages represented in the class. Their linguistics projects culminate with a community research project that focuses on some issue or question related to language in the wider community. For example, students have interviewed members of their communities about bilingual education, dialect, and language prejudice and presented their findings as the last chapter of their linguistics book. Another project involves students writing multilingual children's books on some aspect of language or linguistics (*e.g. How the Chinese Got Language; The Monster that Ate Polish Words,* etc.).

What is most relevant to highlight in this example is the *language planning process* (Corson, 1999, 2001) that educators in the International High School implemented. This planning was designed to resolve problems they identified with respect to the match between the organization of the high school and ELL students' language and academic learning needs. Students entering the high school system with limited knowledge of English were severely handicapped by the inflexibility of the original curricular and assessment requirements. They did not know enough English to gain access to and learn a challenging curriculum at the same pace as native English-speaking students. Despite this they were being assessed with the same tests as native English-speaking students. Consequently, many were failing courses or receiving grades that would preclude them from going on to university or college.

The planning process involved changing the curriculum and assessment procedures to enable students to use their prior knowledge (much of it in their L1) to facilitate their learning and demonstrate what they had learned. Use of students' L1 was encouraged, as was a cooperative and supportive inquiry process. Language itself became a major focus of study within the program. In terms of Figure 7.1, the school moved from a failure-inducing pattern of exclusionary organizational structures and role definitions to one that:

• incorporated students' languages and cultures;

• mobilized parental and community resources in support of student achievement;

• transformed instruction in such a way that students were no longer passively receiving information but actively generating new knowledge;

• instituted rigorous assessment procedures that reinforced the school's instructional goals and fairly assessed the totality of what students had learned.

The latter point is important to emphasize in light of the knee-jerk accountability that has become the norm in many states. The performance assessment implemented in the school was a vital component in the entire restructuring process. There is no way that traditional forms of standardized assessment could have evaluated the learning and project work that students undertook. There is no doubt that standardized "one-size-fits-all" tests would have resulted in a high failure and drop-out rate because most students entering the school with minimal English would not have been capable of passing the tests at each grade level. This is illustrated in the fact that in New York City as a whole the drop-out rate among limited English proficient high school students is close to 30 percent compared to only 3.9 percent at the International High School (DevTech Systems, 1996).

Conclusion

The portraits of "schools in action" outlined in this chapter are intended to illustrate in a concrete way the theoretical framework discussed in previous chapters. To me, these portraits show clearly how culturally diverse students' academic success or failure is crucially dependent on the ways in which identities are being negotiated in the classroom and school. They show also that *empowerment* is generated only through interactions that affirm students' identities and extend their conceptual horizons. The creation of power in these interactions is at the core of genuine educational reform.

One reason why much educational reform has remained at a safe surface level, endorsing the rhetoric of equity and grasping at a few instructional panaceas, is that genuine reform of the kind sketched in this chapter is not safe; it threatens structures of privilege and status within the society. Faced with the escalating rhetoric of diversity as the enemy within, it takes courage for educators to assert the rights of children to develop their home languages and the importance for the nation of fostering these multilingual resources; it takes courage to cross cultural and linguistic boundaries to create structures for genuine parent and community participation and partnership; it takes courage to lift the veil obscuring the social realities around the classroom and unleash students' power to analyze these realities and their own place within them.

The next chapter focuses on the discourse of disempowerment. As discussed in Chapter 2, opponents of bilingual education have attempted to rationalize English-only programs as being in children's best interests. Few of these opponents would acknowledge explicitly that their goal is to preserve a societal power structure that historically has excluded subordinated groups from full participation. To them, bilingual education is self-evidently inferior to English-only programs since it exposes children to less of "the language of equal opportunity."

One can understand how members of the general public and many media commentators might confine their analysis to this "sound-bite" level. Academics, however, are trained in research procedures and analysis techniques. Their *raison d'être* within the society is to generate knowledge and insight. It is thus important to examine more closely the academic arguments against bilingual education. If there truly is a case to be made that bilingual education impedes children's educational progress (as voters in California and Arizona appear to believe), then this would undermine the argument proposed here that the discourse against bilingual education and cultural diversity is a thinly disguised attempt to preserve the societal power structure.

Endnotes to Chapter 8

1. An outstanding example of community-initiated preschool education is the national experiment in Maori language revitalization currently underway in New Zealand (Aotearoa). The indigenous Maori population constitute about 13 percent of the New Zealand population. Sociolinguistic surveys conducted during the 1970s in New Zealand showed that the language was in danger of virtually disappearing within one generation (Benton, 1988). These data acted as a catalyst for community (and, later, government) action to revitalize the Maori language through the institution of preschool programs (called *Te Kohanga Reo* [language nests]) conducted exclusively through Maori. As of 1993, these programs numbered more than 600 and served 14,027 Maori children (96.6% of enrollments), representing almost half of all Maori children enrolled in early childhood education (Bishop & Glynn, 1999; Waite, 1992). Other Pacific Island groups in New Zealand have followed the lead of Maori by instituting their own *Kohanga Reo*. Bishop and Glynn (1999) report that in 1992 there were 170 (non-Maori) programs catering for 3,682 children.

   The *Kohanga Reo* have increased pressure for the establishment of more extensive bilingual and Maori-medium programs at the elementary and secondary level. These Maori-medium programs programs, termed *Kura Kaupapa Maori*, have expanded during the past 15 years and, as of 1999, there were 59 kura kaupapa Maori with an enrollment of close to 4,000 students (Bishop & Glynn, 1999). These programs operate with a coherent set of educational principles derived from Maori culture and tradition and they explicitly aim to affirm Maori values and philosophy in resistance to the dominant discourse in society. Smith (1992) has analyzed the establishment of *Kura Kaupapa Maori* as a form of resistance to the dominant ideology of Eurocentric schools that have systematically excluded Maori language, traditions and belief systems:

   > Kaupapa Maori schooling is an intervention strategy entirely different from the unsuccessful strategies attempted by Pakeha [European-origin New Zealanders] in the past. It is clearly Maori in design, content and practice. Its establishment *outside of the system* questions the right of Pakeha to dominate education to the exclusion of Maori-preferred interests in education. Kura Kaupapa schooling asserts the right to overtly validate Maori knowledge, language, custom and practice. Implied is an analysis of (and a response to) the unequal power relations that led State schooling to serve only dominant Pakeha interests...Maori people have resisted assimilation by Pakeha culture through both individual and collective actions. Within the existing schooling crisis, Maori resistance can be gauged through disproportionate levels of pupil absenteeism, truancy, early school leaving, disruptive school behavior, underachievement, and at times overt cultural expression. Kura Kaupapa Maori has moved Maori resistance to another level and to another site. (pp. 100–103)

   The outcomes of this social experiment in attempting to reverse language shift and resist social subordination remain to be seen over the next several decades. Data from other parts of the world suggest that schools alone are limited in their power to revitalize endangered languages (Fishman, 1991). However, the progress made during the past 20 years by Maori communities is truly remarkable and the outcomes of this struggle for social equality and language rights cannot be prejudged (see Bishop and Glynn, 1999, for a detailed analysis of Maori educational initiatives and their resistance to coercive relations of power; see also Skutnabb-Kangas, 2000, pp. 603–604 for further information on Maori educational initiatives).

The Maori initiatives were highly influential in inspiring even more ambitious language revival efforts in another part of the Pacific, Hawaii. The *Punana Leo* program begins at the preschool level in much the same way as the Maori *Kohanga Reo* and by the mid-1990s had expanded into seven schools with 750 students in grades K-9. According to Crawford (1995), "the total immersion approach postpones English instruction until the 5th grade. Yet, over the long term, students outscore their English-speaking counterparts on standardized tests, according to William Wilson of the University of Hawaii" (pp. 192–193). However, no formal evaluation of the program has been conducted.

2. The advantages and potential disadvantages of recruiting staff from the communities being served were elaborated on by Antonia López in an interview with the periodical Montessori Life:

> The advantages were clear: a staff native to the culture could offer language and cultural compatibility, access to community support, development of local role models, long-term commitment to children and families, and the opportunity for genuine community development.'

> The disadvantages were also very real. 'Most staff members come to us with limited educational backgrounds. But the greatest challenge is the self-doubt compounded by cultural chauvinism and resistance to change, varying degrees of cultural 'self-hate' resulting from their acceptance of the dominant culture's negative attitude about language and cultural minorities and low-income people. (1990, p. 21)

Another outstanding early childhood education program that has emulated many of the Foundation Center's initiatives is the Even Start program in the Lincoln Unified School District in Stockton California that serves a low-income Cambodian-origin community.

3. The California State Department's decision in June 1995 not to renew any of the Foundation Center's contracts was rationalized on the grounds that Marilyn Prosser, executive director of the Center, had been charged with misuse of funds by the Federal Bureau of Investigations (FBI). These charges followed a two-year investigation initiated as a result of anonymous allegations of corruption, money laundering, and attendance fraud. None of these initial allegations were mentioned in the FBI indictment and the case was dismissed by the courts in 1996, but only after the outstanding work of many years had been totally dismantled.

The conflict between the Foundation Center and the Child Development Division of the California State Department of Education go back more than a decade. Twice the Foundation Center successfully brought suit against the Child Development Division for harassment. In both cases, the State was forced to settle out of court in the Foundation Center's favor. The 1996 charges were dismissed by the court on the grounds that State

Department personnel had withheld evidence that would have cleared Dr. Prosser of any wrongdoing.

The allegations against the Foundation Center were the subject of several newspaper articles during 1994. These articles raised the concerns of some sectors of the community as to why public monies should be supporting a "cadillac" program for low-income minority students (with classical music, organic food and toothpaste, and aesthetic surroundings). The fact that, as a result of administrative streamlining, this program was operated at a smaller per-pupil cost than other State-funded programs did not seem to matter. The not-so-subtle implication in much of this debate was that low-income minority children are second-class citizens who deserve only a second-class education.

The charges against the Foundation Center lacked credibility in the extreme and as Rosa Zubizarreta (personal communication, June 1995) points out: "How is it possible to provide the admittedly world-class programs that the Foundation Center runs, on the same low funding that all other State-supported pre-school centers receive, and possibly be 'stealing money from the till?'" The quality of the Foundation Center's programs was never contested by the State; indeed it would be hard to contest their quality in view of the fact that in the late 1980s they were judged one of the two foremost early childhood programs in the world by a New Zealand television documentary.

4. The importance of early childhood education that strongly promotes the child's home language has been demonstrated in the interview study of more than 1,000 families (from various language backgrounds) coordinated by Lily Wong Fillmore (1991b, 2000) in the early 1990s. It was found in this study that a majority of families whose children attended monolingual English daycare or preschool programs reported that their children's L1 skills declined. By contrast, preschool programs, such as those of the Foundation Center, that utilized children's L1 exclusively were associated with significantly less language loss.

The policy implications of these data with respect to the optimal language of preschool programs were debated in the pages of *Education Week* by Porter (1991) and Wong Fillmore (1991b). Porter invoked the principle of "time-on-task" to argue for maximizing preschool children's exposure to English while Wong Fillmore suggested that the predominance of English-only preschool provision was a major contributor to a breakdown of family communication. Wong Fillmore pointed to the alienation of children from their families that typically occurs when children lose their facility in the home language:

> What is lost when English displaces the primary language? If that's the only language the parents speak, children stand to lose much of what parents can teach them. …What children don't need are early educational experiences that destroy their confidence in themselves and their families …In our survey, 64.4 percent of the parents whose children attended English immersion preschools reported negative changes on family communication patterns. Few of the parents spoke English but their children were abandoning the parental language and communicating in English at home. …Parents reported difficulties in talking to their children and in giving them the guidance they needed. …In tumultuous and dangerous times like ours, strong family ties are needed to keep young people out of trouble. It

is plain bad social policy to support educational programs that destroy those ties. ...English immersion for preschoolers is the worst possible solution to a complex problem. If we can't educate young children without harming them, let's leave them alone. (1991b, p. 36)

A Swedish study (Sirén, 1991) of 600 families in the Stockholm area similarly showed extremely rapid language shift from the home language to Swedish among preschool children. Factors that slowed the rate of language loss were consistent parent L1 use and L1 support in the preschool (see Cummins, 1993, for a more detailed summary of Siren's findings).

In the Canadian context, Merylie Wade Houston has outlined a wide variety of strategies for supporting bilingual children's home languages within the preschool. A first step, she argues, is provision of books in the home language. This can be achieved by linking up with the local public libraries which often have collections in languages other than English (at least in multilingual cities like Toronto and Vancouver):

> Even the small local branches had children's books in the languages reflected in the surrounding neighborhoods. Ours, for instance, offered Greek and Cantonese. The librarians believed the books were there to be read...They were willing to lend our [preschool] program bags full of books every two weeks. They even asked us to tell them exactly which languages we needed, so that when they spent the little funding they had for new acquisitions, they would be sure to be getting what the community wanted. (1995, p. 33)

Houston also suggests coordinating with community associations, churches, synagogues, and mosques to solicit donations of L1 books. Families can also be asked to make connections with relatives here or in other countries to obtain L1 books that may have been outgrown by older children. The rationale for reflecting the family's language in the preschool and communicating a positive orientation to the family's language is outlined by Houston as follows:

> If children hear their parents switch to English whenever they are outside the home, whether or not they speak it well, then they may grow up thinking that their home language is second class, that their parents don't belong in their new school world and that they themselves are not as good as the other children. Teachers have a crucial role to play here. It doesn't matter if you don't speak a second language. It is your *attitude* towards language that counts. Because your opinion is so very important to the children's development of values, it is essential that you respect and value their language by reflecting it in your classroom. One of the easiest and most effective ways to do this is through books. (p. 33)

5. Fern (1995) provides the following account (based on interviews with Paquita Holland, school principal in 1993) of how Oyster Bilingual School achieves its two teachers per class organization:

Holland estimates that the additional staff costs about 20 percent more than with traditional staffing patterns; however, she maintains that this added cost is recuperated by saving the school system approximately $100,000 that is allocated to Oyster each year for substitute teachers. If a teacher is absent at Oyster, her teamed teacher is able to teach the class alone. Holland points to the team model as one of the school's ongoing challenges; it does have its disadvantages, it seems. Teachers do not always have the option of choosing their teaching partners, and sometimes generational, philosophical, and personality conflicts develop. (1995, p. 501)

The descriptions of these elementary schools resonate with accounts of recently established "Sweden-Finnish schools" for Finnish-speaking students in Sweden. According to Skutnabb-Kangas (2000, p. 607) there are currently 11 such schools in Sweden. They operate in a similar way to charter schools in the United States. The following excerpts from an article by Markku Peura (2000) entitled *Creating a Successful Minority School* outline the development and accomplishments of these schools during the 1990s:

> A new Swedish law in 1991–92 gave parents the right to choose the type of school they wished for their children, with state funding following the pupil. ...Earlier children were obliged to go to the school in their home area. ...The Sweden-Finnish schools are bilingual schools. Their main aim is to develop the pupils' bilingualism in Finnish and Swedish, their competence in Finnish and Swedish cultures, and a strong bilingual, bicultural identity. ...

> This model [of the school in Upplands Vasby] means that Finnish and Swedish languages are used in parallel. In the lower grades, *Finnish* dominates as the *medium* of instruction. During the higher grades the proportion in *Finnish* and *Swedish* (as *media*) is about 50–50. *Finnish* is taught as a subject throughout all 9 years. Learning to read and write is taught through the medium of Finnish. *Swedish* is taught as a *subject* from the third grade. It is used from the first grade in some context-embedded subjects as the *medium* of instruction, *e.g.* sports and handicraft, taught by teachers who are ethnic Swedes. (2000, pp. 221–223)

Peura explicitly highlights the role of these schools in creating a counter-discourse to the messages the Finnish community have historically received in the wider society. Educators and students negotiate identities in the school in a way that explicitly challenges the historical legacy of coercive relations of power:

> Many Swedes seem to more or less automatically feel superior when meeting a Finn and many Finns feel inferior when meeting a Swede. Especially among Finnish immigrants this supported the development of various kinds of 'strategies' for how to cope with the prejudice and discrimination they met. One was to try to become 'a Swede' (often more 'Swedish' than ethnic Swedes themselves; assimilation). The opposite strategy was to isolate them-

selves from Swedes (self-segregation). If a Finn does not open her mouth with Swedes, nobody knows that she is a Finn (because the physical features of Finns and Swedes are similar). The first generation of Finnish immigrants was often ashamed of being Finnish. The idea of strong self-confidence means that the Sweden-Finnish school tries to work in a way that empowers the pupils, making them proud of their bilingualism and biculturalism. …

Creativity and curiosity are encouraged, a lot of time, effort, and resources go into the use of drama and music to give children the chance to express themselves and to dare to show who they are and what they know and can do. (2000, p. 225).

The academic results in these schools have been excellent. More than 90% of the students attain the qualifications to continue to upper secondary school.

7. One illustration of how teacher education can extend itself into the transformative domains highlighted by Bill Terrazas Jr. has been described by Lois Meyer of San Francisco State University in an article entitled *Barrio buddies: Learning through letters about kids, cultures, communities, and self-confrontation*. In a course entitled *Linguistic and Cultural Diversity in the Elementary School* which all teacher candidates were required to take for the first time in Fall 1992, Meyer initiated various forms of contact between the teacher candidates and inner-city culturally diverse children. The teacher candidates were predominantly White monolingual students whose experience of diversity varied greatly but in many cases was limited. Meyer describes the course as follows:

I arranged for each teacher candidate in my two sections to be paired or "buddied" with one or two children in a fourth or fifth grade classroom at Marshall School…[in the] Mission District, an immigrant Latino barrio that has seen a recent influx of Southeast Asian and Cantonese-speaking families. Since my students were not bilingual, the selected buddy classrooms were English language development classes…Three components became central to the semester's work:

1) Buddy Letters: The university students' primary task was to develop a relationship through letters and finally in person with their buddy(ies), and to document their reflections and learnings in a Buddy Book. The hope was that through the exchange of letters they would learn about the personal histories and experiences of individual children from diverse racial/ethnic backgrounds, at the same time that they reflected upon and shared with their buddy their own personal story…

2) The University Adventure: The university students, in consultation with the buddy teachers, were to organize a field trip which brought their buddies to San Francisco State University at the end of the semester…

3) Reflections on readings, presentations and discussions: Many of my students' most passionate and revealing reflections were written in response to course readings or class sessions that jarred their previous assumptions about the children's lives and communities. As they gained more knowledge from multiple perspectives about their buddies, my students began to analyze themselves as cultural beings, including their own assumptions, stereotypes, biases, and fears concerning cultural perspectives and linguistic practices different from their own, and their assumptions about the purposes and practices of schools. (1994, p. 94)

Meyer describes in detail the conflicting range of emotions the university students went through over the course of the semester as a result of their contacts with their buddies and in reaction to readings such as California Tomorrow's *Crossing the Schoolhouse Border* (Olsen, 1988) and Rethinking Schools' *Rethinking Columbus* (1991). Most developed new perspectives and profound insights on issues of diversity, racism, and second language learning. A few students, however, were infuriated by what they regarded as "offensive" readings (*e.g. Rethinking Columbus*).

Meyer's article makes fascinating reading not only as documentation of a highly creative innovation in teacher education but also as a reminder of how many middle-class students and members of the general public are still almost totally isolated and insulated from the realities of cultural diversity and inner-city life. Teachers are likely to find it much more difficult to connect with inner-city students when they have no direct experience or understanding of diversity than when they understand their students' realities and are willing to learn from their students. Meyer's article illustrates how powerful the learning experience can be when these "two solitudes" come together in a process of negotiating identities.

Chapter 9

From Doublethink to Disinformation: The Academic Critics of Bilingual Education

Research has played a prominent role in the bilingual education debate. Unfortunately, as noted in Chapter 6, the research evidence has been interpreted in very different ways by advocates and opponents of bilingual education. In this chapter, I raise ethical issues about the way in which research evidence has been infused into the public discourse on bilingual education. Unlike courtroom lawyers who advocate for their clients regardless of the merits of the case, academics have an ethical responsibility to analyze the research evidence as objectively as possible and to recommend policy options that are consistent with the evidence. There is also a responsibility to address and to reconcile internal contradictions in their stated positions and interpretation of the research.

The academic debate on bilingual education contrasts markedly with the treatment of the issue in the media. Media articles on bilingual education have tended to be highly negative in their assessment of the merits of bilingual programs (see Crawford, 2000; McQuillan & Tse, 1996). By contrast, the academic debate lines up virtually all North American applied linguists who have carried out research on language learning as advocates of bilingual programs against only a handful of academics who oppose bilingual education. None of those who oppose bilingual education has a background in the discipline of applied linguistics. During the 1990s, the most prominent of those opposing bilingual education have been Rosalie Pedalino Porter, Keith Baker, Christine Rossell, and Charles Glenn. Others such as Nathan Glazer and Herbert Walberg have made occasional forays into the debate to express their skepticism about bilingual education.

Both advocates and opponents of bilingual education invariably claim that they are motivated by what is in the best interests of bilingual children rather than by political considerations. Not surprisingly, each side accuses the other of political rather than educational motivation. The crucially important issue of what types of educational interventions are most likely to reverse the under-achievement of many bilingual students has degenerated into the adversarial rhetoric of courtroom lawyers with each side trying to "spin" the interpretation of research to fit its strongly held beliefs.

In this debate, it is crucial to assess as objectively as possible what the research is saying and what it is not saying. Otherwise it is impossible to separate empirically-supported claims from those that rest only on ideological rhetoric. How can we separate reasonable interpretations of the research data from interpretations that do not fit the facts? There are two basic ways of doing this. First, we look for internal contradictions in the arguments advanced by both sides. Second, we examine claims carefully against the research data.

When we engage in this process of evaluating claims and counter-claims, it becomes very clear that the opposition to bilingual education suffers from blatant internal contradictions and has difficulty reconciling its claims with the research data (as noted in Chapter 6). I refer to these internal contradictions as *doublethink*. The term *doublethink* was coined by George Orwell in his futuristic novel *Nineteen EightyFour* (1949/1983) to refer to the simultaneous belief in two contradictory ideas. Orwell describes the process of *doublethink* as follows:

> Doublethink means the power of holding two contradictory beliefs in one's mind simultaneously, and accepting both of them. The Party intellectual knows in which direction his memories must be altered; he therefore knows that he is playing tricks with reality; but by the exercise of doublethink he also satisfies himself that reality is not violated. The process has to be conscious, or it would not be carried out with sufficient precision, but it also has to be unconscious, or it would bring with it a feeling of falsity and hence of guilt. (1983, p. 865)

The process of *doublethink* is very evident in the current debate in the United States on the merits or otherwise of bilingual education. Specifically, despite arguing vigorously *against* bilingual education, the four commentators considered in this chapter have also explicitly or implicitly *endorsed* certain forms of bilingual education aimed at developing children's bilingualism and biliteracy by means of instruction through the minority language. While basing their opposition to bilingual programs primarily on the *time-on-task* hypothesis (maximum instructional exposure to English will result in maximum learning of English), they simultaneously endorse dual language or two-way bilingual programs that are far more "L1-intensive" for language minority students than the vast majority of transitional bilingual programs.

The public face of doublethink is disinformation. The term *disinformation* refers to the systematic spreading of false information in order to confuse and disorient the opposition. Although the term is usually associated with the activities of groups such as the CIA and former KGB (and more recently, tobacco companies), the phenomenon of disinformation is no less evident in debates on domestic political issues such as the education of bilingual students. In some cases disinformation is spread deliberately; in other cases, the false information is genuinely believed by those spreading it but they have avoided ample opportunities to correct their ignorance or misinformation by means of selective inattention to awkward facts or inconsistencies. In other words, they have engaged in a process of doublethink.

The research on issues such as how long it takes ELL students to catch up academically and the merits or otherwise of bilingual education has been reviewed in previous chapters. In the first section of this chapter, I summarize that research as a basis for evaluating the claims on both sides of the bilingual education debate. Then I consider critically the arguments advanced by commentators who have been prominent during the 1990s in opposing bilingual education and whose writings have contributed to the passage of Propositions 227 in California and 203 in Arizona. [1]

The Applied Linguistics Research Consensus

The following points appear to me to be relatively non-controversial among applied linguists who have examined the research upon which they are based, although they might be expressed differently according to the theoretical orientation of individual researchers.

1. **Bilingual programs for minority and majority language students have been successfully implemented in countries around the world.**
   As documented in many sources (*e.g.,* Baker & Prys Jones, 1998; Cenoz & Genesee, 1999; Cummins & Corson, 1997; Dutcher, 1995; Skutnabb-Kangas, 2000), students educated for part of the day through a minority language do not suffer adverse consequences in the development of academic skills in

the majority language. If there were adverse consequences associated with bilingual instruction, there would hardly be more than 300,000 English-background students in various forms of French-English bilingual programs in Canada. Similarly, in the Basque country of Spain during the past decade, there has been a dramatic increase in the number of students being enrolled in bilingual (Model B) and Basque immersion/maintenance (Model D) programs, as compared to Model A programs that are conducted in Spanish with Basque taught only as a second language (see Chapter 6).

2. **Bilingual education, by itself, is not a panacea for students' underachievement.** Underachievement derives from many sources and simply providing some first language instruction will not, by itself, transform students' educational experience. Bilingual instruction *can* make a significant contribution but the predominant model of bilingual education in the United States (quick-exit transitional programs) is inferior to programs that aim to develop bilingualism and biliteracy, such as developmental (late-exit) and two-way bilingual immersion (dual language). Dual language programs also serve English-background students in the same classes as minority language students, with each group acting as linguistic models for the other (Christian *et al.*, 1997).

3. **The development of literacy in two languages entails linguistic and perhaps cognitive advantages for bilingual students.** There are close to 150 research studies carried out since the early 1960s that report significant advantages for bilingual students on a variety of metalinguistic and cognitive tasks (see Chapter 6).

4. **Significant positive relationships exist between the development of academic skills in L1 and L2.** This is true even for languages that are dissimilar (*e.g.*, Spanish and Basque; English and Chinese; Dutch and Turkish). These cross-lingual relationships reflect the transfer of academic and conceptual knowledge across languages as well as the fact that the same cognitive and linguistic processing system operates on the acquisition and use of both languages.

5. **Conversational and academic aspects of language proficiency are distinct and follow different developmental patterns.** Several large-scale studies (Cummins, 1981b; Hakuta, Butler & Witt, 2000; Thomas & Collier, 1997) have shown that it usually takes at least 5 years for second lan-

guage learners to catch up academically to their native English-speaking peers but conversational fluency in English is often attained within 2 years of intensive exposure to the language.

It is important to note that the research consensus sketched above says nothing about which language (L1 or L2) should be used in initial reading instruction for language minority students. Both advocates and opponents of bilingual programs have sometimes assumed that a central theoretical axiom of bilingual education is that children should be instructed to read in their home language. As noted in Chapter 4, the research suggests that a variety of approaches to initial reading instruction can be successful, ranging from introducing reading instruction in L1, to simultaneous instruction in L1 and L2, to reading instruction initially in L2. With respect to academic outcomes of bilingual programs what is much more important is the extent to which a serious effort is made to promote literacy in both languages throughout elementary school (and beyond) and the affirmation of bilingual students' identity in their interactions with educators in the school.

In the sections below, I examine the arguments of those who claim that "bilingual education doesn't work" and highlight both the internal contradictions and the inconsistencies with empirical data in their views.

Rosalie Pedalino Porter: Expanding Genuine Bilingualism Through Dual Language Programs

Rosalie Pedalino Porter served as Director of Bilingual and English-as-a-Second-Language programs in Newton, Massachusetts and the first two chapters of her 1990 book, *Forked Tongue*, describe what she terms the Newton district's "struggle against bureaucratic vindictiveness" in its attempts to institute an alternative program that involved minimal bilingual instruction. What is communicated to the reader in these chapters is a strong sense of outrage and bitterness against the "self-serving" "defensiveness and paranoia of the bilingual education establishment" (p. 56). According to Porter, the continued implementation of bilingual programs is a function not of research on their effectiveness but of "the impulse for preserving jobs and budgets for the bilingual establishment" (p. 73).

Porter's major argument against transitional bilingual education is that it fails to teach children English effectively and is based on flawed theoretical principles. She rejects what she terms the "vernacular advantage theory," the argument that children learn best through their stronger language, on the grounds that the major variable determining success in language learning is "time-on-task." Thus, one of the lessons she derives from the Canadian experience with early total French immersion programs for majority language (English-background) students is that early intensive exposure to the target language is essential:

> The evidence of direct correlation between early, intensive second-language learning and high level of competence in the second language is inescapable, as is the on-task principle—that is, the more time spent learning a language, the better you do in it, all other factors being equal. (1990, p. 119)

According to Porter, the major problem with transitional bilingual education is that the time spent through the medium of L1 does not contribute to the learning of English. Bilingual education dilutes time-on-task by dividing the instructional time between English and students' L1. She suggests that the success of French immersion programs for majority students in Canada augurs well for the implementation of English immersion for minority students in the United States. She has more recently described bilingual education as "terribly wrongheaded" and "a failure" (Porter, 1998).

There are many problematic aspects to Porter's argument and interpretation of research data. One set of blatant contradictions, however, stands out. Despite insisting that exposure to English is the decisive factor in determining academic success for bilingual students, she nevertheless endorses two-way bilingual programs (involving both minority and majority students) that will normally have far less exposure to English than either English immersion or transitional bilingual education. Most two-way programs continue instruction in both languages throughout elementary school with at least 50 percent of the instruction through the minority language.

According to Porter (1990), a two-way or dual immersion program is:

- "particularly appealing because it not only enhances the prestige of the minority language but also offers a rich opportunity for expanding genuine bilingualism to the majority population" (p. 154);

Such programs promise:

- "mutual learning, enrichment, and respect" (p. 154). They

- "are also considered to be the best possible vehicles for integration of language minority students, since these students are grouped with English-speakers for natural and equal exchange of skills" (p. 154).

Furthermore, two-way programs are:

- "the best opportunity for families that are seriously committed to genuine bilingualism for their children" (p. 154) and these programs

- "do not cost any more than the average single-language classes to maintain" (p. 156).

The *doublethink* process here involves the simultaneous endorsement of (a) English-only immersion programs as the most promising option for bilingual students' academic success because they provide maximum English exposure (time-on-task); and (b) two-way bilingual immersion programs that typically entail *less* English-medium and more L1 instruction than any other bilingual education option. Porter also fails to address the fact that the documented academic success of bilingual students in such programs, despite reduced exposure to English, directly contradicts the "time-on-task" principle (Cazabon *et al.*, 1998; Dolson & Lindholm, 1995; Freeman, 1998; Lindholm-Leary, 2001; Thomas & Collier, 1997). [2]

Keith Baker: Arguing for More Bilingual Programs

Baker has been a prominent critic of bilingual education since 1981 when he co-authored a report entitled *The Effectiveness of Bilingual Education* (Baker & DeKanter, 1981). More recently, he co-authored an article (Rossell & Baker, 1996) that reached essentially the same conclusion as his earlier work: when methodologically-adequate research is considered, there is no evidence that bilingual education is more effective than English-only "structured immersion" programs; on the contrary, the evidence strongly favors structured immersion (Rossell & Baker, 1996).

Baker, however, has also been a strong critic of Porter's work and appears to have little problem drawing diametrically opposite conclusions from the same research study at different points in time. Consider, for instance, his two very different interpretations of the El Paso Independent School District research. The El Paso program was labeled "bilingual immersion" by the district and involved a "native language cognitive development" component of 90 minutes a day at grade 1, gradually reducing to 60 minutes a day by grade 3 and 30 minutes a day by grade 4 (Gersten & Woodward, 1995; Krashen, 1996). In a critical review of Porter's book *Forked Tongue*, Baker (1992b) argues for more intensive forms of bilingual education on the basis of the El Paso data:

> She summarizes a report from El Paso (1987) as finding that an all-English immersion program was superior to bilingual education programs. The El Paso report has no such finding. What Porter describes as an all-English immersion program in El Paso is, in fact, a Spanish-English dual immersion program. The El Paso study supports the claims of bilingual education advocates that most bilingual education programs do not use enough of the native language. It does not support Porter's claims that they should use less.
>
> Like El Paso, San Diego has an extensive two-language program. Like El Paso, there is evidence that the extensive bilingual education program worked better than the typical bilingual education program. ... Like El Paso, the results of the San Diego study argue for more bilingual education programs, not fewer as Porter maintains." (1992a, p. 6)

In a more recent article, however, Baker contradicts this criticism by highlighting how the El Paso data document the harm that bilingual education does to children's academic development:

> El Paso created an SEI [structured English immersion] program in which Spanish instruction was reduced to 30 minutes a day. The district followed students from this program and from the state-mandated bilingual education program for 12 years. The SEI students scored significantly higher on all tests for 11 straight years. In the 12th year, the SEI students still scored higher, but their advantage was no longer statistically significant, suggesting that, after a decade or so, the harm that bilingual education programs do to learning English is more or less wiped out by continued exposure to English outside the classroom. (1998, p. 201)

It is clearly an extreme example of *doublethink* to be able to describe in 1992 a program as "a Spanish-English dual immersion program" whose positive results support the "claims of bilingual education advocates that most bilingual education programs do not use enough of the native language" and 6 years later to describe exactly the same program as a "structured English immersion" program whose positive results illustrate "the harm that bilingual education programs do to learning English." [3]

Christine Rossell:
The Miracle Results of Grade 1 French Immersion

Although Christine Rossell has not directly endorsed any form of bilingual education, a large majority of the studies she employs to argue for English-only structured immersion are in fact bilingual or trilingual programs. Evidence of *doublethink* comes from her use of the documented success of bilingual and trilingual programs to argue against bilingual education. In critiquing her claims, I will focus on her co-authored 1996 paper with Keith Baker since it is the most complete recent statement of her position.

The outcomes of Rossell and Baker's (1996) review of "methodologically acceptable" research studies on the educational effectiveness of bilingual education are clearly stated in the Abstract:

> The research evidence indicates that, on standardized achievement tests, transitional bilingual education (TBE) is *better* than regular classroom instruction in only 22% of the methodologically acceptable studies when the outcome is reading, 7% of the studies when the outcome is language, and 9% of the studies when the outcome is math. TBE is never better than structured immersion, a special program for limited English proficient children where the children are in a self-contained classroom composed solely of English learners, but the instruction is in English at a pace they can understand. (1996, p. 1)

Furthermore, the comparisons of reading scores between TBE and structured immersion showed that structured immersion was superior in 83% of cases and no differences were observed in 17%.

These conclusions, published in a reputable refereed journal, and apparently based on rigorous methodological criteria, would cause any policy-maker to question the merits of transitional bilingual education. However, cracks appear very quickly in the facade of objective rationality that this review of the literature projects. One problem is immediately obvious: When we look more closely at the research studies that supposedly demonstrated the superiority of "structured immersion" over "transitional bilingual education" it turns out that *90% of these studies are interpreted by their authors as supporting the effectiveness of bilingual and even trilingual education.*

Seven of the 10 studies that Rossell and Baker claim support structured immersion over TBE were studies of French immersion programs in Canada. Typically, in these programs English-speaking students are "immersed" in French (their second language [L2]) in kindergarten and grade 1 and English (L1) language arts are introduced in grade 2. The proportion of English instruction increases to about 50% by grades 4 or 5. The closest equivalent to the program in the United States is dual language immersion (*e.g.*, Christian *et al.*, 1997; Dolson & Lindholm, 1995; Lindholm-Leary, 2001; Thomas & Collier, 1997). Note that, as in the U.S. dual language programs, Canadian French immersion programs are bilingual programs, taught by bilingual teachers, and their goal is the development of bilingualism and biliteracy.

Even at the level of face validity, it seems incongruous that Rossell and Baker use the success of the Canadian French-English bilingual programs to argue for monolingual immersion programs taught largely by monolingual teachers with the goal of developing monolingualism. This is particularly the case since 2 of the 7 programs they cite as evidence for monolingual structured immersion were actually *trilingual* programs involving instruction in French, English, and Hebrew (Genesee & Lambert, 1983; Genesee, Lambert, & Tucker, 1977).

In addition to these 7 French immersion program evaluations, one of the 10 studies (Malherbe, 1946) was an extremely large-scale study of Afrikaans-English bilingual education in South Africa involving 19,000 students. The other two were carried out in the United States (Gersten, 1985c; Peña-Hughes & Solís, 1980).

The Peña-Hughes and Solís kindergarten program (labeled "structured immersion" by Rossell and Baker) involved an hour of Spanish language arts per day and was viewed as a form of bilingual education by the director of the program (Willig, 1981/82). I would see the genuine promotion of L1 literacy in this program as indicating a much more adequate model of bilingual education than the quick-exit transitional bilingual program to which it was being compared. Gersten's study involved an extremely small number of Asian-origin students (12 immersion students in the first cohort and 9 bilingual program students, and 16 and 7 in the second cohort) and hardly constitutes an adequate sample upon which to base national policy.

Malherbe's study concluded that students instructed bilingually did at least as well in each language as students instructed monolingually despite much less time through each language. He argues strongly for the *benefits* of bilingual education (however, see Krashen, 1999c, for a critique of the design of this study).

In short, Rossell and Baker's conclusions are immediately suspect as a result of the fact that they use the documented success of bilingual and trilingual programs to argue against bilingual education. There are many other problems with their literature review (see Cummins, 1999; Dicker, 1996; Escamilla, 1996; Krashen, 1996), some of which are noted below:

Rossell and Baker assign labels to different programs in an arbitrary and inconsistent manner. For example, they claim to compare French immersion (structured immersion) programs in Canada with "transitional bilingual education." There are no transitional bilingual education programs in Canada for any group of students. The El Paso Independent School District (1987) program was labeled a "Spanish-English dual immersion" program by Baker in 1992, a "structured English immersion" program by Baker in 1998, and a "submersion" program by Rossell and Baker (1996—Appendix C, p. 72).

Rossell and Baker limit the framework of discourse to exclude bilingual programs designed to promote bilingualism and biliteracy. An additional example of arbitrary labeling is their treatment of Legaretta's (1979) kindergarten study. Originally labeled a "structured immersion" program by Baker and de Kanter (1983), this study demonstrated the superiority of a 50% Spanish, 50% English kindergarten program over both English-only and other bilingual program options with respect to students' learning of English. Rossell and Baker (1996) list this study as showing "no difference" between TBE and submersion (English-only) treatments. Yet the program option that was significantly better than all others was neither TBE nor submersion! The consistently positive outcomes of this kind of "Enriched Education" program (Beykont, 1994; Cloud, Genesee, & Hamayan, 2000) are nowhere represented in Rossell and Baker's review. By limiting the framework of discourse to "transitional bilingual education" versus varieties of English-only programs, they have excluded the type of dual language program option endorsed by virtually all applied linguists and also by several commentators who have been highly critical of bilingual education (Glenn & LaLyre, 1991; Porter, 1990).

Rossell and Baker's reporting of French immersion data is blatantly inaccurate. In response to critiques from Kathy Escamilla (1996) and Susan Dicker (1996) regarding the fact that French immersion programs are fully bilingual in both goals and implementation, Rossell (1996) pointed out:

> In the first two years, the program is one of total immersion, and evaluations conducted at that point are considered to be evaluations of "structured immersion."

It is really not important that, in later years, the program becomes bilingual if the evaluation is being conducted while it is still and always has been a structured immersion program. (1996, p. 383)

The significance of this point is that the major empirical basis of Rossell and Baker's entire argument for structured English immersion rests, according to their own admission, on the performance in French of English-background students *in the first two years* of Canadian French immersion programs when instruction is totally through the second language. They interpret this research as follows:

Both the middle class and working class English-speaking students who were immersed in French in kindergarten and grade one *were almost the equal of native French-speaking students* until the curriculum became bilingual in grade two, at which point their French ability declined and continued to decline as English was increased. The 'time-on-task' principle—that is, the notion that the amount of time spent learning a subject is the greatest predictor of achievement in that subject—holds across classes in the Canadian programs. (p. 22) (emphasis added)

Rossell and Baker seem oblivious to the fact that at the end of grade 1 French immersion students are still at very early stages in their acquisition of French. Despite good progress in learning French (particularly receptive skills) during the initial two years of the program, they are still light years away from native-like proficiency in speaking, listening, reading, and writing. Virtually no grade 1 or 2 French immersion student is capable of carrying on even an elementary conversation in French without major errors and insertions of English. Similarly, it is bizarre to claim, as Baker and Rossell do without even a citation to back it up, that the French proficiency of grade 6 immersion students is more poorly developed than that of grade 1 students, and to attribute this to the fact that the instruction has become bilingual with students' L1 incorporated in the program.

The research data show exactly the *opposite* pattern to that claimed by Rossell and Baker. Lambert and Tucker (1972), for example, report highly significant differences between grade 1 immersion and native French-speaking students on a variety of vocabulary, grammatical and expressive skills in French, despite the fact that no differences were found in some of the sub-skills of reading such as word discrimination. By the end of grade 4, however, (after 3 years of English [L1] language arts instruction), the immersion students had caught up with the French controls in vocabulary knowledge and listening comprehension, although major differences still remained in speaking and writing ability. Similarly, in the United States, the one large-scale "methodologically acceptable" study that investigated this issue (Ramírez, 1992) found that early-grade students in structured immersion were very far from grade norms in English even after *four* years of English-only immersion. After one year only 4% of English learners in structured immersion were fluent in English despite instruction almost totally through English (Crawford, 2000, p. 36).

Another example of *doublethink* on Rossell's part is her endorsement of the "time-on-task" assumption while at the same time acknowledging in a commentary on the Ramírez (1992) report that "large deficits in English language instruction over several grades apparently make little or no difference in a student's achievement" (1992, p. 183). Expressed more positively, instructional time devoted to promoting bilingual students' L1 literacy entails no adverse consequences for English language or literacy development.

Rossell and Baker also fail to acknowledge that the "time-on-task" principle is refuted by every evaluation of French immersion programs (and there are hundreds) by virtue of the fact that no relationship has been found between the development of students' *English* (L1) proficiency and the amount of time spent through English in the program. French immersion students who spend about two-thirds of their instructional time in elementary school through French (L2) perform as well in English as students who have had all of their instruction through English.

In summary, to claim that two years of immersion in French in kindergarten and grade 1 results in almost native-like proficiency in French in a context where there is virtually no French exposure in the environment or in school outside the classroom flies in the face of a massive amount of research data. This can be verified by anyone who cares to step into any of the thousands of grade 1 French immersion classrooms across Canada. If Rossell has some miraculous potion to transform grade 1 French immersion students into virtual native-speakers of French, there are many Canadian educators and parents who would love to find out about it.

It seems clear that Rossell and Baker could have constructed a far more convincing case for the efficacy of dual language programs than the case they attempt to construct for English-only structured immersion. On the basis of their own review of the literature (*e.g.,* Legaretta's [1979] study), and Baker's published statements endorsing the El Paso and San Diego models, Rossell and Baker would appear to agree with Porter that dual language immersion is a model with demonstrated success in promoting bilingual students' academic achievement in English (and L1). Their literature review is totally consistent with the assertion that this model should be promoted vigorously as a viable option in advancing equity for bilingual students. [4]

Charles Glenn: Promoting Schools in Which Two Languages Are Used Without Apology

Charles Glenn is a former Director of Educational Equity and Urban Education at the Massachusetts Department of Education and a well-respected author of several volumes on education and diversity (*e.g.,* Glenn, 1996). Despite his concern with equity, Glenn has supported the passage of Proposition 227 in California (Glenn, 1998). I will focus primarily on his review of the National Research Council (NRC) report on schooling for language-minority children (August & Hakuta, 1997) as representative of his concerns with bilingual education (see also Krashen, 2000a).

Glenn (1997) cites August and Hakuta's statement that "many children first learn to read in a second language without serious negative consequences" (1997, p. 60) as refuting 'one of the central articles of faith of bilingual education' that children must be taught to read first in the language which they speak at home. Glenn appears to believe that this is a core component of the rationale for bilingual education. As noted above, however, the research says nothing about which language should be used for initial literacy instruction and arguments for initial reading instruction in L1 are not in any way intrinsic to the basic rationale for bilingual programs.

Clearly some bilingual program advocates have seen initial reading instruction in L1 as important, endorsing some variant of the linguistic mismatch hypothesis that "children can't learn in a language they don't understand" (see Chapter 6). However, most researchers have argued for more than 25 years that the linguistic mismatch assumption is simplistic and cannot account for the research data (*e.g.,* Cummins, 1979; Engle, 1975; Wagner, 1998). Thus, August and Hakuta's conclusion is simply restating what the research has shown for many years and about which there is no disagreement among researchers.

Glenn's major concern with bilingual programs is that they may segregate students and retain them too long outside the mainstream, with newcomers "simply dumped into a bilingual class of the appropriate age level" (1997, p. 7).

In addition, he suggests that these programs may lack coherent, cognitively challenging opportunities for students to develop higher order English literacy skills.

These concerns may certainly be justified in the case of some poorly-implemented bilingual programs; however, concerns about segregation, low teacher expectations, and cognitively undemanding drill-and-practice instruction equally characterize the English-only programs attended by the vast majority of limited English proficient students. As the research of Harklau (1999) and others has shown, ELL students are much more likely to have low-level drill and practice instruction inflicted on them in all-English classrooms where they lack the English language proficiency to participate fully in discussion and project-based work. The reality is that segregation in schools is primarily a function of housing and neighborhood concentration of particular groups and it exists independently of the language of instruction. A major advantage of dual language programs is that they overcome segregation in a planned program that aims to enrich the learning opportunities of both minority and majority language students. However, even in segregated, low-income, inner-city contexts, the findings of Ramírez (1992), Beykont (1994), and Thomas and Collier (1997) show that well-implemented developmental (late-exit) bilingual programs can achieve remarkable success in promoting grade-level academic success for bilingual students.

Despite his concerns about segregating bilingual students from the mainstream, Glenn is generally positive towards bilingualism and what he regards as appropriate forms of bilingual education. For example, he concurs with August and Hakuta's (1997) recommendation of three components that should characterize any effective program:

• Some native-language instruction, especially initially;
• For most students, a relatively early phasing in of English instruction;
• Teachers specially trained in instructing English-language learners.

To this list I would add the goal of genuinely promoting literacy in students' L1 and continuation of L1 literacy instruction throughout elementary school and, if possible, beyond. Glenn (1996, 1997) approvingly cites the common European (and Canadian) practice of providing immigrant students with the opportunity to continue to study their heritage language and culture as an elective, so presumably he would endorse the goal of L1 literacy development for bilingual students in the United States, at least for Spanish-speaking students where numbers and concentration make this goal administratively feasible.

In fact, Glenn has been one of the strongest and most consistent advocates of two-way bilingual immersion, as the following quotations illustrate:

> More than any other model of education for linguistic minority pupils, two-way bilingual programs meet the diverse expectations that we set for our schools. Properly designed and implemented, they offer a language-rich environment with high expectations for every child, in a climate of cross-cultural respect. Linguistic minority pupils are stimulated in their use of English, while being encouraged to value and employ their home language as well. (Glenn, 1990, p. 5)

> The best setting for educating linguistic minority pupils—and one of the best for educating *any* pupils—is a school in which two languages are used without apology and where becoming proficient in both is considered a significant intellectual and cultural achievement." (Glenn & LaLyre, 1991, p. 43)

I fully agree with Glenn's (1997) concluding statement which demonstrates his personal support for bilingual education as a means of developing children's bilingualism:

> What cannot be justified, however, is to continue substituting a preoccupation with the language of instruction for the essential concern that instruction be effective. Bilingual education, it has become clear, is not of itself a solution to the under-achievement of any group of poor children. It is time that those of us who support bilingual education—in my case, by sending five of my children to an inner-city bilingual school—insist upon honesty about its goals and its limits. Bilingual education is a way to teach children to be bilingual, but it possesses no magic answer to the challenge of educating children at risk. Bilingualism is a very good thing indeed, but what language-minority children need most is schools that expect and enable them to succeed through providing a demanding academic program, taught very well and without compromise, schools which respect the ways in which children differ but insist that these differences must not be barriers to equal opportunity. (1997, p. 15)

A final point of agreement in relation to Glenn's analysis is his statement that "the under-achievement of Hispanics in the United States and of Turks and Moroccans in northwestern Europe, I suggested in my recent book [Glenn,

1996], may have less to do with language differences than with their status in the society and how they come to terms with that status" (p. 10). Among opponents of bilingual education, Glenn is unusual in highlighting issues of power and status as causal factors in students' underachievement. This emphasis is clearly consistent with the framework articulated in the present volume which highlights the direct relationship between power differentials in the wider society and the interactions between educators and subordinated group students in school.

Glenn's distinction between "language differences" and "status in society" suggests that he views language factors as relatively insignificant in comparison to status factors. Thus, bilingual education (as a "language" intervention) may have little role in reversing patterns of academic underachievement. If this is his intent, his argument implies an *either-or* logic that suggests that if underachievement is related to status and power differentials then it has nothing to do with language. Clearly, this is absurd. As Glenn knows better than most, the subordinated status of colonized and marginalized groups in countries around the world has typically been reinforced in the school by punishing students for speaking their home language and making them feel ashamed of their language, culture and religion. As argued in previous chapters, a significant rationale for promoting students' primary language in school through bilingual education is to challenge the subordinated status of the students and their communities, and the coercive power relations in the wider society that gave rise to it. The evidence is overwhelming that strong promotion of literacy in the primary language, in the context of a well-implemented bilingual program, will result in no adverse consequences for literacy in English. Promotion of literacy in the L1 for subordinated group students is obviously not in itself a complete solution, but it can certainly make an important contribution to academic achievement for many bilingual students

In short, Glenn is clearly a strong advocate of using bilingual education to develop students' bilingualism, although highly critical of the way in which many bilingual education programs in the United States have been implemented. He is also willing to acknowledge the central role of coercive power relations in promoting bilingual students' academic underachievement both in Europe and North America. Why then would he support a measure as overtly coercive as Proposition 227 rather than continuing his advocacy for "school[s] in which two languages are used without apology and where becoming proficient in both is considered a significant intellectual and cultural achievement"? I have no idea.

Conclusion

It should be clear at this stage that considerable common ground is emerging between opponents and advocates of bilingual education. So-called advocates have been highly critical of many quick-exit transitional programs on the grounds that they do not aspire to develop bilingualism or biliteracy and also fail to affirm strongly students' cultural and linguistic identity. Virtually all applied linguists endorse developmental or two-way bilingual immersion programs in preference to quick-exit transitional bilingual programs. Surprisingly, the same appears true of the so-called opponents of bilingual education: they are highly critical of transitional bilingual programs but most have strongly endorsed dual language or two-way bilingual immersion programs. As noted above, Porter holds similar views to Charles Glenn's on the benefits of two-way bilingual programs as a means of promoting bilingualism; Baker endorses the El Paso and San Diego bilingual immersion programs, and Rossell and Baker cite the success of bilingual and trilingual programs as an argument for monolingual English immersion. The only "methodologically acceptable" study in their review that compared virtually all the program options from English-only to transitional bilingual to 50:50 dual language (Legaretta, 1979) showed the dual language program to be significantly superior in the development of English proficiency compared to any of the alternative programs.

These commentators have not, however, addressed the contradictions that their endorsement (explicit or implicit) of dual language programs entails. To argue vehemently against bilingual education, while at the same time endorsing the most intensive form of bilingual education, at the very least requires explanation.

There is too much at stake for children's educational and personal development to brush these contradictions aside as a cute exercise of *doublethink* morphing into *disinformation*. There is an ethical responsibility to address and clarify the contradictions both for academic audiences and for the general public. The adversarial nature of the debate on bilingual education, and the resulting widespread disinformation, has hurt children and denied both minority and majority students the opportunity to develop fluent bilingual and biliteracy skills.

There will always be legitimate differences of opinion in the interpretation of academic research. Scientific progress is made possible by means of dialogue, discussion, and further research designed to resolve the differences. This process of dialogue has not happened in the area of bilingual education. A negative spin on the research to the tune of "bilingual education doesn't work" has been fed directly to the media and has polluted public discourse on this topic. I use the strong label *pollution* to convey the fact that the message broadcast by the media ignores the *consensus* among virtually all North American researchers that (a) countless successful bilingual programs have been implemented in countries throughout the world, and (b) dual language or two-way bilingual immersion programs, as well as one-way developmental programs, have produced consistently positive outcomes for both language minority and majority students and constitute a viable policy option for helping to reverse bilingual students' academic underachievement. I believe that academics, in contrast to courtroom lawyers, have an *ethical* responsibility to clean up the info-pollution. Alternatively, they should publicly admit that they have abandoned academic standards in favor of the conventions of adversarial discourse where the goal is to win rather than to contribute to effective policy grounded in solid research.

The last chapter attempts to reframe the issues, arguing that far from being a threat to the coherence of society, effective bilingual programs can contribute significantly to challenging coercive relations of power that constitute the real threat to future generations.

Endnotes to Chapter 9

1. The previous edition of this book considered in some detail arguments advanced against bilingual education since the mid-1970s by a variety of commentators. In this chapter, I am confining my discussion only to the more recent arguments and interpretations of research that have been advanced during the 1990s and beyond. The issues have remained essentially the same during the past 30 years.

   In referring to "academic" critics of bilingual programs, I am using the term "academic" to refer to individuals who have a doctoral degree and whose work has been published in academic journals or books that have focused on research findings. To the best of my knowledge, one of the four commentators considered in this chapter currently holds a university faculty position (Christine Rossell at the University of Boston).

2. There are many other inaccuracies in Porter's account of bilingual education. She appears, for example, to believe that typical transitional bilingual programs in the United States involve almost exclusive L1 instruction in the early grades. She claims that "the teaching of all subjects in the native language of the child for the first few years of schooling has become a non-negotiable condition for the TBE [transitional bilingual education] framework" (p. 71). In fact, large-scale studies have shown that in typical transitional bilingual education programs only about 25% of instructional time is spent through the medium of L1 (Tikunoff, 1983). Teachers typically switch to L1 for clarification of instruction. In many cases the instructional time devoted to L1 is minimal; for example, in a longitudinal study of instructional practices in bilingual classes involving Chinese- and Spanish-background students, it

was reported (Wong Fillmore *et al.*, 1985) that the L1 of students was used for no more than 10% of the instruction. This average time allocation range (10–25%) is consistent with the findings of other reviews (Wong Fillmore & Valadez, 1986).

The level of scholarship in Porter's book can be seen most clearly in her discussion of Canadian French immersion programs. She appears to believe that Canadian French immersion programs serve predominantly working-class students. Furthermore, she makes the bizarre suggestion that Canadian researchers have systematically concealed this "fact" in order to further their own career advancement:

> The linguists, educators, and researchers whose career advancement is linked to the success of immersion education argue protectively that this program is only appropriate for middle-class children who, secure in their majority language and status, are learning a less-valued language. They have clung to this bias despite the fact that the large percentage of children in the Canadian immersion programs are from low-income working-class families. (p. 117)

It is significant, but not surprising, that there is no citation to back up this "fact." The vast majority of students in French immersion programs have always come from middle-class families (Lambert & Tucker, 1972; Swain & Lapkin, 1982).

The importance to Porter's argument of insisting that most students in French immersion programs are from low-income working-class backgrounds is that she wants to be able to generalize the French immersion results directly to the United States context and argue that low-income minority students should be provided with English immersion. As noted in Chapter 6, French immersion programs are relevant to our understanding of bilingual education insofar as their results are consistent with the interdependence principle, thereby increasing the confidence that can be placed in that principle for planning bilingual programs in a variety of contexts.

The debate on Porter's book took an unexpected turn when Keith Baker (formerly [and subsequently] a strong opponent of bilingual education) delivered a scathing critique in the pages of *TESOL Quarterly*. Among his comments after reviewing a host of inaccuracies and misrepresentations in Porter's book:

> Porter violated the most basic trust between reader and author of scholarly works. Porter's level of scholarship falls far short of the most minimal standards of acceptable research. Porter's unmerited scholarly pretensions led to large numbers of people on the far right and in the English-only movement who share Porter's biases giving the book wide publicity as evidence of both the ineffectiveness and political corruption of the bilingual education movement. Neither conclusion is justified...My view is that the research clearly shows bilingual education programs are superior to all-English programs, such as those advocated by Porter, in the early stages of learning English, but I still would not say that a federal mandate is justified. (1992b, pp. 401–402)

Porter (1993), in response, cited Baker's "inexplicable reverses" and "sudden about face" and accused him of character assassination. The vehemence of this exchange clearly reflects a personal as well as an academic conflict.

3. Baker's reporting of the El Paso results in his 1998 article is at variance with Gersten and Woodward's (1995) data. They report that there were no differences between the programs by grade 7 whereas Baker, citing Gersten and Woodward, claims that the "structured immersion" program was "significantly higher on all tests for 11 straight years" (p. 201). Baker (1998) also implies that the El Paso program involved only 30 minutes a day of L1 instruction when, in fact, between 90 and 60 minutes a day of L1 instruction designed to develop Spanish literacy was employed between grades 1 and 3.

This cavalier attitude towards empirical data, which is also evident in Rossell and Baker's (1996) bizarre account of French immersion program results, has not been picked up by the refereed journals in which their articles have appeared. Perhaps more care should be taken by journal editors to ensure that blatant inaccuracies are not present in the articles that appear in their "refereed" journals.

Chapter 10
Babel Babble: Reframing the Discourse of Diversity

Literacy is dangerous and has always been so regarded. It naturally breaks down barriers of time, space, and culture. It threatens one's original identity by broadening it through vicarious experiencing and the incorporation of somebody else's hearth and ethos. So we feel profoundly ambiguous about literacy. Looking at it as a means of transmitting our culture to our children, we give it priority in education, but recognizing the threat of its backfiring we make it so tiresome and personally unrewarding that youngsters won't want to do it on their own, which is of course when it becomes dangerous...The net effect of this ambivalence is to give literacy with one hand and take it back with the other, in keeping with our contradictory wish for youngsters to learn to think but only about what we already have in mind for them (James Moffett, 1989, p. 85).

Genuine critical literacy threatens established systems of privilege and resource distribution because it reduces the potency of indoctrination and disinformation. Critical literacy enables us to read between the lines, to look skeptically at apparently benign and plausible surface structures, to analyze claims in relation to empirical data, and to question whose interests are served by particular forms of communication.

Many social, cultural, and religious institutions throughout the world tend to be wary of both critical literacy and cultural diversity because they bring other perspectives into mind. At issue is the question of whether being willing to look at current issues and historical events from the perspective of the Other will undermine or enrich our original perceptions. North American academics and policy-makers who argue stridently against multicultural and bilingual education view cultural diversity as the enemy within and want to minimize what they see as its destructive effects on the collective psyche of the nation. They want to ensure that students remain within predetermined cultural and intellectual boundaries. They want to retain control of what can be thought in order to ensure the smooth functioning of a democratic society in the service of the current power structure. Their dilemma, of course, is that the economic and diplomatic realities of our interdependent global society in the 21st century demand enormous critical literacy and problem-solving abilities and the constant crossing of cultural and linguistic boundaries.

In this final chapter, I suggest that the enemy within is neither cultural diversity nor critical literacy but a politics of greed and exploitation that is willing to jeopardize not only the lives of individual children but also the coherence of entire societies for its own coercive ends. Core notions that define our societies, such as "liberty and justice for all," have given way to policies that are promoting increased economic polarization and marginalization. The chapter analyzes how coercive relations of power operate to manufacture consent for programs and policies that are not for "the common good" nor in the best interests of the society as a whole. The scapegoating of immigrants and cultural diversity since the late 1980s has reignited *Us versus Them* divisions and fears in order to obscure and distract attention from the increasingly obvious redistribution of wealth in North American societies. Indoctrination and disinformation are the tools whereby consent is manufactured for this process.

In this volume, I have focused on how this process of indoctrination and disinformation has operated in the debate regarding the education of bilingual students. However, as documented by Berliner and Biddle (1995), this is only one part of a larger process of manufacturing and spreading "big lies" about education in the United States context. Their book, which they note was "written in outrage" (p. xi), *The Manufactured Crisis: Myths, Fraud, and the Attack on America's Public Schools*, constitutes a powerful denunciation of what they term the "organized malevolence" (p. xi) orchestrated against public education during the 1980s and 1990s. They acknowledge that there are problems in American public education caused by "huge differences in income, wealth and support for schools in our nation," but contrary to widely-believed myths, "the evidence suggests that, on average, American schools are not only holding their own but are improving in modest ways" (p. 343). They document how this attack "was promoted by specific groups of ideologues who were hostile to public schools and who wanted to divert attention from America's growing social problems" (p. 343):

> The more we poked into our story, the more nasty lies about education we unearthed; the more we learned about how government officials and their allies were ignoring, suppressing, and distorting evidence; and the more we discovered how Americans were being mislead about schools and their accomplishments. ...[M]any of the myths...have been told by powerful people who—despite their protestations—were pursuing a political agenda designed to weaken the nation's public schools, redistribute support for those schools so that privileged students are favored over needy students, or even abolish those schools altogether. To this end, they have been prepared to tell lies, suppress evidence, scapegoat educators, and sow endless confusion. (1995, p. xii)

How can disinformation be identified? As illustrated in the previous chapter, disinformation is achieved by distorting empirical data, limiting the framework of discourse, and ignoring logical contradictions (see Chomsky, 1987, for discussion of these processes in the international arena). As Berliner and Biddle's analysis shows, disinformation can be identified by examining the empirical data. In the debate on the merits or otherwise of bilingual education, the empirical data provides clear evidence that a systematic process of disinformation has been orchestrated to discredit the use of children's L1 in their education.

Distortion of empirical data. On the surface, the claim that bilingual children need English-only instruction to maximize time-on-task appears plausible and well-intentioned. But when this claim is analyzed against the empirical data, it immediately falls apart. There is no evidence in the United States or elsewhere that spending less than 100% of the instructional time through the majority language reduces students' achievement in that language. As noted in Chapter 9, the United States and international data are totally at variance with Rossell and Baker's (1996) claim that in comparisons of reading scores between "structured immersion" and "transitional bilingual education," "structured immersion" was superior in 83% of cases and no differences were observed in 17%. Even a superficial examination of their "evidence" shows that *90% of the studies they cite in support of this claim are interpreted by their authors as showing the effectiveness of bilingual and even trilingual education.*

If bilingual education were harmful, why would elite groups around the world demand it for their children? At this point, there is overwhelming evidence that the best prospects for academic enrichment of all children are provided in programs, such as dual language programs, that aim to develop biliteracy rather than just literacy in one language (Christian, Howard & Loeb, 2000; Cloud, Genesee & Hamayan, 2000; Thomas & Collier, 1997).

A process of disinformation is also evident in the distortion of Canadian French immersion programs as research support for English-only immersion in the United States. The ignorance of these programs shown by the few academics who oppose bilingual education is matched only by their arrogance in posing as experts without having read even a fraction of the relevant research. Among the *extraordinary* statements made by these academics in relation to French immersion programs are the claims that:

- Grade 1 French immersion students attain levels of French proficiency virtually equivalent to that of native French speakers but then fall considerably behind native French speakers after English (L1) instruction is introduced in grade 2 and the program becomes bilingual (Rossell & Baker, 1996). As noted in Chapter 9, the vast majority of grade 1 French immersion students cannot carry on even an elementary conversation in French. By grade 6, however, they have improved sufficiently to approach native-speaker norms in receptive listening and reading skills. Their speaking and writing skills remain far from native-like throughout their schooling.

- "The bulk of the Canadian [French immersion] research was with low-income students" (Gersten & Woodward, 1985a, p. 76) and "there were four studies other than the St. Lambert study, all of which involved children from working-class families" (Gersten & Woodward, 1985b, p. 83). In other words, no more than five empirical studies of French immersion have been carried out and four of these involved low-income children. In fact, there are hundreds of published evaluations of French immersion programs from the late 1960s through to the present day (Swain & Lapkin, 1982) and the vast majority of these programs involved middle class students for the simple reason that the bulk of students in French immersion are from middle-class backgrounds.

In short, the empirical data on bilingual education has been grossly distorted for political ends (see Krashen, 1999a, for further documentation).

Limiting the framework of discourse. Opponents of bilingual education almost never address the outcomes of dual language programs and, in fact,

act as though these programs either did not exist (Rossell & Baker, 1996) or were irrelevant to the bilingual education debate (Glenn, 1997, 1998; Porter, 1990). Rossell and Baker (1996), for example, ignore the superiority of a 50:50 L1/L2 dual language program over all comparison programs (transitional bilingual and monolingual English) in reporting Legaretta's (1979) study. Furthermore, they categorize various kinds of Canadian bilingual and trilingual programs as either "structured immersion" (essentially English-only) or "transitional bilingual education" rather than acknowledge that these are *enriched education* programs (Cloud *et al.*, 2000) whose explicit goal is the development of bilingualism and biliteracy.

If not an attempt at disinformation, how can we explain arguments for monolingual English-only education, taught by monolingual teachers with the goal of promoting monolingualism on the basis of the success of bilingual programs, taught by bilingual teachers, with the goal of promoting bilingualism and biliteracy?

Ignoring logical contradictions. As noted in Chapter 9, both Glenn and Porter ignore the logical contradiction of strongly endorsing two-way bilingual programs while at the same time condemning bilingual education. The two-way/dual language programs typically have far greater amounts of minority language instruction than the quick-exit transitional programs they condemn. Porter compounds the contradiction by endorsing the *time-on-task* principle despite the fact that it is refuted by the results of virtually every bilingual program ever evaluated, including all of the Canadian French immersion programs which she reviews very positively.

An additional contradiction, noted by many authors, is the endorsement of teaching "foreign languages" while at the same time condemning bilingual education as bad for both the individual and the society. Claims that "bilingualism shuts doors" (Schlesinger, 1991) or "bilingual education slows down and confuses people in their pursuit of new ways of thinking" (Gingrich, 1995) are belied by the glossy full page advertisements for language courses, aimed at business people, that have been in virtually every airline magazine I have read during the past five years. The alleged problems of bilingualism for society are also belied by the fact that "the Central Intelligence Agency now has difficulty meeting its needs for critical language skills, even in commonly taught languages such as Spanish" (Stanford Working Group on Federal Programs for Limited-English-Proficient Students, 1993, p. 12). A more appropriate inference from the data would be that American society suffers from a lack of bilingualism rather than an excess. Despite the enormous potential linguistic resources of the United States, the situation has changed little since The President's Commission on Foreign Language and International Studies pointed out that "Americans' scandalous incompetence in foreign languages" "diminishes our capabilities in diplomacy, in foreign trade, and in citizen comprehension of the world in which we live and compete" (1980, p. 12).

I suggested in the previous chapter that these patently flawed arguments serve to reinforce a coercive power structure that historically has denied subordinated communities full access to societal resources. In this chapter, I try to place the xenophobic discourse against cultural diversity into the larger context of which it is a part. I argue that the scapegoating of immigrants and the demonization of bilingual education is part of an exercise to divert public attention away from the massive transfer of wealth from middle-class and poor to the rich that took place in the United States during the 1980s and continues to this day. I also suggest that coercive relations of power have reached a point of diminishing returns, even for those socially advantaged groups whose interests they are intended to serve. The fiscal and social costs of maintaining the current structure of privilege and resource distribution far outstrip the costs that would be involved in shifting to more collaborative relations of power.

Why should educators care about this larger social reality? How is it relevant to the task of teaching English and academic skills to bilingual students?

In the first place, we all have a vested interest in the future of our society, with respect to both its economic health and social cohesion. Our incomes and quality of life (and those of our children and grandchildren) are very much tied to how effectively our society functions and the extent to which our educational systems give students a stake in contributing to their society. If they don't develop the abilities and interest to participate productively in the social and economic life of their society, the chances are that they will drain resources from their society. If schools continue to fail in their attempts to educate students whose communities have been subordinated economically and socially for generations, everyone in society will pay the price. I have argued in this volume that the source of this educational failure is a coercive power structure that is reflected, often inadvertently, in many schools and other societal institutions. Thus, educators who aspire to create contexts of empowerment with their students as the only route to educational success, must understand how disempowerment has all too frequently been created within our classrooms.

Secondly, as educators, we have considerable power to effect change in the lives of those we interact with. As Poplin and Weeres (1992) point out in the quotation that opens this volume, students respond very positively when they sense that their teachers care about them and want to connect with them as people. For teachers, their best experiences were also when they connected with students and were able to help them in concrete ways. These human relationships that form the core of successful schooling determine the social and economic horizon that students see when they look beyond the school.

Our interactions with students in the classroom embody an image of the society they will graduate into and the kind of contributions they are being enabled to make within this society. As educators we are faced with choices and constraints with respect to what and how we teach, the nature of our personal goals in teaching, and the kind of aspirations we have for the students we teach. Classroom interactions collectively shape both our students' future possibilities and those of our society. Thus, understanding the forces that influence the interactional choices we make in our classrooms, and thinking critically about the constraints that are imposed on those choices, is central to how we define our roles in our schools and the society beyond the school.

Because all sectors of our society have strong vested interests in what happens in schools, claims and counter-claims in the media about appropriate directions for education are broadcast loudly into classrooms. Although invariably phrased in terms of what is in the best interests of children, these claims and counter-claims also embody social agendas; they reflect alternative visions of society. The discourse on either side of these debates is intended to mold schools into conformity with particular social, cultural, or religious images.

Educators are committed to helping children learn. However, their choices with respect to issues of language, culture, pedagogy, and parent involvement also reflect the societal discourses that swirl around their classrooms in relation to these issues. If educators are to achieve their goal of helping children learn, it is imperative to analyze critically the societal discourses that are vying for their allegiance. To what extent are different claims supported by verifiable data? Whose interests do these claims serve? What forms of instruction are in the best interests of children and serve the common good of our society? What kinds of knowledge, skills, and values will best serve students as they graduate into a rapidly changing society? Is this the kind of education I would want for my own child?

In the sections that follow, I present my own perspectives on these issues and elaborate the kind of education that I would want for my own children. These perspectives are part of a discourse that values cultural diversity, critical thinking, and social justice. They represent an explicit vision of a society founded on principles of collaborative relations of power, as articulated in Chapter 1. The claim is that the common good of society will be better served by educators and by educational systems that are oriented explicitly to challenging coercive relations of power.

As with any other set of discoursal claims, these arguments should be analyzed critically by educators. Are the data presented convincing? If not, where are the gaps or inaccuracies? Whose interests do these arguments serve? Ultimately, individual educators must define their roles and make their own choices about their instructional and social goals in the classroom. However, making well-informed choices should be an explicit process that takes account of the empirical data and critically examines alternative perspectives. Only through this form of critical analysis will educators challenge the structures in schools and society that serve to disempower them as much as their students.

Graduating into a Rapidly Changing Society

Public schools serve the societies that fund them and they aim to graduate students with the knowledge, skills, and values that will contribute most effectively to their societies. In an era of rapid and intense change, it is often difficult to predict the kinds of "human resources" our societies will need in the future. However, some patterns are beginning to emerge and their implications for education are immense. In the sections below, I describe the changing cultural, economic/scientific, and existential realities that should be reflected in classroom interactions if they are to prepare students to contribute effectively to their societies in the 21st century. [1]

Cultural Realities. Schools intent on preparing students for the realities of the 21st century must take account of the fact that cultural diversity is the norm in both the domestic and international arenas. [2] Around the world we see unprecedented population mobility and intercultural contact resulting from factors such as economic migration, displacement caused by military conflicts and famine, as well as technological advances in transportation and communication. Increased intercultural contact within industrialized countries as a result of decades of migration is matched by growing intercultural contact between countries, reflecting increased global economic and political interdependence.

This escalation of intercultural contact, both domestically and internationally, has major implications for our schools. In the first place, it suggests that the transmission of cultural myopia in schools is a recipe for social disaster. The prophets of doom who warn about the infiltration of the Other in the guise of multicultural curricula and bilingual education have closed their eyes to the urgent need for school programs that promote sensitivity to, and understanding of, diverse cultural perspectives. If we are to learn anything from the racial and ethnic tensions in North American cities and the brutal armed conflicts abroad that have characterized the 1990s, surely it is that our schools have a crucial role to play in helping us live and grow together in our global village. Educators concerned with preparing students for life in the 21st century must educate them for global citizenship. The potential to achieve this goal is obviously greater in a classroom context where cultural diversity is seen as a resource rather than in one where it is either suppressed or ignored.

In the second place, if we take seriously the concerns about the competitiveness of American business in an increasingly interdependent global economy, highlighted by Reagan/Bush era educational reformers, then it is the monolingual/monocultural graduate who is "culturally illiterate" and ill-equipped to prosper in the global economy. Students who grow up and are educated in a monocultural cocoon risk becoming social misfits, totally unprepared for the worlds of work or play in the 21st century. E. D. Hirsch Jr. (1987) got it wrong—students require not just cultural literacy, but intercultural literacy (Cummins & Sayers, 1995). Multinational corporations are increasingly looking for college graduates with bilingual and trilingual skills who can function effectively in a highly competitive multicultural and multilingual global economy. In short, bilingual and multilingual individuals are likely to be more attractive to employers involved in international trade as well as those faced with providing service to a linguistically diverse clientele in societal institutions (hospitals, seniors' homes, airports, airlines, schools, etc.).

It doesn't take a rocket scientist to see that nurturing the linguistic and cultural resources of the nation is simply good common sense in light of the cultural realities of the 21st century. Even minimal investment in enriched education bilingual programs for both majority and minority students and a focus on infusing multicultural awareness across the curriculum can contribute significantly both to the nation's economic competitiveness and to its ability to collaborate internationally in resolving global problems. Australian historian and

TIME magazine's Art critic, Robert Hughes, expressed it well in his best selling book *Culture of Complaint*:

> To learn other languages, to deal with other customs and creeds from direct experience of them and with a degree of humility: these are self-evidently good, as cultural provincialism is not…In Australia, no Utopia but a less truculent immigrant society than this one, intelligent multiculturalism works to everyone's social advantage, and the conservative crisis-talk about creating a "cultural tower of Babel" and so forth is seen as obsolete alarmism of a fairly low order…In the world that is coming, if you can't navigate difference, you've had it. (1993, pp. 88–100)

Economic/Scientific Realities. As discussed above, national economies are increasingly implicated in the global economy. A product may be conceived in one country, designed in another, manufactured in yet another, and then marketed and sold throughout the world. The capacity to communicate across cultural and linguistic boundaries is crucial to business success in this environment, as is access to and ability to manipulate information. Thus, the competitiveness of a business or a country in the global marketplace depends on its human resources: the knowledge, learning, information and intelligence possessed by its people; what Secretary of Labor in the initial Clinton administration, Robert Reich (1991), called *symbolic analysis skills*. These include abstract higher-order thinking, critical inquiry, and collaboration—defined as the capacity to engage in active communication and dialogue to get a variety of perspectives and to create consensus when necessary.

Even for relatively deskilled jobs in the fast-growing service sector, where high levels of literacy are not required for adequate job performance, employers have raised educational standards for applicants. This trend appears to be related to the perception that the "trainability" of workers is essential for businesses to adapt in a flexible manner to a rapidly changing economic environment.

In short, many workers today employ literacy skills in the workplace that are far beyond what their parents needed. In a context where information is doubling every two years or so, employers are looking for workers who know how to get access to current information, who can think critically about what information is relevant and what is not, and who know how to collaborate creatively in problem-solving activities across cultural, linguistic, and racial boundaries. What few workplaces need are workers whose heads are full of inert and soon-to-be-obsolete information.

Two implications for education are clear. First, passive internalization of inert content, which, as noted earlier, research suggests is still a common mode of learning in many North American classrooms (*e.g.,* Goodlad, 1984; Ramírez, 1992), and is being reinforced by knee-jerk accountability and state-mandated standardized tests (McNeil, 1999), does not promote the kind of active intelligence that the changing economy increasingly requires in the workforce. To address the economic needs of the societies that fund them, schools must promote students' capacities for collaborative critical inquiry.

Second, the failure of schools to educate all students carries enormous economic (and social) costs. If students do not graduate from school with the symbolic analysis skills to contribute productively to the economy, then they are likely to be excluded from the economy. Individuals who are excluded from the economy don't just fade away and disappear. They frequently end up on welfare or in jail. There is a huge correlation between dropping out of school and ending up in prison—more than 80 percent of prisoners in U.S. prisons are high school dropouts, each costing taxpayers a minimum of $20,000 a year to contain, much more than it would have cost to educate them (Hodgkinson, 1991). The U.S. incarcerates its population at a rate far higher than any other industrialized country (*e.g.,* ten times that of the Netherlands and six times that of Australia) and this pattern has escalated dramatically in recent years at enormous cost to taxpayers. Natriello *et al.* (1990) in their aptly titled book *Schooling Disadvantaged Children: Racing Against Catastrophe* estimated conservatively that the cost to the nation of the dropout problem is approximately $50 billion in foregone lifetime earnings alone: "Also associated with this cost are forgone government tax revenues, greater welfare expenditure, poorer physical and mental health of our nation's citizens, and greater costs of crime..." (p. 43). As one example of the returns on educational investment, it has been estimated that every dollar spent on Head Start programs will save $7 in reduced need for special education, welfare, incarceration and so on (Schweinhart *et al.*, 1986).

In short, compared to the alternatives, education is one of society's most cost-effective investments. To push low-income culturally diverse students out of school at current levels in urban centers across the nation is financially absurd (not to mention socially unjust in the extreme). Thus, to address the economic realities of the 21st century, schools must look rationally at which programs for culturally diverse students are most likely to succeed in developing high levels of literacy. To exclude from consideration genuine bilingual and multicultural programs, whose success has been demonstrated repeatedly, purely on the ideological grounds that they are "unAmerican" is irrational and simply panders to the neurotic paranoia of the patriotically-correct (to borrow Robert Hughes' phrase).

Existential Realities. By "existential realities," I am referring to the increasing sense of fragility that characterizes our relationship to both our physical and social environment. For example, a perusal of virtually any newspaper anywhere in the world will quickly show the extent of environmental deterioration and the enormity of the global ecological problems that our generation has created for our children's generation to resolve. Similarly, the "new world order" of peaceful coexistence that seemed at hand with the end of the Cold War has been overtaken by eruptions of brutal conflicts around the world. Violence in our schools and streets signal the enormous pressures just beneath the surface of our social fabric. Increased incarceration responds to symptoms rather than to underlying causes and consequently has done little to curb crime. In fact, it has probably contributed to crime since it drains dollars from schools and other social programs.

Despite these changed existential realities, many schools appear dedicated to insulating students from awareness of social issues rather than communicating a sense of urgency in regard to understanding and acting on them. In most schools across the continent, the curriculum has been sanitized such that students rarely have the opportunity to discuss critically, write about, or act upon issues that directly affect the society they will form. Issues such as racism, environmental pollution, genetic engineering, and the causes of poverty are regarded as too sensitive for fragile and impressionable young minds. Still less do students have the opportunity to cooperate with others from different cultural and/or linguistic groups in exploring resolutions to these issues.

A major reason why schools try to maintain a facade of innocence in relation to social and environmental issues is that such issues invariably implicate power relations in the domestic and international arenas. Promoting a critical awareness of how power is wielded at home and abroad is not a task that society expects educators to undertake. In fact, renewed demands for a core curriculum and for imposition of "cultural literacy" can be interpreted as a way of controlling the information that students can access so as to minimize the possibility of deviant thoughts. As Donaldo Macedo (1993, 1994) argues, in the shadows of the list of facts that every American should know is the list of facts that every American must be *discouraged* from knowing. Prominent among these is the history of imperialism and colonialism of Western powers from 1492 to the present (see, for example, *Rethinking Schools*, 1991), the history of slavery as told by those who experienced its full brutality, and myriad other historical realities that are uncomfortable to address, as documented, for example, in Howard Zinn's (1995) *A People's History of the United States*. Virtually every country presents a selective and sanitized version of its history to its young people.

In short, this analysis suggests that issues related to the organization of society, specifically the division of resources and power, be taken off the taboo list of what is appropriate to explore in school. Students whose communities have been marginalized will increasingly perceive the omission of these fundamental issues as dishonest and hypocritical, and this will reinforce their resistance to achievement under the current rules of the game. By contrast, a focus on critical inquiry, in a collaborative and supportive context, will encourage students to engage in learning in ways that will promote future productive engagement in their societies. The research, critical thinking, and creative problem-solving skills that this form of education entails will position students well for full participation in the economic and social realities of their global community. By contrast, excluding students from the learning process at school is pushing us toward a society where everyone loses because every dropout carries an expensive price tag for the entire society.

This analysis of the cultural, economic/scientific, and existential realities that students will graduate into in the 21st century suggests that priorities for our schools should be:

• Promoting bilingual or multilingual skills and intercultural sensitivity among all students;

• Promoting not just basic functional literacy but critical literacy that would include capacities for abstract higher-order thinking and collaborative problem-solving; in other words, collaborative critical inquiry should be the predominant learning focus in our schools;

• Creatively exploring ways to help all students graduate with high academic achievement; since subordinated group students are massively over-represented among dropouts and low-achievers, this essentially means restructuring schools to challenge and reverse the causes of subordinated group under-achievement;

- Promoting an awareness of, and concern for, the common good in our societies; this will entail collaborative critical inquiry into domestic and international social justice issues related to the distribution of resources, status and power in our societies.

These educational directions represent direct inferences from an analysis of clearly observable social trends. Why is it that so few schools across the North American continent are actively pursuing these directions? Why is it that even suggesting directions such as these is likely to be castigated as "radical?" Why do so many working- and middle-class Americans feel such frustration and anger about issues such as immigration and diversity (as illustrated in the overwhelming support for Propositions 187 and 227 in California, and Proposition 203 in Arizona)?

To answer these questions we need to examine some data about how the power structure operates to deflect challenges and minimize dissent.

Coercive Relations of Power in Action

The Polarization of Income. Consider some of the data outlined in *Philadelphia Inquirer* reporters Donald Barlett and James Steele's (1992) book *America: What Went Wrong?* Chapter 1 of their book is entitled "Dismantling the Middle Class" and the statistics show clearly how this has been achieved. These trends of increasing disparities between rich and poor have escalated rather than diminished during the 1990s:

- In 1989, the top 4% in income earned as much as the bottom 51%. Thirty years earlier, in 1959, the top 4% earned as much as the bottom 35%—a 16 point difference. According to Barlett and Steele "The wage and salary structure of American business, encouraged by federal tax policies, is pushing the nation toward a two-class society" (p. ix).

- During the 1980s, salaries of people earning $20,000 to $50,000 increased by 44% while salaries for those earning $200,000 to $1 million increased by 697%; if you were fortunate enough to earn more than $1 million, the icing on the cake was that you received a whopping salary increase of 2,184%! In Barlett and Steele's terms: "Viewed more broadly, the total wages of all people who earned less than $50,000 a year—85 percent of all Americans—increased an average of just 2 percent a year over those ten years. At the same time, the total wages of all millionaires shot up 243 percent a year" (p. 4).

- As a result of the Tax Reform Act of 1986 those earning up to $50,000 saw tax cuts of between 6% and 16% while those earning more than $500,000 saw tax cuts of between 31% and 34%. This represented an average 1989 tax savings per return of $300 for those earning $20,000 to $30,000 compared to an average savings of $281,033 for those earning $1 million or more.

- During the 1950s the corporate share of U.S. income tax collected was 39% compared to 61% for individuals; in the 1980s the corporate share had dropped to 17% while individuals' share rose to 83%.

- The percentage of workers receiving fully paid health insurance fell from 75 percent to 48 percent between 1982 and 1989.

Barlett and Steele argue that as a result of the way the rules of the game have been rigged "the already rich are richer than ever; there has been an explosion in overnight new rich; life for the working class is deteriorating, and those at the bottom are trapped" (p. 2). They summarize the data as follows:

Indeed the growth of the middle class—one of the underpinnings of democracy in this country—has been reversed. By government action. Taken as a whole, these are the results of the rules that govern the game:

- They have created a tax system that is firmly weighted against the middle class.

- They have enabled companies to trim or cancel health-care and pension benefits for employees.

- They have granted subsidies to businesses that create low-wage jobs that are eroding living standards.

- They have undermined longtime stable businesses and communities.

- They have rewarded companies that transfer jobs abroad and eliminate jobs in this country.

- They have placed home ownership out of reach of a growing number of Americans and made the financing of a college education impossible without incurring a hefty debt.

Look upon it as the dismantling of the middle class. And understand that, barring some unexpected intervention by the federal government, the worst is yet to come. For we are in the midst of the largest transfer of wealth in the nation's history. (pp. 2-3)

Noam Chomsky (1995) is even more blunt in his assessment of the causes of crime and violence in American society. He points to the fact that "we're the only industrial nation that doesn't have some sort of guaranteed health insurance. ...Despite being the richest society we have twice the poverty rate of any other industrialized nation, and much higher rates of incarceration" (pp. 128-129). In pointing to the powerful state protection for the rich (illustrated in Barlett and Steele's data), he suggests that:

The United States has, from its origins, been a highly protectionist society with very high tariffs and massive subsidies for the rich. It's a huge welfare state for the rich, and society ends up being very polarized. Despite the New Deal, and the Great Society measures in the 1960s, which attempted to move the United States toward the social contracts of the other industrialized nations, we still have the highest social and economic inequality, and such polarization is increasing very sharply. These factors—high polarization, a welfare state for the rich, and marginalization of parts of the population—have their effects. One effect is a lot of crime. (p. 129)

One of the major sources of subsidies for the rich is the Pentagon, which is why, according to Chomsky, it hasn't declined substantially with the end of the Cold War. In fact the U.S. is still spending almost as much on the military as the rest of the world combined. [3] In addition to the Pentagon, Chomsky highlights straight welfare payments to the rich in the form of home mortgage tax rebates, about 80% of which go to people with incomes over $50,000 (who represent just 15% of the population, according to Barlett and Steele). He justifies labeling these welfare payments on the grounds that "it's exactly the same if I don't give the government $100 or if the government does give me $100" (p. 131). Another example of social welfare for the rich is business expenses as tax write-offs which far outweigh welfare payments to the poor.

In summary, the economic pressures that many middle-class people are feeling (despite the 1990s boom economy) has come from the transfer of resources from middle-class and poor families to the wealthy. This combined with the Savings and Loan bailout of hundreds of billions of dollars and the obscene level of military expenditures during the 1980s and 1990s has resulted in hard times for ordinary people. They feel angry about it and want to blame someone.

Finding Scapegoats. The escalation of rhetoric against immigration, bilingual education, and cultural diversity in general is a convenient way of accomplishing two goals: First, it directs people's anger against a potential threat to the established power structure. The projected rapid growth of minority populations, particularly Spanish-speakers, is a source of concern; if these groups retain some cultural and linguistic distinctiveness, it is feared that they may be less subject to persuasion (control) than other Americans. If they were ever to exercise their right to vote in substantial numbers then, in columnist James Reston's view, they might "not only influence but hold the decisive margin in state and local elections" (The Journal, Milwaukee, WI, February 5, 1981). In order to prevent this catastrophic scenario, it is imperative to reverse the infiltration of alien languages and cultures into American institutions as rapidly as possible. [4]

Second, directing people's anger against immigrants, bilingual educators, welfare mothers, single parent families, and the like, serves to divert attention from the massive transfer of wealth from middle-class and poor to the rich. It very effectively obscures the real causes of school failure among marginalized groups and how the power structure operates to reproduce educational disparities. Once again, Chomsky lucidly identifies how this scapegoating process works:

> The building up of scapegoats and fear is standard. If you're stomping on people's faces, you don't want them to notice that; you want them to be afraid of somebody else—Jews, homosexuals, welfare queens, immigrants, whoever it is. That's how Hitler got to power, and in fact he became the most popular leader in German history. People are scared, they're upset, the world isn't working, and they don't like the way things are. You don't want people to look at the actual source of power, that's much too dangerous, so therefore, you need to have them blame or be frightened of someone else. (1995, p. 134)

The same process of finding scapegoats is evident in the debate on reading that was considered in Chapter 4. The "consensus" view put forward by many academics (*e.g.,* Mathes & Torgeson, 2000; Snow, Burns & Griffin, 1998; Stanovich & Stanovich, 1998) is that "whole-language" instruction is responsible for the failure of many students to acquire adequate reading skills as a result of the fact that whole-language does not sufficiently emphasize the explicit systematic teaching of phonemic awareness and phonological processing skills. The remedy is direct systematic explicit instruction in phonemic awareness and phonics. Apart from issues of research interpretation considered in Chapter 4, a major problem here is the fact that this approach limits the framework of discourse to a specific and isolated instructional intervention and largely ignores the role of broader social and cultural factors in determining reading success and failure.

This point is clearly expressed by James Paul Gee (1999) in a response to the National Academy of Sciences report *Preventing Reading Difficulties in Young Children* (Snow, Burns & Griffin, 1998). Gee points out that the report focuses primarily on decoding (what it calls "real reading") rather than on the broader issues of language, literacy, and learning as they are situated in and influenced by sociocultural practices both in and out of schools. He notes that "the report admits (though draws no interesting inferences from this fact) that high levels of poverty in a school are a better predictor of children who will have reading problems than is a lack of early phonemic awareness, an issue to which the report devotes a great deal of space" (1999, pp. 360–361).

Gee highlights the fact that in the United States, as acknowledged by the National Academy report, poor readers "are concentrated in certain ethnic groups and in poor, urban neighborhoods and rural towns" (Snow, Burns & Griffin, 1998, p. 98). He points out that:

> For some time, from the late 1960s to the early 1980s, the Black-White gap (and that between several other minority groups and Whites), in both IQ test scores and other sorts of test scores, was fast closing. …Some of this heartening progress, especially in regard to achievement tests, ceased in the 1980s. A report that was genuinely interested in increasing the reading scores of at-risk children would ask what factors had been closing the Black-White gap, and why they ceased to operate. (1999, p. 359)

Gee points out that the factors that were closing the Black-White gap were powerful "reading interventions," because they significantly increased the reading scores of marginalized low-income groups. He suggests that the factors responsible were, in all likelihood, closely connected to the sorts of social programs (stemming originally from [President] Johnson's War on Poverty) that were dismantled in the 1980s and 1990s. The problem with the approach adopted by the National Academy that focused on "real reading" (decoding) is that it eliminates from the framework of discourse the influence on reading achievement of social programs designed to combat poverty and educational discrimination of various sorts (*e.g.,* the huge disparities in per-pupil spending between affluent school districts and those in inner cities or poor rural areas).

Gee concludes that if one is genuinely interested in improving reading, it is imperative to acknowledge that social, cultural, institutional, and political issues and interventions are intimately related to literacy development and not mere "background noise." In terms of the present framework, the broader context of widespread and persistent coercive relations of power in the wider society is directly related to educational outcomes in reading, math, and other curricular areas. To exclude these issues from consideration results in research interpretations that are distorted and potentially damaging to children:

> There is also the issue of power and racism, a matter not touched at all in the report. Some people believe that bringing up such issues is merely "political" or, at the very least, not directly relevant to reading. But this is simply not true. The fact that children will not identify with, or even will disidentify with, teachers and schools that they perceive as hostile, alien, or oppressive to their home-based identities and cultures is as much a cognitive as a political point. …To ignore these wider issues, while stressing such things as phonemic awareness built on controlled texts, is to ignore, not merely what we know about politics, but also what we know about learning and literacy as well. (Gee, 1999, p. 360)

In other words, the negotiation of identity in schools is much more fundamental in promoting academic achievement among low-achieving communities than any particular instructional strategy for teaching phonemic awareness or any other aspect of reading. Reading achievement is totally embedded in patterns of societal power relations. To focus only on one isolated instructional element (however significant it might be) is to limit the framework of discourse so that social interventions that benefit low-income children, families and communities do not even enter into consideration as relevant to the improvement of overall reading achievement.

Resolving Contradictions. The roots of the contradictions identified earlier become more intelligible in light of this analysis of coercive relations of power. To reiterate the contradictions:

• Our societies urgently need more people with fluent bilingual skills, yet we demonize bilingual education, the only program capable of delivering bilingualism and biliteracy.

- Our economy increasingly requires people with symbolic analysis skills who are capable of collaborative critical inquiry, but we still insist that schools "get back to basics" (as though they ever left) and police this process with standardized tests.

- In order to increase economic performance and decrease the escalating costs of incarceration, we need to enable more low-income young people to graduate from high school with the possibility of more than a below-the-poverty-line job; only in this way will they have a stake in contributing to our society; yet we resist the kind of educational reforms that would promote contexts of empowerment for low-income students, preferring instead to warehouse them indefinitely in prisons built at enormous cost to the taxpayer.

- Finally, our society desperately needs to restore some sense of coherence and community to its people, founded on notions such as social justice and the common good; yet, any attempt to desanitize the curriculum and look at historical and current issues of social justice from multiple perspectives is still vehemently resisted.

The reason our school systems are discouraged or prevented from pursuing these directions that respond rationally to the changing social realities of the 21st century is that, in one way or another, these directions potentially threaten the coercive power structure that manufactures consent for grossly inequitable resource distribution in our societies. If bilingualism or intercultural literacy were encouraged, it would legitimate the presence of the Other within societal institutions; if critical literacy were encouraged, it might undermine the process of manufacturing consent through indoctrination and disinformation; if we seriously contemplated reversing underachievement among low-income inner city youth, it would require "an investment in education comparable to what has been spent on building a high-tech military machine" (Wirth, 1993, p. 365)—in other words, a significant transfer of wealth from the rich to the poor. Finally, it is virtually unthinkable in most societies around the world to invite educators to desanitize the curriculum and examine the ways in which power has been, and is, wielded for coercive ends. [5]

To what extent can educators, operating within these constraints, realistically create contexts of empowerment that would challenge the impact of coercive relations of power on themselves and their students? Chomsky is pessimistic:

It's just not going to be allowed, because it's too subversive. You can teach students to think for themselves in the sciences because you want people to be independent and creative, otherwise you don't have science. But science and engineering students are not encouraged to be critical in terms of the political and social implications of their work. In most other fields you want students to be obedient and submissive, and that starts from childhood. Now teachers can try, and do break out of that, but, they will surely find if they go too far, that as soon as it gets noticed there'll be pressures to stop them. (1995, p. 141)

I am somewhat more optimistic than Chomsky about what educators, individually and collectively, can achieve. This is elaborated in the final section.

Towards Collaborative Relations of Power in the Classroom

In the dismal scenario sketched above, there are two beacons of hope. One is the fact that power structures are not monolithic. There are many individuals and institutions within North American societies that are committed to challenging inequality and exploitation. In fact, at one level, the United States has committed itself to educational equity more vigorously than most other Western nations. Since the mid-1960s considerable resources have been expended on research to try to understand the causes of school failure and on intervention aimed at reversing a legacy of educational exclusion. This public commitment has been matched by the enormous dedication of many educators who go far beyond their job descriptions to promote contexts of empowerment in their classrooms. However, as documented above, at another level, a very different process is operating that attempts to neutralize potential challenges to the coercive power structure.

A reason for some optimism at this point is that the operation of coercive relations of power has reached a point of diminishing returns. The contradictions are becoming more obvious. Fiscal deficits are unlikely to be reduced when more police are required to combat crime and more prisons are being built to contain undereducated young people; business is unlikely to thrive when fewer people have the disposable income to buy its products; and so on. I am optimistic enough to believe that, in the coming years, coercive power structures will become visible to a greater number of people, thereby providing more scope for educational and other institutions to pursue an agenda of social justice and collaborative empowerment.

A second source of optimism lies in the power that schools, communities, and individual educators have to create contexts of empowerment even under unfavorable conditions. [6] Scattered throughout this volume are examples of this process. School systems are increasingly showing an interest in two-way bilingual immersion programs that explicitly, and very successfully, challenge the *Us versus Them* ideology promoted by groups such as U.S. English. Periodicals such as *Rethinking Schools* create a community of inquiry among educators that counteracts processes of indoctrination and disinformation. In many cases, culturally diverse communities themselves are mobilizing to demand respectful and high quality education for their children.

As emphasized throughout this volume, individual educators are never powerless, although they frequently work in conditions that are oppressive both for them and their students (see, for example, Kozol, 1991). While they rarely have complete freedom, educators do have choices in the way they structure the micro-interactions in the classroom. They do determine for themselves the social and educational goals they want to achieve with their students. They are responsible for the role definitions they adopt in relation to culturally diverse students and communities. Even in the context of English-only instruction, educators have options in their orientation to students' language and culture, in the forms of parent and community participation they encourage, and in the way they implement pedagogy and assessment (see for example the International High School at LaGuardia Community College in New York City discussed in Chapter 8).

In short, through their practice and their interactions with students, educators define their own identities. Students, likewise, go through a process of defining their identities in interaction with their teachers, peers, and parents. This process of negotiating identities can never be fully controlled from the outside, although it will certainly be influenced by many forces. Thus, educators individually and collectively, have the potential to work towards the creation of contexts of empowerment. Within these interactional spaces where identities are negotiated, students and educators together can generate power that challenges structures of injustice in small but significant ways. Each student who graduates into the 21st century with well-developed critical literacy skills, intercultural sensitivity, and an informed commitment to the ideals of "liberty and justice for all," enshrined in the American constitution, represents a challenge to coercive relations of power.

When classroom interactions are fueled by collaborative relations of power, students gain access to ways of navigating difference that our domestic and international communities are sadly lacking at the present time. Bilingual students who feel a sense of belonging in their classroom learning community are more likely to feel "at home" in their society upon graduation and to contribute actively to building that society. Schools that have brought issues related to cultural and linguistic diversity from the periphery to the center of their mission are more likely to prepare students to thrive in the interdependent global society in which they will live. The goal for all of us as educators is to strive to make our classrooms and schools microcosms of the kind of caring society that we would like our own children and grandchildren to inherit. I strongly believe that this is an attainable goal.

Endnotes to Chapter 10

1. The analysis presented here is elaborated in more detail in Cummins and Sayers (1995). The analysis in the chapter as a whole elaborates on a keynote presentation I gave at the 1995 California Association for Bilingual Education conference in Anaheim entitled *Resisting Xenophobia: Proposition 187 and its Aftermath.*

2. Increased linguistic and cultural diversity is a phenomenon affecting many countries in addition to the United States. In Canada, for example, more than 50 percent of the student population in Toronto and Vancouver have a first language other than English. In the Netherlands, 40 percent of students in Amsterdam schools are of non-Dutch origin and in the country as a whole close to 20 percent of the population is of non-Dutch origin.

    In the United States, immigrants' share of total population growth has increased significantly from 11 percent between 1960 and 1970 to 39 percent between 1980 and 1990. Latinos/Latinas will account for more than 40 percent of population growth over the next 60 years and become the nation's largest minority in the year 2013. The Asian American population is expected to increase from 8 million in 1992 to 16 million by 2009, 24 million by 2024, and 32 million by 2038. African Americans are expected to double in number by the year 2050. At current growth rates, the U.S. foreign-born population will probably exceed ten percent by the year 2000 (Hispanic Link Weekly Report, 1995, Vol. 13, No. 31). Waggoner (1999) summarized the demographic realities as follows:

    > The United States became much more culturally and linguistically diverse in the 1980s than in previous decades. The foreign-born population grew from 14.1 million in 1980 to 19.8 million, and the population of people who speak languages other than English at home grew from 23.1 million to 31.8 million. While the total population increased by 10% between 1980 and 1990, the foreign-born population increased by 40% and the population speaking languages other than English at home by 38%. (1999, p. 14)

    Consistent with these projected growth trends, the proportion of culturally diverse students is rapidly increasing in U.S. urban centers. To illustrate, the National Coalition of Advocates for Students (1988) estimated that by the year 2001, minority enrollment levels will range from 70 to 96 percent in the nation's 15 largest school systems. In California, so-called minority groups (*e.g.,* Latinos/Latinas, African Americans, Asian Americans) already represent a greater proportion of the school population than students from the so-called majority group. By the year 2030, half of all the children in the state are projected to be of Latino/Latina background while Euro-Americans will compose 60 percent of the elderly population, a reality that historian Paul Kennedy (1993) terms "a troublesome mismatch" that raises the prospect of "a massive contest over welfare and entitlement priorities between predominantly Caucasian retirees and predominantly nonwhite children, mothers, and unemployed, each with its vocal advocacy organizations" (p. 313).

3. Macedo (1994) reminds readers of the fraud rampant in the military-industrial complex during the 1980s as illustrated in the Pentagon paying $700 for a toilet seat and $350 for a screwdriver. He also illustrates the process of social welfare for the rich with current examples such as a $220 million subsidy paid to bail out McDonnell Douglas in 1990 and military action abroad to protect the interests of U.S. corporations. Among the examples he cites are the following:

   • In 1954 the CIA spent millions of dollars to organize the overthrow of the elected president of Guatemala in order to protect the interests of the United Fruit Company.

   • In 1973 the U.S. government spent millions of dollars in concert with IT&T Corporation to overthrow the democratically-elected socialist leader of Chile, Salvador Allende.

   • The average tax rate for the top twelve American military contractors, who made $19 billion in profits in 1981, 1982, and 1983, was 1.5 percent. Middle-class Americans paid 15 percent. (p. 93)

   Along the same lines, Chomsky (1995) points out that Newt Gingrich's congressional district, a very wealthy suburb of Atlanta,

   gets more federal subsidies—taxpayers' money—than any suburban county in the country, outside the federal system itself. ...The biggest employer in his district happens to be Lockheed. Well, what's Lockheed? That's a publicly subsidized corporation. Lockheed wouldn't exist for five minutes if it wasn't for the public subsidy under the pretext of defense, but that's just a joke. The United States hasn't faced a threat probably since the War of 1812. Certainly, there's no threat now. (p. 129–130).

4. Although it has since been overshadowed by Proposition 227, the debate on Proposition 187, intended to eliminate all services to undocumented immigrants, unleashed a lot of pent-up anti-immigrant emotion in California during 1994. In a presentation to the California Association for Bilingual Education conference in February 1995, I tried to draw out some of the lessons of this debate as follows:

   "Proposition 187 represents a turning point in the social history of California and probably in the social history of all of North America. Obviously those who support it intend for it to be a turning point—a first step in reclaiming the nation, reversing direction after 30 years of increasing multicultural fragmentation, increasing crime, increasing economic difficulty. All the social ills of the nation are symbolized within this Proposition and the culprit for these social ills has been identified. The cause of the fear and the loathing embodied in this Proposition is all around us in everything that we as bilingual educators collectively represent. Proposition 187 expresses the fear of diversity, the fear of difference, the fear of the Other, the fear of strangers—xenophobia.

It is also intended as a statement of identity—a statement of national unity, a statement of who the landlords of this country are and who are the tenants; a warning to the tenants that their lease is close to expiring and if they don't lower their voices, withdraw their demands, become silent and invisible, they will be evicted without ceremony.

Proposition 187 is about power, who has it and who intends to keep it. It is about intimidation and it is about racism and we must recognize these realities if we are to fight against it.

However, if we are to fight it effectively we must understand it better than I think we do. It is not enough to dismiss it as racist because certainly a large proportion of those who supported it do not see themselves as racist and are not racist in the usual sense of the term. If we are to reverse this process and work towards a saner more tolerant society, we must communicate and dialogue with many of those who currently see diversity as a threat. In fact, we must join forces with them to articulate a vision of our society where there is cooperation rather than competition across cultural boundaries, where cultural difference enriches the whole rather than scatters the parts. We have to find those areas where different cultural groups have common vested interests and join forces to achieve these common goals.

The general public, largely white- and blue-collar working people have bought into the message that diversity threatens their way of life. They believe the disinformation that has been transmitted about the costs of immigration, about immigrants taking jobs from residents, about students not learning any English in schools because of bilingual education, about multicultural advocates dismantling the history of this country. These people are afraid not only because of the increase in diversity but also because the media have skillfully associated diversity with increases in crime and economic hardship. Willie Horton may have stopped revolving in the prison door, but George Bush's message lives on: the Other is out there and he's waiting to get you.

Let's look at the realities:

Immigration. *Business Week* (July 13, 1992) reports that at least 11 million immigrants are working and from their earnings of $240 billion are paying more than $90 billion annually in taxes, a great deal more than the $5 billion they are estimated to receive in public assistance. In fact, despite their difficult economic situation as new arrivals, only 8.8% of immigrants receive public assistance, compared with 7.9% of the general population. Furthermore, the average immigrant family pays $2,500 more in tax dollars annually than they receive in public services (New York Times, June 27, 1993, p. A1). The American Council on Civil Liberties (ACLU) has also summarized data regarding the economic impact of immigration; among the information it compiled is the following:

- In a 1990 American Immigration Institute Survey of prominent economists, four out of five said that immigrants had a favorable impact on economic growth. None said that immigrants had an adverse impact on economic growth.

- According to a Los Angeles Times analysis summarizing the best available research, "Immigrants contribute mightily to the economy, by paying billions in annual taxes, by filling low-wage jobs that keep domestic industry competitive, and by spurring investment and job-creation, revitalizing once-decaying communities. Many social scientists conclude that the newcomers, rather than drain government treasuries, contribute overall far more than they utilize in services." (January 6, 1992).

- Studies by the Rand Corporation, the University of Maryland, the Council of Economic Advisors, the National Research Council and the Urban Institute all show that immigrants do not have a negative effect on the earnings and employment opportunities of native-born Americans. A 1989 Department of Labor study found that neither U.S. workers in complementary jobs, nor most minority workers, appear to be adversely affected by immigration (ACLU, Department of Public Education, June 10, 1994).

5. In response to a question about how greed and the pursuit of profit are infused in the histories of the U.S. and other countries, Chomsky discussed how the educational system works to make certain thoughts "unthinkable:"

Well, [the teaching of history is] a little better than it used to be, but not much. Much of history is just wiped out. We just went through a war in Central America in which hundreds of thousands of people were slaughtered, and countries destroyed—huge terror. U.S. operations were condemned by the World Court as international terrorism. It's nevertheless described in this country as an effort to bring democracy to Central America. How do they get away with that? If you have a deeply indoctrinated educated sector, as we do, you're not going to get any dissent there, and among the general population who may not be so deeply indoctrinated, they're marginal. They're supposed to be afraid of welfare mothers and people coming to attack us, and they're busy watching football games and so on, so it doesn't matter what they think. And that's pretty much the way the educational system and the media work. (1995, p. 139)

6. A more elaborated account of the collaborative creation of power (empowerment), and its opposite, can be found in Norwegian peace researcher Johan Galtung's (1980) description of what he calls *autonomy*:

Autonomy is here seen as power-over-oneself so as to be able to withstand what others might have of power-over-others. I use the distinction between ideological, remunerative and punitive power, depending on whether the influence is based on internal, positive external, or negative external sanctions. Autonomy then is the degree of 'inoculation' against these forms of power. These forms of power, exerted by means of ideas, carrots and sticks, can work only if the power receiver really receives the pressure, which presupposes a certain degree of submissiveness, dependency and fear, respectively. Their antidotes are self-respect, self-sufficiency, and fearlessness. …'self-respect' can be defined as 'confidence in one's own ideas and ability to set one's own goals,' 'self-sufficiency' as the 'possibility of pursuing them with one's own means,' and 'fearlessness,' as 'the possibility of persisting despite threats of destruction.' …

The opposite [of autonomy] is penetration, meaning that the outside has penetrated into one's self to the extent of creating submissiveness to ideas, dependency on 'goods' from the outside, and fear of the outside in terms of 'bads.' (1980, p. 58–59)

Appendix A

Language Policy Considerations for Bilingual Students Proposed by the Scottish Consultative Council on the Curriculum (adapted from Landon *et al.*, 1994)

The document *Languages for Life* published by the Scottish Consultative Council on the Curriculum illustrates the kind of enlightened consideration of students' bilingualism that is sorely lacking in many North American school systems at the present time. Below, I have paraphrased some of the suggestions which the Consultative Council groups under the headings *Realizing a Child's Language Assets* and a *Checklist for Action*. My intent is to provide a sense of the kinds of suggestions they make rather than a complete summary. In some cases, I have interpreted and/or elaborated on the suggestions made by the Consultative Council. The Council's suggestions are intended for children from 5-14 years of age and obviously some will more appropriate for children at younger rather than older ages within this range, and vice-versa.. However, many of the suggestions are appropriate across the entire grade spectrum, including high school.

Realizing a Child's Language Assets

School Environment and Ethos

- Provide signs and posters in the various languages of the community at the school entrance and other prominent places in order to welcome members of the community and showcase the school's commitment to bilingualism. Parents and other community members can be involved in producing these bilingual notices, labels, and signs.

- Parents from various language backgrounds can be invited to help in the classroom, library, and playground, and encouraged to use their home language whenever possible.

- Greetings and information in various home languages can be incorporated in newsletters and other forms of communication with parents and the community.

Support for Learning

- In pair or group work on at least some occasions, provide opportunities for children from the same language background to use their L1 in carrying out assignments or projects.

- Ensure that the school and classroom libraries include books written in different languages, including dual language books.

- Acknowledge children's L1 achievements whenever possible (*e.g.* school displays, newsletters, report card). This may involve liaison with community-based language classes. In addition, encourage children to study their home language, *or the home language of their peers*, in extracurricular clubs or during free-choice periods.

- Demonstrate a positive approach to children spending time visiting their countries of origin. Encourage parents to let the school know of such visits in good time so that teachers can set tasks or projects for children to complete (using their L1). For example, children can gather material for display and sharing with their teachers and peers when they return to school.

Opportunities for Home Language Development Within the Curriculum Language

- Invite parents to tell stories to the class in languages other then English. Children who are not from that home language background can speculate on the meaning of the story from gestures, expressions, pictures etc. used by the story-teller.

- Children who are proficient in their home language can be encouraged to write stories or poems in that language. These stories and poems can be translated either by the child herself/himself or with help from peers, school staff, parents, or community members, for sharing with those from other home language backgrounds. They can also be published within the classroom for the classroom library or for the school newsletter, magazine, or web site.

- Children can be offered the opportunity to use the home language during assemblies or class presentations. In a school climate of celebrating children's linguistic accomplishments, children are likely to be less reluctant to display their bilingual/multilingual proficiency; however, children should not be put on the spot or pressured to do this.

- All children should be given the opportunity to learn and try out common expressions in the languages present in the community or classroom.

Mathematics
- Explore number systems in different languages (*e.g.* Chinese) and encourage children to carry out computations using their home language numbers (parents can be a useful resource for this activity).

- Learn number rhymes in different home languages.

Expressive Arts
- Listen to and perform songs or games (*e.g.* Simon Says..) in different home languages.

- Children can produce dramatic scripts, and perform drama, in which different home languages are used. English can also be integrated in these dramas/role plays, possibly depicting cross-cultural communication situations that they or their families have experienced in migrating into a new culture and community. This can be linked with observing people using different languages on film or video and discussing cultural traits (*e.g.* gestures) and dramatic techniques and conventions.

- Use different writing systems as a basis for calligraphy or creative design.

- Have children compare how the media report world events in different languages. Parents once again can be an important resource in providing access to, or information from, newspapers, television programs, etc. in their home languages. Web sites from news media in different languages can also be explored by children and parents.

Environmental and Global Studies

- Provide children with the opportunity to carry out projects in the local community where they will use their home languages (*e.g.* interviewing local residents, collecting life stories or the history of the local community, etc.).

- Cultural and environmental exploration in the local community can be enhanced if the school or class collaborates with a sister class in a different community (either within the country or internationally). Strategies for using the Internet and World Wide Web to carry out these exchanges and collaborative projects have been discussed in Cummins and Sayers (1995).

- Provide children with the opportunity to investigate the global distribution and history of major languages such as Chinese, Spanish, Arabic, Hindi etc. Children can also consider the history and distribution of their home languages and what makes these languages unique (*e.g.* literature, script, relationship with other languages, etc.).

A Checklist for Action on School Language Policy

School Ethos

- Is the ethos of the school communicated clearly enough for children to feel confident to identify with and use their home languages in class and other school contexts?

- Are children's diverse language accomplishments celebrated and acclaimed in different spheres of the school's life?

Staff Development

- Are *all* class teachers and support teachers/classroom assistants aware of the benefits of maintaining and developing children's home languages?

- Are *all* class teachers able to provide appropriate support to children developing as bilinguals at all stages of ESL development?

- Are *all* class teachers prepared to explore with support staff (*e.g.* ESL and bilingual teachers) the most effective ways of cooperating in order to make the curriculum accessible to bilingual students?

Partnerships with the Home and Community

- Are records kept of the home languages of children and made available to all school staff?

- Are trained interpreters used, and translations of home communications made, to facilitate communication with parents whose English is limited?

- Are parents encouraged to participate actively in school life and to contribute to class activities?

- Are references to the development of the child as a bilingual made in reports on the child?

- Are parents actively encouraged and supported in developing their children's home language outside the school? Are they made aware of how fragile, and subject to significant loss of fluency, the home language can be when it is not strongly supported in the home and community?

Classroom Practice—Home Language Development

- Do children use their home languages in the classroom and school to communicate freely with other children from that background? If they do not, do you know what might be inhibiting them and how their inhibitions might be reduced?

- Are instructional opportunities provided to explore language diversity across the curriculum and to affirm and support children's fascination with different languages as tools for expression of identity and action/influence on the world?

Classroom Practice—Second Language Development

- Are appropriate supports for second language development provided within the mainstream classroom as a matter of course? These supports should include:

    1. graphic organizers and other forms of visual scaffolding;

    2. opportunities for purposeful interaction in L1 or L2 between students as they pursue academic tasks;

    3. placement of the bilingual child as a working member of a supportive group within the class;

- Are opportunities provided for bilingual children to share their prior knowledge of curriculum-relevant content and their cultural/life experience if they wish to do so?

- Is the approach to English language errors sensitive and supportive, with the primary emphasis (particularly in the early stages of ESL development) on the quality of content rather than on the accuracy of expression?

- Are accurate and non-discriminatory records maintained of the child's overall learning development and his/her progress in acquiring conversational and academic English?

- Are children provided with appropriately-scaffolded and intellectually challenging instruction both in the early stages of acquiring social fluency in English and in the later stages of catching up academically in English?

School Policy

Does the school's language policy:

1. articulate the benefit to all of recognizing and exploring language diversity?

2. make a strong commitment to home language development?

3. make a strong commitment to providing second language support for students to access the mainstream curriculum within the mainstream classroom?

4. make clear the role and function of ESL and bilingual support teachers (where available)?

5. provide guidance and specific procedures as to how these aspects of the school's language policy can be achieved?

- Are all school staff (including assessment specialists and special education personnel) made aware of the school's language policy and invited to discuss its provisions and make contributions to its improvement?

- Is the language policy made available to parents in a form and in a language that they can understand?

- Does the school regularly monitor the policy and make modifications to procedures, provision, and practice as a result of this monitoring?

Postscript

The enlightened orientation evident among Scottish educational authorities in relation to the importance of encouraging children to develop their home language brings to mind another Scottish reality from more than 150 years ago. Jane Gibson, a former Heritage Language coordinator of the East York Board of Education in Toronto brought to my attention a passage in a book recently published regarding the experience of a Scottish immigrant to Canada in the 1830s. The book itself was written in Gaelic, as a guide to future immigrants, by Robert McDougall, a fluent Gaelic speaker. The Introduction to the book describes the situation in Scotland in the early 1800s that caused many to seek a better life in North America.

The passage quoted below focuses on the educational system. It highlights both the efficacy of dual language programs and the strong relationship between Gaelic (L1) proficiency and the acquisition of English as a second language. Clearly, acute observers have known for a very long time what the research findings are uncovering about the benefits of dual language instruction and the interdependence between L1 and L2 academic development:

> "Not all regions in Scotland had schools, even well into the nineteenth century. And where schools existed, students and educators alike faced another dilemma: largely for political reasons, English was the preferred medium of instruction, despite obvious problems in communication. Worse, many schools ignored Gaelic entirely, both because it was politically expedient and because there were no Gaelic texts to use. Fortunately, by the early nineteenth century, attitudes had softened somewhat; the Scots had not risen against the English recently, and *educators discovered that Gaelic students learned to read English more easily if they had a basic grounding in Gaelic grammar and literature.* The fluency of MacDougall's written Gaelic indicates that he was one of the lucky ones, taught in both Gaelic and English."

> (From Elizabeth Thompson's Introduction to Robert MacDougall's *The Emigrant's Guide to North America*, published originally in 1841 in Gaelic and republished in English translation, 1998, pp. x-xi; emphasis added)

References

Abi-Nader, J. (1993). Meeting the needs of multicultural classrooms: Family values and the motivation of minority students. In M. J. O'Hair &. S. Odell (Eds.), *Diversity and teaching: Teacher education yearbook I* (pp. 212-236). Fort Worth, TX: Harcourt Brace Jovanovich.

Ada, A. F. (1988a). The Pajaro Valley experience: Working with Spanish-speaking parents to develop children's reading and writing skills in the home through the use of children's literature. In T. Skutnabb-Kangas & J. Cummins (Eds.), *Minority education: From shame to struggle.* (pp. 223-238). Clevedon, England: Multilingual Matters.

Ada, A. F. (1988b). Creative reading: A relevant methodology for language minority children. In L. M. Malave (Ed.), *NABE '87. Theory, research and application: Selected papers.* (pp. 97-112). Buffalo: State University of New York.

Allington, R. L., & Woodside-Jiron, H. (1999). The politics of literacy teaching: How "research" shaped educational policy. *Educational Researcher, 28*(8), 4-13.

Anderson, R. C., Hiebert, E. H., Scott, J. A., & Wilkinson, I. A. G. (1985). *Becoming a nation of readers: The report of the Commission on Reading.* Washington, DC: The National Institute of Education.

Au, K. H. (1979). Using the experience-text-relationship method with minority children. *Reading Teacher, 32*(6), 677-679.

Au, K. H. (1998). Social constructivism and the school literacy learning of students of diverse cultural backgrounds. *Journal of Literacy Research, 30*(2), 297-319.

Auerbach, E. R. (1993). Reexamining English only in the ESL classroom. *TESOL Quarterly, 27*, 9-23.

August, D., & Hakuta, K. (1997). *Improving schooling for language-minority children: A research agenda.* Washington: National Research Council, Institute of Medicine, National Academy Press.

Baker, C. (1996). *Foundations of bilingual education and bilingualism*. Clevedon, England: Multilingual Matters.

Baker, C., & Prys Jones, S. (1998). *Encyclopedia of bilingualism and bilingual education*. Clevedon, England: Multilingual Matters.

Baker, K. (1992a). Review of *Forked Tongue*. *Bilingual Basics* (Winter/Spring), 6-7.

Baker, K. (1992b). Comments on Suzanne Irujo's review of Rosalie Pedalino Porter's *Forked tongue: The politics of bilingual education*. A reader reacts. *TESOL Quarterly, 26*, 397-405.

Baker, K. (1998). Structured English immersion: Breakthrough in teaching limited-English-proficient students. *Phi Delta Kappan* (November), 199-204.

Baker, K. A., & de Kanter, A. A. (1981). *Effectiveness of bilingual education: A review of the literature*. Washington, DC: U.S. Department of Education.

Baker, K. A., & de Kanter, A. A. (1983). *Effectiveness of bilingual education: A review of the literature*. Washington, D.C.: Office of Planning and Budget, U.S. Department of Education.

Balderas, V. A. (1995). To be alive in struggle: One teacher's journey. In J. Frederickson (Ed.), *Reclaiming our voices: Bilingual Education, critical pedagogy & praxis* (pp. 260-273). Ontario, CA: California Association for Bilingual Education.

Barlett, D. L., & Steele, J. B. (1992). *America: What went wrong?* Kansas: Andrews & McMeel.

Beardsmore, H. B. (1993). The European schools model. In H. B. Beardsmore (Ed.), *European models of bilingual education* (pp. 121-154). Clevedon, England: Multilingual Matters.

Becker, A. (1990). The role of the school in the maintenance and change of ethnic group affiliation. *Human Organization, 49*, 48-55.

Becker, W., & Gersten, R. (1982). A follow-up of follow through: The later effects of the direct instruction model on children in the fifth and sixth grades. *American Educational Research Journal, 19*, 75-92.

Becker, W. (1977). Teaching reading and language to the disadvantaged: What we have learned from field research. *Harvard Educational Review, 47,* 518-43.

Benton, R. A. (1988). The Maori language in New Zealand education. *Language, Culture and Curriculum, 1,* 75-83.

Berliner, D. C., & Biddle, B. J. (1995). *The manufactured crisis: Myths, fraud, and the attack on America's public schools.* Reading, MA: Perseus Books.

Berman, P., Chambers, J., Gándara, P., *et al.* (1992). *Meeting the challenge of linguistic diversity: An evaluation of programs for pupils with limited proficiency in English.* Berkeley: BW Associates.

Beykont, Z. F. (1994). *Academic progress of a nondominant group: A longitudinal study of Puerto Ricans in New York City's late-exit bilingual programs.* Unpublished Doctoral dissertation presented to the Graduate School of Education of Harvard University, Harvard University.

Bialystok, E. (1987a). Influences of bilingualism on metalinguistic development. *Second Language Research, 3*(2), 112-125.

Bialystok, E. (1987b). Words as things: Development of word concept by bilingual children. *Studies in Second Language Learning, 9,* 133-140.

Bialystok, E. (1988). Levels of bilingualism and levels of linguistic awareness. *Developmental Psychology, 24,* 560-567.

Bialystok, E. (1991). Metalinguistic dimensions of bilingual language proficiency. In E. Bialystok (Ed.), *Language processing in bilingual children* (pp. 113-140). Cambridge: Cambridge University Press.

Bialystok, E., & Hakuta, K. (1994). *In other words: The science and psychology of second language acquisition.* New York: Basic Books.

Biber, D. (1986). Spoken and written textual dimensions in English: Resolving the contradictory findings. *Language, 62,* 384-414.

Biemiller, A. (1999). *Language and reading success.* Cambridge, MA: Brookline Books.

Bild, E. R., & Swain, M. (1989). Minority language students in a French immersion programme: Their French proficiency. *Journal of Multilingual and Multicultural Development, 10*(3), 255-274.

Bishop, A. (2000). Technology trends and their potential for bilingual education. *Issue Brief, No. 7.* Washington DC: National Clearinghouse for Bilingual Education. (www.ncbe.gwu.edu).

Bishop, R., & Glynn, R. (1999). *Culture counts: Changing power relations in education.* Palmerston North: Dunmore Press.

Blauner, R. (1969). Internal colonialism and ghetto revolt. *Social Problems, 16,* 393-408.

Bracey, G. W. (1999, November 2, 1999). Poverty issues get short shrift in today's education debate. *USA Today,* p. 19A.

Brisk, M. E. (1998). *Bilingual education: From compensatory to quality schooling.* Mahwah, NJ: Lawrence Erlbaum Associates.

Brisk, M. E., & Harrington, M. M. (2000). *Literacy and bilingualism: A handbook for ALL teachers.* Mahway, NJ: Lawrence Erlbaum Associates.

Brown, K. (1999). Global learning networks: Heartbeats on the Internet. In J. V. Tinajero & R. A. DeVillar (Eds.), *The power of two languages 2000* (pp. 309-319). New York: McGraw-Hill School Division.

Brown, K., Cummins, J., Figueroa, E., & Sayers, D. (1998). Global learning networks: Gaining perspective on our lives with distance. In E. Lee, D. Menkart, & M. Okazawa-Rey (Eds.), *Beyond heroes and holidays: A practical guide to K-12 anti-racist, multicultural education and staff development* (pp. 334-354). Washington, DC: Network of Educators on the Americas.

Bruner, J. S. (1975). Language as an instrument of thought. In A. Davies (Ed.) *Problems of language and learning.* London: Heinemann.

Buss, M., & Laurén, C. (1995). Language immersion: Teaching and second language acquisition: From Canada to Europe. *Proceedings of the University of Vaasa Research Papers. Tutkimuksia No. 192.* Vaasa: University of Vaasa.

California Department of Education. (1996). *Teaching reading: A balanced, comprehensive approach to teaching reading in prekindergarten through grade three.* Sacramento: California State Board of Education.

California Department of Education (2000) *California Two-Way Bilingual Immersion Programs Directory*. Sacramento: California Department of Education.

California State Department of Education. (1985). *Case studies in bilingual education: First Year Report*. (Federal Grant #G008303723.).

Californians Together. (2000). *Schools with large enrollments of English learners and substantial bilingual instruction are effective in teaching English*. Oakland.

Campos, J., & Keatinge, R. (1988). The Carpinteria language minority student experience: From theory, to practice, to success. In T. Skutnabb-Kangas & J. Cummins (Eds.), *Minority education: From shame to struggle* (pp. 299–308). Clevedon, England: Multilingual Matters.

Cashion, M., & Eagan, R. (1990). Spontaneous reading and writing in English by students in total French immersion: Summary of final report. *English Quarterly, 22*(1-2), 30–44.

Cazabon, M. T., Nicoladis, E., & Lambert, W. E. (1998). *Becoming bilingual in the Amigos two-way immersion program*. Washington, DC: CREDE/CAL.

Cazden, C. B., & Snow, C. E. (1990). English Plus: Issues in bilingual education, *The Annals of the American Academy of Political and Social Science*. Newbury Park, CA: Sage Publications.

Cenoz, J. (1999). Multilingual education in the Basque country. In J. Cenoz & F. Genesee (Eds.), *Beyond bilingualism: Multilingualism and multilingual education* (pp. 175–191). Clevedon, England: Multilingual Matters.

Cenoz, J., & Genesee, F. (Eds.). (1999). *Beyond bilingualism: Multilingualism and multilingual education*. Clevedon, England: Multilingual Matters.

Cenoz, J., & Valencia, J. F. (1994). Additive trilingualism: Evidence from the Basque Country. *Applied Psycholinguistics, 15*, 195–207.

Chall, J. S., Jacobs, V. A., & Baldwin, L. E. (1990). *The reading crisis: Why poor children fall behind*. Cambridge, MA: Harvard University Press.

Chamot, A. U. (1996). *Accelerating achievement with learning strategies*. Glenview, IL: Scott Foresman.

Chamot, A. U. (1998). Effective instruction for high school English language learners. In R. M. Gersten & R. T. Jiménez (Eds.), *Promoting learning for culturally and linguistically diverse students: Classroom applications from contemporary research* (pp. 187-209). Belmont, CA: Wadsworth Publishing Company.

Chamot, A. U., Barnhardt, S., El-Dinary, P. B., & Robbins, J. (1999). *The learning strategies handbook.* White Plains, NY: Longman.

Chamot, A. U., & O'Malley, M. (1994). *The CALLA handbook: Implementing the cognitive academic language learning approach.* Reading, MA: Addison-Wesley.

Chang, H. N.-L. & Sakai., L. (1993). *Affirming children's roots: Cultural and linguistic diversity in early care and education.* San Francisco: California Tomorrow.

Chomsky, N. (1987). The manufacture of consent. In J. Peck (Ed.), *The Chomsky reader* (pp. 121-136). New York: Pantheon Books.

Chomsky, N. (1995). A dialogue with Noam Chomsky. *Harvard Educational Review, 65,* 127-144.

Christian, D., Howard, E. R., & Loeb, M. I. (2000). Bilingualism for all: Two-way immersion education in the United States. *Theory into Practice, 34*(4), 258-266.

Christian, D., Montone, C. L., Lindholm, K. J., & Carranza, I. (1997). *Profiles in two-way immersion education.* Washington, DC: Center for Applied Linguistics and Delta Systems.

Churchill, S. (1986). *The education of linguistic and cultural minorities in OECD countries.* Clevedon, England: Multilingual Matters.

Cloud, N., Genesee, F., & Hamayan, E. (2000). *Dual language instruction: A handbook for enriched education.* Boston, MA: Heinle & Heinle.

Cohen, D. K. (1970). Immigrants and the schools. *Review of Educational Research, 40,* 13-27.

Coles, G. (2000). *Misreading reading: The bad science that hurts children.* Portsmouth, NH: Heinemann.

Collier, V. P. (1987). Age and rate of acquisition of second language for academic purposes. *TESOL Quarterly, 21,* 617-641.

Collier, V. P. (1995). *Promoting academic success for ESL students.* Elizabeth, NJ: New Jersey Teachers of English to Speakers of Other Languages-Bilingual Educators.

Collier, V. P., & Thomas, W. P. (1999) Making U.S. schools effective for English language learners, Part 2. *TESOL Matters,* 9(5), 1,6.

Comer, J. P. (1980). *School power: Implications of an intervention project.* New York: The Free Press.

Corson, D. (1993). *Language, minority education and gender: Linking social justice and power.* Clevedon, England: Multilingual Matters.

Corson, D. (1995). *Using English words.* New York: Kluwer.

Corson, D. (1997). The learning and use of academic English words. *Language Learning, 47*(4), 671-718.

Corson, D. (1999). *Language policy in schools: A resource for teachers and administrators.* Mahwah, NJ: Lawrence Erlbaum Associates.

Corson, D. (2001). *Language diversity and education.* Mahwah, NJ: Lawrence Erlbaum Associates.

Coxhead, A. (2000). A new academic word list. *TESOL Quarterly, 34*(2), 213-238.

Crawford, J. (1992a). *Language loyalties: A source book on the Official English controversy.* Chicago: University of Chicago Press.

Crawford, J. (1992b). *Hold your tongue: Bilingualism and the politics of "English Only".* New York: Addison Wesley.

Crawford, J. (1995). *Bilingual education: History, politics, theory, and practice.* (Third edition ed.). Los Angeles: Bilingual Education Services, Inc.

Crawford, J. (2000). Proposition 227: A new phase of the English-only movement. In R. D. González & I. Melis (Eds.), *Language ideologies: Critical perspectives on the Official English movement. Volume 1. Education and the social implications of Official Language* (pp. 28-61). Urbana, IL: National Council of Teachers of English.

Criddle, J. D., & Mam, T. B. (1987). *To destroy you is no loss: The odyssey of a Cambodian family*. New York: Doubleday.

Crystal, D. (1987). *Cambridge encyclopedia of language*. Cambridge: Cambridge University Press.

Cummins, J. (1976). The influence of bilingualism on cognitive growth: A synthesis of research findings and explanatory hypotheses. *Working Papers on Bilingualism, 9*, 1–43.

Cummins, J. (1979a). Linguistic interdependence and the educational development of bilingual children. *Review of Educational Research, 49*, 222–251.

Cummins, J. (1981a). The role of primary language development in promoting educational success for language minority students. In California State Department of Education (Ed.), *Schooling and language minority students: A theoretical framework*. (pp. 3–49). Los Angeles: Evaluation, Dissemination and Assessment Center California State University.

Cummins, J. (1981b). Age on arrival and immigrant second language learning in Canada: A reassessment. *Applied Linguistics, 1*, 132–149.

Cummins, J. (1984). *Bilingualism and special education: Issues in assessment and pedagogy*. Clevedon, England: Multilingual Matters.

Cummins, J. (1986). Empowering minority students: A framework for intervention. *Harvard Education Review, 15*, 18–36.

Cummins, J. (1989). *Empowering minority students*. Sacramento: California Association for Bilingual Education.

Cummins, J. (1991b). The development of bilingual proficiency from home to school: A longitudinal study of Portuguese-speaking children. *Journal of Education, 173*, 85–98.

Cummins, J. (1991d). Interdependence of first- and second-language proficiency in bilingual children. In E. Bialystok (Ed.), *Language processing in bilingual children* (pp. 70–89). Cambridge, England: Cambridge University Press.

Cummins, J. (1997). Minority status and schooling in Canada. *Anthropology & Education Quarterly, 28*(3), 411–430.

Cummins, J. (1999). Beyond adversarial discourse: Searching for common ground in the education of bilingual students. In C. Ovando & P. McLaren (Eds.), *The politics of multiculturalism and bilingual education: Students and teachers caught in the cross fire* (pp. 126-147). Boston: McGraw Hill.

Cummins, J. (2000). *Language, power and pedagogy: Bilingual children in the crossfire*. Clevedon, England: Multilingual Matters.

Cummins, J., & Corson, D. (Eds.). (1997). *Bilingual education*. (Vol. 5). Dordrecht, The Netherlands: Kluwer Academic Publishers.

Cummins, J., & Danesi, M. (1990). *Heritage languages: The development and denial of Canada's linguistic resources.* Toronto: Our Schools Ourselves/ Garamond.

Cummins, J., Harley, B., Swain, M., & Allen, P. A. (1990). Social and individual factors in the development of bilingual proficiency. In J. Cummins, B. Harley, M. Swain, & P. A. Allen (Eds.), *The development of second language proficiency* (pp. 119-133). Cambridge: Cambridge University Press.

Cummins, J., & Sayers, D. (1995). *Brave new schools: Challenging cultural illiteracy through global learning networks*. New York: St. Martin's Press.

Cummins, J., & Swain, M. (1986). *Bilingualism in education: Aspects of theory, research and practice*. London: Longman.

Cummins, J., Swain, M., Nakajima, K., Handscombe, J., Green, D., & Tran, C. (1984). Linguistic interdependence among Japanese and Vietnamese immigrant students. In C. Rivera (Ed.), *Communicate competence approaches to language proficiency assessment: research and application.* (pp. 60-81). Clevedon, England: Multilingual Matters.

Cunningham, A. (1990). Explicit versus implicit instruction in phonemic awareness. *Journal of Experimental Child Psychology, 50,* 429-444.

Daiute, C. (1985). *Writing and computers*. Reading, MA: Addison-Wesley.

Darder, A. (1991). *Culture and power in the classroom: A critical foundation for bicultural education*. New York: Bergin & Garvey.

DeFazio, A. J. (1997). Language awareness at The International High School. In L. Van Lier & D. Corson (Eds.), *Knowledge about language* (Vol. 6, pp. 99-107). Dordrecht, The Netherlands: Kluwer Academic Publishers, Inc.

Delgado-Gaitan, C. (1994). Sociocultural change through literacy: Toward the empowerment of families. In B. M. Ferdman, R.-M. Weber, & A. Ramirez (Eds.), *Literacy across languages and cultures* (pp. 143-170). Albany: SUNY Press.

Delpit, L. (1995). *Other peoples' children: Cultural conflict in the classroom.* New York: The New Press.

Delpit, L. (1998). Ebonics and culturally responsive instruction. In T. Perry & L. Delpit (Eds.), *The real Ebonics debate* (pp. 17-26). Milwaukee, WI: Rethinking Schools.

Delpit, L. D. (1988). The silenced dialogue: Power and pedagogy in educating other people's children. *Harvard Educational Review, 58,* 280-298.

Delpit, L. D. (1992). Education in a multicultural society: Our future's greatest challenge. *Journal of Negro Education, 61,* 237-249.

DevTech Systems Inc. (1996). *A descriptive study of the ESEA Title VII educational services provided for secondary school limited English proficient students: Final report.* Washington, DC: National Clearinghouse for Bilingual Education.

Dewey, J. (1963). *Experience and education.* New York: Collier Books.

Deyhle, D. (1995). Navajo youth and Anglo racism: Cultural integrity and resistance. *Harvard Educational Review, 65,* 403-444.

Diaz, R. M. (1985). Bilingual cognitive development: Addressing three gaps in current research. *Child Development, 56,* 1376-1388.

Diaz, R. M., & Klinger, C. (1991). Towards an explanatory model of the interaction between bilingualism and cognitive development. In E. Bialystok (Ed.), *Language processing in bilingual children* (pp. 167-192). Cambridge: Cambridge University Press.

Dicker, S. (1996). RTE Forum: Letters from readers. *Research in the Teaching of English, 30*(1), 373-376.

Dolson, D., & Lindholm, K. (1995). World class education for children in California: A comparison of the two-way bilingual immersion and European Schools model. In T. Skutnabb-Kangas (Ed.), *Multilingualism for all* (pp. 69-102). Lisse: Swets & Zeitlinger.

Donaldson, M. (1978). *Children's minds*. Glasgow: Collins.

Dressman, M. (1999). On the use and misuse of research evidence: Decoding two states' reading initiatives. *Reading Research Quarterly, 34*(3), 258-285.

D'Souza, D. (1991). *Illiberal education: The politics of race and sex on campus*. New York: Vintage Books.

Dunn, L. (1987). *Bilingual Hispanic children on the U.S. mainland: A review of research on their cognitive, linguistic, and scholastic development*. Circle Pines, Minnesota: American Guidance Service.

Dutcher, N. (1995). *The use of first and second languages in education: A review of international experience*. Washington, DC: The World Bank.

Eccles, F., Kirton, E., & Xiong, B. (1994). *The family connection: Hmong parent education project*. Merced, CA: Merced County Office of Education.

EdCon International. (2000). *Formative biennial evaluation of Project Y.A.L.L.A. Young Americans Learning Languages Actively*. Dearborn, MI.

Edelsky, C. (1986). *Writing in a bilingual program: Habia una vez*. Norwood, NJ: Ablex.

Edwards, J. (1994). *Multilingualism*. London: Routledge.

Edwards, V. (1998). *The power of Babel: Teaching and learning in multilingual classrooms*. Stoke-on-Trent, England: Trentham Books Limited.

El Paso Independent School District. (1987). *Interim report of the five-year bilingual education pilot 1986-87 school year*. El Paso, Texas: Office for Research and Evaluation.

Elley, W. B. (1991). Acquiring literacy in a second language: The effect of book-based programs. *Language Learning, 41*, 375-411.

Elley, W. B., & Manghubai, F. (1983). The impact of reading on second language learning. *Reading Research Quarterly, 19*, 53-67.

Ellis, R. (1994). *The study of second language acquisition*. Oxford: Oxford University Press.

Engle, P. (1975). *The use of the vernacular language in education*. Washington, DC: Center for Applied Linguistics.

Epstein, N. (1977). *Language, ethnicity and the schools*. Washington, D.C.: Institute for Educational Leadership.

Erickson, F. (1987). Transformation and school success: The politics and culture of educational achievement. *Anthropology & Education Quarterly, 18*, 335-356.

Escamilla, K. (1996). RTE Forum: Letters from readers. *Research in the Teaching of English, 30*(1), 371-373.

Estrada, H. M. (1986, Friday October 31). 'Pajaro experience' teaches parents how to teach kids. *Santa Cruz Sentinel*, pp. A4.

Evans, E. (1978). Welsh (Cymraeg). In C. V. James (Ed.), *The older mother tongues of the United Kingdom*. London: Centre for Information on Language Teaching and Research.

Faltis, C. J. & Wolfe, P. (Eds.) *So much to say: Adolescents, bilingualism, & ESL in the secondary school*. New York: Teachers College Press.

Fern, V. (1995). Oyster school stands the test of time. *Bilingual Research Journal, 19*(3 & 4), 497-512.

Fielding, L. G., & Pearson, P. D. (1994). Reading comprehension: What works. *Educational Leadership, 51*(5), 62-68.

Fillmore, L. W. (2000). Loss of family languages: Should educators be concerned? *Theory into Practice, 34*(4), 203-210.

Fishman, J. A. (1976). *Bilingual education: An international sociological perspective*. Rowley, MA: Newbury House.

Fishman, J. A. (1991). *Reversing language shift*. Clevedon, England: Multilingual Matters.

Fitzgerald, J. (1995). English-as-a-second-language learners' cognitive reading processes: A review of research in the United States. *Review of Educational Research, 65*, 145-190.

Foorman, B. R., Fletcher, J. M., Francis, D. J., & Schatschneider, C. (2000). *Response:* Misrepresentation of research by other researchers. *Educational Researcher, 29*(6), 27-37.

Foorman, B. R., Francis, D. J., Fletcher, J. M., Schatschneider, C. S., & Mehta, P. (1998). The role of instruction in learning to read: Preventing reading failure in at-risk children. *Journal of Educational Psychology, 90*(1), 37-55.

Fordham, S. (1990). Racelessness as a factor in Black students' school success: Pragmatic strategy or Pyrrhic victory? In N. M. Hidalgo, C. L. McDowell, & E. V. Siddle (Eds.), *Facing racism in education* (Reprint series No. 21 ed., pp. 232-262): Harvard Educational Review.

Foster, J. L., & Swinney, R. (1995). *The dual language program of Manhattan's District Three*: Unpublished manuscript.

Foucault, M. (1980). *Power/Knowledge*. New York: Pantheon.

Frederickson, J. (Ed.). (1995). *Reclaiming Our Voices: Bilingual Education, Critical Pedagogy & Praxis*. Ontario, CA: California Association for Bilingual Education.

Frederickson, N., & Cline, T. (1990). *Curriculum related assessment with bilingual children: A set of working papers*. London: University College London.

Freeman, D. E., & Freeman, Y. S. (1994). *Between worlds: Access to second language acquisition*. Portsmouth, NH: Heinemann.

Freeman, R. D. (1998). *Bilingual education and social change*. Clevedon, England: Multilingual Matters.

Freeman, Y. S., & Freeman, D. E. (1992). *Whole language for second language learners*. Portsmouth, NH: Heinemann.

Freeman, Y. S., & Freeman, D. E. (1998). *ESL/EFL teaching. Principles for success.* Portsmouth, NH: Heinemann.

Freeman, Y. S., & Freeman, D. E. (2000). Preview, view, review: A useful technique. *Bilingual Basics, 3*(1) (Fall/Winter), 10-11.

Freire, P. (1970). *Pedagogy of the oppressed*. New York: Continuum.

Freire, P., & Macedo, D. (1987). *Literacy: Reading the word and the world*. South Hadley, MA: Bergin & Garvey.

French, M. (1992). *The war against women*. New York: Summit Books.

Gabina, J. J. et al. (1986). *EIFE. Influence of factors on the learning of Basque*. Gasteiz: Central Publications Service of the Basque Country.

Gale, K., McClay, D., Christie, M., & Harris, S. (1981). Academic achievement in the Milingimbi bilingual education program. *TESOL Quarterly, 15*, 297-314.

Galtung, J. (1980). *The true worlds: A transnational perspective*. New York: The Free Press.

Gándara, P. (1999). *Review of research on instruction of limited English proficient students: A report to the California Legislature*. Santa Barbara: University of California, Linguistic Minority Research Institute.

Gándara, P., Maxwell-Jolly, J., García, E., Asato, J., Gutiérrez, K., Stritikus, T., & Curry, J. (2000). *The initial impact of Proposition 227 on the instruction of English learners*. Davis, CA: University of California Linguistic Minority Research Institute.

García, E. (1991). *Education of linguistically and culturally diverse students: Effective instructional practices* (Educational Practice report 1). Santa Cruz: The National Center for Research on Cultural Diversity and Second Language Learning.

García, O. (1999). Educating Latino high school students with little formal schooling. In C. J. Faltis & P. Wolfe (Eds.), *So much to say: Adolescents, bilingualism, & ESL in the secondary school* (pp. 61-82). New York: Teachers College Press.

Gee, J. P. (1996). *Social linguistics and literacies: Ideologies in discourses*. New York: Falmer Press.

Gee, J. P. (1999). Critical issues: Reading and the new literacy studies: Reframing the National Academy of Sciences report on reading. *Journal of Literacy Research, 31*(3), 355-374.

Gee, J. P. (2000). New people in new worlds: Networks, the new capitalism and schools. In B. Cope & M. Kalantzis (Eds.). *Multiliteracies: Literacy learning and the design of social futures.* (pp. 43-68). London: Routledge

Genesee, F. (1979). Acquisition of reading skills in immersion programs. *Foreign Language Annals, 12*, 71-77.

Genesee, F., & Lambert, W. (1983). Trilingual education for majority-language children. *Child Development, 54*, 105-114.

Genesee, F., Lambert, W., & Tucker, G. (1977). *An experiment in trilingual education.*. Montreal: McGill University.

Genishi, C., & Strickland, D. (1999). Foreword. In G. B. Thompson & T. Nicholson (Eds.), *Learning to read: Beyond phonics and whole language* (pp. vii-ix). New York: Teachers College Press.

Gersten, R. (1985). Structured immersion for language minority students: Results of a longitudinal evaluation. *Educational Evaluation and Policy Analysis, 7*, 187-196.

Gersten, R., & Woodward, J. (1985a). A case for structured immersion. *Educational Leadership* (September), 75-79.

Gersten, R., & Woodward, J. (1985b). Response to Santiago. *Educational Leadership* (September), 83-84.

Gersten, R., & Woodward, J. (1995). A longitudinal study of transitional and immersion bilingual education programs in one district. *The Elementary School Journal, 95*(3), 223-239.

Geva, E., & Ryan, E. B. (1993). Linguistic and cognitive correlates of academic skills in first and second languages. *Language Learning, 43*, 5-42.

Gibbons, J., White, W., & Gibbons, P. (1994). Combatting educational disadvantage among Lebanese Australian children. In T. Skutnabb

Kangas & R. Phillipson (Eds.), *Linguistic human rights: Overcoming linguistic discrimination* (pp. 253-262). Berlin: Mouton de Gryter.

Gibbons, P. (1991). *Learning to learn in a second language.* Newtown, Australia: Primary English Teaching Association.

Gibson, H., Small, A., & Mason, D. (1997). Deaf bilingual bicultural education. In J. Cummins & D. Corson (Eds.), *Bilingual education. Volume 5. Encyclopedia of Language and Education* (pp. 231-240). Dordrecht, The Netherlands: Kluwer Academic Publishers.

Gibson, M. (1995). Patterns of acculturation & high school performance. *University of California LMRI, 4*(9), 1-3.

Gibson, M. A. (1997). Complicating the immigrant/involuntary minority typology. *Anthropology & Education Quarterly, 28*(3), 431–454.

Gingrich, N. (1995). English literacy is the coin of the realm. *Los Angeles Times* (August 4).

Giroux, H. A. (1991). Series Introduction: Rethinking the pedagogy of voice, difference and cultural struggle. In C. E. Walsh (Ed.), *Pedagogy and the struggle for voice: Issues of language, power, and schooling for Puerto Ricans* (pp. xv–xxvii). Toronto: OISE Press.

Glazer, N., & Cummins, J. (1985). Viewpoints on bilingual education. *Equity and Choice, 2*, 47–52.

Glenn, C. (1996). *Educating immigrant children: Schools and language minorities in twelve nations.* New York: Garland.

Glenn, C., & LaLyre, I. (1991). Integrated bilingual education in the USA. In K. Jaspaert & S. Kroon (Eds.), *Ethnic minority languages and education* (pp. 37–55). Amsterdam: Swets & Zeitlinger.

Glenn, C. L. (1990). Introduction, *Two-Way Integrated Bilingual Education.* Boston: Department of Education, Office of Educational Equity.

Glenn, C. L. (1997). *What does the National Research Council study tell us about educating language minority children?* Washington, DC: READ Institute.

Glenn, C. L. (1998). Declaration, *United States District Court, Northern District of California, July 15, 1998, Case No. C98-2252.*

Gold, N. (2000). *Bilingual schools make exceptional gains on the state's Academic Performance Index (API).* Sacramento: Californians Together.

Goldenberg, C. (1998). A balanced approach to early Spanish literacy instruction. In R. M. Gersten & R. T. Jiménez (Eds.), *Promoting learning for culturally and linguistically diverse students: Classroom applications from contemporary research.* Belmont, CA: Wadsworth Publishing Company.

González, L. A. (1986). *The effects of first language education on the second language and academic achievement of Mexican immigrant elementary school children in the United States.* Unpublished Doctoral dissertation, University of Illinois at Urbana-Champaign.

González, L. A. (1989). Native language education: The key to English literacy skills. In D. J. Bixler-Márquez, G. K. Green, & J. L. Ornstein-Galicia (Eds.), *Mexican-American Spanish in its societal and cultural contexts* (pp. 209-224). Brownsville: Pan American University.

Goodlad, J. I. (1984). *A place called school: Prospects for the future.* New York: McGraw Hill.

Goodman, K. (1997). California, whole language, and the NAEP. *CLIPS: A Journal of the California Reading & Literature Project, 3*(1), 53-56.

Gottlieb, M. (1999). Assessing ESOL adolescents: Balancing accessibility to learn with accountability for learning. In C. J. Faltis & P. Wolfe (Eds.), *So much to say: Adolescents, bilingualism, & ESL in the secondary school* (pp. 176-201). New York: Teachers College Press.

Graves, D. (1983). *Writing: Teachers and children at work.* Exeter, NH: Heinemann Educational Books.

Greene, J. P. (1997). A meta-analysis of the Rossell and Baker review of bilingual education research. *Bilingual Research Journal, 21*(2 & 3), 1-20.

Greene, J. P. (1998). *A meta-analysis of the effectiveness of bilingual education.* Claremont, CA: The Tomas Rivera Policy Institute.

Hacker, A. (1995). *Two nations: Black and white, separate, hostile, unequal.* New York: Ballantine Books.

Hakuta, K., Butler, Y. G., & Witt, D. (2000). *How long does it take English learners to attain proficiency?* Santa Barbara: University of California Linguistic Minority Research Institute.

Hakuta, K., & Diaz, R. M. (1985). The relationship between degree of bilingualism and cognitive ability: A critical discussion and some new longitudinal data. In K. E. Nelson (Ed.), *Children's language* (Vol. Volume V). Hillsdale NJ: Erlbaum.

Handscombe, J., & Becker, N. (1994). *A week of school.* North York: North York Board of Education.

Harklau, L. (1999). The ESL learning environment in secondary school. In C. J. Faltis & P. Wolfe (Eds.), *So much to say: Adolescents, bilingualism, & ESL in the secondary school* (pp. 42-60). New York: Teachers College Press.

Harley, B., Allen, P., Cummins, J., & Swain, M. (1990). *The development of second language proficiency*. Cambridge, England: Cambridge University Press.

Harré, R., & Gillett, G. (1994). *The discursive mind*. Thousand Oaks, CA: Sage.

Harris, S. (1990). *Two way aboriginal schooling: Education and cultural survival*. Canberra: Aboriginal Studies Press.

Harry, B. (1992). *Cultural diversity, families and the special education system*. New York: Teachers College Press.

Hatcher, P., Hulme, C., & Ellis, A. (1994). Ameliorating early reading failure by integrating the teaching of reading and phonological skills: The phonological linkage hypothesis. *Child Development, 65*, 41-57.

Hayes, C. W., Bahruth, R., & Kessler, C. (1991). *Literacy con cariño: A story of migrant children's success*. Portsmouth, NH: Heinemann.

Heath, S. B. (1983). *Ways with words*. Cambridge: Cambridge University Press.

Heath, S. B. (1986). Sociocultural contexts of language development. In California State Department of Education (Ed.), *Beyond language: Social and cultural factors in schooling language minority students*. Los Angeles: Evaluation, Dissemination, and Assessment Center.

Heath, S. B. (1993). Inner city life through drama: Imagining the language classroom. *TESOL Quarterly, 27*(2), 177-192.

Hirsch, E. D. J. (1987). *Cultural literacy: What every American needs to know*. Boston: Houghton Mifflin Co.

Hodgkinson, H. (1991). Reform versus reality. *Phi Delta Kappan, 73* (September), 9-16.

Hopkins, D. S. (1987). *Improving the quality of schooling*. Lewes, England: The Falmer Press.

Houston, M. (1995). Tell me a story (Then tell it again): Supporting literacy for preschool children from bilingual families. *Interaction* (Spring), 32-35.

Hughes, R. (1993). *Culture of complaint: A passionate look into the ailing heart of America*. New York: Warner Books.

Huguet, A., Vila, I., & Llurda, E. (2000). Minority language education in unbalanced bilingual situations: A case for the linguistic interdependence hypothesis. *Journal of Psycholinguistic Research, 29*(3), 313-333.

Igoa, C. (1995). *The inner world of the immigrant child.* New York: St. Martin's Press.

Imhoff, G. (1990). The position of U.S. English on bilingual education. In C. B. Cazden & C. E. Snow (Eds.), *English Plus: Issues in bilingual education* (pp. 48-61). Newbury Park, CA: Sage Publications.

Iverson, S., & Tunmer, W. E. (1993). Phonological processing skills and the Reading Recovery program. *Journal of Educational Psychology, 85,* 112-126.

Izumi, S., & Bigelow, M. (2000). Does output promote noticing and second language acquisition? *TESOL Quarterly, 34*(2), 239-278.

Jasso, A., & Jasso, R. (1995). Critical pedagogy: Not a method, but a way of life. In J. Frederickson (Ed.), *Reclaiming our voices: Bilingual education, critical pedagogy & praxis* (pp. 253-259). Ontario, CA: California Association for Bilingual Education.

Jessner, U. (1999). Metalinguistic awareness in multilinguals: Cognitive aspects of third language learning. *Language Awareness, 8*(3/4), 201-209.

Kalantzis, M., & Cope, B. (1993). Histories of pedagogy, cultures of schooling. In B. Cope & M. Kalantzis (Eds.), *The powers of literacy: A genre approach to teaching writing* (pp. 38-62). London: The Falmer Press.

Kanno, Y. (2000). Bilingualism and identity: The stories of Japanese returnees. *International Journal of Bilingual Education and Bilingualism, 3*(1), 1-17.

Kaprielian-Churchill, I., & Churchill, S. (1994). *The pulse of the world: Refugees in our schools.* Toronto: OISE Press.

Kemp, J. (1984). *Native language knowledge as a predictor of success in learning a foreign language with special reference to a disadvantaged population.* Unpublished Thesis submitted for the M. A. Degree, Tel-Aviv University.

Kennedy, P. (1993). *Preparing for the twenty-first century.* New York: Harper Collins Publishers Ltd.

Klesmer, H. (1994). Assessment and teacher perceptions of ESL student achievement. *English Quarterly, 26*(3), 8-11.

Kloss, H. (1977). *The American bilingual tradition*. Rowley, MA: Newbury House.

Kozol, J. (1991). *Savage inequalities: Children in America's schools*. New York: Crown Publishers.

Krashen, S. (1981). *Second language acquisition and second language learning*. London: Pergamon Press.

Krashen, S., & Biber, D. (1988). *On course: Bilingual education's success in California*. Sacramento: California Association for Bilingual Education.

Krashen, S. D. (1991). Bilingual education: A focus on current research, *Occasional Papers in Bilingual Education* (Spring 1991). Washington, DC: National Clearinghouse for Bilingual Education.

Krashen, S. D. (1993). *The power of reading*. Englewood, CO: Libraries Unlimited.

Krashen, S. D. (1996). *Every person a reader: An alternative to the California Task Force report on reading*. Culver City, CA: Language Education Associates.

Krashen, S. D. (1999a). *Condemned without a trial: Bogus arguments against bilingual education*. Portsmouth, NH: Heinemann.

Krashen, S. D. (1999b). Effects of phonemic awareness training on delayed tests of reading. *Perceptual and Motor Skills, 89,* 79-82.

Krashen, S. D. (1999c). Why Malherbe (1946) is NOT evidence against bilingual education. *NABE News, 22*(7), 25-26.

Krashen, S. D. (2000a). Bilingual education: The debate continues. In R. D. González & I. Melis (Eds.), *Language ideologies: Critical perspectives on the Official English movement. Volume 1. Education and the social implications of Official Language* (pp. 137-160). Urbana, IL: National Council of Teachers of English.

Krashen, S. (2000b). What really happened in New York and California: BILINGUAL EDUCATION DID NOT FAIL. *Bilingual Basics*, 3(1) (Fall/Winter), 1-4.

Kwan, A. B., & Willows, D. M. (1998, December). *Impact of early phonics instruction on children learning English as a second language.* Paper presented at the National Reading Conference, Austin, TX.

Labov, W. (1970). *The logic of non-standard English*. Champaign, IL: National Council of Teachers of English.

Ladson-Billings, G. (1995). Toward a theory of culturally relevant pedagogy. *American Educational Research Journal, 32,* 465-491.

Laing, R. D. (1969). *Self and others*. Harmondsworth, England: Penguin Books.

Lambert, W. E. (1975). Culture and language as factors in learning and education. In A. Wolfgang (Ed.), *Education of immigrant students*. Toronto: OISE Press.

Lambert, W. E., & Tucker, G. R. (1972). *Bilingual education of children: The St. Lambert experiment*. Rowley, MA: Newbury House.

Landon, J., Cambell, J., Hassan, B. U. L., Rehman, S., Hindle, A., Armstrong, R., & Robertson, R. (1994). *Languages for life: Bilingual pupils 5-14*. Edinburgh: Scottish Consultative Council on the Curriculum.

Landry, R., & Allard, R. (1991). Can schools promote additive bilingualism in minority group children? In L. Malavé & G. Duquette (Eds.), *Language, culture, and cognition: A collection of studies in first and second language acquisition* (pp. 198-231). Clevedon, England: Multilingual Matters.

Lasagabaster, D. (1998). The threshold hypothesis applied to three languages in contact at school. *International Journal of Bilingual Education and Bilingualism, 1*(2), 119-133.

Laufer, B. (1992). How much lexis is necessary for reading comprehension? In H. Bejoint & P. Arnaud (Eds.), *Vocabulary and applied linguistics* (pp. 126-132). London: Macmillan.

Legaretta, D. (1979). The effects of program models on language acquisition by Spanish speaking children. *TESOL Quarterly, 13,* 521-534.

Levin, H. M. (1998). Accelerated schools: A decade of evolution. In A. Hargreaves, A. Lieberman, M. Fullan, & D. Hopkins (Eds.), *International handbook of educational change (Part Two)* (pp. 807-830). Dordrecht: Kluwer Academic Publishers.

Lewis, E. G. (1976). Bilingualism and bilingual education: The ancient world to the renaissance. In J. A. Fishman (Ed.), *Bilingual education: An international sociological perspective* (pp. 150-200). Rowley, MA: Newbury House.

Lightbown, P. M. (1992). Can they do it themselves? A comprehension-based ESL course for young children. In R. Courchene, J. J. Glidden, J. S. John, & C. Therien (Eds.), *Comprehension-based second language teaching*. Ottawa: University of Ottawa Press.

Lindholm-Leary, K. J. (2001). *Dual language education*. Clevedon, England: Multilingual Matters.

Lloyd, S. (1992). *The phonics handbook*. Essex, UK: Jolly Learning.

Llwellyn, R. (1968). *How green was my valley*. Toronto: Signet.

Lockwood, A. T., & Secada, W. G. (1999). *Transforming education for Hispanic youth: Exemplary practices, programs, and schools* (12). Washington, DC: NCBE Resource Collection Series.

López, A. (1988, October). *The infant-toddler and child development centers and parent education and support*. Paper presented at the Workshop on Early Development of Hispanic Infants and Children: Options for Intervention to Improve School Readiness and Long-Term Academic Achievement, New York.

Lucas, I. (1981). *Bilingual education and the melting pot: Getting burned* (The Illinois Issues Humanities Essays 5). Champaign, IL: The Illinois Humanities Council.

Lucas, T., Henze, R., & Donato, R. (1990). Promoting the success of Latino language-minority students: an exploratory study of six high schools. *Harvard Educational Review, 60*, 315–340.

Lucas, T., & Katz, A. (1994). Reframing the debate: The roles of native languages in English-only programs for language minority students. *TESOL Quarterly, 28*(3), 537–562.

MacDougall, R. (1841/1998). *The emigrant's guide to North America*. Toronto: Natural Heritage Books.

Macedo, D. P. (1993). Literacy for stupidification: The pedagogy of big lies. *Harvard Educational Review, 63*, 183–207.

Macedo, D. P. (1994). *Literacies of power: What Americans are not allowed to know*. Boulder, CO: Westview Press.

Mackey, W. F. (1970). A typology of bilingual education. *Foreign Language Annals, 3,* 596–608.

Mahshie, S. N. (1995). *Educating deaf children bilingually.* Washington, DC: Gallaudet University.

Malakoff, M., & Hakuta, K. (1991). Translation skill and metalinguistic awareness in bilinguals. In E. Bialystok (Ed.), *Language processing in bilingual children* (pp. 141–166). Cambridge: Cambridge University Press.

Malherbe, E. G. (1946). *The bilingual school.* Johannesburg: Bilingual School Association.

Mason, B., & Krashen, S. (1997). Extensive reading in English as a foreign language. *System, 25,* 91–102.

Mathes, P. G., & Torgesen, J. K. (2000). A call for equity in reading instruction for all students: A response to Allington and Woodside-Jiron. *Educational Researcher, 29*(6), 4–14.

Mathews, P. (1997). *The concise Oxford dictionary of linguistics.* Oxford: Oxford University Press.

McCaleb, S. P. (1994). *Building communities of learners: A collaboration among teachers, students, families and community.* New York: St. Martin's Press.

McCarty, T. L. (1993, March). Language, literacy, and the image of the child in American Indian classrooms. *Language Arts, 70,* 182–192.

McKay, S. L., & Wong, S. C. (1996). Multiple discourses, multiple identities: Investment and agency in second-language learning among Chinese adolescent immigrant students. *Harvard Educational Review, 66*(3), 577–608.

McLaughlin, B. (1984). Early bilingualism: Methodological and theoretical issues. In M. Paradis & Y. Lebrun (Eds.), *Early bilingualism and child development.* Lisse: Swets & Zeitlinger B. V.

McLaughlin, B. (1986). Multilingual education: Theory east and west. In B. Spolsky (Ed.), *Language and education in multilingual settings.* Clevedon, England: Multilingual Matters.

McLaughlin, D. (1992). Power and the politics of knowledge: Transformative schooling for minority language learners. In D. E. Murray (Ed.), *Diversity as resource: Redefining cultural literacy* (pp. 235-258). Alexandra, VA: TESOL.

McNeil, L. M. (2000). *Contradictions of school reform: Economic costs of standardized testing.* New York: Routledge.

McQuillan, J. (1998). *The literacy crisis: False claims, real solutions.* Portsmouth, NH: Heinemann.

McQuillan, J., & Tse, L. (1996). Does research matter? An analysis of media opinion on bilingual education 1984-1994. *Bilingual Research Journal, 20*(1), 1-27.

McWilliam, N. (1998). *What's in a word? Vocabulary development in multilingual classrooms.* Stoke on Trent: Trentham Books.

Medina, M. J., & Escamilla, K. (1992). Evaluation of transitional and maintenance bilingual programs. *Urban Education, 27,* 263-290.

Mehan, H., Hertweck, A., & Meihls, J. L. (1986). *Handicapping the handicapped: Decision making in students' educational careers.* Palo Alto: Stanford University Press.

Meloni, C. (2000 (October/November). Word building on the web. *TESOL Matters, 10*(4), 14.

Merino, B. (1999). Preparing secondary teachers to teach a second language: The case of the United States with a focus on California. In C. J. Faltis & P. Wolfe (Eds.), *So much to say: Adolescents, bilingualism, & ESL in the secondary school* (pp. 225-254). New York: Teachers College Press.

Meyer, L. (1994). Barrio buddies: Learning through letters about kids, cultures, communities, and self-confrontation. *California Perspectives: Special Issue: Community Canons, 4*(Fall), 92-109.

Meyer, L. (2000). Barriers to meaningful instruction for English learners. *Theory into Practice, 34*(2), 228-236.

Moffett, J. (1989). Censorship and spiritual education. *English Education, 21,* 70-87.

Mohanty, A. K. (1994). *Bilingualism in a multilingual society: Psychological and pedagogical implications.* Mysore: Central Institute of Indian Languages.

Morison, S. H. (1990). A Spanish-English dual-language program in New York City. In C. B. Cazden & C. E. Snow (Eds.), *English Plus: Issues in bilingual education* (pp. 160–169). Newbury Park, CA: Sage Publications.

Morse, J. (2000, March 6). Sticking to the script. *TIME*, 60–61.

Muñiz-Swicegood, M. (1994). The effects of metacognitive reading strategy training on the reading performance and student reading analysis strategies of third grade bilingual students. *The Bilingual Research Journal, 18*(1&2), 83–97.

Muñoz-Sandoval, A., Cummins, J., Alvarado, C. G., & Ruef, M. L. (1998). *Bilingual verbal ability tests.* Itasca, IL: Riverside Publishing.

Nagy, W. E., Herman, P. A., & Anderson, R. C. (1985). Learning words from context. *Reading Research Quarterly, 20*(2), 233–253.

Nation, I. S. P. (1990). *Teaching and learning vocabulary.* Boston, MA: Heinle & Heinle Publishers.

Nation, P. (1993). Vocabulary size, growth, and use. In R. Schreuder & B. Weltens (Eds.), *The bilingual lexicon* (pp. 115–134). Amsterdam: John Benjamins Publishing Company.

Nation, P., & Coady, J. (1988). Vocabulary and reading. In R. Carter & M. McCarthy (Eds.), *Vocabulary and language teaching* (pp. 97–110). London: Longman.

National Coalition of Advocates for Students. (1988). *New voices: Immigrant students in U.S. public schools.* Boston: National Coalition of Advocates for Students.

National Reading Panel. (2000). *Teaching children to read: An evidence-based assessment of the scientific research literature on reading and its implications for reading instruction.* Washington, DC: NICHD.

Natriello, G., McDill, E. L., & Pallas, A. M. (1990). *Schooling disadvantaged children: Racing against catastrophe.* New York: Teachers College Press.

New Zealand Department of Education. (1988). *New Voices: Second language learning and teaching. A handbook for primary teachers.* Wellington: Department of Education.

Newman, D., Griffin, P., & Cole, M. (1989). *The construction zone.* Cambridge: Cambridge University Press.

Nieto, S. (1996). *Affirming diversity: The sociopolitical context of multicultural education. 2nd edition.* White Plains, NY: Longman.

Nieto, S. (1999). *The light in their eyes: Creating multicultural learning communities.* New York: Teachers College Press.

Oakes, J. (1985). *Keeping track: How high schools structure inequality.* New Haven: Yale University Press.

Ogbu, J. (1978). *Minority education and caste.* New York: Academic Press.

Ogbu, J. U. (1992). Understanding cultural diversity and learning. *Educational Researcher, 21*(8), 5–14 & 24.

Ogle, D. (1986). The K-W-L: A teaching model that develops active reading of expository text. *The Reading Teacher, 39,* 564–570.

Olsen, L. (1988). *Crossing the schoolhouse border: Immigrant students and the California public schools.* San Francisco: California Tomorrow.

Olsen, L., Chang, H., De La Rosa Salazar, D., Leong, C., McCall Perez, Z., McClain, G., & Raffel, L. (1994). *The unfinished journey: Restructuring schools in a diverse society.* San Francisco: California Tomorrow.

Olsen, L., & Minnicucci, C. (1992, April). *Educating limited English proficient students in secondary schools: Critical issues emerging from research in California schools.* Paper presented at the American Education Research Association, San Francisco.

Olson, D. R. (1977). From utterance to text: The bias of language in speech and writing. *Harvard Educational Review, 47,* 257–281.

O'Malley, J. M., & Pierce, L. V. (1996). *Authentic assessment for English language learners: Practical Approaches for the K-12 classroom.* Reading, MA: Addison-Wesley.

Organization for Economic Cooperation and Development (OECD). (1991). *Education and cultural and linguistic pluralism: Synthesis of case studies. Effective strategies and approaches in schools.* Paris: OECD/CERI.

Orr, J. E., Butler, G., Bousquet, M., & Hakuta, K. (2000). *What can we learn about the impact of Proposition 227 from SAT-9 scores? An analysis of results from 2000 with a postscript on Oceanside and Californians Together Report, updated August 27, 2000.* Stanford: Stanford University.

Ortiz, A. A., & Yates, J. R. (1983). Incidence of exceptionality among Hispanics: Implications for manpower planning. *NABE Journal, 7*, 41-54.

Orwell, G. (1983). *The Penguin complete novels of George Orwell*. London: Penguin Books.

Oyster Bilingual School. (1999). *Local school plan*. Washington, DC: Oyster Bilingual School.

Patthey-Chavez, G., & Goldenberg, C. (1995). Changing instructional discourse for changing students: The instructional conversation. In R. Macías & R. García Ramos (Eds.), *Changing schools for changing students: An anthology of research on language minorities, schools and society* (pp. 205-230). Santa Barbara, CA: University of California Linguistic Minority Research Institute.

Payne, K. J., & Biddle, B. J. (1999). Poor school funding, child poverty, and mathematics achievement. *Educational Researcher, 28*(6), 4-13.

Peirce, B. N. (1995). Social identity, investment, and language learning. *TESOL Quarterly, 29*(1), 9-31.

Peña-Hughes, E., & Solís, J. (1980). *ABCs* (Unpublished report). McAllen, TX: McAllen Independent School District.

Pérez, B. (1998a). Literacy, diversity, and programmatic responses. In B. Pérez (Ed.), *Sociocultural contexts of language and literacy* (pp. 3-20). Mahwah, NJ: Lawrence Erlbaum Associates.

Pérez, B. (1998b). Language, literacy, and biliteracy. In B. Pérez (Ed.), *Sociocultural contexts of language and literacy* (pp. 21-48). Mahwah, NJ: Lawrence Erlbaum Associates.

Peterson, B. (1994). Teaching for social justice: One teacher's journey. In B. Bigelow, L. Christensen, S. Karp, B. Miner, & B. Peterson (Eds.), *Rethinking our classrooms: Teaching for equity and justice* (pp. 30-38). Milwaukee, WI: Rethinking Schools.

Peura, M. (2000). Creating a successful minority school. In R. Phillipson (Ed.), *Rights to language: Equity, power, and education*. Mahwah, NJ: Lawrence Erlbaum Associates.

Peyton, J. K., & Staton, J. (Eds.). (1993). *Dialogue journals in the multilingual classroom: Building language fluency and writing skills through written interaction*. Norwood, NJ: Ablex.

Platero, D. (1975). Bilingual education in the Navajo Nation. In R. C. Troike & N. Modiano (Eds.), *Proceedings of the First Inter-American Conference on Bilingual Education*. Arlington, VA: Center for Applied Linguistics.

Poplin, M., & Weeres, J. (1992). *Voices from the inside: A report on schooling from inside the classroom*. Claremont, CA: The Institute for Education in Transformation at the Claremont Graduate School.

Porter, R. P. (1990). *Forked tongue: The politics of bilingual education*. New York: Basic Books.

Porter, R. P. (1991, June 5). The false alarm over early English acquisition. *Education Week, 36*.

Porter, R. P. (1993). Comments on Suzanne Irujo's review and Keith Baker's commentary on *Forked tongue: The politics of bilingual education*. *TESOL Quarterly, 27*(1), 150-154.

Postlethwaite, T. N., & Ross, K. N. (1992). *Effective schools in reading: Implications for educational planners. An exploratory study*. The Hague: The International Association for the Evaluation of Educational Achievement.

President's Commission on Foreign Languages and International Studies. (1980). *Strength through wisdom: A critique of U.S. capability*. Washington, DC: U.S. Government Printing Office.

Ramírez, C. M. (1985). *Bilingual education and language interdependence: Cummins and beyond*. Unpublished Doctoral dissertation, Yeshiva University.

Ramírez, J. D. (1992). Executive summary. *Bilingual Research Journal, 16*, 1-62.

Rees, O. (1981). Mother tongue and English project. In Commission for Racial Equality (Ed.), *Mother tongue teaching conference report*. Bradford, UK: Bradford College.

Regnier, R. (1988). Indians 'r' us: The experience of a survival school pedagogy. *Our Schools, Ourselves, 1*(1), 22-44.

Rehbein, J. (1984). *Diskurs und Verstehen: Zur Role der Muttersprache bei der Textarbeitung in der Zweitsprache*: University of Hamburg.

Reich, R. (1991). *The work of nations: Preparing ourselves for 21st century capitalism*. New York: Knopf.

Reid, E., & Reich, H. (1992). *Breaking the boundaries: Migrant workers' children in the EC*. Clevedon, England: Multilingual Matters.

Rethinking Schools. (1991). *Rethinking Columbus: Teaching about the 500th anniversary of Columbus's arrival in North America*. Madison, WI: Rethinking Schools Ltd.

Reyes, M. de la Luz (1992). Challenging venerable assumptions: Literacy instruction for linguistically different students. *Harvard Educational Review, 62*, 427-446.

Reyes, M. de la Luz. (2000). Unleashing possibilities: Biliteracy in the primary grades. In M. de la. Luz Reyes & J. Halcón (Eds.), *The best for our children: Critical perspectives on literacy for Latino students* (pp. 96-121). New York: Teachers College Press.

Ricciardelli, L. (1989). *Childhood bilingualism: Metalinguistic awareness and creativity.* Unpublished Ph. D. dissertation, University of Adelaide, Adelaide.

Ricciardelli, L. A. (1992). Bilingualism and cognitive development in relation to threshold theory. *Journal of Psycholinguistic Research, 21*, 301-316.

Ricciardelli, L. A. (1993). An investigation of the cognitive development of Italian-English bilinguals and Italian monolinguals from Rome. *Journal of Multilingual and Multicultural Development, 14*(4), 345-346.

Robson, A. (1995). The assessment of bilingual children. In M. K. Verma, K. P. Corrigan, & S. Firth (Eds.), *Working with Bilingual Children* (pp. 28-47). Clevedon, England: Multilingual Matters.

Rodriguez, R. (1982). *Hunger of memory: The education of Richard Rodriguez*. Boston: David R. Godine.

Rogosa, D. R., & Willett, J. (1985). Understanding correlates of change by modelling individual differences in growth. *Psychometrica, 50*, 203-228.

Rossell, C. H. (1992). Nothing matters? A critique of the Ramírez et al. longitudinal study of instructional programs for language-minority children. *Bilingual Research Journal, 16*(1&2), 159-186.

Rossell, C. H. (1996). RTE Forum: Letters from readers. *Research in the Teaching of English, 30*(1), 376-385.

Rossell, C. H. (1998). Mystery on the bilingual express: A critique of the Thomas and Collier study. *READ Perspectives, 5*(2), 5-32.

Rossell, C. H., & Baker, K. (1996). The effectiveness of bilingual education. *Research in the Teaching of English, 30*, 7-74.

Rueda, R. (1989). Defining mild disabilities with language-minority students. *Exceptional Children, 56*, 121-128.

Rumbaut, R. G., & Ima, K. (1987). *The adaptation of Southeast Asian refugee youth: A comparative study*. San Diego: Office of Refugee Resettlement.

Ryan, W. (1972). *Blaming the victim*. New York: Vintage.

Sánchez, G. (1943). Pachucos in the making. *Common Ground, 4*, 13-20.

Sanz, C. (2000). Bilingual education enhances third language acquisition: Evidence from Catalonia. *Applied Psycholinguistics, 21*(1), 23-44.

Saville-Troike, M. (1984). What *really* matters in second language learning for academic achievement? *TESOL Quarterly, 18*, 199-219.

Schifini, A. (1994). Language, literacy, and content instruction: Strategies for teachers. In K. Spangenberg-Urbschat & R. Pritchard (Eds.), *Kids come in all languages: reading instruction for ESL students* (pp. 158-179). Newark, DE: International Reading Association.

Schlesinger, A. Jr. (1991). *The disuniting of America*. New York: W. W. Norton.

Schlossman, S. (1983). Self-evident remedy? George I Sánchez, segregation, and enduring dilemmas in bilingual education. *Teachers College Record, 84*, 871-907.

Schweinhart, L. J., Weikart, D. P., & Larney, M. B. (1986). Consequences of three preschool curriculum models through age 15. *Early Childhood Research Quarterly, 1*, 15-45.

Share, D., & Stanovich, K. (1995). Cognitive processes in early reading development: Accommodating individual differences into a model of acquisition. *Issues in Education: Contributions from Educational Psychology, 1*(1), 1-57.

Shohamy, E. (1999). Unity and diversity in language policy. Paper presented at the AILA conference, Tokyo, August.

Shor, I. (1992). *Empowering education: Critical teaching for social change.* Chicago: The University of Chicago Press.

Shuy, R. W. (1978). Problems in assessing language ability in bilingual education programs. In H. Lafontaine, B. Persky, & L. Golubchick (Eds.), *Bilingual education* (pp. 376-380). Wayne, NJ: Avery Publishing Group Inc.

Siegel, J. (1995). Neighborhood as laboratory. *Electronic Learning*(September), 26-29.

Sierra, J., & Olaziregi, I. (1989). *EIFE 2. Influence of factors on the learning of Basque.* Gasteiz: Central Publications Service of the Basque Country.

Sierra, J., & Olaziregi, I. (1991). *EIFE 3. Influence of factors on the learning of Basque. Study of the models A, B and D in second year Basic General Education.* Gasteiz: Central Publications Service of the Basque Country.

Sirén, U. (1991). *Minority language transmission in early childhood: Parental intention and language use.* Stockholm: Institute of International Education, Stockholm University.

Sirotnik, K. A. (1983). What you see is what you get—consistency, persistency, and mediocrity in classrooms. *Harvard Educational Review, 53,* 16-31.

Sizer, T. R. (1984). *Horace's compromise: The dilemma of the American high school.* Boston: Houghton Mifflin.

Skutnabb-Kangas, T. (1984). *Bilingualism or not: The education of minorities.* Clevedon, England: Multilingual Matters.

Skutnabb-Kangas, T. (1988). Resource power and autonomy through discourse in conflict—a Finnish migrant school strike in Sweden. In T. Skutnabb-Kangas & J. Cummins (Eds.), *Minority Education: From Shame to Struggle* (pp. 251-277). Clevedon, England: Multilingual Matters.

Skutnabb-Kangas, T. (Ed.). (1995). *Multilingualism for all*. Lisse: Swets & Zeitlinger.

Skutnabb-Kangas, T., & Phillipson, R. (1995). *Linguistic human rights*. Berlin: Mouton de Gruyter.

Skutnabb-Kangas, T., & Toukomaa, P. (1976). *Teaching migrant children's mother tongue and learning the language of the host country in the context of the sociocultural situation of the migrant family*. Helsinki: The Finnish National Commission for UNESCO.

Smith, G. H. (1992). Kura Kaupapa Maori: Contesting and reclaiming education in Aotearoa. In D. R. Ray & D. H. Poonwassie (Eds.), *Education and cultural differences: New perspectives* (pp. 89–108). New York: Garland Publishing Inc.

Snow, C. E., Burns, M. S., & Griffin, P. (Eds.). (1998). *Preventing reading difficulties in young children*. Washington, DC: National Academy Press.

Snow, C. E., Cancino, H., De Temple, J., & Schley, S. (1991). Giving formal definitions: A linguistic or metalinguistic skill? In E. Bialystok (Ed.), *Language processing in bilingual children* (pp. 90–112). Cambridge: Cambridge University Press.

Snow, C. E., & Hoefnagel-Höhle, M. (1978). The critical period for language acquisition: Evidence from second language learning. *Child Development, 49,* 1114–1128.

Spires, H. A., & Donley, J. (1998). Prior knowledge activation: Inducing engagement with informational texts. *Journal of Educational Psychology, 90*(2), 249–260.

Spolsky, B., & Cooper, R. L. (1978). *Case studies in bilingual education*. Rowley, MA: Newbury House.

Stanford Working Group. (1993). *Federal education programs for limited-English proficient students: A blueprint for the second generation* (Report of the Stanford Working Group). Stanford, CA: Stanford University.

Stanovich, K. E. (1992). Speculations on the causes and consequences of individual differences in early reading acquisition. In P. B. Gough, L. C. Ehri, & R. Treiman (Eds.), *Reading acquisition* (pp. 307–342). Hillsdale, NJ: Erlbaum.

Stanovich, K. E., & Stanovich, P. J. (1998). Ending the reading wars. *Orbit, 28*(4), 49-55.

Stedman, L. C. (1987). It's time we changed the effective schools formula. *Phi Delta Kappan, 69,* 215-224.

Suárez-Orozco, M. (1987). Towards a psychosocial understanding of Hispanic adaptation to American schooling. In H. T. Trueba (Ed.), *Success or failure? Learning and the language minority student* (pp. 156-168). Cambridge, MA: Newbury House.

Suárez-Orozco, M. (1989). Psychosocial aspects of achievement motivation among recent Hispanic immigrants. In H. T. Trueba, G. Spindler, & L. Spindler (Eds.), *What do anthropologists have to say about dropouts? The first centennial conference on the children at risk* (pp. 99-116). New York: The Falmer Press.

Swain, M. (1979). Bilingual education: Research and its implications. In C. A. Yorio, K. Perkins, & J. Schacter (Eds.), *On TESOL '79: The learner in focus.* Washington, DC: TESOL.

Swain, M. (1997). Collaborative dialogue: Its contribution to second language learning. *Revista Canaria de Estudios Ingleses, 34,* 115-132.

Swain, M., & Lapkin, S. (1982). *Evaluating bilingual education.* Clevedon, England: Multilingual Matters.

Swain, M., & Lapkin, S. (1991). Heritage language children in an English-French bilingual program. *The Canadian Modern Language Review, 47*(4), 635-641.

Swain, M., Lapkin, S., Rowen, N., & Hart, D. (1991). The role of mother tongue literacy in third language learning. In S. P. Norris & L. M. Phillips (Eds.), *Foundations of literacy policy in Canada* (pp. 185-206). Calgary: Detselig Enterprises.

Taylor, B. M., Anderson, R. C., Au, K. H., & Raphael, T. E. (2000). Discretion in the translation of research to policy: A case from beginning reading. *Educational Researcher, 29*(6), 16-26.

Taylor, W. L., & Piché, D. M. (1991). *A report on shortchanging children: The impact of fiscal inequality on the education of students at risk.* Washington, DC: U. S. House of Representatives, Committee on Education and Labor.

Terrazas, B. Jr., & Students for Cultural and Linguistic Democracy (1995). Struggling for power and voice: A high school experience. In J. Frederickson (Ed.), *Reclaiming our voices: Bilingual education, critical pedagogy & praxis* (pp. 279-310). Ontario, CA: California Association for Bilingual Education.

Tharp, R., & Gallimore, R. (1988). *Rousing minds to life.* Cambridge: Cambridge University Press.

Thomas, W. (1992). An analysis of the research methodology of the Ramírez study. *Bilingual Research Journal, 16*(1&2), 213-245.

Thomas, W. P., & Collier, V. (1997). *School effectiveness for language minority students.* Washington, DC: National Clearinghouse for Bilingual Education.

Thompson, E. (1998). Introduction. In R. MacDougall (Ed.), *The emigrant's guide to North America* (pp. vii-xxix). Toronto: Natural Heritage Books.

Tikunoff, W. J. (1983). *An emerging description of successful bilingual instruction: An executive summary of Part I of the SBIF Descriptive Study.* San Francisco: Far West Laboratory.

Tizard, J., Schofield, W. N., & Hewison, J. (1982). Collaboration between teachers and parents in assisting children's reading. *British Journal of Educational Psychology, 52,* 1-15.

Torres-Guzman, M. (1995). Recasting frames: Latino parent involvement. In O. Garcia & C. Baker (Eds.), *Policy and practice in bilingual education: Extending the foundations* (pp. 259-272). Clevedon, England: Multilingual Matters.

Tower Hamlets Education & Community Services. (1995). *An analysis of the 1995 London reading test.* London: Borough of Tower Hamlets.

Treadway, J. (1997). Response to Ken Goodman's critique of the NAEP Report. *CLIPS: A Journal of the California Reading & Literature Project, 3*(1), 57-58.

Troike, R. (1978). Research evidence for the effectiveness of bilingual education. *NABE Journal, 3,* 13-24.

Trueba, H. T. (1988). Culturally based explanations of minority students' academic achievement. *Anthropology & Education Quarterly, 19,* 270-287.

Tschanz, L. (1980). *Native languages and government policy:An historical examination* (Native Language Research Series No. 2): Centre for Research and Teaching of Canadian Native Languages, The University of Western Ontario.

Tunmer, W. E., & Chapman, J. W. (1999). Teaching strategies for word identification. In G. B. Thompson & T. Nicholson (Eds.), *Learning to read: Beyond phonics and whole language* (pp. 74-102). New York: Teachers College Press.

U. S. Commission on Civil Rights. (1973). *Teachers and students: Differences in teacher interaction with Mexican-American and Anglo students.* Washington, D. C.: U. S. Government Printing Office.

United States v. State of Texas. (1981). Civil action #5281 (Bilingual Education) Memorandum Opinion.

Valdés, G. (1997). Dual-language immersion programs: A cautionary note concerning the education of language-minority students. *Harvard Educational Review, 67*(3), 391-429.

Valdés, G. (1999). Incipient bilingualism and the development of English language writing abilities in the secondary school. In C. J. Faltis & P. Wolfe (Eds.), *So much to say: Adolescents, bilingualism, & ESL in the secondary school* (pp. 138-175). New York: Teachers College Press.

van Dijk, T. A. (2000). Discourse and access. In R. Phillipson (Ed.), *Rights to language: Equity, power, and education* (pp. 73-78). Mahwah, NJ: Lawrence Erlbaum Associates.

Vásquez, O. A., Pease-Alvarez, L., & Shannon, S. M. (1994). *Pushing boundaries: Language and culture in a Mexicano community.* New York: Cambridge University Press.

Verhoeven, L. (1991a). Acquisition of biliteracy. In J. H. Hulsijn & J. F. Matter (Eds.), *Reading in two languages* (Vol. 8, pp. 61-74). Amsterdam: AILA. AILA Review.

Verhoeven, L. (1991b). Predicting minority children's bilingual proficiency: Child, family, and institutional factors. *Language Learning, 41*, 205-233.

Verhoeven, L. (1992). Assessment of bilingual proficiency. In L. Verhoeven & J. H. A. L. de Jong (Eds.), *The construct of language proficiency* (pp. 124-136). Amsterdam: John Benjamins Publishing Company.

Verhoeven, L. (1994). Transfer in bilingual development: The linguistic interdependence hypothesis revisited. *Language Learning, 44,* 381–415.

Verhoeven, L., & Aarts, R. (1998). Attaining functional literacy in the Netherlands. In A. Y. Durgunoglu & L. Verhoeven (Eds.), *Literacy development in a multilingual context: Cross-cultural perspectives* (pp. 111–134). Mahwah, NJ: Lawrence Erlbaum Associates.

Vila, I. (1995). *El català i el castellà en el sistema educatiu de Catalunya.* Barcelona: Horsori.

Vildomec, V. (1963). *Multilingualism.* Leyden: A. W. Sythoff.

Vygotsky, L. (1962). *Thought and language.* Cambridge, MA: M.I.T. Press.

Vygotsky, L. S. (1978). *Mind in society: The development of higher psychological processes.* Cambridge, MA: Harvard University Press.

Waggoner, D. (1999). Who are secondary newcomer and linguistically different youth. In C. J. Faltis & P. Wolfe (Eds.), *So much to say: Adolescents, bilingualism, & ESL in the secondary school* (pp. 13–41). New York: Teachers College Press.

Wagner, D. A. (1998). Putting second language first: Language and literacy learning in Morocco. In L. Verhoeven & A. Y. Durgunoglu (Eds.), *Literacy development in a multilingual context* (pp. 169–183). Mahway, NJ: Lawrence Erlbaum Associates.

Waite, J. (1992). *Aoteareo: Speaking for ourselves. Part B: The issues. A discussion on the development of a New Zealand languages policy.* Wellington: Ministry of Education New Zealand.

Walsh, C. E. (1991). *Pedagogy and the struggle for voice: Issues of language, power, and schooling for Puerto Ricans.* Toronto: OISE Press.

Weinstein-Shr, G., & Quintero, E. (Eds.). (1995). *Immigrant learners and their families.* Washington, DC: ERIC/CAL.

Wells, G. (1999). *Dialogic inquiry.* Cambridge: Cambridge University Press.

White, T. G., Power, M. A., & White, S. (1989a). Morphological analysis: Implications for teaching and understanding vocabulary growth. *Reading Research Quarterly, 24*(3), 283–304.

White, T. G., Sowell, J., & Yanagihara, A. (1989b). Teaching elementary students to use word-part clues. *The Reading Teacher, 42,* 302-308.

Willig, A. C. (1981/82). The effectiveness of bilingual education: Review of a report. *NABE Journal, 6,* 1-19.

Willig, A. C. (1985). A meta-analysis of selected studies on the effectiveness of bilingual education. *Review of Educational Research, 55,* 269-317.

Willis, P. (1977). *Learning to labor: How working class kids get working class jobs.* Lexington: D. C. Heath

Wilson, D. (1991, Wednesday, June 19). Native bands demand action on school's abuse of children. *The Globe and Mail,* pp. A4.

Wirth, A. G. (1993). Education and work: The choices we face. *Phi Delta Kappan* (January), 360-366.

Wong Fillmore, L. (1990a). Latino families and the schools. *California Perspectives, 1 (Winter),* 30-37.

Wong Fillmore, L. (1991b). When learning a second language means losing the first. *Early Childhood Research Quarterly, 6,* 323-346.

Wong Fillmore, L. (1991c, June 19). A question for early-childhood programs: English first or families first? *Education Week,* pp. 32 & 34.

Wong Fillmore, L. (1992). Against our best interest: The attempt to sabotage bilingual education. In J. Crawford (Ed.), *Language loyalties: A sourcebook on the Official English controversy.* Chicago: University of Chicago Press.

Wong Fillmore, L. (1997). Authentic literature in ESL instruction. Glenview, IL: Scott Foresman.

Wong Fillmore, L. (2000). Loss of family language: Should educators be concerned? *Theory Into Practice, 39*(4), 203-210.

Wong Fillmore, L., Ammon, P., McLaughlin, B., & Ammon, M. S. (1985). *Learning English through bilingual instruction: Executive summary and conclusions* (Final Report to the National Institute of Education). Washington, D.C.: U.S. Department of Education.

Wong Fillmore, L., & Valadez, C. (1986). Teaching bilingual learners. In M. C. Wittrock (Ed.), *Handbook of research on teaching* (3rd ed. ed., pp. 648-685). New York: Macmillan.

Zanger, V. V. (1994). "Not joined in": Intergroup relations and access to English literacy for Hispanic youth. In B. M. Ferdman, R.-M. Weber, & A. Ramírez (Eds.), *Literacy across languages and cultures* (pp. 171-198). Albany: SUNY Press.

Zinn, H. (1995). *A people's history of the United States*. New York: Harper Perennial.

Author Index

Subject Index

Notes